EMPIRE OF HUMANITY

EMPIRE OF HUMANITY

A History of Humanitarianism

MICHAEL BARNETT

CORNELL UNIVERSITY PRESS / ITHACA AND LONDON

First published 2011 by Cornell University Press

Printed in the United States of America

Library of Congress Cataloging-in-Publication Data

Barnett, Michael N., 1960–
Empire of humanity : a history of humanitarianism / Michael Barnett.
    p. cm.
Includes bibliographical references and index.
ISBN 978-0-8014-4713-6 (cloth : alk. paper)
1. Humanitarian intervention—History.   2. Humanitarian assistance—
    History.   3. Humanitarianism—History.   I. Title.
            JZ6369.B348   2011
    361.2'6—dc22   2010042042

Cornell University Press strives to use environmentally responsible
suppliers and materials to the fullest extent possible in the publishing
of its books. Such materials include vegetable-based, low-VOC inks and
acid-free papers that are recycled, totally chlorine-free, or partly
composed of nonwood fibers. For further information, visit our
website at www.cornellpress.cornell.edu.

Cloth printing   10 9 8 7 6 5 4 3 2 1

For Victoria

Contents

PART III
The Age of Liberal Humanitarianism

Acknowledgments

THIS BOOK is a lot like humanitarianism in two critical respects: It began with modest ambitions and then expanded beyond belief—perhaps too much for its own good. And it depended on acts of kindness, sometimes from strangers, but in many cases from friends. I cannot thank everyone who helped me over the years, but there are quite a few who deserve recognition.

I have benefited greatly from participating in various events and meetings over the years. In 2003–2004, with the support of Craig Calhoun and the Social Science Research Council, I helped to convene a seminar series on humanitarianism; in addition to influencing my views, it also led to *Humanitarianism in Question,* which I edited with Tom Weiss. A sincere thank you, once again, to the participants in that series and the contributors to the volume. In 2005–2006, Raymond Duvall and I organized a Mellon-sponsored Sawyer Seminar series on "Humanitarianism and World Order," which provided the opportunity for an interdisciplinary group of graduate students and faculty at the University of Minnesota to engage a series of controversies and to invite several truly remarkable scholars and practitioners to reflect on their work. In addition to those who participated in the seminar series, I owe much to my collaborator, Bud Duvall. Around this time I also began delving into the relationship between religion and humanitarianism, which might not have happened (and certainly not in the same way) had it not been for a generous grant from the Luce Foundation. The activities surrounding this grant allowed me to interact with a remarkable group of individuals, including, most importantly, Janice Stein, who became a very dear friend in the process. This grant gave me the opportunity to work with an extraordinary group of individuals, including those from the American University in Cairo, the University of Toronto, New York University, the International Council on Voluntary Associations in Geneva, the Centre for Conflict, Development, and Peacebuilding at the Graduate Institute of International and Development Studies in Geneva, and the Humanitarian Forum in London. Although these events included a cast of dozens, special thanks go to Dr. Hany al-Bannah, James Shaw-Hamilton, and Ed Schenkenberg, who put their time and resources behind the events. Because of my growing interest in religion in world affairs, I was invited to join two other collaborative projects, one at the Social Science Research Council and the other organized by Jack Snyder at Columbia University. Once again, I learned a tremendous amount.

In many ways my deepest gratitude goes to the practitioners I met along the way, at their headquarters, at meetings, and in the field. I don't expect that they will agree with everything I have to say (though I hope they agree with much), and at times I worry that they might find the book overly critical. This is probably the proper place to confess that I committed a grave social science sin: I fell in love with my subject. At times I have found myself living vicariously through those practitioners—admiring that they had the courage of their convictions and, wishing, at times, that I could be more like them. I want to give a special thanks to those aid agencies that opened their doors and provided access to archives and, in some cases, individuals who really made a difference. World Vision (thanks to Steve Gray), Care International (thanks to JoEllen Saeli), Lutheran World Relief, Doctors without Borders (thanks to Nicolas de Torrente) and Catholic Relief Services (thanks to Regina Martin) were incredibly generous with their time.

I have imposed my drafts on many kind readers, and I have greatly benefited from their comments. Stephen Hopgood, Janice Stein, Bud Duvall, Tom Weiss, Bertrand Taithe, Antonio Donini, Fiona Terry, Tim Shah, Kevin Hartigan, Martha Finnemore, Kathryn Sikkink, and the anonymous reviewers at Cornell University Press saved me from lots of errors, some big and some spectacular. I also have had memorable conversations and exchanges; thanks to James Orbinski, David Kennedy, Andrew Natsios, Brian Atwood, Nancy Lindborg, Emanuel Adler, Peter Walker, Kate Wolford, Christopher Kaufmann, Judith Randel, and Dr. Hany el-Banna.

Thanks to Rebecca Cohen, Denis Kennedy, Jennifer Hawkes, Sandra Borda, and Hunjoon Kim for research assistance and to Keith Vargo and Jeremy Gordon for administrative assistance.

I have benefited from feedback at various locations, including Duke University, the University of Minnesota, George Washington University, the University of Pennsylvania, the University of Chicago, Simon Fraser University, the American University in Cairo, and Oxford University. I learned a tremendous amount from the participants at a manuscript workshop at the School of Oriental and African Studies, so much so that a book that I thought was almost finished got delayed by several months by a major rewrite. I am indebted to Stephen Hopgood and Leslie Vinjamuri for organizing the event.

I am especially grateful to the United States Institute of Peace and, especially, the Harold Stassen Chair at the University of Minnesota for their financial support. I reuse some of the material from my "Evolution without Progress? Humanitarianism in a World of Hurt," *International Organization* 63, no. 4 (October 2009) 621–63. Copyright © 2009 The IP Foundation. Reprinted with the permission of Cambridge University Press. For permission to reproduce figure 1, Katharina Ziemke's "Solferino," thanks to Zürcher Studio, New York. For permission to reproduce figure 3, "British giving alms," thanks to Mission 21, Evangelisches Missionswerk, Basel, Switzerland. For permission to reproduce figure 7, "Hoover with Polish Children," thanks to the Hoover Institution. For permission to reproduce figure 8, Felix Nussbaum's "The Refugee," thanks to the Yad Vashem Museum, Jerusalem, Israel. For permission to reproduce figure 9, I thank Bildarchiv Preußischer Kulturbesitz. For permission to use figure 10, I thank the ICRC. For permission to reproduce figure 11, I thank the Israel Museum, Jerusalem, and the Artists Rights Society, New York.

Although all the aforementioned people helped me along the way, Roger Haydon looms larger than life and above them all. I cannot exaggerate how critical he has been to the book's formulation and execution and how fortunate I am to have benefited from his intelligence and friendship on this book (and the others). Also at Cornell University Press, many thanks to Martin Schneider for helping to transform the manuscript into a book, and to Karen Laun for seeing the book through the production process.

I dedicate this book to my wife, Victoria. She reminds me a lot of the aid workers that I have encountered: not quite a selfless, sacrificing saint, but with more compassion than just about anyone I know. Without her care, love, and friendship, this book (and just about everything else I have come to enjoy in life) would not have been possible. This book does not begin to begin to balance the scales, but for now, it will have to do.

EMPIRE OF HUMANITY

Introduction:
The Crooked Timber
of Humanitarianism

ALL COMMUNITIES get their history wrong, and the humanitarian community is no exception. The standard and abbreviated history of humanitarianism features Henry Dunant as accidental patriarch, his moment of inspiration in 1859. The Genevan businessman had left home for Italy, hoping to gain the favor of a French general to help in his planned commercial ventures in Algeria. On his way, he witnessed a battle between French and Austro-Hungarian troops at the Italian village of Solferino. Appalled by the carnage and the miseries of the injured soldiers abandoned on the battlefield, he joined local townspeople to offer what relief he could. Similar to many other dramatic narratives in which the protagonist undergoes a life-transforming experience, Dunant had left Geneva as a man seeking riches and returned home as a man who was about to dedicate his life to higher calling. Unable to shake off the haunting experience, he wrote a memoir to publicize the plight of those discarded in battle and to propose a solution. He succeeded beyond his imagination. *A Memory of Solferino* became a European bestseller and launched a citizens' call to alms, and within three years that grassroots campaign produced the International Committee of the Red Cross (ICRC) and the Geneva Conventions. The Battle of Solferino became to modern humanitarianism what the Treaty of Westphalia was to modern international politics.

In the conventional story, the contest between humanity's capacities for cruelty and compassion continued, with compassion falling ever farther behind but refusing to surrender. The period between ICRC's creation and

World War One show few advances, and many setbacks, for humanitarianism. Military technology, for instance, was becoming more efficient at killing greater numbers of people in ever more agonizing ways, and while the ICRC urged states to outlaw uncivilized weapons, it had limited success. World War One, however, proved the ICRC's prescience regarding the increasingly destructive capacity of warfare, and it suddenly found itself busier than ever, providing medical relief and expanding into new areas such as helping prisoners of war. The combination of the destructiveness and longevity of the war also led to a surge in private voluntary relief organizations, including Save the Children and the seldom-heralded Committee for the Relief of Belgium (the latter founded and overseen by the American businessman and future president Herbert Hoover), which saved millions from starvation. After 1918, states established the first of many international humanitarian organizations, among them the High Commission for Refugees and the International Relief Union, but by the end of the 1930s neither had much of a presence.

During World War II governments and private voluntary agencies expanded relief to new populations, and after the war set about rebuilding Europe. Against the backdrop of a newly decolonizing world, many nongovernmental organizations that once had concentrated on Europe now discovered a whole world waiting to be helped, and many international organizations, originally created for European relief and reconstruction and located within the United Nations system, began to act like global organizations. Humanitarianism had gone global.

This century of humanitarian action posed considerable challenges, but those in the humanitarian community knew what they did and how to do it. They provided life-saving relief. They did so by following several basic principles: impartiality, for they must give aid based on need, not on who is being helped or where they live; neutrality, for they must avoid appearing to act in ways that favor one side or another; and independence, for they must be unconnected to any party with a stake in the conflict. These principles rendered humanitarians apolitical—one of the keys to their success. If states believed that humanitarians were trying to influence outcomes or shape postwar arrangements, then they would refuse entry to meddling do-gooders. Following their version of Matthew 22:21—"render unto Caesar the things that are Caesar's and unto God the things that are God's," humanitarians stuck to ethics and left politics to the world of states.

In the 1990s, everything changed. The Cold War was history, replaced by "new wars" that were creating "complex humanitarian emergencies." In fact, these new wars were not so new, and humanitarian emergencies had always been complex, but the international community acted as if they had never seen anything like them. Covered by twenty-four-hour news agencies, the world could now watch, in real time, the horrific spectacles of state failure and civil war, ethnic cleansing and genocide, the use of children as soldiers capable of committing war crimes, and the flight of millions of people from all forms of violence only to find "safety" in city-sized refugee camps without adequate food, shelter, or medical care.

The humanitarian community did not completely meet these challenges—as if that were even possible—but it did expand dramatically in scope and scale and provided new forms of assistance to more people than ever before. Numbers cannot tell the story of the rapid evolution of the humanitarian sector, but they do give a taste. A growing scrum of humanitarian organizations began migrating from one emergency to the next: There were only a handful of aid agencies in Somalia in 1992 prior to the American intervention. Roughly 200 went to Rwanda in 1994. Around 250 were in Kosovo in 1999. The 2004 tsunami attracted hundreds of aid agencies; there were around 180 NGOs in Banda Aceh, Indonesia, in the aftermath of the 2004 tsunami—and these figures exclude national private voluntary agencies, UN agencies, and members of the Red Cross societies; and about 900 registered with the UN, and many more never bothered to do so, in the aftermath of the 2010 earthquake in Haiti.[1] More organizations meant that there were more aid workers than ever before. One conservative estimate suggests that there are about 210,000 aid workers, representing a near doubling over the last decade.[2] But it takes more than an army of well-intended people to fuel such an expansion—it also takes money, and lots of it. Private contributions have increased steadily over the last two decades, particularly as aid agencies became better at marketing their products. But the big money came from states. Official assistance swelled from two billion dollars in 1990 to six billion dollars in 2000, and today there is nearly eighteen billion available for humanitarian assistance, most of it from the public sector.[3]

In addition to these quantitative increases, there were equally impressive qualitative developments. Humanitarian organizations were doing more things than ever before. The UNHCR's mission expanded from protecting refugees to addressing the root causes of refugee flight. Many other nongovernmental organizations began tackling the root causes of violence, which included a laundry list of possible culprits, including a culture of violence, a lack of respect for human rights, and the absence of democratic institutions. In other words, as humanitarians began imagining how to build peace after war, they slipped into building states. They were not alone. As these traditional humanitarian organizations began to move into new areas, they met up with other international and nongovernmental organizations who were not traditionally counted as part of the humanitarian club, including the United Nations Development Programme (UNDP) and the World Bank.

If this surge in humanitarian action seems to be almost too good to be true, it is because it was. States were helping to bulk up the humanitarian sector for a mixture of motives, but mainly because they believed that humanitarian action would advance their foreign policy interests. The rise in official assistance is due to a handful of states, but the United States gives the most. Still, more and more governments appear to want to see their names on the roll call of givers; in the four years prior to 2008 the number of government donors increased by 40 percent, and in 2008 104 governments reported that they had provided humanitarian assistance.[4] More money from more states with ulterior motives was not necessarily good for humanitarianism. States were doing more than just giving money; they were also creating humanitarian units within their foreign and defense ministries to respond more effectively to future emergencies, providing logistical support and sometimes armed protection for aid agencies in places like Somalia, and increasingly accepting the legitimacy of humanitarian intervention, now renamed a "responsibility to protect." Even the private sector jumped on the bandwagon, with commercial firms competing with nongovernmental organizations for increasingly lucrative government contracts and major corporations associating with media-saturated, high-profile emergencies in order to demonstrate to consumers that they, too, had a heart.

The combination of human nightmares and the expanding population of aid agencies led the humanitarian community to depart from their long-cherished principles and venture into once-forbidden areas, but with mixed results.[5] For many, established principles made little sense in the context of emergencies, ethnic cleansing, war crimes, and genocide. What good did neutrality and independence do for Bosnians and Rwandans? The very principles that had been designed to saves lives now looked like excuses for inaction. Even Médecins Sans Frontières (known in English as Doctors without Borders), which had developed a well-earned reputation for opposing humanitarian intervention on the grounds that war and humanitarianism should not be confused, supported a UN military intervention to stop the genocide in Rwanda. Armed humanitarian intervention no longer looked like an oxymoron, and humanitarian agencies that kept their distance because of the principle of independence were accused of indifference. But there were always possible costs—to their principles, to their legitimacy, and to their autonomy—whenever they aligned themselves with states and treated violence as part of their toolkit.

And what should they do once the war was over? Pack their bags for the next killing zone, giving the survivors one last relief package and best wishes for the future? No longer satisfied with keeping alive the "well-fed dead" and feeling obligated to help traumatized societies find peace and justice, many aid agencies embraced postconflict reconstruction, human rights, development, democracy promotion, and peacebuilding. Humanitarian organizations were now venturing into the formerly taboo territory of politics, cooperating and coordinating with intervening states, treating moments of destruction as opportunities for political change, and taking on functions that had once been the exclusive preserve of governments. Suddenly, humanitarian organizations were becoming involved in politics and exercising power as they involved themselves in matters of governance.

Did these developments humanize the world of politics, or did they politicize the world of humanitarianism? Thanks to assistance from states, aid agencies could help more people in more ways in more places than ever before. But states provided that help because it was in their interests, argued many, not because they had undergone some great awakening about the ethical treatment of individuals. If so, then politics was using humanitarianism, not the other way around. Reflecting the anxieties unleashed by this mixture of politics and principle, commentators spoke of humanitarianism in "crisis" and warned of the dangers of "supping with the devil," "drinking from the poisoned chalice," and "sleeping with the enemy." Indeed, such comments were becoming increasingly common *before* the demoralizing experience of the U.S.-led wars in Afghanistan and Iraq, in which aid agencies were funded by an invading state, namely the United States, that openly treated humanitarianism as an instrument of war. Humanitarianism, many in-house critics suggested, had made a Faustian bargain.

And that is, very roughly, the standard story about humanitarianism. This semi-tragic narrative, however, suffers from the disorienting effects of selective memory. In fact, my initial understanding of humanitarianism was deeply influenced by this conventional version of events. Accepting the premise that the end of the Cold War was the start of a great transformation, I set out to examine humanitarianism's evolution after 1990. My understanding changed radically, though, once I began peering into the "before," reading up on the history of humanitarianism, rummaging in the archives of many of the world's leading agencies, and speaking with veteran aid workers. The more I learned, the more convinced I became that the 1990s were hardly unprecedented—indeed, they contained some well-established patterns. Humanitarianism was not a wholly private affair before the 1990s; over the previous decades states and their international organizations were becoming increasingly prominent funders, coordinators, and deliverers of assistance. The principles of impartiality, neutrality, and independence were not part of humanitarianism's original DNA; rather, they had fallen into place over decades of action and debate and had not become part of the ICRC's codes of conduct until the 1960s. The original humanitarians had predated Dunant by nearly half a century and had never limited themselves to emergency relief; they had tried to end all sources of suffering, including cruelty to animals, destitution, slavery, and inhumane forms of punishment and incarceration. Aid agencies had not taken a no-politics pledge before the 1990s, for they had always been political creatures in one way or another. In sum, the dilemmas of humanitarianism were no product of the 1990s—they had been present from the beginning.

In addition to suffering from historical amnesia, the accepted narrative protects the virtue of humanitarianism, but at the expense of a fuller, and decidedly more complicated, picture of its lived ethics. Stories about humanitarianism tend to be organized around binaries, most prominently ethics versus politics. Humanitarianism presents itself as living in a world of ethics, constantly battling the forces of evil and indifference. Certainly the stories became more complicated over the last two decades, for they now are beginning to recognize that aid agencies, in the words of former UN High Commissioner for Refugees Sadako Ogata, must choose among "the least bad of awful alternatives"; that aid workers are not the self-sacrificing saints portrayed by their admirers; that aid agencies can be fixated on the marketplace; and that good intentions can lead to dreadful consequences. These recent accounts raise important questions about the practice of humanitarianism, but most of the blame for why humanitarianism cannot be as pure as it would like stems from the realities of the world in which it operates. Humanitarianism can never be practiced as preached because, to paraphrase James Madison, we live in a world of devils and not angels. Humanitarians must get their hands dirty, they must make difficult choices and compromises as they live the credo that the perfect should never be the enemy of the good. Humanitarians must be attentive to the marketplace because good thoughts do not save lives, and they must even "profit" from the misery of others because people donate only when they are gripped by haunting images. The problem, though, lies not with humanitarianism but instead with an imperfect world that imposes tough, and sometimes heartbreaking, choices on humanitarians. These compromises are inevitable and are part of the price of doing business—even when that business is saving lives.

But what if humanitarianism has its own native demons? One tradition of scholarship reduces humanitarianism to the interests of the powerful, retaining the binaries of ethics and politics but assuming that the former is merely an extension of the latter. Some see humanitarianism as little more than an ideological prop for the Great Powers. Noam Chomsky is perhaps the most famous, though not the most sophisticated, representative of this view; thirty years ago he was claiming that rumors of genocide in Cambodia were being manufactured by the CIA, and he recently dismissed the "responsibility to protect" as serving the interests of the West.[6] Others, following Marx's view of religion, treat humanitarianism as a "feel-good" ideology that helps maintain global inequalities, and allows the rich to sleep comfortably at night as they are allowed to dream that charity is a substitute for radical change and that they are not benefiting personally from global exploitation.[7] Humanitarianism is one part Trojan Horse, one part opiate.

In this book I reject both an overly romantic and an overly cynical reading of humanitarianism. Instead I treat humanitarianism as a morally complicated creature, a flawed hero defined by the passions, politics, and power of its times even as it tries to rise above them. I am most certainly not the first to write in this spirit. A growing list of essays and books by in-house critics and veteran aid workers addresses the dilemmas of aid, the harms associated with the growing humanitarian sector, and the valiant, but ultimately unsuccessful, attempt by humanitarians to resolve these maladies.[8] The aid workers I have met were hardly in denial; they would recount, without theatrics or self-aggrandizement and with considerable humor and humility, the dilemmas they faced and the doubts they had about their decisions and their profession. In this respect, my modest goal is to join this conversation.

Yet I also have a few immodest goals. This is one of the first histories of humanitarianism. Most of the writings on humanitarianism focus on events after 1990, but to comprehend the history of humanitarianism requires that we go back to the beginning. There are a growing number of very good treatments of the origins of humanitarianism, highlighting the sweeping historical changes that occurred in the late eighteenth and early nineteenth centuries, but they rarely connect these origins to further innovations, developments, and trends in humanitarian action. In short, contemporary historical accounts of humanitarianism leave the past and the present unconnected. This book provides one of the first accounts of modern humanitarianism—reading humanitarianism from its origins gives a very different perspective on its present, and reading its present gives a very different perspective on its past.

The history of humanitarianism can only be understood within its global context. I am hardly the first to make this claim, but I like to think that my approach has three defining elements that, in combination, make it distinctive. While many histories of humanitarianism emphasize either geopolitics, capitalism, or ethics, I emphasize how these three combined to shape the global environment in which humanitarianism operated. And while many accounts of humanitarianism fail to adequately incorporate the changing global context, I identify three distinctive ages of humanitarianism, an age of imperial humanitarianism from the late eighteenth century to World War II, an age of neo-humanitarianism from the end of World War II to the end of the Cold War, and an age of liberal humanitarianism from the end of the Cold War to the present. And last, while many global histories of humanitarianism treat the world solely as a constraint on humanitarian action, I also am interested in how the global moment shapes what humanitarianism *is*.

Examining the history of humanitarianism through these global ages sheds light on its ever-present trends and tensions. Humanitarianism, much like international ethics, has expanded beyond the wildest expectations of its earliest champions. Many others have noted how humanitarianism has grown from being a minor movement in isolated parts of the West into a major feature of global social life. Yet there are several features of this expansion that deserve much more attention than they have received by prior accounts. There has been an expanding international ethics of care that has fueled the growing scale and scope of humanitarianism, driven not only by rounds of extraordinary violence but also by attempts by the international community to rescue its own self-image as civilized, humane, and good. Humanitarianism has become a full-blown area of global governance, meaning that it has become increasingly public, hierarchical, and institutionalized. The simultaneous expansion of an ethics of care alongside the growing governance of humanitarianism leads to another critical but overlooked aspect of humanitarianism's history: the changing forms of an empire of humanity. Humanitarianism more closely resembles empire than many of its defenders might like, but because it is an emancipatory project this accusation does not fit quite as well as many of its harshest critics suggest. The application of power in order to liberate the victims of the world is one of the constants of humanitarianism, but politics, power, and ethics have combined in different ways historically to alter the practice of empire. I try to capture these changes and enduring tensions through the concept of paternalism. In general, by taking the long view, we are better positioned to understand the continuities, disruptions, and trends in international humanitarianism.

Adopting a global-historical view of humanitarianism illuminates not only some neglected features of its evolution, but also some enduring tensions. Although there is a growing line of commentaries of humanitarianism that are sensitive to its paradoxes and dilemmas, because they limit themselves to contemporary events they fail to appreciate fully how these tensions have been present from the beginning. In fact, I will suggest, these tensions are not simply an artifact of humanitarian actors having to operate in a dirty world—they also are nearly intrinsic to humanitarianism. Over the decades humanitarianism has maintained a delicate, and ultimately unstable, balance between different elements (more on these elements in a moment). This is not a dialectic, with a movement from thesis to antithesis to synthesis, suggesting that humanitarianism is moving toward a reconciliation and harmonization of its different parts. Nor is humanitarianism a pendulum, swinging back and forth between the excesses of purity and politics, never quite finding a resting place. Neither of these metaphors quite captures how humanitarianism is defined by an "unstable balance" between potentially contradictory elements that are always present and never reconcilable. The metaphor that comes closest is the double hologram: tilt the picture one way and some parts become prominent and others fade; tilt the other way and there is a reversal.

My narrative of humanitarianism elevates its enduring tensions—the following five have been central to producing the zigs and zags of humanitarianism:

Humanitarianism is a creature of the world it aspires to civilize. Many histories of humanitarianism showcase the moral visionaries, such as William Wilberforce, Henry Dunant, Eglantyne Jebb, Dr. Bob Pierce, and Bernard Kouchner, who dared to imagine new kinds of responsibilities toward the helpless, relentlessly pressured power-obsessed states to deepen and extend their obligations to populations in distress, and created a platform for ethical action whose living legacy is a global architecture of care for distant strangers. They tried to make the world a better place, and in many cases they succeeded, and even when they failed (which was often), they offered a living reminder that it is possible to answer suffering with something more than mourning.

However expansive their moral vision, it was necessarily limited by culture, circumstance, and contingency. The abolitionists of the early nineteenth century were outraged by slavery on faraway plantations but, in retrospect, were remarkably dispassionate regarding the slavelike conditions endured by the working classes in Manchester and London.[9] Dunant offered a revolutionary plea to make European wars less barbaric, but he had little to say about the outrages committed by European powers in the colonies. In the decades following World War II the UNHCR impressively expanded refugee protection to include new places around the world, but it refused to intervene in Biafra on the grounds that internally displaced peoples were outside its jurisdiction. Ethical practices are limited by culture and choice.

There are various ways to understand how context shapes what is imaginable, desirable, and possible, and in this book I foreground the global environment. I observe three ages of humanitarianism, distinguished by a global context defined by the relationship between the forces of destruction (violence), production (economy), and protection (compassion). For Imperial Humanitarianism it was colonialism, commerce, and civilizing missions; for Neo-Humanitarianism the Cold War and nationalism, development, and sovereignty; and for Liberal Humanitarianism the liberal peace, globalization, and human rights. Each of these ages imprinted the meaning of humanitarianism, the constraints on humanitarian action, and the ethical dilemmas faced by humanitarian organizations. Although I am attentive to the global conditions under which humanitarianism makes history, I do not want to lose sight of the possibility that humanitarians, at times, project their moral imagination in ways that reshape the world. Humanitarians can and do reflect critically on their actions and attitudes, ensuring that they do not become a mere facsimile of the world but remain capable of transforming it. Too many critical histories spend too much time exposing the power that lurks behind noble enterprises and not enough time considering how humanitarians rethink the ethics of care.

We live in a world of humanitarianisms, not humanitarianism. Although it is impossible to carbon-date the origins of humanitarianism, the actual term began coming into everyday use in the early nineteenth century. We can certainly understand it as a form of compassion, but in practice it had three marks of distinction: assistance beyond borders, a belief that such transnational action was related in some way to the transcendent, and the growing organization and governance of activities designed to protect and improve humanity. This classification of humanitarianism differs from many books on the subject, which define it as the impartial, neutral, and independent provision of relief to victims of conflict and natural disasters. That definition that comes from the ICRC, which is treated as the guardian of all things humanitarian. However, the ICRC did not discover a definition waiting to be found; rather, it crafted a definition in response to the constraints on its goal of medical aid. After making this definition, it then defended it against rivals. Those harboring different ambitions and facing different challenges adopted alternative conceptions of humanitarianism, some articulating broader ambitions, others not so fastidiously loyal to the principles of impartiality, neutrality, and independence. Indeed, to be called a humanitarian was not always a compliment. During the nineteenth century it could be used a term of derision, to refer to busybodies and people fond of telling others how to live their lives.[10] To be a humanitarian, to put it in modern parlance, was to be a mixture of a bleeding heart liberal and moralizer.

There are many distinctions among and between humanitarian agencies, including national origin, religious or secular affiliation, age, size, and mandate, but two types have dominated thought and practice: an emergency branch that focuses on symptoms, and an alchemical branch that adds the ambition of removing the root causes of suffering. These branches have distinctly different understandings of the meaning of humanitarianism, its principles, and its relationship to politics. These differences help to account for the varying positions adopted by aid agencies in response to the dilemmas of the day—and even whether they acknowledge the existence of a dilemma in the first place. Moreover, for much of humanitarianism's history these branches had parallel lives; in fact, the emergency branch long reigned supreme, and its definition of humanitarianism was the industry standard, whereas those in the alchemical branch tended to avoid the discourse of humanitarianism in favor of the discourses of relief and development. Because they operated separately and portrayed their activities in distinctive ways, for much of their existence neither side worried much about what the other was doing (except in humanitarian emergencies during the Cold War).

This benign neglect changed in the 1990s, however, as these two branches crossed paths in relief and reconstruction operations and struggled over the meaning of humanitarianism. Outsiders may see such disputes as esoteric, but agencies have gotten caught up in them, not least because emergency humanitarians fear that if humanitarianism's meaning expands then it will politicize humanitarianism, compromising the ability of aid workers to save lives and turning them into enemy combatants.

Humanitarian ethics are simultaneously universal and circumstantial. For many of us the best expression of humanity is the desire to help those in need, regardless of their place or face. Impartiality, one of humanitarianism's sacrosanct principles, provides the basis for many discussions in normative ethics regarding how we should live our lives and what our obligations should be to others.[11] Many histories of international ethics adopt a Whiggish narrative— they begin at the end, stride backward through time identifying small but significant victories for ethical action, chronicle the evolution of international ethics as inevitable march of moral progress, and then use some idealized standard to judge how far humanity has come and how far it has left to go.

It is impossible to read widely in the history of humanitarianism without being impressed by how context shapes the desirable and the universal. The humanitarian ethic to intervene to stop suffering and confer dignity cannot be turned into a transhistorical category because it is rooted in contemporary notions of humanity and victimhood.[12] It was fashionable among nineteenth-century Europeans to assume that Europe had scaled a moral mountaintop and that Christianity and modernity were agents of civilization. Many of us now cringe at such beliefs. Will future generations look back at us and wonder why so many in the West were so certain that democracy and human rights are the path to salvation? My point is not to condemn contemporary commitments but rather to note that it is commonplace for a community to assume that its values have a timeless quality. I leave moral philosophers to debate whether it is possible to identify moral laws and instead concern myself with how humanitarianism comes to define the universal for a particular age.

Humanitarianism is defined by the paradox of emancipation and domination. Humanitarianism operates in the best tradition of emancipatory ethics. It aspires to keep people alive, to expand their opportunities, and to give them greater control over their fates. It does so through various interventions, all defended on the grounds that they improve the health and welfare of others who are too weak and powerless to help themselves. One of the truly breathtaking developments of the last two centuries is the extent to which this ethic of care has become internationalized and institutionalized, shaping the very nature and purpose of global governance. In fact, the world has come closer than ever to achieving what Didier Fassin calls a humanitarian government: "The administration of human collectivities in the name of a higher moral principle that sees the preservation of life and the alleviation of suffering as the highest value of action."[13] Global society has placed human suffering at the center of its concerns.[14]

Yet any act of intervention, no matter how well intended, is also an act of control. Humanitarian governance may have its heart in the right place, but it is still a form of governance, and governance always includes power. The simultaneous presence of care and control has become intensified by the growing involvement of states and international organizations in humanitarian affairs over the decades (and in this respect reverses the standard observation that global governance enhances the power of NGOs relative to states). It also results from the very nature of humanitarianism. Humanitarianism is partly paternalism—the belief that some people can and should act in ways that are intended to improve the welfare of those who might not be in a position to help themselves. Paternalism has a bad name for good reasons, but at times we implicitly accept that the world needs a good dose of paternalism; in fact, a world without paternalism might be a world without an ethics of care. That said, there can be too much of a good thing, and too much care can feel oppressive and suffocating. Paternalism is not simply an unsavory legacy of the nineteenth century—it represents both the best and the worst of humanitarianism.

Humanitarianism both undermines and advances moral progress. Observers and practitioners are often uncomfortable using the discourse of progress. It is closely associated with nineteenth-century civilizing missions, Eurocentrism, vainglorious confidence in the superiority of the West, and the general belief that the West represents the "end of history" and shows the rest of the world its future. The meaning of progress is generally in the eye of the beholder, and those with power usually define its meaning. Many who invoke the possibility of progress have a remarkable capacity for forgetting a twentieth century teeming with episodes of mass murder, often engineered by those who claimed to be the paragons of civilization. At such moments it is good to recall Mark Twain's observation on man: "He is the only animal that loves his neighbor as himself, and cuts his throat if his theology isn't straight. He has made a graveyard of the globe in trying his honest best to smooth his brother's path to happiness and heaven."[15] Yet we continue to operate with notions of moral progress, sometimes smuggled in with other concepts and often implicit in our ethical judgments regarding whether we believe that one age is superior to another, whether a movement should be supported, whether some action is consistent with understandings of humanity, the international community, and other inspirational abstractions.

Humanitarianism's history is replete with acts that can be read as simultaneously mocking and advancing notions of progress. We celebrate the abolitionists for rallying the public against the horrors of slavery but forget that many of abolition's leaders were passionately preaching Christian missions and colonialism as a way of helping these "children" become responsible adults. Henry Dunant and the other founders of the ICRC imagined saving soldiers—and Christianity. They believed that rapid modernization was causing a moral crisis in Europe and that the formation of Red Cross societies would strengthen what they believed were uniquely Christian values such as humanity, charity, and compassion.[16] And, because non-Christian peoples were incapable of honoring the laws of war but might be able to do so after a colonialism that produced civilization, the ICRC possessed the ethnocentric, if not outright racist, views that were endemic to the era. Over the last two decades humanitarian agencies have professionalized and developed new systems of accountability, but some evidence suggests that their claims to expertise and attention to donors has made them less sensitive to their "clients," "beneficiaries," and "consumers." Any "-ism" that arrives with promises of progress must be closely watched for signs of domination over those whose lives are supposed to be bettered.

It is virtually impossible to write a book on humanitarianism without confronting head-on the question of moral progress. I certainly did not begin with a Pollyanna view. I had spent several years exploring why and how good international organizations go bad, and so was primed to accept the possibility that self-anointed agents of progress might also be accomplices of misfortune. Moreover, I entered the topic of humanitarianism alert to the debate among humanitarian agencies regarding whether the post-1990s expansion was a good thing, and I tended to see the glass as half-empty. Yet because of my engagement with humanitarianism I discovered that I was drifting toward a definition of moral progress. The reader is entitled to know what lingers beneath the text. My view is that any meaningful notion of progress and a moral community requires a readiness to come to the assistance of those in need; benevolence is the surest sign of a moral community, and the expansion of benevolence to incorporate those once considered outside that community is the surest indicator of progress.[17] If the concept of community has any meaning whatsoever, then it includes the mutual obligations and moral responsibilities felt among its members; reciprocal obligations define the community and the community generates reciprocal obligations.[18] Progress, in this respect, cannot be exclusively defined by stocks of wealth. It must also include the social relations of care (recognizing that wealth can enhance our ability to care).

The expansion of those whose suffering matters is related to changes in the meaning and the boundaries of the international community.

Humanitarian action is frequently seen as both a measure of the sense of international community and a creator of that community. The eighteenth-century Swiss philosopher and legal theorist Emmerich de Vattel used humanitarian action to convey the potential for European solidarity: "If a nation is visited with famine, all those who have provisions enough and to spare should come to its assistance, though not to the extent of self-impoverishment.... Help in such an extremity is so much in accord with the dictates of humanity that no civilized nation could altogether fail to respond.... Whatever the nature of the disaster that overtakes a nation, the same help is due to it."[19] Vattel's vision of humanity, though, was largely restricted to European Christians. Steadily the conception of humanity became more inclusive, to the point that it now operates without formal boundaries. And while I know that many dismiss the concept of international community as, in Jeremy Bentham's famous line about ethics, "nonsense on stilts," the internationalization of relief is a pretty good indicator of community, and on these grounds I defend its use.

Progress depends on more than just widening our circle of sympathy; it also must incorporate the wishes, interests, and values of those who are the objects of sympathy if it is to avoid a politics of pity. As I have already suggested, humanitarianism contains elements of emancipation and domination, so those who play rescuer tend to believe that they can speak on behalf of the victims, that they know their needs better than do the victims, that their privileged positions give them the experience, wisdom, and insight to know how to put victims on the road of progress. There is no safeguard against these excesses of paternalism short of finding ways to ensure the "victims" of the world can speak on their own behalf and define their own vision of progress. Humanitarians are frequently aware of this other dimension of moral progress, even if they have not discovered a formula for balancing the desire to incorporate the voices of others against their belief that they must do the right thing, even if others do not see it as the right thing to do.

Humanitarianism is a crooked timber. I am appropriating Immanuel Kant's celebrated observation about humanity, later popularized by Isaiah Berlin: "Out of the crooked timber of humanity, no straight thing was ever made."[20] Kant was attempting to reconcile his wariness about all idealism with his belief in the possibility of moral progress. Writing in the shadows of twentieth-century utopian projects that led to unimaginable cruelty, Berlin adopted Kant's words to defend a vision of community that respects the autonomy, dignity, and liberty of the individual.

Humanitarianism is about meeting the needs of others and meeting our own needs. This fifth and final tension is perhaps the most controversial and speculative. A question hovers over my text: Why do we see an expansion of humanitarianism when we do? Our needs are always close at hand.

Some are motivated by a feeling of power and superiority, some by guilt, some by the possibility of religious redemption and salvation, some by a desire to demonstrate their goodness to themselves and to others. These and other emotions are possible, but I focus on moments of atonement, when we feel the need to demonstrate remorse for the past and repair our relations with the world around us. Simply put, the international community has tended to rally around humanitarianism at precisely the moment that its humanity is most suspect. The claim that the very act of giving to distant strangers is driven as much by our needs as by the needs of others is not to damn humanitarianism but merely to underscore the intrinsic ambiguities of the humanitarian act and the ever-present possibility that our needs may in fact be driving actions that (presumably) benefit others.

Humanitarianism generates radically divergent storylines and no stable ground. Is the history of humanitarianism defined by the humanization of politics or by the politicization of ethics? Is humanitarianism a romantic or a tragic figure? Does humanitarianism help emancipate the world's forlorn or contain them? Have humanitarian organizations and their leaders bettered the world, however slightly, or have they been compromised and co-opted by global forces that are bigger and stronger than them? Is the awe-inspiring growth of humanitarianism evidence of a more humane, just, and cosmopolitan global society or of the timeless capacity of international politics to absorb principled movements and transform them into traitors to their cause? The answer is: yes. Humanitarianism is all these things and contains all these possibilities.

Even ambitious books are limited by choice, and I made several choices along the way. The reader should know what does and does not lie ahead. This book attempts to explain selected patterns and trends in the history of humanitarianism, and while it is theoretically informed it wears its theory lightly. I do not offer a theory of humanitarianism; I can no more imagine a theory of humanitarianism than I can a theory of human rights, or of war and peace, or of global capitalism. I develop a broad framework for thinking about the dynamics of humanitarianism, but frameworks are not theories; at best they identify the central elements of the narrative and their changing relationship to one another. This framework also is ecumenical, drawing from various theoretical schools. All schools contribute something important to our understanding of the evolution of humanitarianism. I leave the gladiatorial debates for other scholars. The only "-ism" I care about is humanitarianism.

The second warning is: Western bias ahead. This is not a book on the history of all forms of humanitarianism around the world. It ignores the long tradition of Islamic charitable activities as well as forms of organized compassion in other cultures, traditions, and regions. This book does not pretend to be a complete history of charity, philanthropy, and compassion but instead is a history of the emergence and evolution of the international humanitarian order. That order is akin to the global economic and security orders: it is rooted in Western history and globalized in ways that were largely responsive to interests and ideas emanating from the West. I hope the growing interest in humanitarian action will spur others to write the history of other traditions. And to the extent that humanitarianism is developing and organizing outside the existing, Western-dominated system, which I think it increasingly is, then there are good reasons to believe that humanitarianism is entering a new stage. More interactions among different networks might change the very character of humanitarianism, perhaps making it more universal, perhaps less so.[21]

Third, the alert reader will notice that I have discussed humanitarianism without discussing its more famous cousin, human rights. Humanitarianism and human rights share various traits, but they are not synonymous, a point that needs stressing because the better-known field of human rights is often assumed to incorporate humanitarianism. It's a confusion that human rights activists and scholars unintentionally propagate. There is no simple way to explain the difference because these rivers share a headwater and have flowed into each other over the decades, and aid workers and human rights activists are frequently trying to sort out the relationship as they work to keep the waters distinct. Violating my belief that humanitarianism and human rights are social constructs and thus have no essential differences, I recognize that over the decades they have had distinct meanings.[22] Human rights relies on a discourse of rights, humanitarianism a discourse of needs. Human rights focuses on legal discourse and frameworks, whereas humanitarianism shifts attention to moral codes and sentiments. Human rights typically focuses on the long-term goal of eliminating the causes of suffering, humanitarianism on the urgent goal of keeping people alive.

Many of those in humanitarian organizations see a critical difference between what they do and what human rights organizations do, and over the last two decades they have spent considerable energy defending their humanitarian space from human rights activists. A good illustration is the 2009 decision by the International Criminal Court (ICC) to indict several Sudanese leaders for genocide. Human rights activists declared it a major victory for justice. Humanitarian organizations, on the other hand, were appalled that the ICC publically thanked aid organizations operating in Darfur for providing critical information and felt no surprise when Sudanese President Omar al-Bashir evicted nearly a dozen aid agencies on the grounds that they were not keeping people alive but rather helping Sudan's enemies. What Darfuris need is not rights but basic protections, these agencies argued, and sometimes the practice of human rights gets in the way. One veteran aid worker told me that when he is in the field, he would much rather have a beer with a soldier than with a human rights activist. In any event, my point is not to man the barricades but rather to stress that human rights and humanitarianism should not be conflated.

Fourth, this is not a history of NGOs, it is a history of humanitarianism, and it is important not to confuse the two. International nongovernmental organizations account for roughly half of the expenditures associated with the humanitarian sector, which leaves out a lot of the important players.[23] Although some NGOs may act as if they have a hammerlock on humanitarianism, they no more have a monopoly of the relief of suffering than clowns have a monopoly on making people laugh, as Hugo Slim wryly observed.[24] A variety of public and private actors contributes to humanitarian action, among them religious bodies, states, commercial outfits, philanthropies, and individuals. That said, most humanitarian organizations—by which I mean organizations whose fundamental purpose is to relieve human suffering—have been nongovernmental and international organizations.

The experience of a few well-chosen organizations can tell us much about how the world has shaped humanitarian action and how humanitarian organizations have lived their ethics. Although many agencies will make cameo appearances, I focus on the ICRC, the United Nations High Commissioner for Refugees (UNHCR), CARE International, Oxfam, Médecins Sans Frontières (MSF), Catholic Relief Services, World Vision International, and Lutheran World Relief. I provide biographical sketches in the various chapters, but I do not attempt an institutional biography of these organizations. Rather, I use critical fragments of their histories to explore the dynamic relationship between global forces and humanitarian agencies, how global forces have shaped the tensions and identities of these organizations, and how agencies have confronted these tensions. I selected these eight for several reasons. They are among the largest and most important aid agencies in the world.[25] They represent both emergency and alchemical agencies and demonstrate varying degrees of financial dependence on major donors. Although my selection criteria and my methods of chronicling my findings will not satisfy the discriminating social scientist, they do identify some important possibilities regarding the relationship between ethical practice and historical change.

The last warning is religion. Social scientists, especially those of us who like explanations based on evidence and not doctrine, sometimes have difficulty fully appreciating the role of religious discourse in shaping modern international life. It is impossible to study humanitarianism without being impressed by the importance of religion. Religious agencies can take credit for pouring the foundations for humanitarianism. Religious discourses continue to motivate, shape, and define various dimensions of humanitarianism. The importance of religion in this book is evident not only in its centrality to the narrative but also in the allegories, concepts, and metaphors that I use; it is extremely difficult to write about humanitarianism without falling under the sway of religious iconography. But humanitarianism has forced me to do more than locate the place of religion in world affairs. It also has led me to accept that humanitarianism is a matter of faith.

Humanitarianism is nothing less than a revolution in the ethics of care. This revolution, like all revolutions, was created through a mixture of transcendental visions, politics, and power, and it has generated an assortment of successes and excesses. This revolution was carried out in the name of the international community, a community that was not as universal, transcendental, and cosmopolitan as its leaders presumed and that contained the politics that inhere in all communities. Expressive of an international community that is made up of ethics and politics, of solidarity and diversity, of emancipation and domination, humanitarianism's history tells us much about the changing global order in which we live. It is a sobering counterpoint to those who insist that transnational connections are humanizing global politics and diluting power. It is a rejuvenating counterpoint to those who believe that international history is best understood as cycles of tragedy with no possibility of progress. Humanitarianism is ethics vanquished and victorious. Humanitarianism's history is modern international history—and its future.

1

⚍

Co-Dependence:
Humanitarianism and
the World

THROUGHOUT HISTORY, religious, spiritual, and philosophical commitments have inspired acts of compassion. If we equate humanitarianism with compassion, then humanitarianism is as old as history. But if we decide to limit the history of humanitarianism to when individuals started using the concept to characterize their actions and those of others, then humanitarianism is roughly two centuries old. Specifically, around the turn of the nineteenth century *humanitarianism* slowly entered into everyday vocabulary. Although there is no bright line to distinguish humanitarianism clearly from previous and current forms of charity, compassion, and philanthropy, three characteristics arose in the early nineteenth century, and have been present ever since, that are marks of distinction.

It slowly became associated with compassion across boundaries. In the beginning humanitarianism included both international and domestic action; it could refer to either abolitionists or advocates for child labor reform. Precisely when and why the concept of humanitarianism became reserved for border-busting action is unclear, though the creation of the ICRC in 1863 as the world's first official international humanitarian organization probably was a tipping point. The specific association of compassion across boundaries is related to the presumption that humanitarianism implies going beyond the call of duty. Who has duties to whom? People, organizations, and governments provide local assistance on a daily basis, and most of the time we describe them as fulfilling their duties and do not call them or their actions "humanitarian." Parents feed, clothe, and shelter their children, and it would sound odd to describe such actions as humanitarian. A police officer responding to a crime is not a Good Samaritan—she is doing her job. Villages often have a moral economy that materializes when famine, destitution, and hardship strike; members of the community are doing their duty.[1] We expect citizens and the government to act when another part of the country is struck by a natural disaster. Few in the United States characterized the Bush administration's response to Hurricane Katrina in 2005 as humanitarian; it was acting (or failing to act) according to its responsibilities. It is only when such assistance crosses a boundary that we tend to call it humanitarian. What duties do we have to each other? It is impossible to identify them in advance precisely because they are formed in and around changing material forces and moral sentiments; are understood differently in different kinds of humanitarianism; and vary with the moral boundaries of the community.

Humanitarianism's vow to help strangers in distant lands is related to a second defining characteristic: its transcendental significance. Although this is not a feature that is normally associated with humanitarianism, it figures prominently enough in the chapters that follow that I feel compelled to include it as a defining characteristic. By the transcendental I mean, quite simply, the belief that there is something larger than us. It is not unlike what some characterize as religious experience, which John Dewey, following William James, described thus: "The self is always directed toward something beyond itself and so its own unification depends upon the idea of the integration of the shifting scenes of the world into that imaginative totality we call the Universe."[2] In this manner the transcendental can embody a religious form, but not necessarily. Religious beliefs were critical to the origins of humanitarianism and continue to influence its unfolding. Yet humanitarianism tracks, in some ways, with the mythic versions of secularization, in which the secular replaces the religious as a source of authority and meaning. The world, of course, never became secularized, and neither did humanitarianism, which is why the sector maintains the distinction between faith and secular agencies. But secularly driven humanitarianism also has elements of the transcendental, which are especially evident in notions of humanity. For many who staff secular agencies, humanitarianism is a way of both expressing and bringing into existence an international community. In no way am I suggesting that humanitarians are saintly creatures because they are connecting the everyday to the transcendental. As I have already suggested and will soon elaborate, humanitarianism exists to attend to the needs of the giver and not only to those of the receiver. Nor am I suggesting that other forms of compassion are not also connected to some notion of the transcendent. Instead, I want to highlight how humanitarianism's purpose is intertwined with the desire to demonstrate and create a global spirit.

Although humanitarianism might have this otherworldly quality, it also is very much of this world. Humanitarianism is imprinted by modernity, the Enlightenment, and the belief that it is possible to engineer progress. In this way, humanitarianism is connected to governance, and a stunning development of the last two centuries is the deepening and growing governance of humanitarianism. For much of human history acts of compassion were a largely private affair, the domain of the privileged, the pious, and the philanthropic. When individuals were in need, because of either their everyday circumstances or exigencies, they had to rely on the kindness of others. Beginning in the nineteenth century and continuing in the twentieth century, there was a growing zeal for creating institutions and other standing bodies, increasingly and selfconsciously organized around the principles of rationality that are the hallmark of the modern organization. Also, the humanitarian movements of the nineteenth century, including those that were devoutly religious, frequently articulated a confidence in using modern scientific techniques and public interventions to improve the human condition. They largely imagined perfecting society, though, through markets and not with the heavy hand of the state. The nineteenth-century laissez-faire ideology slowly receded in the early twentieth century, as the state accepted more responsibilities for its citizens. Many of the same factors that led to the expansion of the welfare state also contributed to a growing willingness by Western states to expand various kinds of aid and assistance to vulnerable populations. Since World War I the organization of humanitarian action has largely followed the tremendous internationalization, institutionalization, and rationalization of global affairs. Today there exists an international humanitarian order.

What distinguishes humanitarianism from previous acts of compassion is that it is organized and part of governance, connects the immanent to the transcendent, and is directed at those in other lands. But, as discussed in the introduction, I treat humanitarianism not as a coherent whole but rather as a concept in motion that has several enduring tensions—the existence of multiple humanitarianisms; an ethics that are simultaneously universal and circumstantial; a commitment to emancipation that can justify forms of domination; the possibility (or not) of advancing moral progress; and ministration to the needs of both the giver and the recipient. Although these tensions are nearly intrinsic to humanitarianism, a global arena shaped their character, content, and intensity. Specifically, the forces of destruction, production, and compassion combined to generate three discernible ages of humanitarianism—an imperial humanitarianism, a neo-humanitarianism, and a liberal humanitarianism—and these ages shaped the meaning and practices of humanitarianism.

Although these global forces pushed and pulled humanitarianism over the decades, humanitarian organizations have some discretion over its dealings with the world that, at times, appears to leave them with no good choices. The simple recognition that aid agencies are constantly struggling over what to do, that different agencies arrive at different answers, makes this discretion apparent. Although various factors influence these choices, three are particularly important.

Humanitarianism comes in many shapes and forms, but a critical difference is between a humanitarianism that largely limits itself to saving lives at risk—emergency humanitarianism—and a humanitarianism that adds a desire to remove the causes of suffering—alchemical humanitarianism. These different humanitarian identities lean toward different responses to two fundamental problems faced by all humanitarian actors: how to live in a world of states and other actors that are often responsible for the very suffering they want to relieve; and whether and how to take into account the needs of those who are often perceived as being too weak, uninformed, oppressed, or traumatized to help themselves. In response to the first problem, humanitarian agencies have crafted different kinds of principles, and in response to the second they have demonstrated varying sensitivity (though not very much) to the problem of paternalism. Notwithstanding these differences, there is one way in which they are alike: they depend on others for their resources. A longstanding hunch is that the more they depend on states, the more likely they will conform to their wishes, an argument that has some merit but whose extreme claims I find unconvincing. By recognizing the possibility that aid agencies can shape their fate, but not under the conditions of their own choosing, I recover the possibility that they can escape their circumstances to expand the global ethics of care.

The World of Humanitarianism

While humanitarianism has many mothers, and over the ages has been influenced by various bone-chilling events and idiosyncratic developments, critical has been the combination of the forces of destruction, production, and compassion.[3] These forces do not operate in isolation but rather interact in various ways to define the age, opening up and closing off opportunities for humanitarian action, heightening and lessening the practical tensions of humanitarianism, and shaping the evolving meaning and practice of humanitarianism. These are not anonymous forces with a singular identity but rather have historical content and, in combination, produce the age of humanitarianism.

The Forces of Humanitarianism

The *forces of destruction* include acts and patterns of violence that endanger lives and the possibility of safety and security. They also affect how great and lesser powers conceptualize the relationship between state and human security. Violence has been a causeway for benevolence. Massacres, international and civil wars, war crimes, crimes against humanity, and war-induced famines have been a principal "call to alms."[4] Changes in military technology and strategy furthered the desire to expand the laws of war and provide more protections and relief to civilians. Solferino triggered a pattern in which advances in the lethality of military technology led to efforts to ameliorate its destructive potential. The emergence of total war, the obliteration of the very unstable distinction between civilian and soldier, and the willingness of combatants to treat civilians as an object of strategy have led to new forms of protection.

Patterns of war are shaped by the strategic ambitions of great and lesser powers, and these patterns can influence both the opportunities for and the constraints on humanitarian action. If states believe, for whatever reason, that there is a convergence between their security interests and humanitarian action, then aid agencies will find new opportunities in the field and beyond; if otherwise, then they will confront significant barriers. Western states decided to establish the High Commissioner on Refugees following World War I primarily because they feared that mass population displacement in Europe would lead to regional instability. Humanitarian intervention is selective because states are usually willing to put their troops in harm's only way when their security and economic interests are at stake.

Conceptions of international order and the precise relationship between domestic order and international order also have had a profound impact on the character of humanitarianism. There are two stylized views of international order. One claims that sovereignty and the principle of noninterference, alongside a healthy dose of deterrence, can create stability; the other, that domestic order affects international order. These views have enjoyed different periods of acceptance: during the late colonial period, Western states argued that colonial states required lessons in civility before they could be expected to abide by the rules of international society; during decolonization and the Cold War, great hopes were placed on sovereignty and military power; and in the post–Cold War period there is a prevailing belief that states organized around democracy, markets, and rights make good neighbors.

The *forces of production* include capitalism and the global economy and ideologies regarding the state's role in society. The debate over the relationship between capitalism and humanitarianism began the moment that formal organizations first appeared in the early nineteenth century and declared that they were trying to save the world from itself. One view is that capitalism is the structure and humanitarianism is part of the superstructure that aids capitalism's reproduction and expansion. In *The Communist Manifesto*, Karl Marx identified "economists, philanthropists, humanitarians, improvers of the condition of the working class, organizers of charity, members of societies for the prevention of cruelty to animals, temperance fanatics, hole-and-corner reformers of every imaginable kind" as operating to smooth over social grievances and help improve bourgeois society.[5]

An alternative view observes that the dislocations caused by capitalism created the conditions for humanitarianism. Market expansion, industrialization, and urbanization undermined the existing religious and normative order. In response, religious and secular leaders proposed solutions that included new kinds of public interventions that would help restore a moral order, which, not coincidentally, was consistent with capitalism's requirements. For instance, industrialists saw rampant alcohol consumption as a significant hindrance to a stable and compliant labor force, so they supported emerging temperance movements that treated alcohol as part of the devil's bag of tricks and encouraged individuals to become sober, self-disciplined, and responsible.[6]

The expansion of global capitalism, now known as globalization, also has affected humanitarianism's forms and functions, though how is a matter of controversy. Some, following classical Marxist thought, argue that capitalism's unquenchable drive to expand means that there will be a constant need to govern and integrate those that are, in Mark Duffield's phrase, on the borderlands.[7] In this view, the discourse of development, while celebrated by humanitarians in the decades following World War II, was the latest chapter in the continuing saga of capitalism's attempt to incorporate those existing on the margins. Today's antipoverty campaigns follow in their footsteps. Others argue that humanitarianism does not so much integrate the borderlands as contain them. Not everyone will be able to enjoy capitalism's benefits, and in order for capitalism to survive it must quell any possibility that frustrations boil over into rebellion. Humanitarianism is a global welfare institution, and aid workers are social workers—appearing to be emancipatory when operating as mechanisms of social control.[8] Global capitalism needs humanitarianism.

Ideologies regarding the state's proper role in society and economy also have shaped the demand for humanitarian assistance. During the nineteenth century's era of laissez-faire capitalism, individuals fended for themselves, and various charitable and reform-minded organizations stepped in where the state refused or failed to tread. In the United States the combination of a growing urban underclass alongside the rise of oil and manufacturing tycoons led the latter to found various philanthropic and charitable organizations to improve human welfare.[9] The rise of the welfare state after the 1920s increased the resources available for various kinds of aid programs.[10] The post-1980s ideology of neoliberalism and the limited state created a greater demand for humanitarian organizations; Western governments favored NGOs for delivering services because they were presumed to be more efficient than either bilateral or intergovernmental organizations.[11]

The forces of destruction and production help to account for the fluctuating demand for different kinds of assistance, the timing of outbursts of activity, and the stepwise internationalization of humanitarianism, but strategic and economic interests do not explain why individuals feel compassion for others. To do so requires attention to the *forces of compassion*. Why people feel compelled to respond to suffering remains something of a mystery. Theories abound, running the gamut from psychological—I feel guilty; to utilitarian—I like helping others; to religious—God commands me; to biological—I am genetically wired to act in ways that help the survival of the species. These theories, though, cannot explain the rapid development of institutions of compassion over the last two centuries. Nor can they explain the equally impressive change in the beliefs about who deserves assistance, what kind of assistance they require to develop their humanity, and what part they should play in defining their emancipation.

Most explanations of this growth highlight how Enlightenment processes have increased our awareness of suffering, our feeling that we are causally and morally responsible for the misfortunes of others, our confidence that we can make a difference, our belief that humans have certain basic rights, and our sense that our own humanity depends on adhering to certain moral codes.[12] In this view, Enlightenment discourses have dissolved distinctions and made it more difficult to sustain, at least rhetorically, the claim that some lives are worth more than others. The Enlightenment did not create a superior human being, a position that Kant ridiculed by suggesting that we have an "overheated mind."[13] Nor is Enlightenment a code word for secularism. The boundaries between the religious and the secular are porous; religion has motivated individuals to engage in compassionate action toward distant strangers; and secular discourses have not flattened distinctions. Instead, the claim is that a conjunction of material and ideational forces have formed a particular meaning of humanity.

These forces of compassion potentially contain an expansionary logic. The discourse of humanity, with its insistence that differences dissolve, has led to the care of previously neglected and even rejected peoples. Alongside humanity, the principle of impartiality, which claims that all individuals are equally deserving of respect and thus rejects discriminatory behavior, also contributes to a morally flat world. Furthermore, once one set of needs are attended to, then it becomes virtually impossible to refuse an adjacent or connected set of needs. Hugo Slim calls this "ethics creep." "Surely one cannot cure a wounded man," Slim observes, "only to send him back into battle or heal a small child only to discharge her back into a malarial area with no health education and primary health care system? If one sees and knows the deeper causes of a person's sickness, one is duty-bound to address it. Not to do so is morally irresponsible. It is this ethical logic that made most relief NGOs become development NGOs. And it is a good logic."[14] A typical experience for many aid workers entering the field for the first time is to feel especially touched by one child or family, to want to help them by giving them money, sponsoring a child's education, or perhaps adopting the child, securing a job for the father or mother in the field office, or arranging for the family to migrate to the West. Consider the following statement by Paul Farmer:

> Soon you find out that the children you are taking care of for their complex diseases also are not in school. Or you see the thousandth case of typhoid, and you know that is because people don't have clean drinking water. Or you see a whole family living in a very tiny hut, all with tuberculosis, and you realize, of course, that not only do they not have access to care for tuberculosis, but they also don't have adequate housing. And so it sort of opens up a Pandora's Box. Once you start doing a good job taking care of sick people...and become involved in their lives and visit them in their home...and you discover that they are not just sick, but they are facing what seem to be insuperable problems.[15]

In a slightly more cynical tone, MSF's Rony Brauman observes: "As the NGOs are happy to repeat, 'the needs are limitless.' This slogan provides a good interpretation of the humanitarian feeling, which is by definition unlimited because its object is suffering humanity, and it offers a prime fuel for organizational growth."[16] This expansionary logic helps explain the slow but steady accretion of humanitarianism in various nooks and crannies.

Although these explanations help identify the conditions that incorporated more peoples and lengthened the list of needs, they cannot explain outbursts of compassion. My observation is that these ethical awakenings are produced by a crisis of faith and a process of atonement; these, in turn, are caused not by abstractions, God or law, but rather by a cataclysmic event. Ethics, observed the philosopher Emmanuel Levinas, is "first and foremost an event. Something must happen to me in order for me to stop being 'a force that continues on its way' and wake up instead to pangs of conscience."[17] But what is it about these events that deliver this kind of impact? While killing, destruction, and unnecessary suffering can give us pause and move us to act, arguably it is when we feel implicated in the suffering that we undertake the emotionally wrenching process of critical self-reflection. It is our behavior and not the behavior of others that unsettles. Humanitarianism is sustained by a particular story that we tell ourselves—that we are good, loving individuals. There are moments, though, when this narrative of the compassionate and loving self becomes impossible to sustain. There are encounters that can force individuals to reexamine everything they thought they knew about others and themselves, unleashing a spiritual anxiety.

Such moments can lead to a process of atonement—the expatiation of sin. The concept of atonement is deeply religious, central to Judaism and Christianity, and while the practices of atonement have changed over the centuries, some of its fundamental features resemble how humanitarian actors respond to a crisis of faith. To begin with, there must be a recognition that a sin has been committed; this sin might be against God or against another human being, but the consequence is that a relationship has been broken and must be repaired. This recognition demands a response. Historically such responses have included a range of religious practices, and the goal of these acts of repentance is not necessarily to punish but rather to return one's soul to its proper place. One venerable response is sacrifice. In ancient Judaism sins were expatiated by sacrifices at the temple in Jerusalem; after the Jewish expulsion by Rome, prayer became its substitute. A fundamental tenet of Christianity is that Jesus Christ died on the cross to sacrifice and atone for the sins of others. Today the language of sacrifice continues, though not usually with demands for human or animal sacrifice.

However, sacrifice is often not enough. It also is essential that, as demanded by the Jewish prophet Ezekiel, repentance include "a new heart and a new spirit." Outward expressions of this awakening include charity. To work for the poor, then, is not punishment but rather reparation. For those who are already working for the poor and perhaps, in this respect, symbolizing the atonement of others, the journey might be especially intense, emotionally burning. In general, atonement encapsulates the process of regeneration, purification, and restoration of a unity with humankind.

Although the concept of atonement is typically reserved for individuals, a comparable process occurs in the community. Communities also tell stories about themselves, how they define material and moral progress and how they are loving, compassionate, and good. There are, though, events, that violently disrupt such self-conceptions, moments that compel the recognition of a breach between who they say they are and what they do. One of the shocks of World War II was that "civilized" people committed such barbarity toward civilians, not only because they were in the path of war but also because they were seen as inhuman and thus could be cruelly treated and disposed of. Once the community acknowledges its sins and shortcomings, then it must repent in ways that honor the dead. There are various ways to do so, including erecting memorials, creating ceremonies and days of remembrance, and engaging in other symbolic rites that are designed to remember the dead and recognize their suffering. Repentance also can include acting in ways that are intended to stop such action from ever happening again: "Never again."[18] In other words, the living are at the service of the dead, and the dead deserve not only cemeteries but also moral institutions.[19] The living are a bridge between the dead that still walk among us and history's future victims if we do not act differently.[20] After World Wars I and II various religious and secular elites attempted to push forward new moral institutions that they believed would represent true monuments to the dead. We pledge to become the people that we said we were.

This collective process of atonement helps explain the burst of institution-building that follows horrific events that shock not just the conscience but also our own sense of humanity. In this spirit, over two centuries ago Kant wrote:

> Various evidence suggests that in our age, as compared with all previous ages, the human race has made considerable moral progress, and short-term hindrances prove nothing to the contrary. Moreover, it can be shown that the outcry about man's continually increasing decadence arises for the very reason that we can see further ahead, because we have reached a higher level of morality. We thus pass more severe judgments on what we are, comparing it with what we ought to be, so that our self-reproach increases in proportion to the number of states of morality we have advanced through during the whole of known history.[21]

Kant is postulating a self-induced spiral model of moral progress. It begins with an event that challenges our self-affirming narrative. In response, we pledge to do better and begin the process of creating new institutions to carry out our new obligations and duties. Perhaps we will do better on the next occasion, but even if we do, we invariably fall short of our declared pledges, which, in turn, leads to another round of self-questioning followed up by another round of institution-building. It is because we are not the people we say we are but believe we can be that causes us to do better than the last time, even as we fail each and every future challenge.

Disasters, both natural and man-made, are not only moments when we recognize that we are not who we say we are but also moments of possible renewal. In early American evangelical thought, "misfortune...was to be understood as a blessing that could be measured in increments of moral and spiritual development. Amid the growing influence of evangelicalism in the middle years of the eighteenth century, rival preachers seized on disasters specifically as spurs to personal spiritual awakening."[22] This spiritual awakening need not be religious; it also can be secular. One historian of American foreign policy accounts for the rather appreciable difference between the American reaction to World War I and World War II to the gap between facts and norms, between horrifying realities and abstractions such as justice and security.[23] A theme in the United States following the devastating earthquake in Haiti in January 2010 was to treat it as an opportunity to imagine and work for a "new Haiti." Cataclysms are opportunities for regeneration and renewal—and atonement is central to this process.

Although I have singled out the forces of destruction, production, and compassion, an additional source of influence bears mention, even if I will not anoint it as a fourth force: technology. Changes in material and human technologies have not only unleashed the destruction and disintegration that have motivated humanitarian action, they also have expanded the opportunities for it. Changes in transportation technology have shortened the distance between those who have and those who need. Changes in media technology have made claims of ignorance unsustainable.[24] Media imagery, beginning with the emergence of war reporting in the mid-nineteenth century and continuing with today's satellite, telecommunications, and web-based technologies, has increased public awareness, which, in turn, has created a demand that something be done in the face of conscience-shocking suffering. In the late nineteenth century, Edmund Morel and missionaries used the recently invented camera to publicize King Leopold's savagery in the Congo Free State. In Mark Twain's satire of Belgian rule in *King Leopold's Soliloquy,* King Leopold laments, "The Kodak has been a sore calamity to us.... I was looked up to as a benefactor of a down-trodden and friendless people. Then all of a sudden came the crash! That is to say, the incorruptible Kodak."[25] The video footage of the starving people in Korem, Ethiopia, in 1984 helped to galvanize action. Changes in human technologies also have improved the capacity to intervene. There has been radical improvement in emergency medicine, delivery systems, and logistical capacities; the consequence is not only are we more efficient at saving lives, we also have greater confidence that we can.

The Ages of Humanitarianism

There have been three distinct ages of humanitarianism: an imperial humanitarianism, from the early nineteenth century through World War II; a neo-humanitarianism, from World War II through the end of the Cold War; and a liberal humanitarianism, from the end of the Cold War to the present. Each age is distinguished by the constellation of the forces of destruction, production, and compassion, which, in turn, shaped the overall purpose of humanitarianism and constrained how humanitarian organizations confronted the ethical dilemmas of the day. As we move from one age to the next, though, two trends emerge: a discourse of humanity that extends more protections to more populations that were once neglected or reviled; and a growing governance of humanitarianism, rendering humanitarianism increasingly public, hierarchical, and institutionalized. Although there were no clean breaks between one age and the next, cataclysmic events largely associated with war proved to be turning points and accelerators of these trends. The following table summarizes the ages and their elements.

TABLE 1 THE AGES OF HUMANITARIANISM

Forces	1800–1945 Imperial Humanitarianism	1945–1989 Neo-Humanitarianism	1989–present Liberal Humanitarianism
Destruction	Great Power war and colonialism	Cold War and decolonization	Liberal peace
Production	Commerce	Development	Globalization
Compassion	Civilization	Sovereignty	Human Rights

The Age of Imperial Humanitarianism (chapters 2 through 4) spans from the early 1800s through World War II. As the forces of destruction and production destroyed a local sense of community, the forces of compassion encouraged individuals to widen their horizons and to imagine new kinds of obligations to one another. Fueled by new ideologies of humanity and a belief that Christianity and the West defined the values of the international community, liberal and religiously inspired humanitarians set out to nurture new kinds of compassion, accepted new responsibilities, and aspired to release civilizing processes to reduce human suffering. The forces of destruction and compassion led to the establishment of the ICRC and the Geneva Conventions. It also reflected a Eurocentric idea of international community. Motivated by the ideas of spreading Christian fellowship and rescuing the fallen, Dunant imagined voluntary organizations rushing to provide medical assistance on the battlefield. The ICRC assumed that only European states would be able to understand fully and comply with the laws of war; it was not until Japan and Turkey asked for admission that the ICRC debated and decided to expand the club because it might spread European society.

Notwithstanding the ICRC's quasi-public standing, this burst of relief activity was largely a private affair. Sometimes movements would try and use the state for its purposes, most notably when the antislavery societies tirelessly petitioned the British Parliament. But most humanitarian action occurred outside of formal channels of governance; even the ICRC was not quite a public body, falling in the space between a private relief agency and a public international organization. It was only with World War I that states became involved in humanitarian action, creating several international humanitarian organizations, including the High Commissioner for Refugees, which revealed how far states had come in accepting new kinds of responsibilities for the vulnerable—but also how far they had to go.

The Age of Neo-Humanitarianism (chapters 3 through 5) begins with the end of World War II and ends with the cessation of the Cold War. World War II, decolonization, and the Cold War created a new space for imagining new kinds of commitments to the welfare of more populations overlaid by superpowers striving to harness humanitarian action to their interests. The end of colonialism created an institutional vacuum in the Third World, quickly occupied by the superpowers, nongovernmental organizations, and international organizations pledging to bring progress and modernity to the backward populations. Universal versions of humanity and the community of peoples slowly edged out stratified views of humanity. While the infantilizing civilizing ideology was no longer acceptable, the arrival of new forms of global governance alongside ideologies that proclaimed that the rich and powerful had an obligation to "teach" the rest of the world altered the tone more than the workings of paternalism.

The globalizing tendencies of humanitarianism alongside the dangers of a more state-centered architecture became particularly evident during humanitarian emergencies. After World War II, states limited the few existing international humanitarian agencies to Europe, but they capitalized on world events and the discourses of humanity and impartiality to claim a universal jurisdiction. But there was no doubt who was in charge. Now that states and their international organizations were becoming more central to humanitarian action, agencies began emphasizing principles such as neutrality, independence, and impartiality as a way to clear a space for themselves. It would prove painfully difficult to do, especially because aid agencies were increasingly dependent on states and international organizations for their funding. And even those who used their principles to keep their distance from politics were not always happy with the results, including an ICRC whose concept of neutrality led some to accuse it of cowardice in the face of crimes against humanity. In places like Biafra, Vietnam, Cambodia, and Ethiopia, aid agencies discovered that they were part of the war and pawns for combatants, struggling to figure out how close to get to politics without getting burned and how to deliver aid without unwittingly prolonging conflict or suffering.

We now reside in a Liberal Humanitarian Age (chapters 8 through 10). International security shares the stage with human security and ethnic, religious, and nationalist conflict, and the international community's response is to create a liberal peace that might remove the causes of violence. The concern with the dangers failed states posed to themselves and others heightened after September 11, 2001, as major powers and international organizations produced a sense of urgency to those domestic conditions, including poverty and despotism, that were said to be breeding grounds for terrorism. Saving failed states was now a human security issue, too important to be left to nongovernmental organizations. Development suffered its own ideological crisis in the 1980s, but the urge to provide economic relief continued with the emerging globalization agenda. Globalization was creating winners and losers, with a growing fear that there would be a revolt by the losers if their needs were ignored, fueling various global campaigns, including debt relief, development, and disease prevention. The world encountered the "end of history," and while many distanced themselves from this vitriolic formulation, there was no escaping liberalism's rising hegemony— even as the challenge became how to accommodate universalism in a world of diversity and growing forms of provincialism that resulted from globalizing forces that were seen as enemies of tradition. Growing connections, facilitated by technological revolutions in transportation and communication, heightened a sense of community, evident not only in the steady stream of global campaigns to ban landmines, provide debt relief, make medicines accessible to the poor, and on and on, but also in changes in the meaning of state sovereignty and, most prominently and profoundly, the ascendant discourse of human rights.

This new global environment had major consequences for humanitarianism, creating new opportunities alongside new dangers. The eruption of civil wars, complex humanitarian emergencies, and mass murder campaigns around the world led to new forms of humanitarian action—aid agencies attempting to deliver life-saving assistance in the midst of war, states becoming increasingly involved in the protection and delivery of assistance, and a growing number of international organizations engaging in the resolution of war. Until the 1990s, relief, rights, and development agencies engaged in parallel play, rarely contemplating the relationship among their fields of activity. A decade of humanitarian emergencies and postconflict reconstruction projects, though, encouraged these organizations to begin coordinating and integrating their programs and ambitions. Humanitarian agencies became busily involved in postconflict reconstruction and peacebuilding, promoting democracy and human rights, pursuing a human security portfolio, addressing the causes of poverty with the creation of microfinance projects, attacking gender violence and inequality, and teaching local communities how to settle their disputes peacefully. The desire by the international community to extend new kinds of protections to civilian populations led to a "responsibility to protect." Humanitarian intervention, once dismissed as illegitimate, was now in play, and humanitarian organizations that once sought to use states for humanitarian action now found themselves being explicitly used by states as a tool for their political and strategic objectives.

The Humanitarians

Until now I have focused on the world of humanitarianism, giving proper respect to the global conditions that made and remade humanitarianism over the decades. Too much respect, though, imposes a cost. It might cause us to imagine that the world and the humanitarianism of its creation has coherence or that humanitarian organizations are supplicants and replicants, captured by forces greater than them and acting according to their instructions. This is not the case. Humanitarianism is replete with tensions that owe to different traditions of humanitarianism, and different kinds of humanitarian organizations with different missions make different decisions under differently imagined ethical dilemmas and project different kinds of moral imaginations that challenge themselves and the world in different ways. Humanitarian organizations are both of and beyond the world. To recover the ambiguities, below I explore humanitarianism's relationship of power to the powerful and the powerless; the distinction between emergency and alchemical humanitarianism; and whether and how money shapes moral choices.

The Powerful and the Powerless

Power is always present in humanitarian action, but humanitarian organizations tend to be more sensitive to the power that others have over them than they are to the power that they have over others. Humanitarians depend on others to do good, especially on states and others who have political and military power. Humanitarians often need the cooperation of the very groups that are responsible for the suffering or who will help only so long as it furthers their interests. The ICRC needs the cooperation of those states who are suspected of abusing prisoners of war, political prisoners, and detainees. Aid organizations often seek funding from the same governments that they believe have caused the suffering they want to alleviate. Relief convoys often must negotiate with the same rogues that are causing, and frequently benefiting from, mass starvation. Aid agencies try to minimize the compromises they make, but compromise they must.

Over the decades humanitarians have used, in some form, fashion, or combination, four principles to enable them to follow their values and not the interests of others. Humanity commands attention to all humankind. Impartiality demands that assistance be based on not on the basis of nationality, race, religious belief, gender, political opinion, or other considerations.[26] Neutrality demands that humanitarian organizations refrain from taking part in hostilities or from any action that either benefits or disadvantages the parties to the conflict. Independence demands that assistance not be connected to any of the parties directly involved in the conflict or who have a stake in the outcome. One MSF official dramatized the importance of not taking government funds in the following way: "Can you imagine MSF convincing the Taleban [sic] of our neutrality if our operations were funded by your governments [from NATO]? For that matter, can you imagine the reverse? A health organization working in London or New York or Copenhagen funded by the Taleban [*sic*]?"[27] Although there are various ways in which aid agencies have tried to maintain and assert their independence, both real and perceived, most prominent has been their desire to limit their financial dependence on states.

Like weak states that cling to their sovereignty because they have little else to protect them from powerful states, aid agencies clutch at these principles to create what is now called a "humanitarian space," a space where ethics can operate in a world of politics, one that allows aid workers to reach victims during times of war and limits what states can ask of relief agencies.[28] These principles work, in part, because they are seen as "apolitical" and thus allow agencies to be innocent by association. Even though humanitarianism's perceived apolitical character is part confidence trick and part self-delusion, these principles help aid agencies do the impossible.

Nearly all humanitarians, regardless of dialect, claim to be in solidarity with the objects of their compassion—yet the relationship between deliverer and recipient contains its own inequalities. Some can choose altruism; others have no choice but to play the role of the vulnerable but always grateful pauper.[29] Those that presume the authority to represent the suffering of others frequently (mis)appropriate the pain in ways that celebrate the deliverer and limit the capacity of the victims to express in their own words their suffering and sorrow.[30] The very cultivation of compassion can generate little more than feel-good moments that immunize onlookers from real action that can have more tangible effects.[31] The "gift" often comes with obligations and generates new forms of dependency and obligation.[32] The passion of compassion can lead to a "politics of pity" that creates a distance between the observer and the suffering object.[33]

While there exist various ways to dissect the power imbalance between the giver and the recipient, the concept of paternalism encapsulates many of the central ambiguities of humanitarianism. Humanitarianism and paternalism overlap in various ways. Paternalism can be understood as "the interference with a person's liberty of action justified by reasons referring exclusively to the welfare, good, happiness, needs, interests or values of the person whose liberty is being violated."[34] Humanitarian action is dedicated to helping others, and it frequently does so without soliciting the desires of those who are seen to be in need. Both, in this way, are motivated by an ethics of care. And, at the same time, both seek control over the lives of others. The philosopher Avishai Margalit dramatizes the point in the following way: "It is easy to adopt a tolerant attitude toward mistakes made by people to whom we are basically indifferent. But it is difficult with regard to people we care about, perhaps most of all with regard to our children. It is painful, sometimes unbearable, to watch them waste a distinct talent they have, behave irresponsibly regarding their health, or chose an obviously wrong spouse. Caring may easily play out at the expense of respect for the other person's autonomy."[35]

Critical here is the vexing concept of consent. A hallmark of paternalism, especially from the standpoint of liberal political theory, is the willingness to intervene in someone else's life without her consent, thus potentially violating her liberty, autonomy, and dignity. Humanitarians frequently act without asking the recipients what they want, a neglect that they generally justify on the grounds that time is urgent or that their needs are obvious. While humanitarians might claim that they do not violate anyone's liberty because they do not carry guns or use the force of law, they arrive in highly deprived environments with various privileges and resources that make any notion of consent inherently problematic. And this is true not only during emergencies. In the context of a measles epidemic in a small Sudanese village, an MSF doctor recounts the following exchange with a colleague about getting the child to understand why they need to draw blood in order to procure the child's consent. "'Do you mind if we take some blood from some of them? Just to confirm?'" he asked. 'I...um...I guess you had better ask them,' came the reply. The patients, of course, would not refuse. I doubt they recognized their right to do so, the idea of autonomy in the face of authority as unfamiliar as everything else in the hospital."[36] Generally speaking, the more we feel a responsibility for the welfare of others and a capacity to improve their lives, the more likely that we will feel justified overlooking matters of consent and other limits on our power.[37]

While humanitarianism shares traits with paternalism, I want to offer two amendments. To begin with, humanitarianism is not always paternalistic; on many occasions aid is requested and gratefully accepted by local communities. Nor is paternalism necessarily a bad thing. We expect parents to be paternalistic toward their children and the state to intervene in various areas of life to improve the welfare of its citizens.[38] Although those who allege that humanitarianism is paternalistic are not showering it with praise, I prefer to withhold judgment. Several years ago I had a conversation with a former UNHCR official who was painfully recalling the very tortured dilemma he faced in Zaire in 1997 as Hutus from Rwanda were fleeing into the jungle to escape potential harm (hundreds of thousands eventually perished): if the UNHCR allowed them to flee, then they were likely to face certain death, due to starvation, disease, and violence, but if UNHCR compelled their return to Rwanda, the organization would be forcibly repatriating them, a violation of a cardinal UNHCR principle, to a country where they probably would encounter reprisal killings by Tutsi survivors of the 1994 genocide. UNHCR decided to try and force as many back home as possible, perhaps a very justifiable act of paternalism given the circumstances.

Rather than attempting the controversial exercise of assessing, in any particular instance, whether humanitarianism is paternalistic and whether humanitarians are justified in their paternalism, I want to use the concept to highlight two issues central to the history of humanitarianism. First, who is the "human" that demands our compassion? Following Margalit, in order to be paternalistic we have to care enough about the person to worry about his or her welfare. This is relatively easy to do when considering those we know, especially immediate members of our families. But often we do not care enough about the welfare of others to be paternalistic. Although there are various reasons why we choose to care or are indifferent to others in need, critical to humanitarianism is the "human." The very notion of humanity, as the French anthropologist Claude Lévi-Strauss observed, is a recent invention. For most of human history, people tended to draw distinctions and to deny that those that were not like them might also be human, calling them subhumans, vermin, ghosts. There was no place for these outsiders in the community and, by extension, little reason to help them during hard times.[39]

Beginning in the nineteenth century, a more inclusive view of humanity slowly evolved, extending the boundaries of the community and expanding the number of people who were viewed as worthy of assistance. The antislavery societies had to fight against a fairly widespread view that Africans were not quite human, perhaps were not even capable of registering pain, as they urged their fellow citizens to recognize the humanity of people whom they had never seen and whose skin color differed from their own. Dunant wanted Europeans to recognize the humanity of all soldiers, not just their own. Over time the principle of impartiality became wedded to the concept of humanity. Today the inclusive concept of humanity erases the grounds for discriminating against or in favor of a particular population, insisting that we help those in need and not merely those whom we know or like. I do not mean to suggest that people and institutions undertake some kind of objective calculation of need before deciding whom to help; many factors influence whom people help and where aid agencies go, including previous historical ties, proximity, and, not least, international, media-saturated, spectacles. Today we typically give to those for whom we feel "special responsibilities" even as we recognize the principle of impartiality. Humanity might now be all-inclusive, but this took a fair bit of work, and there are many imperfections.

Second, how do we know what is best for another person? Perhaps such needs are self-evident. The emergency room doctor treating an unconscious victim of a car accident cannot and should not ask for the individual's consent. The same is true for the refugee camp doctor who is attempting to save the life of a victim of a landmine or a severely malnourished child. Yet much of humanitarian action does not occur during life-or-death circumstances but instead during less dramatic situations. It is difficult to know someone else's needs, especially when crossing moral, political, social, and cultural boundaries, as humanitarians do. A striking feature of the history of humanitarianism is the rarity with which humanitarians ask the recipients what they want but instead rely on their own judgment. There are many reasons for this confidence: a belief that God is on their side; that they represent the best of humanity; that they have the expertise because of their experience and education; and that a victim's lack of resources or education indicates that he might not know what is in his best interests.

Regardless of the sources of such certitude, the humanitarian frequently wants to reform societies to remove the causes of suffering. However noble, such goals are premised on several, potentially less enlightened, sentiments. Such reforms can only take place through power and politics, which, of course, revisits the possibility of paternalism and the justification for deciding for others what is in their best interests. Although interveners frequently appeal to humanity and universal values to justify their interventions, these seemingly egalitarian principles and values, especially in the context of intervention, nearly always presume a ranking of what is superior and what is inferior. In the very same speech in which Lévi-Strauss recognized the rather dramatic development of the concept of humanity, he also observed that even inclusive views incorporate hierarchical notions of humanity.[40] In short, humanitarians proclaim that they act in the name of universal values; desire to spread those values with the aim of enabling all members of the community to realize their humanity; and, therefore, operate with notions of where communities reside on some continuum of progress.

Emergency Workers and Alchemists

While humanitarianism comes in many shades, two are significant for understanding how humanitarian agencies try to change the world and how they confront the challenges in their path—emergency humanitarianism and alchemical humanitarianism, which differ in their goals, principles, and relationship to politics and therefore have different relationships to the world and to their populations of concern.[41]

Emergency humanitarianism concerns the provision of relief to those in immediate peril; cleaves to the principles of neutrality, impartiality, and independence; and has a hands-off attitude toward politics. Agencies that fall into this camp, including the ICRC and MSF, largely focus on keeping people alive. Nothing more. In an address to NATO officials in December 2009, Christophe Fournier, international president of MSF, drew a line between a bare-bones humanitarianism and everything else:

> Our ambition is a limited one. Our purpose is not to bring war to an end. Nor is it humanitarian to build state and government legitimacy or to strengthen governmental structures. It's not to promote democracy or capitalism or women's rights. Not to defend human rights or save the environment. Nor does humanitarian action involve the work of economic

development, post-conflict reconstruction, or the establishment of functioning health systems. Again, it is about saving lives and alleviating suffering in the immediate term. This marks a fundamental difference between our two ways of thinking. What you do in Afghanistan today is for the Afghanistan of tomorrow. What we do in Afghanistan today is for today. We heal people for the sake of healing people.[42]

The ability of emergency humanitarians to carry out this modest but essential task, they argue, depends on following the principles of humanity, impartiality, neutrality, and independence.[43] These principles create a "humanitarian space," a sanctuary for aid workers and victims. Only by honoring these principles will states give the access to the populations at risk; being viewed as taking sides or playing favorites can cost the lives of those in need and the aid workers.

Emergency humanitarianism labors to separate humanitarianism from politics.[44] The ICRC's mandate mentions explicitly its apolitical character. Many of the postwar international humanitarian agencies created by states, including the United Nations High Commissioner for Refugees (UNHCR), are defined as apolitical and are commanded to stay out of politics. This division of labor works for emergency agencies because it provides a discursive space for agencies to operate. Rony Brauman, a former president of MSF, forcefully argues that "humanitarianism is not a political issue and it should remain separate from political maneuvering."[45] Emergency humanitarians will not get a strong argument from states, who generally prefer humanitarians to know their place.

They can protest all they want, but those in this camp, Brauman included, practice politics. It is about a particular brand of politics. Operating in the spirit of Michel Foucault's famous aphorism that "the misfortunes of men must never become the silent left-overs of politics," they practice a politics of resistance, of humanity, of protest against an international sacrificial order that sacrifices so many in the name of justice, of life.[46] Henry Dunant was outraged that politics might treat its soldiers as disposable victims. As guardian of international humanitarian law, the ICRC continuously lobbies states to honor the Geneva Conventions; these acts resemble politics, especially for those who are accused of violating them.[47] Bernard Kouchner and the others who founded MSF were members of various leftist organizations, participated in the student movement in Paris in May 1968, and then went to Biafra and other war zones because it represented a new style of politics. MSF sent a medical team to Baghdad in the days preceding the American invasion in 2003 not because it wanted to save lives, since it did not expect the Iraqi government to give it authorization to work, but instead to stand in solidarity with the vulnerable and to enact a politics of resistance.[48] Several former MSF presidents or vice presidents have held elected office—including, most famously, Bernard Kouchner, who served as the United Nation's proconsul of Kosovo after the 1999 invasion and is now France's foreign minister. MSF's principle of witness often influences its decision to deploy to or remain in the field; in many circumstances they cannot save lives but can make a political statement by being present.[49] In general, emergency agencies work to maintain the appearance of being apolitical because it helps them practice their kind of politics.

Because emergency humanitarianism generally confines itself to saving lives, it tends to avoid the worst connotations of paternalism—but not completely. Saving lives would seem to avoid many of the possible sins of paternalism because of the presumption that people want to live, a presumption so strong that it can be assumed even in the absence of consent. In fact, I once had a discussion with a longtime member of MSF who commented that one reason why MSF chose not to go beyond emergency relief was that they were worried about becoming paternalistic. But restricting activities to emergency medicine does not eliminate the possibility of paternalism. After all, doctors are frequently accused of treating patients like inanimate objects that are to be manipulated for their own good. As another MSF worker once confessed, they work in environments of radical inequality, and it is impossible to avoid paternalism, no matter how much they try.

Alchemical humanitarianism involves saving lives at risk and addressing the root causes of suffering; operates with a less binding set of principles; and treats politics as a necessary and at times even welcome feature of humanitarian action. What does alchemy have to do with humanitarians who want to make the world a better place? The relationship might be subtle and slightly insulting, but the association is far from contrived or unfair. Although alchemy is now understood as a pseudo-science (at best), and alchemists are associated with the fanciful desire to transform unassuming metals into gold and sliver, alchemists tried to bring together the physical and spiritual worlds in order to produce a new and more valuable object. Alchemists were treated as experts, possessors of knowledge with the capacity to create highly valued and, at times, nearly sanctified objects. And even some of the most revered scientists of the modern age were devotees of alchemy, including Sir Isaac Newton.[50] Although it is fashionable to call humanitarians the new missionaries, it is more accurate to call them the new alchemists, given their attempt to harness the science of the day to transform social, political, economic, and cultural relations so that individuals can lead more productive, healthy, and dignified lives. Those engaged in development, peacebuilding, and community empowerment strategies frequently use empirically grounded research, trial-and-error methods, and close observation to draw inferences that can guide future action; to the extent that they do, then they are on much firmer ground than the original alchemists (and in this sense, the label is unkind and unfair). But when the conversation turns to how to produce peace, or how their individual programs might contribute to peacebuilding, I am less certain that they are any more justified in their confidence than the medieval alchemist in his Midas touch.

Alchemical humanitarianism emerged in the late eighteenth and early nineteenth centuries. Decades before Dunant wrote his stirring memoir, various intellectuals, politicians, jurists, and clergy started an impressive number of reform movements with the intention of arresting the apparent disintegration of moral society as a consequence of rapid industrialization, urbanization, and market expansion. Drawing from a mixture of religious and Enlightenment ideas, they pushed for public interventions to alleviate suffering and restore society's moral basis, concentrating on domestic issues such as temperance, charity for the poor, child labor, public education, and, most famously, the abolition of slavery. The urge to reform and transform intensified over the decades, bringing more of daily life under its domain. This broader movement suggests a connection between early-nineteenth-century abolitionists, the late-nineteenth-century missionary movements, the mid-twentieth-century development agencies, and the early-twenty-first-century peacebuilding programs.

Alchemical humanitarianism judges the merits of impartiality, neutrality, and independence in each individual situation. These principles can help aid workers do their work, but not always. At times combatants will not give them access, no matter how principled these agencies claim to be. Civilians are not only war's unintended victims; they can also, in fact, be its intended targets. Because genocide, ethnic cleansing, and crimes against humanity can occur only if civilians are left unprotected, those carrying out such depravities have little interest in letting in well-intended outsiders. Under these circumstances, how do principles of neutrality and independence help the victims? How did neutrality help the victims of the Rwandan genocide? Moreover, because their ambitions include trying to remove the causes of suffering and vulnerabilities, it is nearly impossible to appear neutral.

Alchemical agencies, therefore, have a more complicated relationship to politics. Like emergency agencies, they cherish being perceived as apolitical because it facilitates their ability to work without triggering the suspicion of the state or local elites; they often present their activities as technical and not political in order to avoid suspicion. Yet if agencies want to remove the causes of suffering, then they will have to get their hands dirty with politics. They will have to advocate for the redistribution of political power, the reallocation of resources, and the enforcement of rights. They certainly can insist that they are not political, but local elites, who would be the likely losers of any reforms, know better. Furthermore, resource-starved humanitarian agencies cannot and need not tackle this ambitious agenda on their own. States can help. It is because of the tireless lobbying, pleading, cajoling, and shaming on the part of humanitarian organizations that, on occasion, states have responded to the tragedies around the world, adopted more progressive foreign policies, and harnessed their considerable power for good. Advocacy is politics by another name. Politics, far from being the enemy, can be a brother in alms.

Given the desire to remove the causes of suffering through various kinds of interventions, for alchemical humanitarians paternalism has always been imminent or present. The nineteenth-century missionaries and liberal humanitarians were paternalistic, often quite unapologetically so, on the assumption that these childlike populations needed adults to civilize them. Today there is such stigma attached to paternalism that no right-thinking humanitarian would ever admit to it, but in many instances paternalism exists in all but name. It is only recently that many humanitarian agencies have undertaken needs assessments or incorporated the views of local populations. As I previously noted, there are many reasons why they have traditionally neglected or discounted local opinion, including the belief that they have superior knowledge and the conviction that they need to ignore the loudest voices, often those who have the guns and who are most committed to defending the status quo, if they are going to promote social change. In any event, I do not want to bury or praise humanitarians for their paternalism, only to insist that, like death and taxes, it is a near-certainty.

For much of humanitarianism's history, emergency workers and alchemists were aware of each other but tended to go about their business without paying too much mind to the other, except during times of war. During the nineteenth century, those wanting to humanize war in Europe and those wanting to improve the lives of the native populations in newly acquired colonial territories had little reason to coordinate their activities or even exchange views. World forces, though, encouraged both sides to expand their horizons. Beginning slowly with World War I, picking up steam in World War II, and then galloping at full speed after the end of the Cold War, humanitarians began actively to consider the relationship between relief and reconstruction. These considerations, toward the end of the century, turned into a full-fledged debate between emergency humanitarians and alchemical humanitarians about what humanitarianism is and how it should be practiced. Tensions run high because a lot is at stake, including lives, resources, and status.

Money and Morals

Humanitarianism requires more than morals—it also requires money. Until a few years ago, the perpetual struggle of NGOs to keep their operations running was barely mentioned, conveying the impression that staff were so consumed by saintly principles that they gave little thought to earthly matters like budgets. This was always far from the truth. Money is scarce, but populations in need certainly are not. Although there are moments, frequently during well-publicized disasters, when humanitarian organizations are flush with funds, usually they are worried about their income. This can be a tiring, endless, and stressful problem. Fundraising might have killed Eglantyne Jebb, the founder of Save the Children. By her account she was terrible at fundraising, was wearing herself out in the process, but felt that she had to lead by example. "It was strange," Jebb writes, "that I knew perfectly well that I was killing myself, and that I was killing myself for nothing."[51] Longtime members of World Vision International (WVI) remember the old days, long before it was one of the world's largest and best-funded aid agencies, when they would hold all-night prayer meetings to pray for contributions to stay afloat.

Because good causes do not sell themselves but rather have to be sold, aid agencies have developed considerable marketing prowess. Relief agencies have used modern marketing techniques, circulating heart-stopping, graphic pictures of human suffering and catchy slogans that communicate both urgency and a confidence that money would make a difference. They obtain celebrity endorsements and tie-ins with companies. They cultivated the media in order to garner favorable coverage, "brand" themselves and their operations, and associate themselves with the defining issues and events of the day.[52] There is nothing new about this marketing acumen. Eglantyne Jebb used all kinds of marketing techniques, including distributing leaflets with pictures of starving babies and taking out newspaper advertisements imploring people to give pennies to save the life of a child. As one founding member of CARE reflected, "If there was any publicity stone left unturned, I can't think what it could have been."[53] Because fundraising can be too important to be left to volunteers, Sunday collection plates, and door-to-door campaigns, many agencies hire professionals to staff new publicity departments and outside consultants to develop and deliver the message. As one high-ranking WVI staff member unapologetically recalled: "We were a marketing machine. We worked with ad agencies. We took it all very seriously." In direct contrast to the British tradition of volunteerism, Oxfam did the heretical and hired professionals.[54] MSF was one of the first relief agencies to experiment with direct marketing, an experiment that paid considerable dividends.

Some activities are easier to market than others.[55] Emergencies have been a relatively easy sell. Individuals can readily see the need and imagine how their contribution can save lives. Accordingly, many agencies put their marketing machines into high gear the moment an emergency erupts. In fact, a good emergency can keep an agency running in the black for months. One WVI staff member assertively defended the tendency to pull out the cameras first and then the energy bars on the grounds that people give most generously during emergencies; however crass and manipulative it might appear to be to use the suffering of others to solicit funds, it works, providing more resources for other programs in need. Many agencies understand that they are walking a fine line between utilitarianism, where the publicized misery of some might generate the resources needed to alleviate the misery of many, and exploitation, where pictures reduce the poor to stick figures and remove their dignity. But they believe that they have to risk commodifying the suffering of strangers because nothing else works quite as well. So, in the spirit of Bernard Kouchner's *la loi du tapage* (the law of hype), they will advertise if not embellish the tragedy in order to tap into the guilt of the rich.[56]

As agencies sell the cause, they also sell themselves. Resembling the humanitarian version of "what is good for General Motors is good for America," many act as if "what is good for the agency is good for the cause." In response to a rather lackluster early few months, CARE in 1947 stepped up its efforts at self-promotion, believing that promoting itself was promoting its cause and that by promoting the cause it was promoting itself.[57] When Lutheran World Relief was deprived of its traditional source of funding in the 1970s, it immediately developed a marketing strategy designed to keep its name in the public eye.[58]

Oxfam's rise owed in part to its astute self-promotion. The agency placed ads in newspapers, journals, and other public outlets in order to raise its visibility, publically thanked its contributors in order to encourage loyalty, and actively attempted to brand itself so that when people thought of, for instance, world hunger they would think of Oxfam.[59] In 1958 it helped to create the World Refugee Year and, later the same year, the very well covered Freedom From Hunger Campaign in order to bring attention to the needy and satisfy its own cravings for publicity and funding. In 1960 Oxfam used the Congo to burn "the image of the starving African child onto the collective British conscience" and, in the process, catapult itself "into public view as the British medium for prompt relief to famine victims in faraway places."[60] Another example of Oxfam's marketing acumen is its well-publicized clothing campaigns; in fact, it may have meant more to the organization than to the those in the Third World. Until the 1950s much of Oxfam's activities revolved around its clothing drives, but shipping clothes is expensive, and the types of clothes that the wool-wearing British tended to donate hardly matched the needs of, say, the famine-stricken Indians in Bihar. Consequently, staff began to question whether to continue Oxfam's emphasis on clothing. For many the answer was an emphatic yes. Clothing was part of its very identity. Even if this was an expensive identity to maintain, clothing had the additional benefit of being registered in accounts as money equivalent, which lowered Oxfam's overhead expenses to around

10 percent, a figure that would impress donors of Oxfam's leanness. Lastly, clothing drives provided a way to maintain Oxfam's grassroots support; the physical act of dropping off clothes at an Oxfam shop created a tangible bond that could not be duplicated by writing a check. Oxfam continued as is.[61] While Oxfam might not make clothes, clothes helped to make Oxfam.

The vital question is: will aid agencies sell out their principles as they sell themselves and suffering? One increasingly popular portrait is of aid agencies "scrambling" for resources, ready to do and say (and to not do and to not say) whatever it takes to win the affections of their donors.[62] Humanitarian staff have told me tales of organizations holding their tongue because they did not want to bite the hand that fed them, or deciding to go into one area and not another because that was where the money was. One former senior staff member of a major relief agency recalls the reaction of a colleague in the foundation office to the news that he and others were successfully moving toward a plan for prevention: if we reduce the death toll, then we will have a harder time raising money. Sometimes doing well matters more than doing good.

Although these stories make good copy, the claim that aid agencies are willing to suspend their principles to satisfy their donors is largely based on innuendo, speculation, anecdote, and incidental correlations—not systematic evidence. Several years ago, in fact, I made plans to investigate these claims. Drawing from resource dependence approaches, my straightforward hypothesis was that the more dependent the aid agency is on states, the more likely it will alter its policies so that they are consistent with the states' interests.[63] The hunch, therefore, is that aid agencies, such as MSF and World Vision International, that do not depend on states but instead on public contributions will have an easier time doing what they think is right and not bending their principles to satisfy the interests of states. Conversely, those agencies, such as International Rescue Committee, CARE International, Catholic Relief Services, and UNHCR, that are heavily dependent on states are presumed to be more willing to alter their policies in order to secure their resources. With this resource dependence model in hand, I began collecting the data to test the argument. However, I found myself frustrated time and again by the absence of credible information. Aid agencies are notoriously poor bookkeepers, especially prior to the 1990s, and tended to categorize similar activities in different ways and different activities in similar ways. Correlations regarding the relationship between financial dependence and activities cannot be trusted.

In addition to these methodological obstacles, my thinking also began to evolve in a slightly different direction; I became more interested in those moments when humanitarian agencies interrogate their ethics and less interested in whether their policies line up with what their donors want. Of course there is likely to be a relationship between the two; having money can make it easier to follow one's conscience. But in addition to the possibility that aid organizations might undergo such self-examination without necessarily coming to the conclusion that they must change in a fundamental way, in my research I became convinced that money matters much less than identity in understanding the conditions under which agencies undertake such a process.[64]

Before proceeding to discuss one of the conditions that is likely to trigger such an ethical journey, it is important to note that organizations are built like draft horses, designed to put one foot in front of the other, never looking sideways and certainly never looking backward. There are many reasons why organizational change tends to be incremental and why organizations typically avoid the kind of painful soul-searching that typically must accompany a radical change. Change is costly. Aid organizations will rightly worry about whether they are harming their own existence by moving in new directions. There are the obvious financial costs involved, as well as the potential for rupture with existing donors. Aid agencies, like all of us, are more sensitive to losses that can be measured in the present than future intangible gains. Organizations are built to be suspicious of radical change, obsessed with rules, comfortable with tradition, and addicted to habit. In the end, to undertake true change requires the courage to look oneself in the mirror and risk seeing something unrecognizable—something we generally avoid.

Yet aid agencies can and do undertake the necessary ethical labor, reconsidering not only their strategies but also their missions. Periods of financial crisis—when the agency nears bankruptcy or experiences hard times—are certainly a major cause of organizational change. Desperate times call for desperate measures, as the saying goes. But organizations that are experiencing severe economic pressure, at least the organizations in this book, are not willing to do anything to stay afloat. Instead, they keep one eye on their principles, the other on their donors' perception of their legitimacy. In other words organizations will revise their principles to accommodate the organizational changes they need to make to survive. The history of humanitarianism reveals many examples of this process.

Humanitarian organizations also can undertake wrenching soul-searching when they believe that they have acted in ways that violate their basic principles, contributed to harm and injustice, or prolonged the suffering of others.[65] In other words, relief agencies that suffer crises of faith are potentially more likely to reconsider and potentially change their fundamental principles. Relief workers can vividly recall circumstances that have forced them to reexamine their basic understanding of the community, who is a member, what members need and deserve, how the weakest members might participate in their own emancipation, and how their own humanity has been affected. In this respect, aid agencies experience their own process of atonement. After its silence in the face of the death camps during the Holocaust, the ICRC reexamined a policy of neutrality that appeared to give comfort to the killers. After it finally acknowledged that it had responded to the genocides in Bosnia and Rwanda with indifference, the UN undertook a very painful process of introspection. As many aid agencies discovered over the last decade, sometimes the unintended consequences of their programs are a result of their failure to listen to the people they wanted to help. What triggers a crisis of faith is difficult to predict, and how that crisis is resolved is equally uncertain and dependent on many situational factors, including money, but at the very least it is important to acknowledge the possibility that aid agencies can try to stop focusing on the world at large and interrogate their own motives. Aid agencies are sometimes the first to tell the international community what it must atone for and how to do so, and even they must occasionally look in the mirror and imagine what they have done and what they have become. It is at these very moments of self-doubt that humanitarians demonstrate the capacity to act beyond the here and now.

PART I

The Age of Imperial
Humanitarianism

2

⤙≋⤚

The Humanitarian Big Bang

THE REVOLUTION in moral sentiments and the emergence of a culture of compassion is one of the great unheralded developments of the last three centuries. Although charity and benevolence were part of everyday life, they were not a central part of organized society. In this way the revolution in compassion resembled the corresponding revolution in capitalism and the states system: there were pockets of long-distance trade and even wage labor prior to the seventeenth century, and there were certainly interstate rivalries prior to the seventeenth century, but there was a grand transformation in the global economy and the states system in the seventeenth and eighteenth centuries. Something similar happened to compassion beginning in the eighteenth century as it moved from part of the private realm and into the public realm, and the alleviation of human suffering became a defining element of modern society.

Evidence of this sea change in compassion can be observed from strategically placed historical outposts. Throughout history, various religious and lay figures practiced compassion in their daily lives, but there was no regime of sympathy. In the late seventeenth and early eighteenth centuries, Latitudinarian preachers, in an offshoot of Anglicanism, sought to combat puritan pessimism regarding human nature and introduce a realm of virtue oriented around a new spirit of benevolence. Some historians credit them for laying the groundwork for a new doctrine of sympathy and feeling; regardless of their actual impact, they were pushing a new set of ideas.[1] According to the literary historian R. S. Crane, the doctrine of humanitarianism and the notion of the sympathetic man began to make inroads in the mid-eighteenth century, commenting that this development was "something new in the world—a doctrine, or rather a complex of doctrines, which a hundred years before 1750 would have been frowned upon, had it ever been presented to them, by representatives of every school of ethical thought."[2] Although most of these acts and discussions concerned neighbors helping neighbors, at times they extended to foreigners. In 1755 a massive earthquake crushed Lisbon, inspiring one of the first pan-European relief efforts. In eighteenth-century France, a philosophical movement helped to popularize the concept of *humanité,* implying a deeply felt concern for the welfare of one's fellow human beings.[3] In this spirit, Emmerich de Vattel, a seminal figure in the history of modern international law and international relations, claimed that nations are bound by "humanitarian obligations" (*offices d'humanité*). These humanitarian obligations are "the mutual assistance and duties which men owe one another as social beings who must help each other for their self-preservation and happiness and in order to live according to their nature."[4]

But it was not until the late eighteenth century that organized compassion became part of the everyday. Reflecting on developments in the late eighteenth century, Hannah Arendt observed:

> History tells us that it is by no means a matter of course for the spectacle of misery to move men to pity; even during the long centuries when the Christian religion of mercy determined moral standards of civilization, compassion operated outside the political realm and frequently outside the established hierarchy of the Church. Yet we deal here with men of the eighteenth century, when this age-old indifference was about to disappear, and when, in the words of Rousseau, an "innate repugnance at seeing a fellow creature suffer" had become common in certain strata of European society and precisely among those who made the French revolution.[5]

At another point Arendt observed that by the early nineteenth century, rapidly modernizing Europe began experiencing a "passion for compassion."[6] The extraordinary was becoming ordinary. A rapidly growing number of standing organizations, committees, and societies began forming to alleviate suffering, at first locally and then more remotely.

Additional evidence of the growing centrality of compassion can be found not only among its admirers but also among those who were less than charmed. Arendt was not always fulsome in her praise of compassion. She worried that compassion could become part of a politics of pity, and the basis for violent excesses of modern revolutions. Others, likewise, worried that a politics of pity might have the effect of removing the humanity of the object being pitied or giving the weak a new form of control over the powerful.[7] By the end of the nineteenth century, Friedrich Nietzsche grimaced at how modern philosophers were demonstrating a new "predilection for an overvaluation of compassion," whereas before they appeared to be unified on the "worthlessness of compassion."[8] Love it or hate it, compassion was becoming part of modern life.

There is greater consensus on the fact of this expansion of compassion than on the question of which of its many possible causes were most consequential. The Hobbesian image of a mechanical, nearly soulless, asocial individual lost influence to the growing belief that compassion was a natural human instinct and a measure of a person's worth. Evident in a range of texts, including Adam Smith's *Theory of Moral Sentiments,* there was a growing appreciation for the human capacity to exhibit sympathy, a virtue inextricably related to the emerging discourse of "humanity."[9] While sympathy, much like humanity, exhibited real limits, the emerging language of natural rights helped to dissolve existing categories of inclusion and exclusion. In late-eighteenth-century revolutionary France a rights discourse led to the extension of citizenship to Europe's "other"—the Jews.[10] This period also witnessed the ascending idea of an autonomous self that was capable of using reason and making moral judgments, which, in turn, gave rise to a concern with those factors that hindered that autonomy and the capacity for learned thought.[11] Technological advances in communication and transportation caused individuals to become more aware of the suffering of others in distant lands, ways they might have contributed to that suffering, and approaches to alleviating it.[12] The clergy viewed these developments as consistent with and nurturing Christian notions of love, compassion, and charity. Humanitarianism represented a new "historical stage in the education of the emotions."[13]

Enlightenment processes helped to translate sympathy into collective action. The Scientific Revolution and a growing science of government that concerned the protection of individual liberties and intervention for the public good stimulated a newfound confidence in the human capacity to make a difference and encouraged a "collective belief in the possibility—and desirability—of disinterested service in the cause of human moral improvement."[14] These evolving beliefs contributed to a change in the organization of society for relief and charity. Whereas once the local religious institution oversaw the collection and distribution of charity, increasingly individuals organized into citizens' groups, associations, and committees to provide immediate relief and to agitate for greater public attention to the destitute and the vulnerable. As the historian Frank Klingberg astutely remarked: "All the humanitarian currents and forces of the [nineteenth] century may be thought of as the struggle for the organization of a civilized social life, with the economist, the churchman, the reformer, the poet, the satirist, and the legislator each working in many related 'causes' for the change of social conditions."[15]

The third development was a logical extension of the first two and perhaps the most revolutionary of them all: the desire to go beyond relief and to attack the very causes of suffering. Traditionally, charity translated into various forms of alms-giving and helping people survive one day to the next. Increasingly, though, it had come to be seen as not enough, a shift that owed to several factors. The growing confidence in scientific knowledge and its application to human affairs translated into a belief that it was possible to improve the human condition.[16] Moreover, charity was feared to bring out the worst in people, encouraging a dependent, irresponsible, undisciplined personality.[17] As J. D. Roberts wrote, moral reform became tied up with a

> set of culturally evolving assumptions about the responsibility of individuals for their own actions—about their capacity to choose between vicious and virtuous conduct. . . . At core it became a debate about the cultural control of the "animal appetites"—greed, lust, violence and (if it counts as an appetite) indolence—all human propensities which have the potential to disrupt the fulfillment of social obligation to family, employer, neighbors, civil authority and God.[18]

To address the causes of suffering required new forms of intervention that would alter society and humankind.

This humanitarian revolution was made possible not only by a change in moral sentiments and intellectual technologies but also by a period of rapid societal transformation marked by an expanding market, urbanization, and modernization.[19] Political, social, and economic forces were breaking down existing political communities and encouraging individuals to envision new forms of solidarity and responsibility that were at a greater social distance.[20] These transformations were also producing dislocations. The agricultural and industrial revolutions that increased economic output were also eroding rural society, causing populations to search for economic opportunities in increasingly dense cities. Settling into overcrowded urban slums far from their homes, these newcomers labored and loitered outside their traditional safety nets, fended for themselves in disorienting environments, and became seduced by all kinds of opprobrious activities. Public hangings were treated as public sport and seemed to bring out the vilest responses by crowds. Prostitution thrived and was supported by men of all classes. Alcohol was consumed with incredible passion and regularity, leading to all kinds of unsavory behavior according to many reformers of the age. Children were hardly a protected category and routinely witnessed—and often participated in—these salacious, lustful public activities.[21]

The economic and social ferment catalyzed a period of tremendous religious experimentation, though evangelicalism was perhaps most important for the development of humanitarianism.[22] Evangelicalism is a broad-brush term that can refer to any of the many Christian denominations that emerged with the Reformation, but in the late eighteenth century the evangelical movement was defined by several features: an emphasis on the conversion experience and being saved; the Bible as the only source of religious authority; a duty to share one's beliefs with others in various kinds of settings; and a focus on Jesus' death on the cross and his good works as the pathway to salvation.[23]

Evangelicalism was closely associated with "awakenings."[24] An awakening occurs when an individual emerges from a religious slumber and becomes spiritually alive. These awakenings occurred largely in and through revivals, emotional events in which sinners confessed and begged for salvation. While there were various strands of revivalism, they shared a belief that: the individual can approach God on his or her own and has the free will to choose whether or not to be saved; an emotional, life-changing event aroused salvation; and the individual "maintained religiosity and salvation through continued experiences, inward piety, and right moral behavior."[25] Evangelists were central to this process, and the best of them were charismatic and theatrical, using sophisticated methods of persuasion that raised the emotional temperature conducive to inducing religious conversion.[26]

The very idea of an awakening represented a brush against the religious grain of the time. The doctrine of predestination, the belief that all humans are inherently sinful and can do little to save themselves, dominated religious interpretation. Evangelicalism and the revivalist movement, though, was premised on the belief that individuals possessed free will—they could chose to be saved, shifting salvation from God to the individual. Evangelicals began to spread the good news, and with considerable urgency. The great awakenings were bound up with millenarianism, the doctrine that the final judgment was fast approaching. To prepare themselves for the end of days, they needed to create a more perfect religious society.[27] Such religious sentiments, of course, were hardly new; they were prominent among the first settlers in the United States and became a part of American culture, perhaps best known in John Winthrop's famous 1630 sermon, "A Model of Christian Charity." The New World would prepare for the next one.[28] In any event, the increasingly powerful evangelical movement was acting with greater urgency.[29]

The evangelical movement led to charitable activities and a burst of social reform.[30] By no means did religious activists monopolize the reform movement. Also present were secular humanitarians, who shared with the religiously minded a belief that a lack of justice in contemporary society required a change in the conditions for the improvement of societal welfare, even as they disagreed on who was to blame, with some secular humanitarians claiming that Christianity itself was the problem.[31]

Yet it is difficult to imagine this rather robust social reform movement without religion. Evangelicalism transformed religion into reform. Evangelicals believed that the purpose of life was to serve God, which translated into a struggle for personal salvation and to "save the souls of others."[32] This missionary impulse demanded urgent action because of the fear that "men were going to hell around them: they *had* to make every effort to save as many as they could."[33] And there was every reason to believe that society was going to hell. They were surrounded by evidence of society's rot and all manner of sinning. These contemporary evils were being nourished by overpopulated, dreary industrial cities that were eroding traditional family life, the existing religious order, and society's mores.[34] The discovery of one moral ill invariably led to the identification of another.[35]

In response, evangelicals, along with secular elites, established myriad organizations that seemed prepared, as one association later put it, to "redress...every oppression that is done under the sun....For the cure of every sorrow by which our land or our race can be visited, there are patrons, vice-presidents, and secretaries. For the diffusion of every blessing of which mankind can partake in common, there is a committee."[36] They created aid societies of all kinds: for aiding stranded seamen and the widows of clergymen; for recovering the bodies of the drowned; for establishing good Christian families; and for converting Gypsies to Christianity.[37] In Britain a "Tory humanitarianism school of thought" connected feelings of revulsion against oppression and misery with social action, claiming such graduates as the abolitionist William Wilberforce and Tory labor reformers like the elder Robert Peel, Richard Oastler, and Michael Thomas Sadler.[38] In the United States religious sentiments associated with evangelism gave rise to various kinds of social reform and charitable movements that had a defining impact on the development of civil society.[39]

Evangelicals, who wanted to save souls through acts of individual conversion and to build a more perfect, civilized, society, were hardly antimodernist or leery of politics. While evangelicals were reacting against the Enlightenment's assault on religion, their emphasis on reason and rationality meant that they saw no contradiction between reason and religion. In fact, modernization could stimulate religiosity and was interpreted as a sign of Christianity's superiority.[40] Although evangelical political thought included a healthy wariness of the state—for they were worried that the state might intervene in religion if the boundaries became blurred—evangelicals nevertheless were ready to work through and with the state to accomplish their goals.[41] Politics, in short, was essential for creating a proper Christian nation. As George M. Thomas observes:

> Revivalism radicalized...mainstream Protestantism: A moral citizenry must actively construct the Kingdom of God. Viewing themselves blessed by God

with foundational documents of democracy, Christians were to push forward and directly transform the nation. This led to an emphasis on social reform movements that had as their goal the defining of citizenship by building moral categories into the legal order, citizenship, education, and work. These reforms included temperance, abolition, observation of the Christian Sabbath, and public schools.[42]

Anything that obstructed salvation had to be remedied or removed, and rather than let nature take its course, it was possible to harness the modern science of government to accelerate the process.[43]

Humanitarianism revealed an emancipatory spirit that included dissolving boundaries of indifference, creating new forms of community and obligations among its members, and instilling new kinds of commitments on the part of the fortunate to the welfare of the less fortunate. Migrating from the backstreets of London to colonial outposts in northern India and West Africa because of colonialism, capitalism, and Christianity, these humanitarians began preaching a unity of mankind, encouraging individuals to identify with the suffering of others and demonstrating compassion to all living creatures. Those involved in missions of charity, including both alchemical and emergency agencies, were aware that in any era of empires power was never far behind, and they tried to find ways to distance themselves from the powerful. And as they engaged in their humanitarian actions, they were aware that the powerful and the civilized could sin with the best of them and thus were part of the problem.

This humanitarian spirit also incorporated ideologies of paternalism. Although humanitarianism contained discourses of human equality, they also existed alongside discourses of Christianity, colonialism, and commerce that deemed the "civilized" peoples superior to the backward populations. This superiority, in turn, gave them a moral obligation to assuage their suffering and help them improve their lot by ridding them of the traditions that had condemned them to a life of misery. Intervention, in other words, was intended to produce emancipation and liberation as defined by the civilized. In this way humanitarianism's emancipatory spirit also contained mechanisms of control. It targeted specific populations that might be particularly restive and used a variety of nonviolent techniques to contain the possibility of violence and rebellion. These interventions would not only give food, shelter, and hope to the indigent and thus take the edge off of rebellion, they would also help to weave the new moral order.[44] What humanitarianism could give, humanitarianism could also take away.

Although the emergency and alchemical branches of humanitarianism shared the general commitment to helping distant strangers and deepening new forms of transnational solidarity, the commitment of the former to protecting soldiers and of the latter to saving humans and humanity led to important differences between the two. Both worried about being too closely associated with those in political power, but those in the alchemical camp had more to gain by using the power of the colonial administrators and foreign merchants. Both were influenced by many of the same forces of compassion, namely a Christian and civilizational mentality, but those on the emergency side rarely ventured outside of the geopolitical realm and had difficulty, at first, imagining codes of compassion being accepted by non-Christian powers; those in the alchemical camp were more keen to see compassion not only as saving lives but also as saving souls and societies. Both had a transnational orientation, but the emergency humanitarians tended to limit themselves to Europe, while those in the alchemical camp expressed a truly global perspective. Both were wary of politics, but given the desire by those in the alchemical camp to engage in sweeping reforms that would remove the causes of suffering, they had difficulty not venturing into sensitive areas claimed by the state. Their differences notwithstanding, they are part of the same family.

3

⧯

Saving Slaves, Sinners, Savages, and Societies

F OR MANY students of humanitarianism and human rights, it all began with the antislavery movement.[1] Because of the volumes dedicated to its history, I need briefly mention only a few points that are critical to my argument. The antislavery movement was an historic breaching of established categories of humanity. As Adam Hochschild observes, "It was the first time a large number of people became outraged, and stayed outraged for many years, over someone *else's* rights. And most startling of all, the rights of people of another color, on another continent."[2]

There was no single cause of this moral awakening. Instead, various world-turning developments combined to produce an outcome that only a few decades before few had reason to believe would ever exist. The age of rights and an unprecedented willingness to see all humans as capable of reason and thus born with some natural rights played a role. The Enlightenment and a newfound passion for human liberty influenced Granville Sharp, one of the early and relatively unheralded abolitionists, and many other pioneers of humanitarian action.[3] New religious doctrines created new possibilities for salvation and for seeing others as having humanity. Nearly all of the founding abolitionists were evangelicals, and Quakers were overrepresented in the ranks, preaching that all humans were the Lord's children and thus should be treated with equal respect and decency.[4] Other evangelical sects dominated the leadership and the rank and file, who viewed slavery as inhumane and as a moral and physical barrier to the spiritual awakening of the slaves.[5] Protestant missionaries also contributed to the growing antislavery sentiment, as they tried to reconcile their desire to convert the slaves with the barbaric treatment of the slaves by slave owners who were hardly demonstrating Christian virtues. Indeed, many of the early antislavery leaders were not opposed to slavery as such; instead, they were horrified by the treatment of the slaves and the failure to give them proper religious instruction and, accordingly, championed a "Christian moral economy centered on reciprocal duties and obligations rather than on a liberal political economy organized around individual rights and liberties."[6] The antislavery slogan, "Am I Not a Man and a Brother?" though probably coined by a rationalist Cambridge churchman in 1788, gained currency among evangelicals because it paired their religious identity with a sense of moral responsibility toward others (figure 2).[7]

The antislavery leadership engaged in various tactics to encourage the British population to sympathize with the plight of the slaves. They authored pamphlets that detailed the practices and consequences of slavery. They put a human face on slavery by sponsoring tours of former slaves who told stories of their enslavement and emancipation. They assembled traveling displays that showcased slavery's brutality and its weapons of

Figure 2 Medallion created by Josiah Wedgwood as part of antislavery campaign, 1787. Library of Congress Rare Book and Special Collections Division, LC-USZ62–44265.

discipline, including thumbscrews, whips, and manacles. They challenged the public to consider whether they were implicated in this cruelty because every morning and afternoon they enjoyed their tea, in which they put sugar produced by the slave islands in the Caribbean. On this note, William Wilberforce preached how all Britons "ought to plead guilty, and not to exculpate ourselves by throwing the blame on others."[8] The abolitionists attempted to get the British people to imagine the meaning of losing one's freedom, as many could because of the practice of impressment by the British Royal Navy. They challenged the religious establishment to defend a practice that inflicted such cruelty.[9] Demonstrating considerable ingenuity and boundless determination, and possessing many of the characteristics that are now associated with successful social movements, the abolitionists drew from the experiences of their fellow crusaders in the American colonies and their experiences in other reform campaigns as they invented new techniques of persuasion to convince the British public that there was no principled or pragmatic justification for slavery and that Britain's very moral character was on trial.

Yet not all streams of antislavery sentiment, including some of its famous leaders and sects, were motivated primarily by the welfare of others. As examined in his detailed study of the abolitionist movement, Christopher Brown argues that antislavery activists might not have had economic interests, but they campaigned against slavery as a way of commenting on public morals, critiquing the conduct of the British Empire, expanding evangelicalism, shielding themselves from further guilt, and laying claim to a new kind of moral purpose from the British nation. "A few, to varying degrees, did take a genuine interest in the welfare of the enslaved," writes Brown, but what truly moved the abolitionists can be understood as being driven by self-regarding, self-concerned, and even self-validating impulses.[10] In other words, they viewed the antislavery movement not only as an end in itself but also as a means to ends that were much closer to home and deeply personal.

The campaign to end slavery was swimming against the strong tide of history and economic and political interests, but it achieved a series of victories. The original campaign aimed at ending the Atlantic slave trade and the slavery of the Africans and their descendants in the Caribbean and North America. The first victory was the Abolition Acts of 1806–07; twenty-five years later, the climactic victory was the emancipation of the slaves on August 1, 1834. Yet their mission was hardly complete. Slavery was a sin everywhere, not just in the British Empire, so they kept going until the prohibition was universal. And even after they had successfully outlawed slavery, there was the problem of enforcement, debates about what to do with slaves that had escaped from places that still allowed slavery, and the continuing existence of labor practices that kept individuals in slave-like conditions. Various kinds of societies for the protection of native populations, including, most famously, the Aborigines' Protection Society, joined forces with the antislavery movement.

The antislavery movement cultivated considerable compassion for distant strangers—and paternalism too. As the British public increasingly sympathized with the slaves and came to learn of their homelands and lives, they began to entertain obligations that went beyond the slaves' liberation and to consider how they should help develop their humanity.[11] In this way, a sense of shared humanity and claims of mutual obligation could lead to paternalism; in other words, mutual obligation was not so mutual, and obligation meant not leaving them alone but rather becoming more involved for their own good. Slaves were human but not fully so or equal to white Christians. In a few decades biological theories of race would emerge to explain their perceived backwardness, but at this moment the British, many of whom had never seen an African, attributed their primitive state to various features, including race, religion, superstition, and lack of education.[12] Abolitionists could not very well liberate the slaves and then leave them to a life of suffering and damnation. Instead, the Christian peoples had a duty to civilize them.[13] At a dinner in 1816, William Wilberforce declared that free slaves would come to appreciate their protected position: "Taught by Christianity, they will sustain with patience the suffering of their actual lot...[and] will soon be regarded as a grateful peasantry."[14] Far from peculiar, Wilberforce's belief that imperialism and colonialism were creating new opportunities for humanitarian action was standard fare.[15]

There was no moral justification for caring for liberated slave populations when so many others also seemed to be suffering from a combination of backwardness and European exploitation. Accordingly, there was a "new vigor towards those peoples who, while notionally free, were seen as suffering seriously from the impact of European expansion—Canada's Indian peoples, Pacific Islanders, New Zealand's Maoris, the Aborigines of Australia, and the indigenous peoples of South Africa."[16] Although colonialism certainly nurtured such sentiments, they existed long before colonialism entered its most intensive phase.[17] Feelings of compassion mixed with evangelicalism to stir a demand for a benevolent colonialism to atone for past sins. "Atonement," writes the historian Andrew Porter, "involved not acts of contrition alone, but the performance of good works from which the doer might also benefit. Here lay the possibility of marrying Christian duty with secular self-interest, something the humanitarian coalition had already shown could become politically unstoppable."[18]

Colonialism and Compassion

Most of us now summarily dismiss any possible claim that colonialism might have had anything to do with compassion. Although colonial powers frequently depicted their rapacious behavior as for the benefit of the local populations, and many probably even believed it, today we give little credence to such outlandish possibilities. I have no intention of defending colonialism, but do want to suggest that, the relationship between colonialism and humanitarian sentiments is more complicated and, that the relationship contains elements that have a contemporary resonance. Or, to put the matter a little more provocatively, the humanitarians of the period of Imperial Humanitarianism should not be so quickly condemned, and the humanitarians of the period of Liberal Humanitarianism should not be so quickly excused.

The age of European exploitation and conquest forced the powerful to contemplate their relationship to local populations, especially once new discourses of humanity emerged in the late eighteenth century. The central questions were: What was the purpose of colonial power? How might it be legitimately used in relationship to the colonized? Importantly, few feasted on the idea that might makes right, and most wrestled with how to use their considerable power responsibly and in ways that would benefit the ruled. This ideology of trusteeship is closely associated with Edmund Burke's views on the purpose of the empire. Addressing the British Parliament in December 1783 on the occasion of a debate on the East India Bill, Burke spoke of the relationship between the powerful and the powerless in the context of colonialism in the following way:

> All political power which is set over men, and...all privileges claimed...in exclusion of them, being wholly artificial...and derogation from the natural equality of mankind at large, ought to be some way or other exercised for their benefit. If this is true with regard to every species of political dominion, and every description of commercial privilege...then such rights or privileges, or whatever else you choose to call them, are all in the strictest sense a trust; and it is of the very essence of every trust to be rendered accountable; and even totally to cease, when it substantially varies from the purpose for which it alone could have lawful existence.[19]

The British government, he argued at various moments, had a sacred duty to help the civilized peoples prepare for political sovereignty. While the ruled did not give their consent, the imperial ruler could assume a tacit trust because of its superiority if and only if it agreed to tolerate differences, especially in the area of religion.[20] Burke's views gained an important platform when news from abroad suggested that the British were not as enlightened as they made themselves out to be. One notable moment occurred in the late 1780s at the infamous trial of Warren Hastings, the governor-general of Bengal from 1774 to 1784 who was accused of corruption and abuse of power.[21] At stake in the trial was not only the purpose of colonial rule but also its limits—while it could include forms of civilization, it should respect local cultures, traditions, and religions. The campaign against slavery and colonialism on trial exposed how the supposedly civilized British engaged in acts of cruelty, and Burke took the unpopular stand of calling into question British colonial practices. Yet however much he railed against the abuses of empire, he nevertheless "sketched out an ideal of benevolent stewardship."[22] He was not opposed to colonialism but rather objected to a colonialism that was irredeemably exploitative.

Nineteenth-century colonialism included an ideology of trusteeship, with the defining themes of civilization and conversion. Shaking away any possible stigma regarding the relationship between imperialism and slavery, the nineteenth century witnessed a burst of cultural and civilizational confidence among the Great Powers.[23] Nearly all colonial powers justified their expansion and conquest of other peoples in terms of some form of civilizing mission: France had *la mission civilisatrice,* Britain the white man's burden, and the United States manifest destiny. These explicitly paternalistic ideologies were accompanied and fueled by racist theories of human evolution that posited a spectrum of humanity, from the backward dark-skinned races to the civilized Caucasian Europeans. Alongside discourses of humanity and similarity were discourses of difference that created new forms of hierarchy, producing a view that the colored races were not quite fully human and could be treated differently from Caucasians, and the white Christians race had a responsibility to rescue the backward races from disease, destitution, and depravity.

Importantly, evangelical and liberal thought joined forces, burying a Burkean perspective that advocated cultural and religious toleration. Evangelicals had a difficult time tolerating other religions, knowing that the damned could make the choice to be saved.[24] Many liberals of the period held that power and emancipation lived together comfortably.[25] For instance, the liberal John Stuart Mill defended British imperialism in India on the grounds that it would help the Indians develop the mental capacities and social institutions to become free-thinking, reasoning peoples.[26] His views dominated the times, and critics of colonialism and civilizing projects were a minority.[27]

How feelings of obligation to distant strangers in the colonial context could produce tragic forms of paternalism is illustrated by the heartbreaking response of the British colonial authorities to the famine in northern India in 1837–38.[28] Once the British East India Company controlled a sizable area of India in the late eighteenth century, it became implicated in the periodic food shortages and their fatal consequences. In response to the famine of 1803–04, the colonial administrators debated whether they should intervene or let markets rule. Following their Smithian ideology, the desire to ensure that colonies did not become a burden on the public treasury (colonialism was being sold as a self-financing enterprise), and

British military interests, the administrators refused to take any action that might interfere with how the market might distribute the food supply, including banning the exports of food. Millions died who might have been saved.

In 1837 another devastating famine in northern India wiped out an estimated 15 to 20 percent of a population of eight million; dissembled all dimensions of social, political, and economic life; and created everyday spectacles of emaciated people, skeletons alongside roads, and animals feeding on human remains. Much had changed, though, in the thirty years since the previous famine. The antislavery movement had caused the British public to broaden its moral imagination and to recognize its special responsibilities to the colonized. In Britain there now existed a network of welfare societies to help the very poor. Although most of these were church-based societies, there was a growing expectation that the state should help, or at least not aggravate matters. Significantly, in 1834, just three years before the famine, Parliament passed the New Poor Law, which implicitly recognized that the state had an obligation to help the poor (and then move them back into the labor market). These developments influenced the thinking of the British authorities in India. At first they drew from their familiar laissez-faire toolkit, which increased the price of food, the incentive to export food to high-income regions, and suffering. Because the market was killing people, there was growing pressure on the British authorities to take more concerted action. Drawing inspiration from recent welfare policy in Britain, they created a "works of public utility," one of the first instances of the application of "modern principles" to enable famine relief. By putting people to work, they could buy food.

Having undertaken this unprecedented intervention, British colonial authorities now began claiming that the state was humanitarian and describing public works as charity. They imagined doing more than saving lives, however. They also wanted to combat a growing "moral decadence." The famine had produced a breakdown in "law and order," and British authorities hoped that its new public works policy would feed people while teaching them moral discipline. The policy, though, was not working—or perhaps it was working too well. The British were paying starvation wages and working the labor force to the point of collapse. But the desperately poor had no choice but to seek these death-inducing wages, and the line kept growing. The British now worried that this program was becoming too expensive and breeding a dependent, lazy Indian, so it cut wages. When this move had little impact on the demand, it created an every-other-day work policy. The British were caught in a paradox: they wanted to honor basic political economy practices that valorized the market but nevertheless felt compelled to consolidate their ideological position by adopting new methods of welfare provision. And there was only so far they would go in trying to remedy the famine. The British might put food into the mouths of starving Indians, but they refused to address the causes of poverty, which preordained a future of famines and interventions that recreated the conditions for famine. What mattered was limiting mass death, not preventing it. The British were taking the unprecedented step of "protecting" the population, accepting a new humanitarian responsibility consistent with a general reluctance to "adopt open-ended responsibilities and... limit the endlessly rising costs of direct Imperial intervention even inside its own colonies."[29]

The famine that ravaged the Indian population nourished the British colonial state. Although British policy was making little headway against the famine, it refused to consider the possible contribution of traditional, indigenous systems of relief. Assuming that Christian charity was naturally superior to local methods, an attitude that was consistent with the emerging view in Britain that public institutions were superior to private charity because they were believed to be less prone to corruption and abuse, the effect of the famine was to place more of the poor in the hands of a colonial state. Taking on new obligations created a new apparatus of control. Shifting the locus of relief to the state effectively gave the British colonial authorities more power over the populations, though without any appreciable improvement in their welfare. Moreover, Indian labor was building roads and infrastructure, allowing British authorities to expand and tighten their grip on India. Thanks in part to a new ideology of humanitarianism, the early British colonial state was partly built on the skeletal remains of the Indians.

Missionary Humanitarianism

The centerpiece of Christian mission is to cross frontiers, geographical, cultural, economic, social, and political, in the service of Christ and his Kingdom.[30] The period of classical missionary activity, beginning in 1792 with the publication of William Carey's *Enquiry into the Obligations of Christians to Use Means for the Conversion of the Heathens* and concluding with the 1910 World Missionary Conference in Edinburgh, represented the only sustained humanitarian activity during the period of European expansion and colonialism.[31] Evangelicalism was a major reason for this new energy. While Christian missionaries held varying views of non-Western peoples, not all of them enlightened, they imagined a common humanity.[32] Importantly, and in contrast to ideologies built on biological theories of race, they believed in a fundamental unity of humankind.[33] Because all were children of Christ, all could be saved. "The missionary project," emphasizes Brian Stanley, "was only sustainable if there was a belief in the possibility of assimilation and the fundamental unity of humanity."[34] The problem, though, was that the backward populations did not know they had a choice between light and dark. Accordingly, evangelicals set out to spread the gospel and provide all nonbelievers with the opportunity to embrace Jesus Christ as their Lord and savior.[35] Adopting militaristic language like a "crusade against idolatry" and the "war for salvation," missionaries fanned across the world to give heathens the opportunity to restore a "right relationship" with God.[36] Nonbelievers could be saved, and evangelicals could know they had done their duty and atoned for the sins of slavery and colonialism.[37] Figure 3 captures a stereotypical representation, with the nicely civilized missionary showing mercy for the unfortunate peoples of the world.

The missionary and abolitionist movements drank from the same evangelical well.[38] Many individuals belonged to both movements. Consider William Wilberforce. In 1823 and in the context of a campaign to end slavery in the British Empire, he argued that slavery was a sin against Christianity and that Christianity could civilize the liberated slaves. In response to the charge that the slaves' liberation would lead to moral ruin, Wilberforce argued that slavery had led to defects in the human character

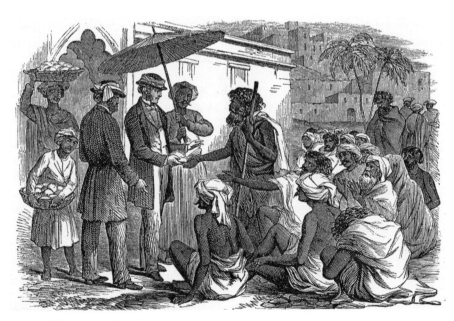

Figure 3 The British giving alms.

and that there was considerable evidence that Christianity could lead the slaves and the backward races out of darkness and into light. He wrote:

> But it is in Sierra Leone, that long despised and calumniated colony, that the African character has been most effectually and experimentally vindicated. The first seeds of civilization were sown there by the Christian philanthropy of Mr. Granville Sharp.... It is in Sierra Leone that the great experiment on human nature has been tried; and there it has appeared that the poor African barbarians, just rescued from the hold of slave-ships, are capable, not merely of being civilized, but of soon enjoying, with advantage, the rights and institutions of British freemen.[39]

His plea excludes the possibility that freed slaves might be left alone; instead, Christianity must deliver slaves and other African populations from backwardness.

The abolitionist and missionary movements also drew inspiration and learned from each other.[40] Missionaries began organizing into societies and seeking the formal assistance of the state around the same time that other aid societies and abolitionist groups were doing so. The London Missionary Society began in a London coffee house in 1794, growing out of the evangelical movement and inspired in part by the antislavery movement, which, in turn, reciprocated some interest.[41] Tactics successfully practiced by one movement were subsequently employed by the other. In 1793 Wilberforce used the occasion of the renewal of the royal license of the East India Company to advocate for opening Christian missions and native schools. Following on the established principle that the British should not mix business and religion, Parliament soundly rejected the amendment. After failing for several years to get the British colonial authorities to authorize and support missionary activities, in 1813 a coalition of missionaries and abolitionists tried a new tactic—tying missionary work to the Indian rite of *sati,* the ritual self-immolation of widows. For them, missionary work was humanitarian, and humanitarianism was best served by Christianity. After decades of failure, the missionary movement won the passage of a law that explicitly recognized the right of a Christian country to propagate Christianity in its colonies.[42]

The missionary movement's difficulty overcoming the objections of the British state and the East India Company illustrates the converging and diverging interests of missionaries, colonialists, and capitalists. Missionaries viewed colonialism and capitalism as providing new opportunities to bring civilization and Christianity to backward populations. Colonialism instilled in missionaries tremendous confidence and allowed them to travel to once-inhospitable lands. In fact, the failure to respond to these new opportunities might well trigger feelings of guilt and remorse.[43] After all, Britain's fortunes were a sign of God's grace, giving Britain and evangelicals special responsibilities for helping the native peoples.[44]

Missionaries also believed that colonialism and commerce could help civilize the local populations. Christianity, commerce, and civilization were a trifecta for progress. The native populations were defined by what they lacked—beginning with Jesus Christ and continuing through a long list of items that they associated with the civilized, Christian West.[45] Drawing from fashionable evolutionary theories of the day in which the environment was presumed to influence the traits of the species, missionaries aimed to introduce modern institutions such as schools and health clinics and emphasized the importance of hygiene (cleanliness was next to Godliness).[46] They also preached new forms of self-control and discipline, including chastity, sobriety, and hard work, which were viewed as essential for a Christian character. Colonial administrators and foreign traders found such projects highly desirable, if only because, if successful, the local population would become more compliant, easier to control, and develop tastes and values that were consistent with the interests of the West.[47]

Missionaries of all kinds trumpeted the dynamic duo of "Christianity and commerce." Beginning with slavery, evangelicals had steadfastly claimed that free labor and commerce were a path to civilization. Commerce would supplant illegitimate dealings such as the slave trade, spread a Christian material culture that would promote consumer desire for additional British goods, and nurture a Protestant virtue of self-discipline as the colonized sought to become part of the wage labor force in order to buy more goods.[48] When the missionary and abolitionist Thomas Fowell Buxton undertook an expedition to Niger to battle slavery, he brought with him the weapons of civilization—the idea of creating modern farms, trading networks, and churches to give the people of the Niger River Valley an economic alternative to slavery. Christianity, commerce, and civilization, he wrote, "can penetrate to the root of evil, can teach [the African] to love and to befriend his neighbor, and cause him to act as a *candidate* for a higher and holier being."[49] The legendary British general Charles George Gordon, who died in Khartoum fighting the Mahdi, personified the mixture of Christianity, civilizing processes, and humanitarianism. Celebrated for his bravery in battle, his Christian piety, his battles against Islam, and his accomplishment of ending the slave trade in the Sudan, Gordon was among the many in England who believed that ending the slave trade required opening up the Sudan to European influence through commerce.[50]

Yet missionaries did not always see eye to eye with colonial administrators or foreign capitalists. Missionaries believed in the unity of humankind and wanted to emancipate the local populations, beliefs not necessarily shared by administrators and settlers who placed power and profits above Christianity.[51] In many places, the settler communities stiffly resisted missionary work, fearing that if the indigenous peoples became Christian, then they would demand to be treated as equals.[52] Administrators and the home office often worried that missionaries wanted to use the state's scarce resources for religious quests that might lead to rebellions.[53] For this reason

British colonial authorities prohibited Christian missionary activity in places such as northern Sudan.[54] When British missionaries first advocated the abolition of the Indian *sati* in the late eighteenth century, they had to fight the official position of the East Indian Company of indifference to all dimensions of Indian society, an indifference that translated into a 1772 company policy of noninterference concerning religion and local institutions. Utilitarian rather than principled factors drove this policy: the company feared that any attempted reform would be interpreted by the local population as proselytization, perhaps igniting a revolt, which would hardly be good for business. When British authorities finally changed their position it was because the governor-general had calculated that it was worth taking the risk of political instability in order to convey to the British public an image of an enlightened rule, to show, by example, good governance, progress, and the superiority of Western civilization.[55]

Missionaries and humanitarians were dependent on the colonial state to provide the proper security, legal, and normative sanctuary, but in one area they were relatively independent: financing. Unlike most contemporary humanitarian agencies that frequently depend on official assistance, missionary societies relied on parishes and congregations at home. To the extent that missionaries and hometown donors shared basic beliefs, missionaries did not have to worry that they might be acting in ways that threatened their funding base. But they did not always see eye-to-eye. Missionaries, at times, could articulate genuine respect for local cultures and traditions, positions that funders sometimes found permissive and indulgent.[56]

Missionaries and foreign capitalists also clashed at various moments. Foreign capitalists often viewed missionaries as meddlesome busybodies, ready to incite unrest among the population, an accusation previously leveled by slave owners.[57] Missionaries looked suspiciously on foreign capitalists who seemed to be willing to do anything to make a profit, who seldom exhibited Christian principles, who desired to transform individuals into consumers, promoting not righteousness but rather hedonism. They repeatedly clashed over free labor.[58] The movement to abolish slavery gave way, at times, to a desire to end other forms of indentured labor and the labor trade. In Australia, missionaries, frequently working closely with the Aborigines' Protection Society and the Anti-Slavery Society, tried to regulate labor, a position that plantation owners found deeply objectionable.[59] In general, because evangelical missionaries recognized that heathens could become civilized and that the civilized could be sinners, they often found themselves in a difficult position.[60]

Although missionaries preached the unity of humankind, many if not most believed that Western, Christian civilization was vastly superior to local cultures in almost all ways. Citing scripture, they argued that the "same new Testament which affirms the oneness of all persons before God also contains the stark antithesis between the children of light and the children of darkness, between the narrow gate and the wide gate, between kingdom of heaven and the kingdom of this world. Jesus himself spoke of his coming as a force that would bring division and not peace, setting sons against fathers and daughters against mothers."[61] Missionaries had a well-earned reputation for viewing derisively the habits and customs of the local populations and treating them as less than fully human, even though they could become Christians. And even if they became Christians, they were still inferior to the highly civilized missionaries. As Gustav Sjoblom put it, "Hierarchies were welcomed and adorned by missionaries. The equality of Africans was a matter of principle and potential, not a suggestion of immediate egalitarianism."[62]

The popular image in the nineteenth century of missionary work and humanitarianism as a paternalist enterprise that wanted to destroy other cultures and transform the native populations into miniature, deeply romanticized, versions of themselves and the West had a strong basis in fact. Yet some missionaries wondered which features of local cultures should be condemned and which ones could coexist with Christianity; reevaluated their own identities, goals, and relationship to other cultures; and even began to doubt the value of proselytization.[63] As one set of 1873 missionary instructions commanded: "Do not ANGLICISE YOUR CONVERTS. Remember that the people are foreigners. Let them continue as such. Let their foreign individuality be maintained. Build upon it, so far as it is sound and good; and Christianize, but do not needlessly change it. Do not seek to make the people Englishmen. Seek to develop and mould a pure, refined Christian character, native to the soil."[64] When missionaries acknowledged that Western civilization brought not only salvation but also unimaginable cruelty—a defining theme of the antislavery movement that appeared periodically over the century, most famously in the campaign to end King Leopold's genocidal reign over the Congo—they were forced to take a hard look at themselves.[65] Many missionaries accepted the criticism that they were paternalistic and imperialistic, which coincided with the growing influence of new interpretations of social gospel that highlighted equality, justice, and solidarity.[66] There was even a new and more positive evaluation of non-Western cultures; the colonial encounter could force them to reevaluate their own identities, values, and understanding of self in relationship to the colonial "other."[67] Over time, many missionaries shifted from saving souls to saving societies, helped along in part by the development of a scientific, professionalized philanthropic sector that was much more interested in the here and now than the hereafter.[68]

The World Missionary Conference (WMC), held in Edinburgh, Scotland, in 1910, captures the politics of community and emancipation that defined the age. The title of the conference says it all: *The World Missionary*

Conference to Consider Missionary Problems in relation to the Non-Christian World. The conference's underlying premise was that the world contains an underlying unity that is currently divided between the Christian and non-Christian Worlds, and the challenge was to expand the former and shrink the latter through a more scientific enterprise.[69] In preparation for the meeting, the conference planners created committees on several themes, including relations with political power and how to prepare the missionary. It is difficult to exaggerate the ambition and the accomplishment. The organizing committee wanted their discussions to be informed by empirical analysis and not guesswork; this "scientific" turn was a natural outgrowth of the development of a professional field of missology—the application of scientific methods to assess missionary practices, a movement led by the American evangelist A. T. Pierson.[70] Accordingly, the committee surveyed hundreds of missionaries, who, in many ways, were the anthropologists of their day, having lived for years among the "natives," observing their cultural and religious practices. The majority of the missionaries responded, many with lengthy, detailed reports. The committee then summarized the findings into eight books that were organized around the quest to increase the impact of missionary work.

Reflecting a world view in which missionary activity was integral to Western expansion, in attendance were some of the period's most important religious, political, and economic figures. The presiding officer was Lord Balfour, who opened the conference with a warm statement from the king of England. The American delegation included Rear Admiral Alfred Thayer Mahan; William Jennings Bryan; John Mott, an eventual winner of the Nobel Peace Prize in 1946 and one of the best-known evangelical ministers of the period; and Seth Low, the former mayor of New York City and president of Columbia University. Theodore Roosevelt could not attend, but he did send a very warm letter of congratulations that reflected on the conference's importance to the Western international order. It was an impressive gathering in a spectacular setting (figure 4).

While all people had the right to hear the gospel and the opportunity to convert, the experience of the missionaries was that not all people were equally receptive. Accordingly, a major concern was identifying where, when, and how missionary work was most successful. Toward that end, and following the fashion of the times, they created a hierarchy of civilizations, arraying societies in terms of where they fell on a civilizational scale. Being closer to civilization, however, was no assurance of greater receptivity to the gospel: missionaries had a difficult time in nearly civilized Japan and a much easier time in less civilized Korea. The conference was particularly worried about "Mohammedism," as missionaries reported their lack of acceptance in Islamic societies and noted that Christianity was losing ground to Islam for the souls of nonmonotheistic peoples in places like sub-Saharan Africa. Registering alarm and anxiety, the conference highlighted the urgent

Figure 4 World Missionary Conference, Edinburgh, Scotland, 1910.

need to confront Islam, limit its gains, and, if at all possible, send it back to Arabia.

The conference also reflected on the relationship of the missionaries to the local populations and the colonial powers. Missionaries obviously wanted to spread the gospel but, reflecting the spirit of the times, also desired to recognize the dignity of other peoples and the possibility of Christianity's expansion without needing to transform all aspects of society. As the Commission proudly observed:

> It is interesting to note the way in which the missionary becomes the champion of the people among whom he lives. Their national unity, their language, their institutions (where plainly anti-Christian or immoral) become dear to him. The reproach that missionaries desire to Europeanise the inhabitants of mission land, if ever true, is now absurdly false. Their anxiety everywhere is that the land in which they dwell should work out its national destiny, aided where need be by the higher cultural of the West.[71]

This was a difficult balancing act: bringing Christianity to backward populations while recognizing the principle of cultural autonomy—even though this culture was viewed as "lower" and Christianity could not be easily contained to one sphere of life. One possible middle ground was the longstanding strategy of indigenization—to create "self-governing" churches that were rooted in the local communities and no longer needed external support. But middle grounds are rarely stable.

The conference viewed colonialism and missionaries as two forces working together to spread civilization. The duty of government, as they put it, is "to restrain evil and promote good," and "both missions and governments are interested in the welfare of nations." Colonialism was central to spreading Christianity. The colonial powers were Christian nations, pursuing not some secularized version of the national interest but rather making possible a Christian world order, providing unprecedented opportunities for spreading the word, and boosting the confidence of missionaries. Consequently, those in attendance did not necessarily perceive a conflict between their own sense of nationalism and a Christian state that would help spread civilization that would better humankind. Colonialism was good for Christianity, as Christianity was good for colonialism. As stated in the seventh book:

> Penetrating into barbarous lands before the advent of any civilised Government, they have, by moral influence alone, mitigated war and slavery, and cruel and abominable usages, and prepared the way for an enlightened and civilised rule; and where civilised rule has followed then, they have proved, both in official and unofficial positions, the best mediators between the new, strict, and exacting Government and the suspicious native races, resentful of interference with their ancient ways, evil and good alike.... They have won an influence which has made the task of governments comparatively easy; and everywhere they continue to manifest and inculcate that loyalty to and co-operation with governments, without which the latter indeed may rule, but without which they cannot fit a people for the higher task of ruling themselves.[72]

Although the conference paraded the marriage of missionary work and colonialism, there are limits to all marriages. The long history of government-mission relations included considerable conflict, particularly when colonial administrators and settler communities tried to enlist missionaries in activities that the religiously minded found unjust or when administrators believed that missionaries were stirring the pot. Consequently, the conference set up various rules that were intended to avoid conflict, including demonstrating loyalty to governments, avoiding political agitation, and teaching the local populations to respect the colonial administrations. They asserted a functional equivalent to the principle of neutrality, as missionaries avoided confronting the colonial government because it might jeopardize access to populations in need. Following the maxim of "rendering unto Caesar the things that are Caesar's and unto God the things that are God's" (Matthew 22:21), they attempted to maintain a line between themselves and politics. Matters of governance were the domain of the state, matters of religion were the domain of the church, and both the government and the church needed to recognize each other's sphere of authority. For some participants, the conference itself was dangerously stepping into a new realm—the political.

Yet there were limits to what missionaries would tolerate from colonial powers. Missionaries had a duty to "exercise their influence for the removal of gross oppression and injustice, particularly where the government is in the hands of men of their own race...provided that in so doing they keep clear of association with any political movement." Much like many contemporary relief organizations of today, missionaries wanted to protect certain fundamental rights of the population but in an apolitical manner, if apolitical is defined as nonpartisan. The conference censured the opium and liquor trade and forced labor for being immoral and un-Christian. Opiates and alcohol numbed the masses and were conduits of evil, and missionaries had a strong track record of condemning all forms of slavery. Importantly, though, while missionaries might take a "demand" approach to these problems (encouraging natives to find Christ and "just say no"), colonial governments and foreign capitalists also could need reforming because, in many cases, they had introduced and profited from these evils. In this regard, the late-nineteenth-century controversy over Belgium's "humanitarianism" in the Congo, where King Leopold's rapacious and genocidal rule left hundreds of thousands dead, provided a solemn reminder that the West could also be cruel. Although the French-born Edmund Morel rightly gets considerable credit for publicizing King Leopold's crimes in the Congo and the hollowness of his humanitarian credentials, missionaries also played an important role. The atrocities in the Congo tapped into a longstanding issue that confronted all those who identified with the abolitionists: there was a thin line between slave labor and some forms of "free labor," and many colonial powers tolerated slavery in everything but name. What made such systems of servitude particularly appalling to many abolitionists and their inheritors was that these imperial labor systems had the declared purpose of removing all forms of gross exploitation.

Those at the World Missionary Conference were meeting against the backdrop of a religious authority that was increasingly competing with, and would soon be eclipsed by, a secularizing world. The first signs of a humanitarianism that once felt little need to justify itself in religious discourse became more fully apparent with the rise of the first generation of human rights activists. There was considerable overlap between the two, especially since both had a strong interest in civilizing and protecting local populations and in ending all form of slavery. Whereas missionaries cited God, the nascent human rights movement, drew from the distinctive liberal, humanist, tradition.

But there were differences between the two. Each offered different assessments regarding whether and when local populations might be ready to govern themselves. Missionaries typically believed that the colonies would require considerable oversight and the local cultures would have to be thoroughly transformed before the population could be entrusted with self-governance. Human rights activists argued in favor of a form of cultural relativism that accepted that Western peoples were indeed superior to the colored races, but, at the same time, local populations had cultures worthy of respect and could soon realize an ability to run their own affairs.[73] Illustrative of this growing tide of human rights was the Liverpool Sect, established in 1896 with the express purpose of campaigning for rights and insisting on forms of cultural relativism.[74] Rights-oriented humanitarianism also got a boost from Mary Kingsley, the spirited explorer whose journeys in Africa gained widespread fame. While holding to the view that Western society was superior to African society, she nevertheless railed against missionaries and cultural conversion. Edmund Morel also broke with the missionaries in the Congo because of the discrepancy between their insistence on conversion and his insistence on cultural relativism and commerce.[75] A religiously inspired humanitarianism was increasingly sharing ground with a secular alternative.

The cross-cutting trends in humanitarianism were particularly evident in the Western orientation toward the colonial peoples after World War I and in the creation of the League of Nations. Influenced by Woodrow Wilson's Fourteen Points and the principle of self-determination, the League of Nations established a mandatory system that gave the colonial powers a "sacred trust"—to prepare the colonial peoples for independence. Article 22 of the League of Nations Covenant used language that was simultaneously novel because of the emphasis on independence and familiar because of the overt paternalism:

> To those colonies and territories which as a consequence of the late war have ceased to be under the sovereignty of the States which formerly governed them and which are inhabited by peoples not yet able to stand by themselves under the strenuous conditions of the modern world, there should be applied the principle that the well-being and development of such peoples form a sacred trust of civilization and that securities for the performance of this trust should be embodied in this Covenant. The best method of giving practical effect to this principle is that the tutelage of such peoples should be entrusted to advanced nations who, by reason of their resources, their experience or their geographical position, can best undertake this responsibility and who are willing to accept it, and that this tutelage should be exercised by them as Mandatories on behalf of the League.

Not only is the sentiment familiar, but, according to Eric Weitz, it was lifted nearly wholesale from the General Act of 1885.[76]

Although the concept of a sacred trust had Christian foundations and many missionaries saw the mandatory systems as premised on Christian principles of trusteeship, for many leaders, and especially for those outside of the West, it explicitly referenced not God but rather humanity. The "civilized" trustee was expected to raise the "savage." Following in the secularizing spirit of the times, humanitarians began using the phrase "native interests" to emphasize the importance of material welfare over spiritual needs, and imperial forces began to drop "Christianity" from the slogan of "Christianity and commerce" and "moral" from the siren call of "moral and material improvement." Illustrating the shift, the most influential postwar statement on empire, Sir Frederick Lugard's *The Dual Mandate in British Tropical Africa* makes no explicit reference to Christian duty.[77] Although religious discourses helped to give legitimacy and substance to many of the new global institutions of care in the twentieth century, one of the striking features of the new era was the apparent willingness of individuals to cite humanity and not God as their reason for caring for the welfare of others. Regardless of whether it was because of God or humanity, the League of Nations, its mandatory system, and its skeletal humanitarian network imagined not only saving lives but also getting at the root causes of suffering.[78]

Imperial humanitarianism reflected the spirit of the times even as it occasionally tried to challenge them. Colonialism, Christianity, and commerce, according to many humanitarians of the period, could provide the will and the way to emancipate slaves, save sinners and souls, and position backward societies on the path of civilization. It embodied the unapologetic paternalism of the period, with missionaries and liberal humanitarians sharing the belief that they had a duty to civilize and improve the lives of the native populations. Because of their commitment to improve their lives, though, they were not always on the same page as colonial administrators and merchants, at times acting as the protector of local peoples and calling attention to the uncivilized behavior of Europeans. And there were even instances in which missionaries and other liberal reformers began to reflect critically on their own attitudes and came to believe that local cultures had their own integrity and value. But whether they cited God or humanity, the humanitarians of the period still saw themselves as agents of the transcendental.

4

⤛⤜

Saving Soldiers and Civilians
during War

UNTIL THE 1860s all was fair in love and war, but after the 1860s
only love operated without rules. It is not as if until then war were
a complete free-for-all. Over the centuries armies had followed religious and historical custom for waging war, for determining what was
manly or civilized behavior, and for shaping their conduct toward vanquished populations. But what we now call the laws of war or international humanitarian law did not exist, and humanitarianism was largely
associated with the general attempt to relieve various kinds of unnecessary
suffering everywhere except the battlefield. Although alchemical humanitarianism had had a fifty-year head start, once emergency humanitarianism
got out of the blocks it quickly became the official face of international
humanitarianism, and humanitarianism and the laws of war became virtually synonymous. Perhaps more important for our purposes, emergency
humanitarianism was born under a very different set of circumstances and
built for a very different set of purposes, so it developed in different directions, even though it shared some traits with alchemical humanitarianism.

Many histories of humanitarianism, and certainly those of international
humanitarian law, begin with Henry Dunant and the conjunctural forces
that catapulted him to new ethical heights. Like all good stories involving
ethical action, the outcome was the result of chance factors that led the protagonist to experience something of a spiritual awakening and to dedicate
his life to humanity. Although no stranger to charitable activities—Dunant

was, after all, part of a Genevan society with a rich history of noblesse oblige—he left Geneva to get a letter of support from Napoleon for his business pursuits in French Algeria. At the end of his journey to Italy, he happened upon a battle between French and Austro-Hungarian troops at the Italian village of Solferino (see figure 5). At this moment, Dunant wrote, he felt overwhelmed by the situation. Although well aware of his lack of training, he nevertheless felt obliged to act: "The moral sense of the importance of human life; the human desire to lighten a little the torments of these poor wretches, or restore their shattered courage; the furious and relentless activity which a man summons up at such moments: all these combine to create a kind of energy which gives on a positive craving to relieve as many as one can." In a climactic passage fondly cited by many histories of the origins of humanitarianism, he writes: "Seeing that I made no distinction between nationalities, following my example, showing the same kindness to all these men whose origins were so different, and all of whom were foreigners to them. '*Tutti fratelli*' [all are brothers], they repeated feelingly. All honor to these compassionate women, to these girls of Castiglione! Imperturbable, unwearying, unfaltering, their quiet self-sacrifice made little of fatigue and horrors, and of their own devotion."

Figure 5 Adolphe Yvon, *Battle of Solferino*, 1859. Réunion des Musées Nationaux / Art Resource, New York.

Still haunted by his experiences months after the event, he decided to write an account of what he had witnessed. It was more than a testimony—it was a jeremiad for action. Exceeding his wildest expectations, the memoir, *A Memory of Solferino,* became a sensation, and nearly a century and a half later it is easy to see why it became the talk of European salons. This was not the Solferino that Europeans remembered as a glorious victory that freed Italy from Austria.[1] Deftly and movingly written, Dunant provided one of the first unvarnished accounts of war. Stripped of its heroism and splendor, war became a series of brutal set pieces in which soldiers were sacrificed and then abandoned to suffer until they died; whole passages describe churches that are turned into hospitals or morgues and hallways that become assembly lines for amputations performed without anesthesia. After juxtaposing the inadequate medical corps, the thousands of soldiers left to suffer, and the heroic but overwhelmed townspeople, Dunant recommended that European elites form charitable societies to march into battle to help the wounded. To further the cause, he proposed an international convention to grant special protection to the wounded and those caring for them, whether uniformed or civilian. This network of charitable relief societies would: help save lives; stimulate Christian principles of charity and giving; nurture among the common people a respect for those wounded or killed in battle, no matter what uniform they wore; and stimulate ideals of civilized society. Humanitarianism, at least this version, would rescue soldiers and nourish Christian civilization.

Without wishing to minimize Dunant's tremendous accomplishments, the impact of the book owed much to being the right message at the right time. Over the previous half-century European societies had established a network of charitable and reform organizations, building a solid presence in Geneva where the elite had a venerable history of social action. Also, the idea of regulating war and providing medical relief to soldiers had gained some ground in previous decades. The first push to regulate war began in the seventeenth century and was the product of advances in military technology that made war more brutal; moral and legal discourses regarding civilized behavior (among Christians); and arguments in favor of international norms to create a stable and just order among (European) states.[2] In the eighteenth century legal and political theorists such as the Genevans Emmerich de Vattel and Jean-Jacques Rousseau advanced the cause of regulated war on both principled and self-interested grounds. Rousseau, for instance, wrote that once soldiers were no longer instruments of the state because they were sick, injured, or captured, then they reclaimed their standing as individuals who had rights that needed to be protected. Also at this time natural law-based theories led to a stronger distinction between combatants and noncombatants, the view that not all violence was necessary or justified, especially as it pertained to the wounded and prisoners of war.

Dunant also was joining a number of others who were agitating for improving medical relief. In the early nineteenth century, militaries began to develop field units for wounded soldiers. At midcentury the push to improve medical assistance for soldiers was occurring on both sides of the Atlantic. A few years after Dunant, during the American Civil War, Florence Nightingale drew from her experiences in the Crimean War to lobby for improved medical relief, Francis Leiber helped to author military codes of conduct, and the Sanitary Commission proposed various reforms, including improved hygiene to reduce disease among the troops. In Europe there was growing interest in doing more for wounded soldiers. Dunant added his voice to theirs, chronicling how the militaries provided little medical relief for their soldiers and how at Solferino they had more "veterinarians to care for horses than they did doctors to care for soldiers wounded in battle."[3] Treating soldiers as disposable might not have caused such an outcry if these had been mercenary troops (though there was a mosaic of soldiers at Solferino), but these were national armies, and the parents of the conscripts hardly expected their militaries to treat their sons as less valuable than horses.[4]

Dunant's message grabbed the attention of the Genevan Society of Public Utility, and in February 1863 it created an exploratory subcommittee, comprised of five Genevan citizens: Henry Dunant; a financier, Gustave Moynier; two doctors, Louis Appia and Théodore Maunoir; and an army general, Guillaume-Henri Dufour. All five were deeply religious and quite concerned about moral progress. Dunant was an evangelical who saw himself as "an instrument in the hands of God."[5] Moynier, who deserves considerable credit for turning Dunant's vision into reality, was a veteran of reform movements, a committed Calvinist and highly respected member of Genevan society who believed that the Calvinist elite had a special role to play in the world; he was particularly taken with the possibility that charitable organizations might stimulate (Christian) notions of progress, charity, and humanity and civilize the lower classes. Christianity contributed to the emergence and perseverance of the ICRC and the Red Cross Movement.[6]

While God and compassion might have inspired Dunant and his compatriots, states answered to a higher authority—themselves—and without their blessing nothing would happen. Their initial, fairly predictable, reaction was negative: they had little interest in seeing a bunch of do-good, moralizing volunteers entering into the thick of battle, could hardly imagine how they might save the lives of soldiers, and dismissed their pretense of cosmopolitanism. They changed their minds, though, after concluding that Dunant's proposal might help them legitimate and save war. As just noted, this was a time when changes in military technology were making war more bloody and states were shifting away from mercenary forces and toward conscripted national armies. Democracy was a bloody mess. War reporting also was coming of age, as journalists were dispatching graphic accounts to their readers back home.[7] Parents could now imagine that at the very moment they were reading battlefield accounts in the newspaper, their loved ones were being allowed to suffer and die. The public response was to question not only conscription but also war itself, stirring pacifist sentiments in some corners. What the military needed, then, was some device to address the concerns of the public, and Dunant's proposals were perfect for the job. After all, Dunant was not a pacifist—he wanted to humanize war, not outlaw it. The military now had a way to save war from itself.

When governments gathered to discuss the proposals, they dumped those they found objectionable and threatening to their interests—that is, virtually all of them. Dunant had imagined European volunteers wandering into war to care for the wounded, but military commanders buried this proposal on the grounds that the battlefield was no place for self-nominated saviors of humanity. Their involvement might undermine military discipline, disrupt operations, and perhaps even distract from the military's own, evolving, field medicine.[8] Accordingly, the congress decided that volunteers could serve far behind the front lines and supplement the army's medical capacities. The only proposal that emerged unscathed was an international convention to grant special protection to the wounded and those caring for them, regardless of whether they were uniformed or civilian. In order to minimize the possibility that medical personnel would become targets or prisoners of war, the Geneva Conventions established the principle of the neutrality of military personnel.[9] On a voluntary basis, states could participate and create local national Red Cross societies, but they would be distinguished by Swiss-branded armbands. But, ultimately, a state's willingness to participate or comply with the Geneva Conventions was entirely voluntary. There was no penalty for not joining or for signing and then violating the pact (though reciprocity could be a powerful motivator). With these limitations international humanitarian law got its start, and the ICRC was created to help develop and protect it.

The creation of the ICRC and the Geneva Conventions, quite obviously, was a decisive moment in the history of emergency humanitarianism, and it is worth stopping to marvel at the moral breakthrough and some of the ways it compared to alchemical humanitarianism. For the very first time there was a convention and a semi-official body that would regulate the conduct of war and the treatment of soldiers. Although few at the time expected that their mere creation would have an immediate and significant impact, even the most cynical acknowledged that something important had changed regarding the standards by which states would be measured. Yet, ultimately, states decided whether they would live up to those standards and whether they would accept the assistance of the ICRC. Accordingly, emergency and alchemical humanitarianism began with different relationships to the state. Those organizations that comprised alchemical humanitarianism sometimes needed the state, particularly when they were trying to influence legislation, but in many instances these voluntary and church-based organizations, what we now call civil society organizations, could operate outside of the state's jurisdiction. Yet the ICRC was encroaching on one of the state's most sensitive areas, security, and started as a quasi-public, quasi-private body, an arm of states even as it was independent of them. Consequently, from the very beginning the ICRC's very existence and effectiveness depended on states, which meant an acute sensitivity to their views. Largely because of its close connections, the ICRC strove to create principles and symbols of independence.

The ability of states to absorb ethics and invert cosmopolitanism became clearer over the first half-decade of the ICRC's existence.[10] Central to Dunant's vision was that Red Cross societies would create a transnational and cosmopolitan movement, stimulating respect for soldiers regardless of their uniform and thus contributing to the idea of a common humanity. However, they became imprinted by the state system and patriotism.[11] States increasingly treated the national Red Cross societies as part of the war effort, and the Red Cross societies, desirous of being accepted by their governments, accommodated. Far from articulating and aspiring to cosmopolitanism, they developed a patriotic nationalism as they reminded citizens of their duty to help their soldiers at the front. Red Cross societies began providing support to the troops, running blood drives, delivering food to soldiers going off to war, staffing recovery hospitals, and encouraging citizens to donate to the war effort. National Red Cross societies became part of the growing militarization of society.

Whereas the discourses of nationalism and patriotism shaped the ICRC's evolution among the community of states, the discourses of Christianity and civilization shaped the ICRC's view toward those outside the European community. Reflecting "the religious and moral assumptions of the nineteenth century European bourgeoisie... [t]hey had naturally assumed that mercy and compassion were uniquely Christian values. The first task for the Red Cross, they believed, was to instill these virtues within Christendom, especially among the common people whose weak moral sense seemed to them to need careful nurture."[12] The issue was not simply a matter of getting their priorities right—it also concerned whether and how these laws of war might apply to those outside of Europe. Consistent with the variegated notions of humanity that prevailed at the time, the ICRC believed that while European Christians could comprehend and honor the Red Cross principles, those outside these boundaries probably could not.[13] For this reason it responded with incredulity to the 1865 message from the sultan of the Ottoman Empire that he was prepared to accept the Geneva Conventions; it could hardly believe that this Muslim state either understood or was prepared to honor the conventions. And, to complicate matters, the Ottoman Empire notified Geneva that, as a Muslim state, it would not adopt the symbol of the cross. While it is quite likely that the delegates to the Congress had selected the cross because of its association with Christian charity and aspirations for a universal, enlightened humanitarianism (and not as a tribute to Switzerland), they nevertheless treated the symbol as nonsectarian and could not imagine that it might give offense.[14] After considerable discussion, the ICRC allowed the Ottoman Empire to use the Islamic-based crescent.

This episode caused the ICRC to rethink its purpose and entertain the possibility of a civilizing mission beyond its borders. As one founder stated in a newsletter in 1873 in the context of ICRC's discussions with Japan, while it would be "puerile" to expect "the savages and barbarians, who are still singularly numerous on the face of the globe, to follow this example" [of Japan], there is the possibility that there are "races which possess a civilization, albeit one different from ours" that desire closer relations with Europe and might be brought into civilized society through the Red Cross societies.[15] Red Cross societies began to expand across the globe. For a dedicated colonialist like Gustave Moynier, the ICRC could help perform a civilizing mission that would "humanize" the "savage peoples" by rescuing them from their "brute instincts."[16] ICRC officials interpreted the popularity of the organization outside of Europe as an opportunity for furthering the dream of universalizing the laws of war and diffusing Christian notions of charity.

Saving Civilians

Most of the attempted innovations in emergency relief in the decades immediately prior to World War I concerned civilizing war by outlawing and regulating certain kinds of military technologies and improving the conditions of wounded and captured soldiers. Civilian populations at risk were not entirely neglected, but whether or not they received attention frequently depended on the existence of a diaspora ready to mobilize on its behalf.[17] Although in many respects World War I continued this tradition of private, fly-by-night charities giving to those who shared their identity, in other ways the war and the subsequent interwar period was a transitional point between the Age of Imperial Humanitarianism and the Age of Neo-Humanitarianism. There were signs that need, not identity, was the increasingly important criterion for deciding who received attention; that a secularized humanity was replacing a religiously based compassion; that institutionalization was replacing improvisation; that public governance of relief was replacing private morality; and that internationally coordinated responses were replacing nationally driven action. In this respect, just as many students of international history treat the thirty years between World War I and World War II as one continuous event from one era to the next, the same can be said of humanitarianism. But all of this is clearer in hindsight than it was at the time.

Although impartial relief was not completely unknown, most societies and governments tended to give to those with whom they had a prior emotional connection or bond; a tribal division of moral labor evolved from a long tradition in welfare and immigration societies that had an ethnic, national, or religious identity. During and after World War I this meant that British- and American-based relief organizations focused exclusively on the needs of their allies. In the United States there were many associations keen on helping the Russians, the Belgians, and the British populations, and after the war the U.S. government established a quasi-private relief agency, the American Relief Administration, which purposefully neglected the Germans, even though it knew that one-third to two-thirds of German children were malnourished. German-American associations were nearly alone in organizing relief for the German population (and were often accused of aiding the enemy for doing so) and after the war German-American associations, well-placed individuals, and the Quakers stepped into the breach.[18] The discourse of humanity, especially one that demanded nondiscriminatory practices and that included friend and foe alike, barely registered.

In this context Save the Children's insistence that the postwar British relief should go to all children, including German children, represented a controversial and courageous stand. Much of the credit deservedly goes to Eglantyne Jebb, the founder of Save the Children, and while her position was ahead of its time, it reflected broader trends that were occurring in British society. Born in 1876 to a well-to-do family, Jebb had the good fortune to be among the first women educated at Oxford. After graduation she set off to make her mark, but there were few occupations open to women in her day, teaching and philanthropy among them. She tried her hand at teaching, but was neither well suited for the position nor all that fond of children. As she wrote, "I have none of the natural qualities of a teacher: I don't care for children, I don't care for teaching."[19] She then worked at the Charity Organisation Society (COS), a conservative charitable organization that largely wanted to improve charity for the deserving poor; assigned the task of studying the charitable societies, she assembled a well-received volume that presented a wealth of data on the sector and summary findings regarding the future of charity. At around the time she was finishing her work at the COS, she was invited to help with the relief

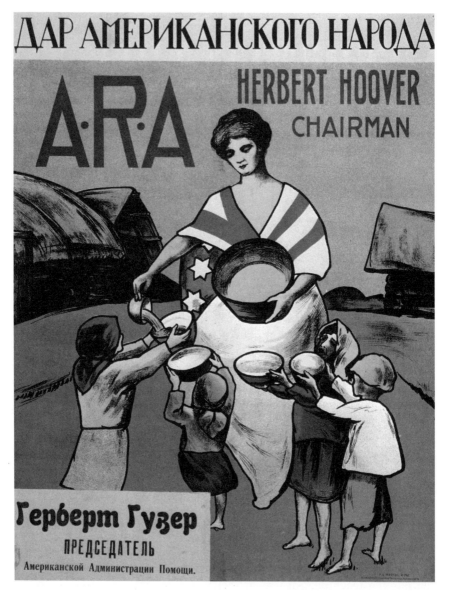

Figure 6 American Relief Administration poster. Image provided by the Hoover Institution of Stanford University.

effort in the Balkans, where she confronted many challenges, including how to operate in multiethnic, multireligious, and multinational societies. Her response was to emphasize the importance of giving based on need and not on identity, a position she held unwaveringly for the rest of her life.[20]

Although Jebb had grown up politically conservative and exhibited little interest in the radical politics of the times, including suffrage, her political views became more liberal at the turn of the century and were influenced by various factors, including her sister, Dorothy Jebb Buxton, who was married to an aspiring liberal politician, Charles Roden Buxton.[21] Jebb's philosophical views were an eclectic fusion of a cosmopolitan view of citizenship, a religiously and spiritually influenced humanity, and social economics. Although she had had a traditional Christian upbringing, the death of her brother and her own spiritual quest led her to various forms of spiritualism, which had quite a following in the late nineteenth and early twentieth centuries, which accommodated her belief in the oneness of the world and a transcendental humanity.[22] She became increasingly convinced that what was required was more than relief but rather a new kind of social responsibility that transcended but included the state. Her closest friend was Margaret Keynes, the wife of John Maynard Keynes, and she and John Maynard occasionally corresponded and exchanged views.

Her previous work experience, social philosophy, and desire to alleviate the famine in postwar Europe forged her determination to make Save the Children a leading international relief and philanthropic organization. Said otherwise, it was not because of a deep and abiding love for children. She never had children, never expressed any regrets over it, and showed little interest in her nieces and nephews. As she sarcastically wrote to a friend after she founded Save the Children, "I suppose it is a judgment on me for not caring about children that I am made to talk all day long about the universal love of humanity toward them."[23] If she was not necessarily fond of children, then why make them her focus?: Britain's continued blockade of Europe after the war and its direct effect on the famine ravaging the continent. Along with others, she formed the Famine Council on January 1, 1919, with the direct desire to end the British blockade. Soon thereafter Jebb and her sister decided that more direct action was needed, so they took to the streets, distributing a "Starving Baby" leaflet, and the authorities arrested the two on the grounds that they were spreading antipatriotic propaganda. Acting as her own attorney, she claimed that the leaflets were humanitarian and not political. Although she was found guilty, the judge gave her a light sentence, a victory of sorts. Undeterred, even emboldened, she exploited the discourse of children as innocent representatives of humanity and encouraged everyone, especially women, to protect the children. Thus Save the Children was born. Importantly, she insisted that all children, including the children of former enemies, be eligible for relief. Her famous supporter, George Bernard Shaw, wrote at the time, "I have no enemies under the age of seven."

Her commitment to impartiality derived not only from a child-centered focus but also from a desire to use the organization as a vehicle for creating a unity of humankind. Former enemies could unite around the idea of the innocence of the child and agree that children are the building blocks for a better future. It was not the child known or recognized but rather the child as an abstraction, as a symbol of what the world might become. By providing relief and charity to children, Jebb believed that she was helping them develop to their fullest material and spiritual capacity and, along with it, growing the seeds for a new internationalism.[24] As her niece wrote, Jebb saw Save the Children as a demonstration and "assertion of the oneness of mankind, of the human race being, as it were, one family."[25]

Relatedly, Jebb was attracted to humanitarianism because it allowed her to act outside of formal politics.[26] She worked hard, and succeeded, at distancing Save the Children from traditional religious and political divisions; she received public support from Pope Benedict XV, who called for collections from the Catholic Church, and Protestant denominations and moved Save the Children's headquarters to Geneva not only to be closer to the new League of Nations but also to symbolize Save the Children's separation from power politics. But Jebb's ambitions, in many ways, were far more political and radical than the left-liberal politics of her sister. She imagined saving children by changing the societies in which they lived. She wrote that it would be "heartbreaking indeed if it comes about that we have only saved them from starvation one year in order to leave them to starve the next."[27] She even wrote to her friend John Maynard Keynes to propose a program for European reconstruction, believing that the future of children, and thus the future of humankind, rested on a radical reform of European politics. Although religion remained a powerful force for many who gave and became involved in relief activities, Save the Children illustrated the growing influence of a secularized humanity. The Jebbs had founded one of the first great ecumenical agencies and decided that in order to maintain its nonsectarian identity and help it manage its growing number of branches throughout Europe, they would create Save the Children International Union and locate it in Geneva.

The war and the tremendous relief effort highlighted the limitations of improvised charity and the necessity of an institutionalized philanthropic and aid sector. The severity and duration of the war meant that private voluntary agencies had to become bigger and develop the qualities of permanent organizations, with staff, rules, procedures, and headquarters. Particularly noteworthy was the effort by Herbert Hoover, the American businessman and future American president, on behalf of civilian populations facing famine in German-occupied Belgium and northern France. Because of the occupation and the slowdown of the economy, disruption of food production, a flood of stricken refugees, and, most importantly, a blockade imposed by the Allies of the North Sea ports, a famine fell over Belgium. Local relief organizations attempted to do what they could, but they were overwhelmed by the task of keeping alive over nine million people. In September 1914 a local committee approached Hoover, who had recently earned some fame in London for helping to organize the relief and evacuation of nearly two hundred thousand Americans stranded in London at the beginning of the war, to help secure a shipment of grain. In cooperation with the United States and the German occupation authorities, Hoover formed the American Committee for the Relief of Belgium (later renamed the Commission for Relief in Belgium) to ship and distribute food aid. Demonstrating tremendous patience and considerable diplomatic acumen, Hoover convinced both sides that they would gain little from the starvation of the occupied population; the British that relief would go to the civilian population and not the German military; and the Germans that food aid would not advantage the allies. During its nearly five-year run, the CRB became one of Belgium's primary sources of food, delivering more than five million tons, valued at the time at over $800 million. Remarkable in international affairs, the CRB was a private international organization that nevertheless had many of the functions associated with the state, as it could conclude agreements with states, and states conferred on it political neutrality and operational independence.[28] In many respects, the CRB offered humanitarianism a glimpse of its future.[29]

World War I also signaled the beginning of the end of private charity's monopoly of relief, for states were becoming more actively involved in the organization of aid. After the war President Wilson declared that the time was ripe for the "second American intervention" and established the American Relief Administration (ARA), retiring the CRB but keeping Hoover as the head of the new organization, a role that brought him into various parts of Europe (see figure 7). Although it had an official imprint, in fact it relied heavily on the nine existing private relief agencies, nearly all of them religious. It had two noteworthy features. It delivered food and medical supplies to Central Europe and, most famously, to Russia during the famine of 1921, an operation requiring considerable diplomatic and logistical skill to avoid giving the appearance of either strengthening the Bolshevik government, and thus falling afoul of American public opinion, or attempting to use relief as a way of destabilizing the Bolsheviks, and thus being evicted by the new Soviet regime.[30] Also, it responded to existing demand among the American people for a way to help their relatives and friends affected by the war, creating a program whereby individuals could buy standard food packages and have them delivered. U.S. officials were realizing that they could harness the humanitarian spirit for their broader foreign policy goals.[31]

Another development was the growing readiness of states to accept new kinds of responsibilities to vulnerable populations and build international organizations to help them carry out those responsibilities. The good news was that such developments were reflections of the growth of international opinion in favor of providing relief to the needy, an emerging view among

Figure 7 Hoover and Post–World War I Relief. Image provided by The Hoover Institution of Stanford University.

states that humanitarian action could be consistent with various state interests, and the general belief that the humanitarian emergencies and the desire
to do something about them were now a permanent feature of international
political life and thus demanded a multilateral response. The not-so-good
news was that states were careful to design these organizations so that they
had little chance of jeopardizing their interests or taking advantage of their
hospitality. Two initiatives, the High Commissioner for Refugees (HCR)
and the International Relief Union (IRU) demonstrate the breakthroughs in
humanitarian action and their state-imposed boundaries.

Growing state controls over their borders, a world war that created
unprecedented numbers of displaced persons; the breakdown of the multinational empires in Russia, Austria-Hungary, and Turkey; the creation of
national states (often by ethnic cleansing); and the Russian Revolution and
the famine that followed created a situation in which millions of people
were unable to either go home or find sanctuary elsewhere. In 1921 the
League of Nations responded by establishing the HCR. States decided to act
for two principal reasons. Overwhelmed by the sheer number of displaced
persons and their demands, many private charity groups lobbied states to
create a new international agency to aid the relief effort.[32] Also, and perhaps most important, states believed that mass population movement was
destabilizing Europe. Yet there were real limits on the number of people
they were prepared to help. Although refugees were strewn across Europe,

Western states were unwilling to recognize their presence and restricted the HCR's mandate to the Russian refugees. Also, the category of refugee was defined in part as someone forced to flee because of persecution—a politically loaded charge that they were prepared to level only at the Soviet Union. States also limited the HCR to coordination and refused to give it any operational capacity. And because the HCR was not expected to do all that much, states gave it a meager budget to match.

Despite the initial shackles states placed on it, the HCR managed to expand its scope. It ventured far beyond the Russian refugee crisis to become involved elsewhere in the region and to articulate a set of refugee rights. The organization's first High Commissioner, the renowned Norwegian explorer Fridtjof Nansen, deserves much of the credit. In part because of his previous experience dealing with the repatriation of Russian war prisoners, he had some credibility with Western governments that he was able to exploit to expand the agency's activities. Over the objections of these governments, Nansen soon insinuated himself into the political and refugee crises in Greece, Turkey, Bulgaria, and elsewhere. Such interventions proved to be a powerful precedent for international involvement in refugee issues. In addition to this geographical expansion, the HCR successfully negotiated a set of refugee rights, including travel documents (the so-called Nansen passport), education, and employment (Nansen worked with the International Labor Organization to help refugees find jobs). For the first time, there was an international agency that was assisting refugees—helping to define populations in need and what rights they might possess. However, while the HCR was able to broaden its geographical scope, elevate issues, and set agendas, it remained a coordinating agency with no implementation capacity. It was wholly dependent on states to carry out its recommendations; when states did not want to cooperate, little happened.

In 1933 governments convened to consider a refugee convention. Largely written by Nansen's office, the draft treaty proposed a more categorical and open-ended statement regarding the future refugee regime alongside a lengthy list of refugees' rights.[33] States, however, rejected the idea of refugees' rights, an expanded definition of refugees, and an expanded mandate for the HCR. Their discussions led to a draft treaty that failed to define a refugee, refused to guarantee the right of asylum, skirted the issue of refugee rights, and neglected to deliver a categorical prohibition against returning refugees to their homeland without their consent. Even this weak document proved too radical for most states, for it received only eight signatures. The unwillingness of Western states to shelter "undesirable" groups became tragically clearer over the next few years, as they denied entry of Jews and other persecuted people from Nazi Germany. Nansen's successor High Commissioner, James McDonald, attempted to help the victims of Nazi persecution by publicizing their plight and imploring Western governments to follow through on their obligations, but he found no takers. He resigned in protest, calling on the League to "remove or mitigate the causes which create German refugees."

The tension between trying to work with the growing refugee situation caused by Nazi Germany and the League's desire to remain outside of "political matters" caused it to define refugee problems as "technical." As the Dutch minister of foreign affairs acidly stated in his plea to the League to assist the refugees, there was "no wish to examine why these people have left their country, but we are faced with the undeniable fact that thousands of German subjects have crossed the frontiers of neighbouring countries and are refusing to return to their homes, for reasons which we are not called upon to judge. For us, therefore, it is purely a *technical problem*."[34] The League Assembly referred the matter to the committee on technical organization, not political questions.

The International Relief Union (IRU) was another interesting example of the willingness of states to break new ground but retreat at the first sign of inconvenient demands. The brainchild of an Italian senator and president of the Italian Red Cross—Giovanni Ciraolo dreamed of creating an international organization to provide aid in response to natural disasters— it was established on July 12, 1927 and, on the occasion of the twelfth signatory, went into force on December 27, 1932. The IRU had a rather undistinguished and short-lived existence, ultimately unable to get states to do much beyond setting up the organization. In addition to the usual nemeses, the IRU's eventual demise also owed to another development related to the institutionalization of relief—interorganizational competition. The ICRC viewed the IRU as a potential competitor and did what it could to undermine its rival.[35]

Yet the debate surrounding the organization captured the past and the future. Many supporters asserted that any meaningful international solidarity must include relief, claiming, for instance, that the IRU was part of a "holy mission, that of international solidarity."[36] Although the great bursts of humanitarianism that emerged after the "Great War" were now in retreat, conceded one observer, "intersocial feelings are constant. The idea is too Christian to die by the way....Man may weary of some eternal values, but he cannot do without them."[37] What is particularly noteworthy is that even skeptics of the IRU were impressed by the background factors that made such an organization imaginable. Although grossly exaggerating the extent to which the principle of "mutual assistance" had become widely accepted (even assuming that everywhere includes Europe), one commentator at the time observed that this basic principle of humanity, which had the force of "private international morality," was now becoming part of international public morality.[38] It was always possible to criticize the IRU of sentimentality and naiveté, and wonder about whether aid does any good at all. Along these lines, one observer approvingly cited Anatole France's wicked criticism of those who believe that acting good is doing good: "The giving of alms is no more comparable with doing good than a monkey's grimace is to the smile of the Gioconda. Beneficence is as effective as alms is futile. It is careful to see that what is done is commensurate with need."[39] But only the most committed cynic would dismiss out-of-hand the forces that were bringing into view the outlines of an organization such as the IRU.

The ICRC, a strange hybrid of a private and public international organization, found itself confronting a variety of challenges from states after the war, and it adopted a variety of evasive maneuvers. To begin, World War I rejuvenated a demoralized ICRC. Its first fifty years were distinguished only by its stumblings, in-fighting, conflicts with an increasingly independent Red Cross movement, and reluctance to undertake creative, bold, or risky action that might rankle states. It had little to show for its decades-long struggle to regulate advances in military technology in order to avoid a future firestorm. Yet during the war it distinguished itself. Although it played little role in the distribution of relief to the civilian populations, its involvement in monitoring and assisting prisoners of war gave it considerable prestige and helped it win the Nobel Peace Prize in 1917. Moreover, the horrors of the war led to a strong tide of international opinion in favor of humanizing war, and the ICRC's prior efforts demonstrated its prescience and raised its status, evidenced when the League of Nations highlighted its centrality for regulating and lessening the brutality of war.[40]

The ICRC's renown brought it some unwelcome attention. The possibility that it might do and be more became part of the postwar discussion in large measure because of the considerable ambitions of an American, Henry P. Davison, who chaired the war council of the American Red Cross during the war and then imagined an American-led Red Cross that became active in all forms of war and peacetime relief, combating both war and disease-induced death.[41] The possibility of the ICRC delivering relief during times of natural disaster and engaging in other life-saving activities such as disease prevention had been discussed at various moments since its inception. One argument in favor of an expanded mandate was that the ICRC could gain invaluable logistical and operational experience through these peacetime activities. Another was that the ICRC was practicing selective humanitarianism because of its failure to treat all lives as equal, choosing to respond only to those who were affected by violence and ignoring those in comparable straits but affected by natural disasters.[42] Although the ICRC was well aware of the need to change, it viewed Davison's proposal as threatening to transfigure the organization. The ICRC would become a small fish in a bigger lake of relief, its moral authority would be suffocated by a U.S.-led enterprise, a voluntary-based organization comprised of patrician Genevan citizens would be replaced by technical and professional experts in public health, and it would become something of a global welfare agency.

The ICRC blocked the proposal, in part by distinguishing its impartiality, neutrality, and independence from a more regionally focused, U.S.-run venture.[43] In other words, these elementary principles of humanitarianism were good for helping the ICRC save the lives of others—as well as its own.

Although the ICRC was opposed to an expansion that would undermine its autonomy, it was quite willing to follow its identity into new areas. It became involved in refugee matters in response to the Russian Revolution. In the Spanish Civil War it appealed repeatedly to the combatants to distinguish between civilian and military targets.[44] Extending its involvement in monitoring prisoners of war during World War I, it sought access to those in civil wars and invented language in order to widen its mandate without stirring controversy, including those "detained by reasons of events." As David Forsythe put it, "If prisoners of war morally mattered in international armed conflict, why not detained combatants in internal wars; and why not other 'political enemies' when detained? Were not all of these detainees in potential danger and thus in need of a humanitarian intermediary when in the hands of an adversary?... Hence the ICRC's moral imperative to protect detained 'enemies' transcended the categories of conflict so beloved by states with their fixations on the murky notion of state sovereignty and domestic jurisdiction."[45] The ICRC was on the move—but only so far.

The ICRC's response to the Italian invasion of Ethiopia in 1935 and its various crimes, including the use of poison gas, shows how its policies were shaped by the times.[46] Italy invaded Ethiopia, then known as Abyssinia, on October 3, 1935, and four days later the League of Nations unanimously declared Italy an aggressor but without taking any other action. Although eventually the ICRC was embarrassed into taking a more active role, at first it was very reluctant because of its prejudices. The ICRC operated with a civilizational mentality, in which Western Christian powers were superior to non-Western peoples. Although Ethiopia was that rare African state that had never experienced colonialism and was a member of the League of Nations, the mandatory system and prevailing European beliefs held that African peoples could benefit from European oversight. Ethiopia, in other words, was an anomaly, but perhaps to its disadvantage. One high-ranking ICRC official characterized the Ethiopian Red Cross as a "facade" and said that it was a contestable decision for the League to admit a "state" whose "civilization" was questionable. Whether its prejudices contributed to its passive response to Italian crimes is a matter of debate, but its civilizational attitudes hardly encouraged sympathy for the Ethiopians.

The geopolitical context also influenced the ICRC's languid response. The very patrician and exclusive eighteen individuals that were the full members of the ICRC were members of right-wing parties, anticommunists, and those who believed that the rise of fascism would help contain the spread of Bolshevism. In other words, many at the ICRC sympathized with Italy (and the Italian Red Cross also became thoroughly and willingly co-opted by Mussolini).[47] The desire to avoid a squabble with Italy at all costs led to a policy of public silence by the ICRC on known atrocities committed by the Italian forces and to interpret neutrality in ways that allowed it to avoid appearing too sympathetic to the Ethiopians. In order to enforce this policy of neutrality in the face of war crimes, the ICRC silenced staff who wanted to speak out. For instance, Geneva dismissed its head of mission, Sidney Brown, when he complained too much and too loudly. Brown begged headquarters to "defend the interests of the Red Cross with a little more vehemence"; Geneva rewarded him by sending him home and then firing him, an outcome that an Italian Red Cross member boasted he had made happen because he revealed that Brown was a homosexual. This was not the first time that the ICRC kept silent, and it would not be the last.

One last development deserves mention—NGOs were beginning both to build and to take advantage of a global platform to expand humanitarian action. Save the Children, once again, illustrates the new possibilities. Under Eglantyne Jebb's direction, it began tackling problems related to child labor in Iran and China, child marriage in India, and primary education in Africa. In keeping with the times, Jebb also moved to institutionalize her commitments in various legal instruments and international bodies. She and others began working on a "Children's Charter" to cover the fundamental, inalienable rights of children, which led to the "Declaration of Geneva," a document listing the rights of children and endorsed by League of Nations in September 1923.[48] The following year the League of Nations established the Child Welfare Committee, and Save the Children officials used this platform to push children's rights outside of Europe.

The Conference on the African Child in 1931, organized by the Save the Children International Union, illustrates several aspects of humanitarianism's changing nature. To begin with, it was becoming more truly humanitarian—children were the innocent of the world, and a child's needs in India deserved the same consideration as a child's needs in Liverpool. Humanitarianism was becoming better institutionalized, not only in terms of the adoption of new norms and legal instruments but also in the creation of new networks of activists that joined together under a common cause. There was considerable emphasis and faith placed in the value of data, empirical analysis, and statistics. Scientific knowledge was the analogue to humanitarianism—both were neutral and universal in scope and application. The conference organizers took a page from the World Missionary Conference in Edinburgh and undertook a worldwide survey of children's health as a way to generate new data that might justify new forms of intervention.

Also, the conference reflected an interesting development in the relationship of religion to humanitarian action. Missionaries did play a critical role in providing the knowledge, labor, and organizing skills that were critical for the conference's success. But the conference had the strong veneer of nonsectarianism (which is hardly surprising given that many of the conference organizers were members of or heavily influenced by Save the Children). Importantly, missionaries and secular humanists found common ground in the language of rights. The missionaries who were at the conference had spent decades in the bush with the local peoples, which had left them with a pluralistic view of African culture that acknowledged that African laws, organizations, and customs had their own integrity.[49] Their tolerance did not necessarily mean that they saw local cultures as on the same plane as Christianity; they were still missionaries, and they believed that by changing the spirituality and moral codes of the African people they could lift them into civilization. But they also believed that education was the mechanism of conversion, and that native populations had rights like those in the West. Although it was increasingly difficult to tell where the religious ended and the secular began, the softening of humanitarianism's religious discourse was both evident at the conference and a sign of the changing times.[50]

The world was moving between two global ages, and humanitarianism bore its marks. The world was becoming increasingly secular, and humanitarianism's once-explicit religious discourse was losing ground to the discourse of humanity and international community. States had grudgingly accepted new kinds of international assistance and protections for radically vulnerable populations after World War I, and their halting creation of various kinds of safety nets during the interwar years suggested that states were accepting new responsibilities for their populations. Far from being the war to end all wars, World War I was more of a dry run, with dress rehearsals occurring around the world during the 1930s, in China, Spain, Ethiopia, and elsewhere. The relatively few humanitarian institutions that states had built after the war were completely inadequate to the task—little surprise, since states were only beginning to warm up to the idea of public international organizations for humanitarian action against the backdrop of a world gone mad.

PART II

The Age of
Neo-Humanitarianism

5

~≈~

The New International

WORLD WAR II transformed the world of humanitarianism. Europe's destruction catapulted the United States and the Soviet Union to Great Power status. The United States fought two major wars simultaneously, demonstrated a military capacity unprecedented in world history, and emerged from the war as the sole possessor of nuclear weapons. The economies of the major industrial countries lay in shards, except for the United States, whose economy strengthened as the war went on. While the rest of the world scavenged for food, the United States wondered what to do with its agricultural surplus. Importantly, after believing that its decision to remain aloof from global affairs after World War I had contributed to the Great Depression and given comfort to fascism, U.S. officials now accepted the role of "leader of the free world." The Soviet Union's victory came at an obscenely high cost. It lost roughly 26 million citizens, the majority of whom were civilians. Whole cities had been destroyed, becoming nearly uninhabitable for the survivors. Vitebsk, a small Russian city that changed hands between the Russians and the Nazis eleven times, lost more lives than the total number of Americans killed during the war.[1] An agricultural sector that had been shattered by Stalin's forced collectivization of the 1930s was now struggling to feed its population. Little remained of its hard-won industrialization from the interwar period. The Soviets confronted the herculean challenge of postwar reconstruction, but unlike the Europeans and even the defeated Axis powers, who received American assistance, the Americans refused to help their wartime ally.

The marriage of convenience between the Americans and the Soviets collapsed into a bitter divorce after the war, defining a new historical period—the Cold War. They were fated to be bitter enemies, according to realists, because of the bipolar distribution of power. Perhaps. But they also possessed grandiose self-images—the United States as leader of the "free world" and a "city on a hill" and the Soviet Union as the vanguard of the world revolution. As Hans Morgenthau, the father of postwar realism, observed, the United States and the Soviet Union were promoting their visions of a universalistic nationalism, "a secular religion, universal in its interpretation of the nature and destiny of man."[2] These were dueling visions, with each side typecasting the other as a strategic and existential threat. For the next forty-five years this bipolar "cold" war caused more violence, mayhem, and night sweats than a good many hot wars.

Europe's devastation also led to the fall of colonial empires and the rise of a newly independent Third World. Only a few decades earlier, the self-satisfied and confident colonial powers had completed their hostile takeover of the world. Although World War I and the mandatory system suggested that colonialism would have a more difficult time legitimating its existence, the colonial powers displayed remarkably little anxiety. World War II, though, began the process of finishing off what World War I had started. The war-weary British and French publics turned vocally against colonialism, insisting that all resources had to be directed to a home front that had sacrificed mightily over the previous decade. Also, the war loosened the grip of the colonizer on the colonized, and many anticolonial leaders used the cracks to build nationalist movements whose calls for revolution were increasingly backed by force. The United States and the Soviet Union were neither nostalgic for colonialism nor able to connect its continuation to their immediate strategic and economic interests; in fact, because both saw themselves as freedom fighters in their own right, their sympathies lay with the ruled, at least rhetorically. The United Nations Charter contained the writing on the wall, inscribing in various places that it would work for the peaceful end of colonialism. Colonialism's days were numbered, and the global debate shifted from whether the colonies would gain their independence to how soon.

The combination of the Cold War and decolonization unleashed new conflict patterns in the emerging Third World. On the eve of decolonization, many in the West predicted that the independence of the Third World would unfurl global violence, because the colonies were unprepared for self-governance and sovereignty; these forecasts were wrong because they failed to recognize how keen Third World leaders were to embrace sovereignty and its principle of noninterference, if only because it aligned with their survival strategy. In many cases, though, the transfer of power triggered a brutal struggle for domestic supremacy. In addition to causing tremendous human suffering, it also opened the door to new forms of Great Power intervention. Imitating in various ways the nineteenth century's Great Power scramble for colonies and acting as if the principle of noninterference applied to everyone but themselves, the Soviets and Americans, couched firmly in their zero-sum view of the world, began carving up the globe into spheres of influence and using all covert and overt means at their disposal to cultivate friends and punish enemies. Although many Third World leaders declared themselves to be nonaligned, by word and deed the Soviets and Americans denied such an option. The superpowers carried their conflict to the Third World, frequently fighting each other through proxies in part because it was safer than confronting each other directly. The global South was, once again, swept up into the high-stakes game of global geopolitics.

An equally momentous shift occurred in the forces of production, though most consequential for the future of humanitarianism was the transformation of the state's role in economic life. Prior to World War I the prevailing view was that the best state was the limited state, present when defending the homeland and private property but otherwise conspicuously absent. With limited exceptions, individuals were on their own during hard times; they might find comfort from their neighbors, their churches, and their fellow citizens, but not the state. This self-righteous indifference increasingly became a thing of the past, and several factors produced a shift from the state-as-night-watchman to the state-as-caretaker. The global depression of the 1930s caused states as ideologically diverse as the United States, France, Britain, and Germany to accept that the state had a responsibility to protect its citizens during tough times. Keynesianism, in its many guises, was nudging government leaders to accept that when the market failed, the state could and must play a greater economic role and protect the welfare of its citizens. Using the great flood of the Mississippi Delta in 1927 to capture the revolutionary change in government's role when Americans were down on their luck, Herbert Hoover reflected, "Those were the days when citizens expected to take care of one another in time of disaster and it had not occurred to them that the Federal Government should do it."[3]

There was the additional reconsideration of the relationship between the economy and security. The belief that a strong economy was essential for national security was hardly new, present in various forms of economic nationalism at home and abroad. However, relatively novel was the conviction that economic stability underpinned domestic and international stability. In the domestic sphere, state officials increasingly included economic rights alongside what we now call political and civil rights as fundamental rights; voiced an affirmative responsibility to protect the individual on the grounds that it was both the right thing to do and necessary for stability; and linked the language of rights, protection, and security.[4] Government officials began extending these claims to global politics. President Roosevelt's "Four

Freedoms" speech to Congress in 1941 held that the freedoms of speech, of religion, from want, and from fear were interconnected, and the readiness to even hint at economic rights represented a remarkable change, at least for American policymakers.[5] Prior to World War I, free trade was the reining ideology, and society had nowhere to hide when the global economy darkened; during the interwar period, states increasingly erected protectionist barriers, which were widely believed to have exacerbated the depression and fueled international instability. After the war policymakers searched for a new type of international economic governance that would remove the fetters to international commerce but nevertheless allow the state to protect its populations during periods of economic decline.[6] U.S. officials projected the New Deal onto the global stage and insisted that postwar Europe must include new kinds of welfare protections.[7] John Maynard Keynes, whose prescient views on how to win the peace after World War I were ignored, was now given a ringside seat and watched his ideas about how a market-friendly state could produce growth, protect general welfare, and promote security become the foundation for the emerging Bretton Woods system.

This new ideology of economic governance contributed to an era of development. The discourse of development predated World War II, first appearing in the context of colonial administrators trying to legitimate a colonialism that increasingly looked exploitative to those back home.[8] Then, after World War II, development, at least as a project, took off. What was good for the state in the West was now good for the state in the developing world; in fact, late-industrializing countries needed a more active and muscular state to mobilize the needed resources and channel them to the right sectors. There emerged a new field of development economics and a cadre of development economists preaching that the science of economics, with its universal and timeless insights, could benefit the Third World.[9] In many cases the same individuals, nongovernmental organizations, and international organizations that were central to European reconstruction used their experiences to confront the new challenges in the global South.[10]

These ideologies, bodies of knowledge, and development institutions might never have decamped in the decolonizing world had potential donor states not tied development to their security interests. While heading the United Nations Relief and Reconstruction Association, Herbert Lehman, the former governor of New York, argued that American interests and international political and economic stability depended on ensuring that "the men, women, and children who make up the nations, are not driven by starvation and desperation to embrace ideas as horrible as those of the Axis which we are seeking to exterminate."[11] In 1946 the head of Truman's Famine Emergency Committee, Newbold Morris, warned that "democracy on an empty stomach is a luxury. Totalitarianism...is a political philosophy and a political system which thrives on despair, and despair begins with hunger and ends in war."[12] The signature moment occurred at President Harry Truman's 1949 inauguration, when he famously proclaimed a "development age," pledging that the United States would act as midwife to a new era that nourished minds and bodies.[13] Along similar lines, President John Kennedy said: "To those peoples in the huts and villages of half the globe struggling to break the bonds of mass misery, we pledge our best efforts to help them help themselves.... If a free society cannot help the many who are poor, it cannot save the few who are rich."[14] Development and modernization became intertwined in doctrines of anticommunism.[15]

And what of the forces of compassion? They disappeared. The decades following World War I, the war to end all wars, delivered unimaginable human suffering. The Great Depression ravaged societies and, if any aid was to be given, it would be to fellow citizens and not strangers. The modest gains that had been made in establishing the foundations for international humanitarian assistance after World War I became warehoused; the international refugee regime, which got off to a great start, was disregarded by states at the moment it was most needed, as Jews and other persecuted populations tried to flee Nazi Germany but had nowhere to run. And after 1939, to be a humanitarian was to work for the defeat of the Axis powers; relief could only do so much, with tens of millions trapped behind enemy lines. War, not compassion, was the answer.

With the end of the war, the victors discovered that rumors once dismissed as too outrageous to be true had in fact minimized the evil. The liberators of the concentration camps discovered mounds of human remains surrounded by the walking dead. Whole communities had been emptied by both occupiers and neighbors-turned-opportunists. The lucky among the survivors could think about rebuilding their lives, but for many the war meant the end, not the beginning. If the victors had looked at themselves in the mirror, they might have questioned their own humanity. In the belief that nearly anything could be justified to bring an end to the war and save lives, the Allied forces unleashed scorched-earth campaigns against German cities; firebombed most major Japanese cities, leaving, by some estimates upward of 500,000 dead and millions homeless; and dropped nuclear weapons on Hiroshima and Nagasaki. These actions probably helped to shorten the war, but at a horrific cost to civilians. In fact, former secretary of defense Robert McNamara, who helped plan firebombings of Japan, recalled that his boss, General Curtis LeMay, concluded that if the Allies had lost the war they could have been prosecuted for war crimes.[16] The laws of war were now interned with the victims in nameless, unmarked graves. The fine line between humanity and evil had been erased in the very place that had offered itself up as evidence of civilization and God's love.

For some, the Holocaust and the other spectacles of inhumanity led to a denial of the possibility of religion, God, or anything resembling the transcendent, but for others the urgent task became the recovery of a global spirit. The great Marxist scholar Louis Althusser, writing after World War II, observed that "we are confronted with a phenomenon that is international in scope, and with a diffuse ideology which, though it has not been precisely defined, is capable of assuming a certain organizational form...one senses...a mentality in search of itself, an intention eager to embody itself in concrete form, an ideology seeking to define itself, entrench itself, and also furnish itself with a means of action. If this mentality is international, and in the process taking institutional form, then a new 'International' is in the making."[17]

In this inchoate atmosphere, in the gray zone between the recent memories of devastation and the eternal hope for a better world, rose the discourse of the "international community." In many respects, it represented the latest attempt to find a common humanity. During the nineteenth century the discourse of civilization had been hegemonic, favored especially by the Christian-minded; during the late nineteenth century the class-conscious and the reform-minded privileged the discourse of "internationalism"; and in the early twentieth century legal theorists and diplomats favored the language of the community of nations.[18]

While the discourse of international community might be mistaken as just another in a long line of self-medicating ideologies, there was an important difference: whereas these other border-busting concepts operated with a not very subtle distinction between individuals and groups—the saved versus the damned, a civilized West versus the barbarians, the haves against the have-nots, and states against peoples—the language of international community denied difference. After a war in which cruelties were often justified because of perceived differences, it became essential to remove these differences, or at least to discredit them. There existed an international community formed not by God but rather by a common humanity.[19] Atonement demanded nothing less.

As imagined at the time, and ever since, the international community existed in awkward relationship to a world of evil, a world of states, and a world of humanity. At a moment when humanity demonstrated its considerable capacity to terrorize, the international community was supposed to play the role of superego. As Michael Ignatieff perceptively writes: "The human rights instruments created after 1945 were not a triumphant expression of imperial self-confidence but a war-weary generation's reflection on European nihilism and its consequences...part of a wider reordering of the normative order of postwar international relations, designed to create firewalls against barbarism."[20] The Genocide Conventions were not an expression of humanity's boundless desire to make the world a better place—it was an acknowledgment of its capacity to commit unspeakable crimes. The Geneva Conventions were less a breakthrough for humanity than a belated recognition that the brutality of war had exceeded acceptable limits. The

Universal Declaration of Human Rights was less a climactic moment in the indefatigable march of human rights than a mournful recognition of humankind's deficit of humanity. These human rights institutions, and many of the edifices constructed after World War II, were testimony not to compassion but rather to the fear of further acts of barbarism.[21]

The international community included the additional meaning of interstate cooperation. States were the bedrock of the international community. Ideally, these states represented political communities and a national interest. A world of states pursuing their national interests could lead to conflict, violence, and war. However, states also believed that they were not fated to live in constant fear but rather could construct institutions that would allow them to further their collective interests. Although the idea that states might create international institutions and organizations to tame their worst instincts had been tarnished by the failure of the League of Nations, many policymakers concluded that the proper interpretation of the League's shortcomings was not that cooperation was impossible but rather that it must be based on "reality." The postwar institutions were predicted to be more durable precisely because they were inspired not by utopias but rather by interests.

Yet there remained an anxiety that an international community that depended on enlightened state interests was permanently precarious and destined to be chronically vulnerable; after all, states had repeatedly demonstrated that they were quite capable of allowing short-term gratification to bury their long-term interests. Few held out the hope that a harmony of interests alone would save the world; instead, an international community based on a common identity, a global spirit, offered a more likely source of salvation. During the nineteenth century God and religion defined the transcendent for many (especially in the West). During the twentieth century a secularized humanity became more fashionable and more widely regarded as providing the transcendent foundations for an international community defined by considerable diversity.[22]

The international community represented a global spirit that could not be reduced to individual interests—and there was no better evidence for that than the growth of a global aid society.[23] For those who treated international relief and humanitarianism as both sign and creator of a sense of community, the surge of relief activities associated with World War II must have been gratifying, exceeding anything Dunant, Jebb, and Hoover might have imagined. Once the Allied forces defeated the Axis forces, relief agencies spread out across the liberated areas. Although their immediate task was to save lives from disease, exposure, and hunger, they also began the process of "rehabilitating" these war-destroyed societies. While they were working in Europe, a new world of suffering came into view; armed with discourses of humanity and impartiality, they developed a global reach.

Although this massive increase in assistance activities represents a break from the past, it is the presence of continuities that justifies my claim of a shift from Imperial Humanitarianism to Neo-Humanitarianism. Radical scholars and politicians deployed the concept of neocolonialism to capture how Third World states had formal sovereignty even as Western powers retained considerable privileges and mechanisms of power over them. Neocolonialism had a soulmate in Neo-Humanitarianism. Humanitarianism's emerging principles of humanity, impartiality, independence, and neutrality were crafted to lift humanitarianism from the muck of politics and power in much the same way that international policymakers tossed around sovereign equality. But humanitarianism had little chance of escape.

In fact, humanitarian governance was moving in directions that made escape even less likely. States were increasingly central to the funding, regulation, and organization of humanitarian action. Prior to World War I voluntary agencies looked for funding from parishioners and households and, beginning in the latter part of the nineteenth century, the occasional philanthropist. After World War II, though, these patterns changed as governments began to provide more funding because they now imagined a relationship between security and foreign aid.[24] In a typically unromantic assessment, in 1976 Secretary of State Henry Kissinger said, "Disaster relief is becoming increasingly a major instrument of our foreign policy."[25] Relief as instrument, not goal.

American food aid illustrates the mixture of motives that comprised much of official assistance. At the request of President Truman, Herbert Hoover reprised his previous role as director of humanitarian aid when he became head of the Famine Emergency Committee. As already mentioned, while the rest of the world was starving, American agriculture was facing the problem of surplus. In 1947 Republican Pennsylvania James G. Fulton, working closely with the American Council of Voluntary Associations (ACVA), published a report lauding NGOs as implementing partners. Following on the spirit of Fulton's report, the need to do something with America's bounty, and the desperate straits of those abroad, in 1949 Congress, working closely with ACVA, agreed to provide food aid and to help defray the shipping costs. In June 1954 ACVA and members of Congress teamed up to create P.L. 480, which became American's primary food aid program.[26] It was not only the starving peoples of the Third World that benefited from this program; so, too, did many agencies, most centrally CARE and Catholic Relief Services. Between 1945 and 1983 CARE delivered nearly $2.8 billion in food to over sixty-five countries, and most of that food came from the Food for Peace program.[27] Given their reliance on official assistance, NGOs had difficulty sustaining images of independence and impartiality. Similarly, international humanitarian organizations might claim to be apolitical and independent, but they were more dependent on states than ever. States created these organizations to help them fulfill their obligations, and while the good news was that their felt obligations had expanded, they nevertheless imposed various constraints to make sure that these humanitarian agencies did not undertake action that might interfere with their fundamental interests.

The purpose of postwar humanitarianism also retained features of the past. "Official" humanitarianism remained identified closely with the ICRC and other relief agencies. Yet many of the same agencies that once provided relief expanded into development, moving from "help" to "self-help." Most of the time emergency and alchemical agencies did not cross paths, compete for attention, or use the same labels to define their different activities. During war and conflict, though, their differences became immediately apparent, particularly when emergency agencies appeared to worry more than alchemist humanitarian agencies about the principles of impartiality, neutrality, and relief, and keeping away from politics.

To further their ambitions, humanitarian organizations became increasingly centralized and bureaucratized. Whereas prior to World War II aid agencies came and went with the emergency—constantly improvising and experimenting as they did so—they now settled in for a long campaign and became quasi-bureaucratic, rationalized organizations that could apply continuous force on the world. The intermittent and scattershot approach to transformation of the prewar years was steadily replaced by a more sustained, relentless, and boundless tack. Several decades later aid agencies would reflect on these decades as free from rule.

Neo-Humanitarianism resembled Imperial Humanitarianism in one final way: paternalism. To be sure, the paternalism of postwar humanitarians differed from imperial humanitarians in three significant ways. With the missionaries losing ground to the development experts, humanitarians were more likely to cite humanity than God to explain why they cared. They were more sensitive to infantilizing language and discarded any hint that these people were "backward" or "child-like," even though distinctions between "undeveloped" and "developed" retained evolutionary images in which the West would show the rest of the world its future. And, they used expert knowledge and utilized quasi-technocratic language to justify their interventions. Although these changes could suggest a more respectful approach, humanitarianism was still something done for and to others, not with them. Reminiscent of how the abolitionists reasoned that colonialism would help atone for the sins of slavery, those arguing in favor of various kinds of assistance pointed to the responsibilities the rich had to the poor, not just because of moral but also because of causal responsibilities, inherited by the West because of colonialism. Also as with the abolitionists, many were arguing that freedom, independence, and sovereignty would mean little without the intellectual and material tools necessary for self-governance, development, and progress. This is where the West came in—yet again.

And, they were blissfully ignorant of their power over the objects of their compassion. The discourse of humanity and international community had a magical way of making power and paternalism disappear—at least in the minds of the humanitarians.

6

~⊜~

Neo-Humanitarianism

BEGINNING WITH World War II, the world got serious about humanitarianism. Until then first responders to an emergency left the impression that this was the first time that they had ever responded to an emergency. In most instances relief agencies popped up with the emergency, frequently organized by an immigrant, religious, or labor association, staffed by volunteers who rushed to the scene to do whatever they could. And because these organizationally challenged agencies were descending on the same emergency with little coordination among them, the level of activity was more impressive than the actual results. As James Shotwell, the prominent internationalist and a member of President Woodrow Wilson's brain trust at the 1919 Paris Peace Conference, observed with considerable frustration, until World War II relief was largely an uncoordinated affair.[1] How many more lives might have been saved with more preparation?

Getting serious about saving lives required planning.[2] Private agencies began to show signs of professionalization, in part a natural consequence of the length of the war and the presence of veterans of the last great relief efforts during World War II. But planning, one of the buzzwords of the war, was something that states increasingly assumed was their responsibility and forte. The willingness of states to become more involved in the organization and delivery of relief owed not only to a newfound passion for compassion but also to a belief that their political, economic, and strategic interests were at stake. In short, states began to put their stamp on humanitarianism. Humanitarian agencies and states entered into a codependent relationship, though the former was clearly more dependent on the latter than the reverse. These developments associated with World War II—a growing humanitarian sector that was increasingly planning-minded and influenced by states and their interests—became defining elements of emerging architecture of humanitarianism.

This was an architecture that was increasingly global and organized around principles of humanity. Relief agencies founded to help those in Europe turned their sights on the rest of the world once Europe was on its feet. Agencies that once practiced a politics of identity and profiling, helping those like them and not many others, now practiced a politics of impartiality. If the logic of humanity and need-based aid meant that the defeated Germans were just as deserving as the rescued French, then aid agencies working in Europe could not, in good conscience, ignore what was happening in China, Korea, South Asia, and the Middle East. And, just as they had in postwar Europe, agencies that began with help soon moved to self-help. Transporting their experiences in Europe to other parts of the decolonizing world and carrying on a long tradition of humanitarianism during colonialism, these relief-turned-development agencies now imagined transforming traditional into modern societies, and doing so without touching politics, which would have been an even grander feat of magic.

World War II

Although the United States did not monopolize humanitarian action during World War II, it dominated the effort and helped to establish a new pattern of humanitarianism that lingered after the war.[3] There were moments prior to World War II that foreshadowed the growing involvement of the United States. After World War I it created the American Relief Agency. In 1936 U.S. Secretary of State Cordell Hull addressed his concerns that American political and economic organizations might embroil the United States in the Spanish Civil War by extending the 1935 Neutrality Act to control their actions. In 1939, and in response to the outbreak of war in Europe, Hull recommended that the United States regulate the fundraising campaigns of private voluntary agencies to ensure that they did not violate America's neutral status; in November Congress passed the Neutrality Act of 1939, extending the regulation of relief from Spain to nearly all of Europe.

Upon entering the war in 1941 the U.S. government began treating the humanitarian sector in a manner nearly identical to its management of society and economy—imposing the state's control in order to further its war aims. Ostensibly to give the American people the confidence that they were donating their money to bona fide charities and not being swindled by flim-flam men, on March 13, 1941, President Franklin Roosevelt created the

State Department–associated Committee on War Relief Agencies, a "small, self-appointed committee" to coordinate, supervise, and consolidate relief "by endorsing certain organizations and refusing to endorse others."[4] Headed by Joseph Davies, the former ambassador to Russia, the Committee had no formal regulatory powers, but it nevertheless managed to retire many organizations.

The government tightened its control of the relief sector on July 25, 1942, when President Roosevelt, by executive order, created the War Relief Control Board (WRCB), an independent agency with ties to the State Department. All relief societies, no matter how big or small, had to register, and once they did they were under the jurisdiction of a board that could approve budgets; oversee methods used in appeal campaigns; command organizations to publicize their American funding in order to enhance U.S. prestige; and decide who would get an export license.[5] In short, the WRCB had the power of life and death, and it used that power. Mainly because of its actions, the number of agencies declined from several hundred in 1941 to sixty-seven in 1943. Some, though, thrived from favoritism, including the American Red Cross and the United States War Bond.[6] Although the WRCB justified its decisions on the grounds of reducing waste and improving the delivery of relief, America's war aims loomed large. For instance, the U.S. government graced Catholic Relief Services with $12 million between 1943 and 1946 for various projects in part because it hoped that the Catholic agency would cultivate intelligence contacts in Europe.[7] The government retired the WRCB at the end of the war, but it was still quite interested in regulating the aid sector; the government replaced the WRCB with an equally powerful Advisory Committee on Voluntary Foreign Aid. The government's desire to align the relief sector with its war aims transformed private agencies into nearly parastatal agencies, which some government officials of the time called "volagencies."[8]

The record (at least of the surviving agencies) suggests that aid agencies sympathized with the reasons behind government's growing regulatory powers and were prepared to do their patriotic part. Still, they rightly understood that regulation would reduce their autonomy, and religious agencies were doubly worried that regulation might be a back door for the state to intrude on religious life. Agencies resorted to various organizational, rhetorical, and principled devices to limit the possibility that regulation would become absolutism. Private agencies established the American Council of Voluntary Agencies in response to both the government's demand for an umbrella organization to further its goal of interagency cooperation and coordination and their own desire to band together to defend their interests. Moreover, they insisted that they could best serve U.S. war aims if they were independent in both reality and appearance.[9] If recipient countries viewed American relief agencies as operatives of the American state, they observed, then they would have difficulty getting access. Maintaining their distance from American military would be good for the needy, for the agencies, and for the U.S. government.

Similar to what was occurring on the American scene, the global governance of humanitarianism also was becoming more organized and symbolic of the international community, caught, in many ways, between multilateralism and internationalism. The defining moment occurred on November 9, 1943, when forty-four countries, led by the United States and Great Britain, established the United Nations Relief and Rehabilitation Administration (UNRRA), World War II's first bona fide international relief agency, mandated to coordinate the allies' aid efforts in liberated Europe. Like many of the postwar multilateral ventures, the Americans took the lead, for many familiar reasons. They believed that greater regulation would save more lives. Many of the Americans who helped create the UNRRA were veterans of the relief effort in World War I, who believed that better coordination would have saved more lives, and New Dealers, who believed in the virtues of planning and wanted to project the modernizing American welfare state onto the global stage. They believed that American war interests were best served through multilateral coordination.[10]

Because the allies were planning the UNRRA at the very moment that they were discussing the shape of the postwar arrangements, they treated the UNRRA as a symbol of the possibility of a more desirable international order. Many American participants hoped that the UNRRA would steer America away from isolationism and toward engagement. American leadership, in their view, would be necessary for any postwar order, and international relief was a good place to demonstrate its virtues.[11] The UNRRA, in this respect, symbolized the necessity and benefits of future international collaboration. Arising "in the context of... broad debates on issues such as the nature and function of modern nation-states, the potential formats for international collaboration and the mechanisms for making an international authority work," the UNRRA reflected the dreams of the postwar planners and represented the device for turning those dreams into reality.[12] Frank Boudreau, a high-ranking official with the League of Nations Health Organization, wrote that the war had created fertile soil for a new era of international progress.[13] But it would to be based not on a League of Nations utopianism but rather the demands of states and their interests. The UNRRA would demonstrate the possibilities of enlightened self-interest on a global scale. But, like all such moments when people dream of a new international order, it also was invested with a broader spirit. For many participants, the UNRRA reflected their faith in the ability to bind compassion and technocracy, to create a muscular, modernized, spirit of progress.[14]

One of the immediate consequences of the growing regulation of humanitarian action was that aid agencies that once enjoyed considerable autonomy and independence were obliged to face new constraints. Whereas the League of Nations viewed charity as primarily owned and operated by private voluntary agencies, with the establishment of the UNRRA charitable organizations now became "subservient to Allied occupying armies and international agencies."[15] But this would not be a temporary or fleeting development. Instead, it would become a central feature of the emerging landscape. In 1944 Francesca Wilson, whose career in relief began in World War I and continued through World War II, wrote perceptively:

> Voluntary societies will have less scope this time than after the last war. This is partly because of the overwhelming scale of the need.... But there is another reason...and this is because we have at last become planning-minded. In the interim of the two wars the idea that it is better to plan beforehand than muddle through anyhow has gained ground and we have this time an official *superState* body in charge of relief, the U.N.R.R.A.[16]

Humanitarianism was entering a new phase of global governance.

Although many imagined that military victory was the surest way to save lives, the end of the war imposed greater demands on relief agencies. Those who had barely survived the war now faced the equally daunting challenge of surviving the peace. The survivors of the death and labor camps now faced death due to malnutrition, exposure, and disease; after years of unimaginable deprivations, they needed to be nursed back to health, slowly and carefully. Much of Europe was on starvation diets, and tuberculosis was running at epidemic levels. Buildings and homes had been demolished, so temporary shelters had to be constructed. Basic necessities, including food, heating oil, and medicine, were scarce. Millions of people were now far from home; many had fled to escape war and persecution, while millions of others had no choice in the matter, herded into cattle cars or forcibly marched hundreds of miles. Before the displaced could imagine their future, they wanted to know if their loved ones were still alive and, if they were, to be reunited with them as soon as possible. Some could go home, but many refused to return to the scene of the original crimes; in many cases, their communities had vanished in the inferno. If they could not return home and could not stay where they were, then where would they go?

A handful of international organizations and hundreds of private relief agencies tried to respond to the soul-crushing demands. In addition to the UNRRA, states created other international humanitarian agencies: in 1945 the Food and Agricultural Organization, to rebuild Europe's agricultural, fishery, and forestry sectors; in 1946 the United Nations Children Fund, as a temporary agency for postwar reconstruction with a specific focus on health; also in 1946 the World Health Organization, to provide technical assistance and aid to governments in the area of public health;[17] and then in

1947 the International Relief Organization, to handle Europe's remaining refugees and displaced peoples (succeeded three years later by UNHCR). Private voluntary agencies, though, remained the workhorses of relief and reconstruction. In addition to those existing during the war, between 1945 and 1949 nearly two hundred organizations joined the ranks, most of them from the United States.

Aid agencies were increasingly using the language of impartiality and the principle of aid based on need, but in fact the established pattern of giving aid to one's own continued to define the distribution of relief. In the United States Jewish agencies threw all their energies at the urgent task of saving Europe's remaining Jews, getting them out of displaced persons camps, and helping them rebuild their lives, often in Palestine if only because Western states were following a policy of "not in my backyard"—happy to help Jews settle anywhere but within their borders.

In 1945 American Lutherans founded Lutheran World Relief (LWR). Although formally accepting the principle of aid based on need, it used the language of "family" to justify its focus on Lutherans, particularly German and Austrian Lutherans.[18] American Lutherans were responding not only to an obvious need but also to an intentional oversight by the UNRRA. The Allies created the UNRRA to help the victims of *German* aggression, so there was little interest in giving equal weight to the needs of the Germans. American Lutherans picked up the slack and lobbied the U.S. government to change its policy of neglect, arguing that the surest test of America's humanity would be how it treated not the victims of Nazism but rather the Germans (U.S. policy eventually changed in 1947).[19] During its first five years, 80 percent of its assistance went to Germany, much of it from Marshall Plan aid, with nearly all the rest going to the Palestinians and Japan.

The American Catholic Bishops founded Catholic Relief Services in 1941. This was not the first time that the American Catholic community had organized for relief, but it was the first time that it managed to succeed in establishing a central agency.[20] In 1917 President Woodrow Wilson encouraged different religious agencies to consider joint fundraising, and in response the American Catholics created the National Catholic War Council (NCWC). However, American Catholics, suspicious of bureaucratic enterprises, even those run by the Church, and wanting to make sure that their contributions went to the homeland, avoided this new agency in favor of existing "national" and "ethnic" parishes.[21] During the interwar period the American Catholic Bishops tried again to create a central organization to oversee the thousands of existing Catholic societies—in 1922 they renamed the National Catholic War Council the National Catholic Welfare Council, and in 1936 they established a committee to help Catholic victims of Nazi persecution. In every instance American Catholics kept their distance.[22]

In 1941 the NCWC created the Catholic Relief Service; it began operations in 1943.[23] Although various factors help to explain how it succeeded where previous ventures had failed, one critical variable had changed: the direct support of the United States government. The very decision by the American Catholic Bishops to create yet another agency owed in part to the White House's desire to encourage a possible partnership between the NCWC and the Vatican as a way to support the Allies. And the government backed up its support with money. One of CRS's first projects was to help thousands of Polish Catholics enduring an extraordinary and perilous trek in search of safety; they had been forced to move from Poland to Central Asia and Iran, from there to eastern Africa and then, finally, to northern Mexico, where they waited for admission to the United States. CRS claimed to operate on the principle of need but proceeded to justify an exclusive focus on Catholics.[24]

Created in 1945, the Cooperative for American Remittances to Europe, best known as CARE, in many ways represented the shift from the old to the new style of humanitarianism. It was originally founded on the familiar pattern of delivering relief based on identity and not on need. World War I's American Relief Administration (ARA) proved to be the inspiration for CARE. Arthur Ringland, a well-respected Washingtonian and consultant to the War Relief Control Board, having fond memories of how the ARA had provided Americans with the opportunity to send packages to their loved ones in Europe, wanted to rekindle its spirit. When Ringland and other ARA veterans first aired the idea of creating an ARA for the World War II generation, U.S. officials balked at a new venture that might distract from ongoing efforts. Wait, officials told Ringland, until after the war. He did, only to discover a blocking coalition in the form of a relief community that had little interest in welcoming a rival organization and American officials who believed that the UNRRA was already doing what Ringland wanted to do. Undeterred, Ringland argued that a new collective organization was needed because existing agencies were not prioritizing food aid they way they should—they were too busy dividing their time between food delivery and rebuilding Europe's agricultural sector and were targeting their favored constituencies, leading to competition and waste. The challenge, he argued, was to get agencies of all stripes, colors, and affiliations to form a new organization dedicated to food delivery.

After considerable discussion, ACVA voted in early 1945 to create a nonprofit cooperative, which was to be owned by existing relief agencies and interested constituencies, in order to give Americans the opportunity to send food parcels to friends and family in Europe. The vote was followed by months of inactivity until that summer, when the Cooperative League of the USA, the Catholic Relief Service, and the American Friends Service Committee decided to reinvigorate discussions. The agency's very future depended on getting government accreditation and support because the State Department decided who got a license, and it was initially quite skeptical of the venture. Meanwhile, a different "problem" had cropped up. The U.S. Army had 7.6 million ten-in-one rations, designed specifically for Asia, and capable of feeding a family for two weeks.[25] Ringland ingeniously proposed that these rations be used for relief, and the idea began to gain considerable support in Washington. However, it turns out that the UNRRA had hit on the same idea and had already negotiated a contract. Because the UNRRA was already stretched thin, it was willing to transfer the task, but only if Ringland could get the army's approval and secure financing. The army was initially reluctant because it wanted to get these rations out of its valuable storage space and distributed as quickly as possible, and entrusting the task to an untried venture had its obvious downsides. Eventually, though, the army agreed. The financing was a different matter. The only way the new organization could get the necessary capital was if the WRCB allowed the existing relief agencies to use some of their war funds for capital contributions. After some hard politicking and last-minute threats, the WRCB relented.

In mid-October, twenty-two private, civic, cooperative, labor, and religious organizations formally launched the Cooperative for American Remittances to Europe.[26] It had a very rough first few months. Although these agencies had agreed to band together to support this venture, that was about the extent of their cooperative spirit:

> The members represented agencies with divergent interests, and themselves came from widely disparate backgrounds. As a result, all the tensions and conflicts that existed in external society were reflected in CARE's Board. For example, differences of opinion could be found on the role of consumer cooperatives as opposed to free enterprise and profit-seeking capitalism; on the functions of unions and of management, and of many other current issues. In addition, some of the agencies were full-time, permanent relief bodies while others considered that their functions in that field were limited and temporary. The various religious sects did not see eye to eye, except on the problem of preventing the state from becoming too influential within CARE, and on this point they were generally not supported by the secular agencies, who did not feel so involved in the traditional church-state conflict.[27]

No surprise, then, that CARE had an inauspicious start. It would take strong leadership to create coherence, but CARE had problems at the top from the very beginning. The person who originally agreed to head the organization, a highly respected executive from Sears and Roebuck who would bring some merchandising flair and credibility to the organization, soon resigned after it became clear to him that the job was a lot bigger than he had been told. CARE had difficulty locating the right office space and ended up renting some fairly expensive real estate near Wall Street.[28] The American people were not rushing to subscribe, and the army's fears were becoming a reality. It had to tweak the packages to ensure that the contents were appropriate for civilians and did not contain any items that might offend its members (for instance, the Seventh-Day Adventists, an important member of CARE, objected to the inclusion of cigarettes). After considerable delay, the first "CARE packages" arrived in Le Havre, France, in May 1946.

After months of worries that CARE might be a losing venture, it became an overnight sensation and "took on a life of its own."[29] There were several keys to its success. Perhaps most important was marketing acumen. It developed slick campaigns, secured celebrity sponsorship, received President Truman's endorsement in a public ceremony at the White House, mobilized children and communities to canvas on its behalf, arranged a tie-in with Princess Elizabeth's wedding, set up booths at Sears stores and other commercial outlets, had a weekly radio show on ABC, and even got the United Fruit Company, hoping to benefit from CARE's good name, to sponsor a competition for the best new recipe using bananas with a pledge to contribute twenty-five cents for every entry. The more famous CARE became, the more individuals and companies wanted to share the stage, and the onslaught of promotions was turning CARE into a household name, even if most households did not know what the acronym stood for.[30] If people were buying the product, though, it was because, as Ringland had predicted, it was selling something Americans wanted: the opportunity to send a package to a special someone. And, because CARE was explicitly secular and apolitical, it stood out from the crowd of other agencies.[31]

All this success gave CARE the opportunity and incentive to expand the kinds of assistance it provided and groups it served. Because people need more than food to survive, CARE eventually added blankets and clothing, medicines, and other basic needs. After Europe successfully passed from the emergency stage, CARE staff wanted to move into new kinds of assistance activities that would enable individuals to rebuild their lives. Although some members worried that CARE was encroaching on their turf, the CARE board voted overwhelmingly to provide other kinds of assistance, including tool kits for tradesmen involved in postwar reconstruction. Like other agencies after the war, CARE was moving from "help to self-help."[32]

CARE also gained the authority to decide who should get aid, and shifted from the principle of association to the principle of need. Because CARE allowed Americans to buy packages to ship to specific individuals, the question of who received a package depended on the presence of a caring friend or relative in the United States. In other words, the fed could become the well-fed, not necessarily in keeping with the idea of relief to those most

Figure 9 Hans Hubmann, "Making Care Packages in Germany," 1948. Bildarchiv Preussischer Kulturbesitz / Art Resource, New York.

in need. However, CARE's growing fame was leading Americans to send checks without identifying a person or even a country. This development was hardly unwelcome or unexpected—CARE enjoyed having the discretion over who got a package, and its advertising emphasized that CARE provided relief and deliberately downplayed the fact that contributors were supposed to designate a recipient. Until early 1948 CARE refused to set a policy, sometimes accepting the checks and sometimes returning them, attempting to avoid what it knew would be a highly contentious debate among its members about what to do with undesignated contributions.

The board confronted the controversy, and, as predicted, passions ran high. Arthur Ringland warned that CARE might lose its license if it limited assistance to individuals who have an "uncle in America."[33] Harold Miner, CARE's treasurer, wrote that CARE was preferable to its parents because CARE cut across denominations and produced a unified appeal that tended to draw in those who had not previously contributed to a cause.[34] Other members strongly argued the other side. Some complained, with good evidence, that CARE's fundraising efforts were harming their own.[35] Religious agencies feared that the government's strong involvement in CARE would blur the boundaries between church and state and encourage government interference.[36] In the end, the best predictor of an agency's position was whether or not it currently had a relief program—those that did opposed giving CARE more authority, and those that did not, and who tended to see CARE as their relief agency, favored it.

After considerable debate, the board voted eleven to ten to return undesignated checks. However, when it revisited the matter later that month one board member switched sides, allowing CARE staff to decide what to do with the checks. In a fury, several prominent board members, including the original founders of CRS and the American Jewish Joint Distribution Committee, resigned. Their resignation had a lasting impact on CARE, giving it a more secular identity, allowing it to expand as it saw fit, and easing any worries about being too closely associated with the U.S. government.

Although I have focused on American agencies, other countries with a long tradition of humanitarianism also made their presence felt. Most prominent was Britain. Beginning with the abolitionists, continuing through the missionary movement and the campaign to end King Leopold's rape of the Congo, and passing through World War I and the Jebbs' founding of Save the Children, the long tradition of British humanitarianism continued during the interwar period and quickened after the outbreak of war in 1939. Among the various agencies that came into existence at this time, perhaps the most famous was the Oxford Famine Relief Committee, today known as Oxfam. It began as a response to famine in occupied Greece. Citing the 1907 Hague Conventions that stipulated that the occupying power had the responsibility either to feed the population or to allow the population to feed itself, at the outset of the war Prime Minister Winston Churchill imposed an embargo on those European countries occupied by Nazi Germany. Notwithstanding the tremendous suffering, he rejected any action that might conceivably help the Germans and prolong the war, and relief agencies had difficulty arguing against the embargo without appearing unpatriotic. However, in the fall of 1941 news of mass starvation began to trickle out of Greece. The Greeks had fiercely resisted the Germans, only to fall in the spring of 1941; the Germans were merciless in their retaliation and began to requisition private stocks of food, medicine, and clothing to help the German troops in the North African campaign. Over the winter nearly two hundred thousand Greeks died of starvation.

In the spring of 1942, British citizens, including many clergy and veterans of relief activities during World War I, started a campaign to ship food to Greece. Because Greece was not formally part of the British embargo, British citizens could plead for action without appearing unpatriotic or critical of Churchill. Created on May 29, 1942, Oxfam focused on the Greek population for the next two years, and when the war ended it followed its charitable instincts to other parts of Europe. What truly distinguished Oxfam from many of the other aid agencies was its insistence that Germans were equally deserving. Much like the situation after World War I, it was difficult for British populations to accept the proposition that the defeated

Germans should jump to the front of the food line because they were suffer-ing more than, say, the Dutch.[37] Much like Save the Children after World War I, Oxfam struck on the idea of a campaign to "Save Europe Now," ex-plicitly appealing to all those in need in Europe and emphasizing the prin-ciple of aid based on need. Although Oxfam had backed into the principle of impartiality, it was now part of its identity.[38]

The New Alchemists Go Global

Humanitarianism went global after World War II. To some extent it always had been. But now all the elements that had been assembled in Europe glo-balized to a rapidly decolonizing world—propelled by discourses of hu-manity and international community, powerful states increasingly ready to underwrite a humanitarianism that they viewed as vehicles of influence, and networks of international and nongovernmental organizations applying the principle of need to create a borderless humanitarianism. Aid agencies, then, were facing new opportunities and constraints. They rode ascending moral obligations and greater support from powerful states to new heights. But they also were risking overexposure by becoming more closely associ-ated with them. To avoid getting burned, aid agencies increasingly sought protection from the principles of independence, neutrality, and impartial-ity. Emergency agencies had an easier time avoiding overexposure than did alchemical agencies: whereas the former agencies had little ambition to try to tackle the causes of suffering, the latter did—and that impulse caused them to encroach constantly on politics.

By 1948 Europe's postwar recovery had moved solidly from relief to reconstruction, and the private voluntary agencies that had once played a central role in distributing assistance to families now stepped aside, as governments, aided considerably by the U.S. European Recovery Program, best known as the Marshall Plan, undertook the heavy lifting of repairing roads, ports, communication lines, and transportation networks; rebuild-ing industries; and recovering farmlands. In these new circumstances, many aid agencies congratulated themselves on a job well done and closed their doors. But others, armed with a discourse of humanity and needs, looked outside of Europe and discovered colonized peoples encountering even greater challenges. Lutheran World Relief captured the perceived enormity and urgency of the challenge when it wrote that "a billion people...emerg-ing from their backwardness in the direction of twentieth century social and economic progress such as has characterized other areas of the world. Great numbers are seeking quick emancipation from superstition, hunger, sickness and imprisonment of minds and souls. To these people, and oth-ers like them, the compassionate arms of the Church will need to reach out with material gifts for the foreseeable future to alleviate hunger, exposure, and illness."[39]

The discourse of humanity and needs affected how aid agencies presented their calling, where they worked, and what they did. Prior to World War II religious agencies dominated the field, and religious discourse influenced whose suffering mattered the most, namely those who appeared ripe for conversion and who had not yet heard the gospel. But in the postwar environment the secularized discourse of humanity elevated the salience of material—and not spiritual—needs, and agencies talked about filling bellies rather than teaching the Bible. If missionaries felt overwhelmed by the sheer number of souls that needed saving, the postwar humanitarians were overwhelmed by the sheer number of lives that needed saving. And because everyone's needs mattered equally, there was no obvious metric for choosing one population over another. Indeed, there is no evidence that any agency ever did a "needs assessment" or adopted a humanitarian version of triage, which could have been justified given that it was possible to defend almost any randomly selected spot.

Where an agency ended up generally resulted from several factors. Sheer chance and opportunity played a role. Those disasters that were well covered and that captured the attention and imagination of the West were more likely to receive assistance. Beginning with World War II governments became major funders, and their concern was not the needs of others but their own interests. Identity also figured prominently. Many agencies had a built-in constituency, whether religious, ethnic, or national, and it was always easier to feel compassion and raise money for those who were part of the family. No single factor, not money and not identity, completely explains the emerging pattern.

CARE, according to its former head, Philip Johnston, followed a needs-based logic from Europe to the rest of the world. At first it justified its excursions outside of Europe with explicit reference to areas "implicated by WWII," a bow to its original mandate and U.S. funders; in April 1947, CARE established operations in China, Japan, and Korea. But soon thereafter CARE simply identified the need and then forged ahead.[40] By the mid-1950s CARE's ambitions were far exceeding its budget and, according to its executive director, Paul French, at an unsustainable rate. In response, French proposed that CARE declare victory and close the organization. Predictably, staff rejected a cure that seemed worse than the disease and opted to reduce its operations from forty-two to twenty countries, with one group getting food packages and the other P.L. 480 surplus.

Oxfam's initial focus on Greece expanded with the end of the war, first to other parts of Europe and then to the Third World. Oxfam's staff, which formed a broad church in which no single denomination prevailed and an almost secularized spirituality existed, rededicated themselves to the cause of ending suffering everywhere—not just in Europe. Accordingly, in early 1949 the central committee voted unanimously to change its mandate to "the relief of suffering arising as a result of wars or of other causes in any part of the world."[41] In other words, the world was their domain.

Religious agencies also were using the discourse of need to following the trail of suffering from Europe to rest of the world. According to LWR's Paul Empie and Henry Whiting: "It seems obvious that the concern of Christians for their fellowmen should be sufficiently inclusive to embrace all types of their need and cannot be limited to those involved in 'war-created needs.'" Yet the problem, as they immediately noted, was that LWR might become dangerously overcommitted. Its solution was to formally acknowledge that while all humans deserved to be protected, LWR could legitimately prioritize Lutherans:

> However, concern and activity are two different things! It cannot be the responsibility of Lutheran World Relief to occupy itself with every human need in every part of the world. It must be limited not only by its resources but also by its recognition of the roles of other agencies, both Lutheran and non-Lutheran, concurrently active in meeting the needs of mankind. Insofar as the two can be separated, Lutheran World Relief deals in material rather than in spiritual needs, and has in practice accepted a primary obligation to areas in the world where Lutherans are to be found, even though it is explicitly stated that distribution shall be on the basis of need rather than upon other considerations.[42]

Although many agencies increasingly committed themselves to the principles of impartiality and nondiscrimination, in practice they had to decide who had first claim on their resources—and identity remained a powerful criteria.

In Asia a combination of chance events and accidental meetings led to the creation of a new religiously based aid organization that in a few decades would become the largest private aid agency in the world—World Vision International. There are several versions of its origins, but most agree on the basic outline. In 1947 Chinese president Chiang Kai-shek invited Billy Graham to come to China; already scheduled to tour Europe, Graham tapped a young, enthusiastic member of his organization, Bob Pierce, to go in his place.[43] Pierce proved to be a worthy substitute, preaching the gospel wherever and whenever he could to receptive audiences. Toward the end of his visit a Dutch missionary who worked in an orphanage thrust a young girl, "White Jade," into his arms, telling him that she had come to the orphanage because she had been kicked out of her house for having committed the sin of bringing home a Bible and disgracing the family. Now the girl was homeless, the missionary continued, but the orphanage could not feed another mouth. Pierce's preaching was partly responsible for the girl's situation, so what did he intend to do about it? Surprised and shaken, Pierce emptied his wallet, a total of five dollars. The missionary replied, in effect, that this was a good start but she expected a regular donation from America. He agreed.

Pierce returned to the United States a changed man and with a vision of evangelicals combining personal evangelism with social action. Appreciating the originality of the message requires knowing something about the central divisions among fundamentalists at this time. Most fundamentalists, much like many of their co-religionists, believed that religion and the state should stick to their assigned roles—religion saves souls and governments perform social action. Moreover, fundamentalists looked down on what they believed were the excesses of liberal church organizations, which, beginning at the turn of the century, seemed to be more passionate about humanitarianism than salvation. And, there were divisions within the evangelical movement, most importantly between the fundamentalists and the new evangelicals. Fundamentalists subscribed to "dispensationalism," which included a strong version of millenarian antimodernist thought, held a literal interpretation of the Bible, and opposed all modernizing trends, especially those that challenged religion. Beginning in the 1940s the "new evangelicals" began to make their presence felt. In addition to doctrinal differences, the new evangelicals were more disposed to social and cultural engagement; they created the Fuller Theological Seminary to give them an institutional basis to emphasize social concerns. Before Pierce, though, they had not crossed the line from emphasizing social concerns to undertaking social action—but Pierce dared them to do so.

In 1950 Pierce visited South Korea to preach to the American forces and to the Koreans—and at the same time founded World Vision with the specific mission of supporting and establishing orphanages in Korea. Over the next decade Pierce and World Vision became indistinguishable, and World Vision's future commitments could be predicted by Pierce's travel schedule—everywhere he went he saw children in need, and he would impetuously pledge to provide or extend some services, leaving his staff to worry about the funding. Describing this period, Dr. Paul Rees, a vice president at large, wrote: "There was something remarkably unpremeditated about our origin. A vision of need in Asia! The passion to act in meeting that need! It was almost as simple as that. No long-range planning. No elaborate mechanisms of administration. Emergency by emergency, crisis by crisis, it was a summons from Christ to act, and act now."[44]

The founders of World Vision International were aware of the political consequences of their actions. In fact, there is considerable evidence that they intended to be political to the extent that the evangelism might counterbalance the spread of communism. Writing in 1958, Pierce observed that "the Communists are further ahead of us in evangelizing the world than they are in science. All over the world the Russians are outpreaching us, outsacrificing us, outworking us, outplanning us, outpropogandizing us and outdying us in order to gain their ends."[45] In other words, changing souls was both a means and an end.

In addition to having to determine whose needs mattered most, aid agencies had to decide what those needs were. Basic needs that helped individuals physically survive were easily defined. But what happened after survival? Whereas emergency agencies tended to close up shop and head for the next disaster, the new alchemists began to consider what people and societies needed to insulate them from the causes of suffering. It is fashionable among many critically minded postwar narratives of international development to treat these new development agencies as direct descendants of the missionaries and the liberal humanitarians of the colonial period. However much they might have played a similar function, the language of planning, development, and reconstruction was very much rooted in the wartime experience of many aid agencies. The UNRRA, after all, stood for relief *and* rehabilitation. Although relief was easy to define, not so rehabilitation, and the creators of the UNRRA chose not to define it partly because it was less clear-cut and partly because all eyes were understandably focused on relief.[46] The UNRRA's policies suggested two dimensions of rehabilitation. Destruction was the opportunity for creation. Societies had to be rebuilt, and there were lots of reasons to try to build them such that they would have the promise of a better future. Plans for reconstruction, in short, revealed dreams of a better society.[47] Also, planners increasingly believed that everything was connected to everything else, encouraging a more complex picture of the world and complicating all attempts to manage it. In 1943, as Elizabeth Borgwardt put it, policy planners "were...striving to separate relief, rehabilitation, and reconstruction from trade, finance, and currency policies, and from more overtly 'political' considerations as well. It was through the experiences of the united nations conferences of mid-1943 to mid-1944 that these planners learned just how interrelated these various fields actually were."[48] Postwar aid agencies and planners faced the challenge of trying to master a world that they viewed as inherently complex as they tried to help societies move toward a better future.

Aid agencies working in the rapidly decolonizing world found themselves first trying to attend to the basic needs of the population and then, as they had in Europe, entertaining thoughts of moving from "help to self-help." Many of the documents of the period contain some version of the "fish story": give a man a fish and he eats for a day; teach a man to fish and he eats for a lifetime. Among the many factors that account for their growing ambition, arguably two were most prominent. Many agencies determined that it was more cost-effective to stop or reduce the damage caused by disasters than to respond after the damage had been done. An ounce of prevention is worth a pound of cure, as the proverb has it, although no one knew what the miracle elixir was. Also, agencies often determined that when a program failed it was because they had overlooked something important. To return to the fish story, aid agencies realized that being able to make a living at fishing was more complicated than teaching a man to fish and giving him a line and a lure. He also needed to get the fish to the market, learn from Western NGOs how to invest his meager profits in new technology (and not waste it on beer), educate his children in schools being built by Western NGOs, stay healthy in Western-funded clinics, and benefit from Western-sponsored community development projects.[49]

Oxfam's early years nicely illustrate these dynamics. From the time of its creation in 1942 through the late 1950s, Oxfam focused on famine relief, leaving others to worry about long-term development. Beginning in 1960, inspired partly by the UN's declaration of a "Decade of Development" in 1960, Oxfam began to examine the causes of hunger. For an organization with relief-oriented mindset, this was a conceptual leap. Oxfam began modestly, trying to educate farmers in new agricultural techniques and establish rural cooperatives. But when these programs did not produce the expected results, some at Oxfam began to wonder if they were failing to see the bigger picture, including how the world economy shapes the prospects for local development. Others proposed even more radical recommendations, tying development to fundamental questions of justice. Debates in Oxfam over how far to go turned not only on what was causing the lack of development but also what Oxfam might reasonably tackle and where it might make a difference.[50]

World Vision International followed a similar path. Beginning in the 1960s, WVI began to look beyond relief to the causes of suffering. In its first decade it ran orphanages and soon thereafter began establishing child sponsorship programs, which were extraordinarily popular with donors, who now had the opportunity to help an underprivileged child. There was only one problem: some of the sponsorship programs were not always having a positive impact. The sponsored child's family would shift resources to other family members. Sometimes the sponsored child was the target of attacks, often motivated by jealousy. Feeding and educating a child had little permanent impact in an impoverished environment. Consequently, World Vision staff began looking beyond sponsorship and to community development, working to try to change the neighborhood. As one World Vision field staff recalled, "It was not as if we said, let's do development, but we wanted to do something besides traditional sponsorship."[51]

Relief agencies were becoming development agencies, forcing many to debate whether to change their names to reflect their expanding mandates. CARE went through various name changes. The formal name, Cooperative for American Remittances to Europe, was outdated from the very start. But once CARE became a household name, then all adaptations were obliged to stay true to its famous acronym. In 1953 it became the Cooperative for American Relief Everywhere and then in the 1990s the Cooperative for Assistance and Relief Everywhere. The CRS debated whether to eliminate "relief" from its name altogether or to expand its name to include "over-seas" and "development."[52] In the contest between truth-in-advertising, and name recognition the latter won out. In 1979 LWR also debated whether to change its name to provide a "more accurate picture of our work," which would also "provide a fresh opportunity for attracting attention and inter-preting the new emphasis that we are following, namely a larger emphasis on development." Accuracy was all well and good, the report concluded, but it could be a "fund-channeling disaster." They decided to keep the name but change the publicity materials.[53] For these and other agencies, branding came first.

Like their predecessors, the humanitarians of the postwar period were quite nervous about their relationship to the major powers and to politics. Their presence opened up grand opportunities for the humanitarians, and the sudden interest by major powers in humanitarianism meant that they were better treated and supported than ever before. Yet they were at con-stant risk of being seen as political for two reasons. One was their close association with the agendas of the West. States were integrating humani-tarianism into their foreign policies, erasing the distinction between them-selves and aid agencies. In 1950, for instance, Congress increased foreign assistance, but, unlike the previous legislation that described the purpose of aid as for "economic assistance," the new legislation justified aid for the "mutual security of the free world." As Bruce Nichols astutely observes, "With this brief change in wording, any hope that humanitarian activities could be distinguished from military and national security concerns ap-peared to have been eliminated."[54] Alongside these changing state interests was a change in the funding patterns: whereas during the era of colonial humanitarianism, humanitarian institutions relied on publics, parishion-ers, and philanthropists—not the state—for their financial wherewithal, the postwar humanitarians were growing more financially dependent on the state. No surprise, then, that aid agencies were increasingly using their reli-ance on government funding as a measure of their independence; it had an elegant simplicity, reflecting the general belief that money corrupts and that big money from big powers corrupts absolutely.

An agency's anxiety regarding its dependence on government funding depended on whether it saw itself and the government as having shared aims. Many of the largest American agencies, especially those that received generous funding from the government, were sympathetic to and acting in a manner that was consistent with U.S. interests. The U.S. government funded CARE not because it believed it would influence CARE's agenda, but rather because it was a reward for an organization that the government believed furthered its interests, particularly as it was dissolving "barriers between nations and creating everywhere a feeling of friendship for America and Americans."[55] For its part, CARE readily acknowledged their complementary values while denying that such correspondence meant that CARE was little more than an instrument of the United States. Although CARE officials might not have been suffering from cognitive dissonance, they labored to salvage their independence while getting so much money and support from the United States. In a particularly revealing verbal tap dance, Murray Lincoln, a former president of CARE, tried to distinguish CARE from the United States in the following way:

> We are not engaged in political ventures to entice people away from Communist leanings (however worthy such an effort may be). We are not trying to buy friends for America (even though we succeed, as a byproduct, in making many friends for our country). We are not attempting to convert the recipients of our help to Christianity or to any other religious belief (even though we are sure that the work of the agencies so engaged is more effective with people whose stomachs are no longer empty, whose bodies are clothed, and who have regained hope and dignity). We are not attempting to argue the American people into the support of CARE on the grounds of enlightened self-interest (a more palatable expression than "selfishness"). We ask the people of America to give of their plenty that these under-privileged peoples may be fed, healed, and helped to become self-supporting, self-respecting members of the world society.[56]

Or, to put it slightly differently, to support humanitarianism was to support CARE, the United States, and humanity.

Because of traditional church-state boundaries, many religious aid agencies appeared to be particularly sensitive to the appearance of lacking independence,[57] but some were more sensitive than others. One general observation of the period is that Protestant organizations were much more sensitive than were either Jewish or Catholic organizations. Protestant agencies were generally more circumspect. LWR was constantly worried about its independence and attempted to minimize the potential costs of any association.[58] Again, financial independence was a telltale metric. Fortunately, it was largely funded by Lutheran World Action, in-kind contributions, and donations generated by appeals by LWA and local pastors. Using the occasion of his testimony to the Senate Foreign Relations Committee in 1959, LWR's Paul Empie asserted the agency's independence from the U.S. government and explained its importance. Any relationship with the government, even something as seemingly benign as surplus food, he asserted, "may alter to some degree its character as a voluntary religious agency."

Unlike a secular agency, he observed, "a voluntary religious agency exists for reasons which go beyond those of human compassion or 'enlightened self-interest.'" Specifically,

> *the primary thrust of the programs of a voluntary religious agency is that of giving specific witness to the implications and fruits of the faith and its constituents.* If a religious agency takes government money then its own witness will be compromised. Moreover, once an agency partners with the government then the recipients might suspect that it is an *instrument* of government, thus compromising its character and undermining the ideological foundations of its existence. There is a serious threat to its usefulness—indeed, to its life![59]

Catholic and Jewish organizations, who might be expected to be more wary of the state, given American religious history, were surprisingly more accepting. Despite a history of anti-Semitism, many Jewish organizations believed that state support was essential for their objectives.[60] Catholic groups were particularly open to government assistance, in part because the Catholic Church has a long history of reasonably close relations with the state, and in part because of a strong anti-communism. A CRS that was highly dependent on U.S. assistance fit this mold. According to one biographer of the agency, its anticommunist ideology had various sources. Catholics believed that there was a "need for an international political authority to promote and protect the common good," and the United States was the logical candidate. Although the Catholic Church had a reputation for befriending authoritarian regimes, American Catholics, like much of the American population, believed that democracy was best. These two commitments bred a passionate anticommunism, which swelled as the Soviets curtailed religious and church activity in heavily Catholic Eastern Europe. Also, the Church, especially in the European context, was accustomed to quasi-formal relations with the state, especially as government-church relations operated on a principle of subsidiarity and recognized the importance of the church's role in local matters. Lastly, the Catholic Church was calling for economic assistance to and political liberty for less-developed countries.[61] Although testifying to congress in his capacity as head of ACVA, in 1961 Bishop Edward Swanstrom enthusiastically reported that aid agencies enjoyed working closely with the United States, a position that many aid agencies believed was fairly accurate about CRS but less so about other groups.[62]

Yet not all supporters of American Catholic bishops or CRS were as comfortable as Bishop Swanstrom with this association. Sensitive to the appearance of being an agent of the United States, CRS issued a string of statements assuring its constituency of its independence. Rivaling CARE's

Murray Lincoln for being able to hold two contradictory ideas at the same time, CRS argued the very fine point that food aid "was then and remains a gift from American citizens—not government—to those suffering hunger in other parts of the world."[63] In response to rumors that CRS was being too subservient to American policy, the American Catholic bishops launched an investigation into whether CRS had ever been subject to or complied with demands from the U.S. government; the team found CRS innocent of the changes.[64]

A slightly more objective assessment, however, concluded that CRS's "association with the government blurred the lines between private and public aid and made [its] claims of being 'nonpolitical' tenuous at best. Their constant interchange with federal officials and agencies increasingly tied their programs to government aims. Their acceptance of subsidies and membership in government organizations helped broaden their operations, but also made them subject to more persuasive government supervision and recommendations."[65] As we will see in Vietnam, the combination of anticommunism and U.S. funding turned CRS into an arm of the U.S. government.

The willingness of aid agencies, religious or otherwise, to stick to their principle of (financial) independence had its costs. LWR could have benefited from official assistance to underwrite the cost of administering its projects.[66] WVI was living paycheck to paycheck. One veteran WVI official recalled attending all-night prayer meetings in the mid-1960s where they prayed to be able to cover the payroll, and such prayers were a staple at WVI through the mid-1970s as well. There were no easy solutions. Although its child sponsorship programs were doing well, these earmarked funds could not be used for other programs. Nor was WVI able or willing to seek government contracts: as a faith-based organization, the government would not fund religious programming; by this time WVI's programming had a pronounced evangelical and missionary orientation, and WVI feared that government funding would invite meddling. In 1962 it establish a shell organization, the World Vision Relief Organization (WVRO), as an independent entity in order to receive some government funding for disaster relief. But WVI did not want or expect the government to become a principal source of support.[67]

Aid agencies were at constant risk of being viewed as political not only because of who their financial backers were but also because they were moving from relief to development, from help to self-help. Although it might seem inconceivable to work for social change without doing politics, aid agencies nevertheless tried to appear distant from politics and quickly retreated whenever they were seen as encroaching.[68] One way they maintained their distance was by restricting politics to matters of the formal political system and governance. Typical in this respect was CRS's statement that its programs "are, and must remain, apolitical. While understanding the need and desirability, in some instances, of those types of social change *which require a restructuring of the political system* in a host country, CRS...has no mandate of this kind. Its mandate is aimed at the individual at the lowest end of the economic ladder. Its objectives relate primarily to those efforts which can bring to the individual, through the agencies of the Church, an improvement in the economic, social, and spiritual aspects of life."[69] LWR similarly claimed that it "attempts to divorce its operations from politics at home and abroad. All development work has political implications, however; populations in need, in addition to being the target groups of humanitarian programs, constitute a political entity....A program that helps small farmers in a developing country obtain a fair price for their produce creates a situation of economic—and political—confrontation with those who previously profited from unreasonably cheap food. No matter how 'apolitical' LWR wishes or strives to be, impartial observers will see actions as having political consequences." In order to avoid becoming political, the group should not evaluate governments on their democratic character or openly second-guess their priorities. All that should matter is whether "their policies encourage or even permit meaningful development change."[70]

Oxfam's worries about being political owed little to its government funding, which was relatively modest. Rather, the problem was that it had run afoul of the British Charities Commission. In order for nongovernmental organizations to receive significant tax breaks, exemptions, and various kinds of incentives from the government, it needs to be certified as a charity by the Commission. In 1962 the Commission ruled that propaganda, advocacy, and solidarity were not charitable but instead were political activities, a warning shot for an organization that was increasingly lobbying governments to expand development assistance and organizing grassroots campaigns for social and political change.[71] In 1963 the British Charities Commission ruled that Oxfam was both a charitable and a political organization because it delivered relief and performed other noncharitable activities. Heeding the warning, Oxfam recast its mandate so that it conformed more closely to the Commission's definition of a charity. Yet it was nearly impossible for an agency so clearly associated with a program of radical change to avoid trouble with the Commission. Also, its high-profile advocacy had also brought Oxfam fame and fortune.[72] Oxfam was constantly pushing the limits, at times choosing to label its advocacy as education and at other times taking a step backward before moving forward again.[73] In July 1979 Oxfam settled on a new formulation. As stated in "Oxfam: An Interpretation," the trustees articulated a new policy statement on humanitarian neutrality—"need above political divide." Once again, the language of needs was chosen because of its depoliticizing qualities.

Aid agencies also avoided human rights. The avoidance of human rights is striking if only because humanitarians demonstrated no such fear in the periods that preceded and proceeded Neo-humanitarianism. Before World War I, colonialists and missionaries had evoked the language of rights in their civilizational discourse, and in the 1990s one of the central controversies in the humanitarian community was about how closely to associate itself with an impressively ascendant human rights. Although various factors contributed to the temporary silence during this period of Neo-humanitarianism, figuring centrally was that newly independent countries had lost patience with high-minded Westerners and a Cold War that had little sympathy for human rights. For the time being, human rights would have to be advanced by the few existing human rights organizations, such as Amnesty International.

The belief among aid agencies that they could operate outside of politics also owed to their bureaucratization and technocratic ethos. WVI's evolution is instructive in this regard. As an evangelical organization, WVI was created to proselytize. Reflecting on these early days, one document contained this description: "Thirty-five years ago there was a polarization between those who believed that we should only preach the gospel and save souls, and those who placed their emphasis on feeding people with little spiritual consideration. Bob Pierce caused both camps to imagine a third way. His challenge to Christians was simple. You don't fulfill Christ's mandate simply through proclamation. You don't evangelize the world only by giving a cup of cold water."[74] When Stan Mooneyham, a disciple of Billy Graham's, became president of WVI in 1969, he brought with him his teacher's tools. "He would hold evangelistic crusades," recalled one WVI official. Motivated by the urgency to spread the gospel and to give individuals a choice to be saved, World Vision staff were, as a staff member put it, "rice bowl Christians," as keen to save souls as to save lives.

World Vision's tremendous growth during the 1980s strained its evangelical identity. WVI was now moving headlong into development and was attempting to be known as one of the world's premier development organizations. Toward that end, it was increasingly utilizing the most sophisticated techniques and "best practices." Yet was it possible to be both a development organization and a Christian organization? What exactly was a Christian development agency? For some the answer was that it provided opportunities to spread the gospel and perform conversion.[75] In 1978 WVI issued evangelism guidelines for the field: "We urged the Fields to ensure that an individual or group had a valid opportunity to accept or reject Jesus Christ, and, where applicable, to move an individual or group or people through the *process* of deciding for Christ and being incorporated into a fellowship of a viable body of believers.... In 1979 the WVI

Board approved specific policy on Development which described the components of Christian Development. "The policy stated that WVI *plans* to give the Gospel and the outward opportunity for a community to confront Jesus Christ during the course of our ministry in a community."[76] Other statements suggested that Christian development had a different process, defined by alternative values, including participation and finding religious meaning in the possibility of progress. Rather than speaking of evangelical development, WVI began to use the phrase "Christian witness" as a way to express its identity in various contexts.[77]

By the end of the 1980s, however, the word *evangelical* began to disappear from its materials. The days of large tent revivals were gone, replaced by more technically oriented missions; measuring outcomes now revolved around how many lives, not souls, were saved. This did not mean that WVI had lost interest in spreading the gospel and helping individuals realize their spiritual as well as their physical needs. It had not. But the religious, evangelical fervor had been dampened by its more technical and internationalized orientation. These developments reflect a notion of what individuals needed not only to survive but also to become fully human.

If the label *Neo-Humanitarianism* is deserved, it is because there was relatively little change in the practices of paternalism. There had been a revolution in the organization of world politics, moving from an era of empires to an era of sovereignty, and this revolution was accompanied by the expectation of a new set of relationships between the West and the newly emerging Third World. Visions of self-determination, independence, and sovereignty were emerging against the backdrop of the international community. Overt references by Westerners to themselves as the parents and to the newly decolonizing peoples as children were no longer tolerable (even if they were often present in their minds).

Yet there remained the practices of paternalism. While I have met few staff from the period who recall likening themselves to parents and the local populations as children, they nevertheless have vivid memories of believing that their training, education, and background gave them superior knowledge and the right to intervene in the lives of those who did not know what was in their best interests. Recalling his experiences in Indonesia in the 1970s, one veteran World Vision official said, "We used to read the new development manuals at night and then teach the villagers what we learned the next day."[78] If previous humanitarians, especially of the religious variation, believed that God was on their side, these new humanitarians believed that science was on their side. This attitude was present not only among aid workers but also among a generation of development economists, who believed that their training and knowledge would allow them to accelerate the development of the Third World, rarely questioning their assumptions that they knew what was best and how to get there.[79] Technocratic authority replaced religious authority. Although harsh, Kenyan leader Jomo Kenyatta's critical words for aid agencies had an element of truth: "Those professional friends of the African who are prepared to maintain their friendship for eternity as a sacred duty, provided only that the African will continue to play the part of the ignorant savage so that they can monopolize the office of interpreting his mind and speaking for him."[80]

7

༺❧༻

Humanitarianism during Wartime

THE NOVELTY of the postwar humanitarian emergencies has less to do with their objective features and more with the simple fact that they generated more attention from more people from greater distances than ever before. Although the history of the nineteenth century demonstrates that the plight of those from the global South could, at times, capture the attention and sympathy of those in the West, by and large their suffering went unnoticed or even excused as part of progress. After World War II, though, places once neglected by those in the West became objects of concern at times of war or natural disasters.

This remarkable postwar development owes to several factors. The discourse of humanity and international community made it more difficult to defend selective attention. The Cold War invested nearly all conflicts around the world with geopolitical significance, incidentally bringing attention to mass suffering in otherwise forgotten places. A growing network of print and visual media was carrying news nearly instantaneously into the homes of ordinary citizens thousands of miles away. The rising population of development NGOs was bringing immediate attention to emergency situations, offering themselves as saviors, and finding that association with high-profile disasters was good for business. It was easier than ever before to mobilize action on behalf of distant strangers and more difficult to justify indifference.

These developments provided more opportunities for aid agencies to get involved, which brought not entirely unfamiliar but certainly more intense challenges. Although they presented themselves as apolitical, acting on behalf of humanity and operating according to the principles of impartiality, neutrality, and independence, aid agencies could no more insulate themselves from politics than Third World states could remove themselves from the Cold War. Major powers increasingly treated humanitarianism as an instrument of their foreign and economic policies, and knowing that lives were on the line did not change their policies. Many who joined relief agencies did so because they wanted to enact their political commitments in practical ways, making such an act a political statement. And, many states, regimes, and opposition groups, especially those fighting for their causes and their lives, discovered that mass misfortune could attract massive amounts of attention and aid, which, in turn, could be converted into diplomatic and military capital.

Aid agencies had to figure out how to navigate these crosscurrents, and there was no rule book, not then and not today, to tell them how to do so. They understood that there was no way to avoid being implicated in and compromised by global, regional, and local rivalries. They even worried that by providing aid they might be prolonging war and, with it, horrific suffering. What to do? In the absence of such a rule book, they relied on their instincts, political leanings, and organizational identities; and knowing that status and money generally came to those who delivered aid meant there were strong incentives to remain on the ground regardless of the cost to principles. Although it is dangerous to generalize, emergency and alchemical agencies clustered around two different kinds of responses. Because they were more singlemindedly focused on relief, emergency agencies tended to be more respectful of the principles of impartiality, neutrality, and independence. Such a move, they believed, constituted them as humanitarian, kept them outside of politics, and enabled them to reach the victims. Alchemical agencies, by contrast, were more comfortable with politics and more willing to align themselves with states if they believed it would help further their interest in relief and social justice. Many high-profile emergencies illuminated these dynamics, but Biafra, Vietnam, Cambodia, and Ethiopia were defining events, forcing aid agencies to take a hard and uncomfortable look at themselves and introducing them to a world that would become increasingly familiar after the Cold War.

Biafra

Biafra is rightly credited with opening a new chapter in humanitarian action; while the suffering was hardly unprecedented, the international response was. After achieving its independence from Britain in 1960, Nigeria collapsed into a violent fight for political supremacy that had ethnic and religious dimensions. In 1966, after a string of coups, the Nigerian army and various ethnic groups began attacking the Ibos, especially in the northern regions, where they were a visible and vulnerable minority. Thousands of Ibos died, and two million more fled east to the region of Biafra, where the Ibos were the ruling majority. On May 30, 1967, the Ibo government declared its independence, and the Nigerian government's response was swift and severe, leaving even more dead and displaced.

As part of its military strategy, Lagos imposed a blockade on Biafra, hoping to starve the rebels into submission. The move was partly successful: a famine soon descended on Biafra and tens of thousands lay dying; but the rebels refused to surrender. In early 1968 a fact-finding mission by the ICRC estimated that three hundred thousand children were suffering from kwashiorkor, a form of malnutrition that produces symptoms of shriveling skin and bloated bellies. Soon thereafter there were estimates that upwards of eight million Biafrans were in peril.

For months the international community ignored Biafra in the same way it ignored other conflicts in the decolonizing world, and then suddenly in early 1968 the famine became worldwide news, transforming Biafra into a cause. Although various factors rescued Biafra from anonymity, considerable credit is due to the legacy of missionary activity and the continuing presence of religious groups. Unlike the rest of the Nigeria, which was predominantly Muslim, Biafra and the Ibo population were heavily Christian because of a long history of Protestant and Catholic missionary activity. Consequently, church organizations were among the first to focus on Biafra, highlighting its religious features; on March 20 the World Council of Churches and the Vatican issued a joint appeal on behalf of the Biafrans.[1] Soon thereafter church organizations were joined by an assortment of other international parties insisting that the West do something about the famine.

Outgunned and outmanned by the Nigerian military, the Ibo leadership observed that the only reason why the international community cared about Biafra was because of the famine, and so it began to use the famine as an instrument for its military and political goals. Specifically, the Ibo leadership benefitted in several ways from the famine. Those in the West who might not have cared about the political agenda of the Biafran leadership suddenly became supporters because of the famine, assuming that a people suffering such hardship must have a worthy political cause; the Biafran leadership could then translate this sympathy into political capital.[2] Because relief agencies had to negotiate with the leadership as the official representatives of the Biafran people, it handed the leaders legitimacy. There also were material benefits that flowed from such a large relief operation, including generating employment and opportunities for corruption. The leadership did not passively cultivate these various benefits from the famine—it actively pursued them. The Biafris hired a public relations firm, Markpress, to publicize their plight and then exaggerated and manipulated the effects of the famine in order to generate more international assistance. And, because they now had an incentive to keep the famine alive, the Ibo leadership showed little urgency in trying to get an agreement with Lagos to open the relief spigot. Only years later did aid agencies realize how much the savvy Biafran rebels had manipulated them.[3]

The famine and the public relations campaign placed Western governments and NGOs under tremendous pressure to act. For various reasons, though largely because of Cold War politics, at the outset the Western governments supported Nigeria, but as the famine continued and intensified they were accused of being heartless and acting as an accomplice of the Nigerian government. The relief agencies were caught between the desire to provide relief and the need to get Lagos's approval. How long they were willing to wait for permission depended in part on their political leanings. The Irish Fathers, a particularly outspoken pro-Biafra group that had little government financing, began using food shipments to smuggle weapons to the rebels. Other organizations also tried to mobilize political and military support on behalf of the rebels and often looked away as gun runners used aid shipments. But to ease the effects of the famine would require a major international relief effort, which, in turn, would require Lagos's consent, which it withheld for several reasons. It insisted that the operation be organized and monitored to ensure that food would go to the victims and not to the rebels, a reaction in part to the knowledge that certain NGOs with open sympathies for the Biafrans were allowing their aid shipments to be used by arms smugglers. The rebels, however, were in no hurry to conclude an agreement, because they believed that the existence of starving people enhanced their political and military position.

Early on, many NGOs agreed to get the government's acquiescence before acting, but as the negotiations dragged on and more people died from the famine, "neutrality" began to look like a poor excuse for inaction. Oxfam sprinted ahead of the pack, developed a relief campaign, and publically supported the rebels, undermining any pretense of neutrality. Precisely why Oxfam broke unilaterally from its previous agreement with other NGOs to coordinate their policies is not exactly clear, though the combination of the pressure to do something and the temptation to be rewarded generously with good publicity were undoubtedly important factors.[4] Not only were aid agencies such as Oxfam and Catholic Relief Services risking the wrath of the Nigerian government, they were also opposing American and British foreign policy, which, along with a coalition of Western and Muslim countries, was aligned with the Nigerian government.

The ICRC was at the center of the negotiations with the Nigerian government and, in many respects, the lead agency in the relief effort. It was hardly the obvious choice, or the choice of many, to play this role. Historically the ICRC preferred working outside the limelight. The Soviet Union also was no fan of the ICRC, viewing it as part of the bourgeois West. The ICRC might not have the global support it needed to undertake such a delicate mission.[5]

More importantly, its record on protecting populations at risk was hardly sterling. Although critics could have pointed to its record in Ethiopia in the 1930s they understandably fixated on its controversial actions during the Holocaust. Simply put, the ICRC refused to speak out against, or say what it knew about, the treatment of the Jews and others imprisoned in the death and labor camps. Although its policy was not unlike those of many other governments and the Vatican, presumably what separated the ICRC from these other actors was that it had a protection mission. Accordingly, soon after the war its policy came under fire. In a 1948 booklet it answered its critics in the following way:

> Protest? The International Committee did protest—to the responsible authorities. . . . A whole department of the Committee's work was to make on long series of protests: countless improvements in the [concentration] camps, for example, were due to steps of this kind. . . . Every man to his job, every man to his vocation. That of the Red Cross is to nurse the wounded where it can with the means at its disposal. For the Committee to protest publicly would have been not only to outstep its functions, but also to lose thereby all chance of pursuing them, by creating an immediate breach with the government concerned.[6]

In short, there was not a lot that ICRC could do. Its mandate cautioned against doing too much. Going public would not have saved any lives. Accordingly, its best course of action was to improve the conditions in the labor and death camps (whatever that might mean, in this context).[7] In the immediate postwar period its response to the criticisms were much like its response to the Holocaust: "[T]he ICRC continued for the most part to operate as an amateur with relatively modest objectives; when attacked for its passive stance vis-à-vis the Nazi concentration camps, its standard response was to sidestep the issue, refusing to examine the implications of its silence."[8]

Yet because the challenge of protecting civilians in the postwar world remained a central challenge, eventually the ICRC re-examined its core principles. In some respects the ICRC was taking not a fresh look but a first look—in the nearly one hundred years since its birth, the ICRC's formal and informal principles had evolved incrementally and in reaction to the horrors of the day, creating a jumble of principles with no agreement on their interpretation. Consequently, this postwar dialogue was one of the agency's first sustained and systematic effort to deconstruct and construct first principles, to try to give some precision to its foundational concepts, and, in so doing, establish the commandments of "official" humanitarianism. Fully aware that they were debating not only the principles of the ICRC but also humanitarianism writ large, the debate, led by longtime ICRC official Jean Pictet, turned on the categorical and the consequential, on a consideration of which principles defined ICRC and its humanitarianism and which principles might be useful for accomplishing its work.

After several years of debate, in 1965 the ICRC adopted a document called "Fundamental Principles of the Red Cross." The ICRC identified seven principles, of which the most important were impartiality, neutrality, and independence. These were hardly new to humanitarianism. In various episodes and for various aid agencies, they had been essential in allowing them to do their work. The ICRC had long stressed the importance of impartiality and neutrality. Even missionaries, often influenced by a respect for the separation of church and state, worried about the boundaries between themselves and the state and thus advocated forms of independence. But beginning with the age of neo-humanitarianism, aid agencies increasingly treated these principles as constitutive of humanitarianism, influenced by the ICRC's conclusions. Indeed, these principles increasingly came to define who is and is not a bona fide humanitarian actor.

This recent history provides an important part of the context for understanding ICRC's activities regarding Biafra. It did have relatively little room for maneuver because of the combination of the freshly debated principles, a mandate that required it to act with the consent of member states, and the fourth Geneva Convention, which gave the blockading power the right to inspect and supervise shipments.[9] The difficult task of trying to negotiate an agreement with Nigeria and the Ibo leadership was given to the ICRC's Auguste Lindt, a former United Nations High Commissioner for Refugees. He and the ICRC wanted to act, knowing that each additional day of negotiations could be measured in hundreds if not thousands of dead, but he had to conclude an agreement with the Nigerian government. There was always the option of acting without its permission, but this posed considerable risks to the safety of its staff and the possibility of creating a permanent lifeline to Biafra. If the ICRC was going to get an agreement, then it had to stick to its principle of neutrality. Indeed, the ICRC needed to do more than remain neutral, it had to be perceived as neutral.[10]

After months of frustrating and fruitless negotiations, in August 1968 an exasperated ICRC did something very un-ICRC-like: it declared its intention to send relief to Biafra without Lagos's permission, knowing that running the blockade could make them targets for the Nigerian military.

Sure enough, soon after the announcement of the operation, the Nigerian army advanced on an ICRC refugee camp and warned staff to leave—or else. Defying the threat, Geneva ordered its staff of 120 to remain at their posts. Nigeria attacked the camps, killing four French Red Cross workers. Several months later, on June 5, 1969, Nigeria shot down an ICRC aircraft bringing in provisions. After months of playing a dangerous game of cat and mouse with the Nigerian military, the ICRC decided to end all flights until it received Lagos's consent.

Although the international community appeared to be in a frenzy about Biafra, the United Nations was the picture of calm. UN Secretary-General U Thant argued that because the UN's mandate did not include domestic politics, there was little he could do because Biafra was an internal affair. Yet he did more than hide behind his mandate—he actively discouraged members of the Security Council from bringing Biafra before the council. The reasons for his aloofness remain unknown, though evidence suggests that recent memories of Congo, which became the resting place of the UN Secretary-General Dag Hammarskjöld and any notion of an activist UN, and the Cold War had a major impact.[11] The UN assumed its traditional "make no waves and do not call attention to yourself" posture.

The UNHCR also remained on the sidelines. Its refusal to become part of the international relief effort, which in retrospect appears all the more remarkable given that Biafra was a refugee crisis, can be best understood by its finely tuned radar for knowing when to push beyond its mandate and when to keep its head down. During and immediately after World War II, Western states created a series of international organizations dedicated to the needs of refugees and displaced peoples caused by World War II. Responding to the apparent contradiction between a principled desire to help refugees in Europe and an unwillingness to extend such protections outside of Europe, the UN's Economic and Social Council began discussing the termination of the International Relief Organization, the latest of the World War II–era refugee organizations, and the creation of a permanent refugee agency with a global reach.

Although there was widespread sympathy with the general idea, the United States objected on various grounds. Washington did not want to issue a blank check at a moment when it was, in effect, the world's humanitarian benefactor or create a global organization that handed the Soviet Union an equal role. Instead, it preferred to work through bilateral programs and organizations that it could control. It also believed that the surest solution to refugee problems was economic development, the remedy provided by the Marshall Plan.[12] Refugees might be a permanent feature of world politics, but this did not mean that the United States had to support a permanent organization with real resources and a real mandate.

Although it was unable to table the possibility of an international refugee organization, it did successfully limit its ambitions and discretion. A refugee was defined as:

> any person who, as a result of events occurring before 1 January 1951 and owing to well-founded fear of persecution for reasons of race, religion, nationality, or political opinion, and is outside the country of his nationality and is unable or, owing to such fear, is unwilling to avail himself of the protection of the government of the country of his nationality.

The contrast between what was imaginable and what was politically desirable could hardly have been greater. States knew that the world would continue to produce an endless stream of refugees, but the UNHCR was limited to refugees produced in Europe as a consequence of World War II. By extending the definition only to those who had crossed an international border, the UNHCR was precluded from helping those who were forced to flee but were unable to get to the other side. A refugee, also, was defined as an individual escaping persecution, even though states knew that peoples might flee because of economic hardship and political events such as international and internal wars, famines, and government oppression.

The UNHCR was limited to legal assistance, offering refugees an "international legal bridge between periods of national sovereign assimilation."[13] Put another way, while it could assist refugees by "identifying them, issuing travel documents, assisting in obtaining recognition of their various legal statuses, and advocating ever more precise guidelines for handling recognized refugees," it could not offer material protection.[14] "Protection" became legal protection. Reflecting on the meaning of international protection during the Cold War, former High Commissioner Sadako Ogata said:

> UNHCR essentially waited on the other side of an international border to receive and to protect refugees fleeing conflicts. This approach was determined by the very concept of international protection of refugees which would come into play if, and only if, victims of persecution or violent conflict fled their homeland. It was also dictated by the concept of state sovereignty and the consequent reluctance of intergovernmental organizations, such as UNHCR, to be seen as being too involved in the internal conditions of countries of origin that might give rise to refugee movements.[15]

An agency that was to provide legal assistance to help pre-1951 refugees was not expected to have a long life expectancy, and the United States imposed a three-year expiration date. Just to foreclose any possibilities of escape, the UNHCR had to rely on voluntary contributions, almost all of which came from states.[16]

Importantly, states insisted that because the UNHCR is a humanitarian agency, it should avoid politics. States rejected an already existing definition of protection that included both "legal and political" elements in favor of "international protection" because politics was viewed as divisive, controversial, and likely to produce violations of state sovereignty. Moreover, states substituted "humanitarian" for "political." As a humanitarian and apolitical organization, states created the UNHCR to help coordinate the operations of states and NGOs and to provide legal assistance to refugees. Stated negatively, states did not expect or want the UNHCR to become an operational agency or to address how to eliminate the causes of refugee flight, which, by definition, were political matters and therefore encroached on state sovereignty.[17] In general, states intended the UNHCR to be an "apolitical" and "humanitarian" organization that focused on relief and ignored the causes of flight. Paragraph Two of the UNHCR's statute insists that "the work of the High Commissioner shall be of an entirely nonpolitical character; it shall be humanitarian and social." The nonpolitical clause was an artifact not only of the prevailing view of humanitarianism but also of East-West tensions.

Although the UNHCR, much like the refugees it was mandated to protect, was in a state of limbo, with no resources and few prospects, it managed to beat the odds. Its shoestring budget barely covered the basics, and in 1955 its financial situation was so perilous that a three-million-dollar Ford Foundation grant became the difference between bankruptcy and survival. Because its mandate was limited to refugees produced by events in Europe prior to 1951, it was quickly going out of business as the number of "cold war" refugees (refugees arriving from the Soviet bloc) dwindled. The United States refused to have much to do with the agency, provided little diplomatic and no financial support, and worked through organizations it could control, such as the International Committee for European Migration and United States Escapee Programme.[18] Perhaps the only thing in its favor was a determined High Commissioner, Dr. Gerrit Jan van Heuven Goedhart, who saw himself as the refugees' representative and champion of their interests.[19]

Over the next two decades the UNHCR capitalized on world events and used its growing authority to rescue itself from oblivion and to significantly extend its activities, mandate, and working definition of a refugee.[20] Beginning in the mid-1950s, a series of conflicts created refugee crises that were formally outside the UNHCR's jurisdiction either because the refugee-causing events occurred after 1951 or because they were outside of Europe, or both. In each case a similar sequence of events occurred. The High Commissioner, who believed that the agency was morally obligated to assist all refugees, not just those made homeless and stateless because of events that occurred in Europe before 1951, would go to the Executive Committee of the UNHCR and the UN and ask for a one-time exemption. Once it received an exemption, this exemption would become a precedent for future exceptions and a more permanent expansion of the UNHCR's mandate. With each and every cycle of this dynamic the UNHCR expanded its global coverage and assistance programs.[21] This expansion would never have happened without the permission of states, though the state that was the hardest to convince was its original doubter, the United States. Over time, though, the United States warmed to the possibility that the UNHCR could play a valuable stopgap role, if only because there was no viable alternative.

But the UNHCR also demonstrated considerable ingenuity in insinuating itself into refugee crises before receiving permission. Toward this end it got considerable mileage from the concept of "good offices," which essentially signaled that the UNHCR is simply using its established position to see if it can be of assistance.[22] The good offices concept had two principal advantages. It allowed the UNHCR to extend protection and assistance to new groups and to transform what might have been a deeply politicized issue into a humanitarian and apolitical matter.[23] This depoliticization benefited not only refugees but also the UNHCR, for the concept alerted governments that the agency was "not guided by any political intentions or considerations."[24] Also, it separated the issues of solution and protection from what was increasingly understood as the main issue of international concern—material assistance: "Solution and protection were considered for the most of this period as 'political' questions to be distinguished from the 'humanitarian' questions of relief: the former were to be outside UNHCR's concern, the latter was not so to be considered if the main states involved were to be of that opinion in each particular case."[25] Although states had tagged the UNHCR with a humanitarian identity as a way of limiting its activities, the UNHCR cagily used its identity as a stealth tool to burrow into new areas and activities.

By the time Biafra erupted, therefore, the UNHCR had figured out when to push and when to duck—and Biafra was most definitely in the latter category. While the UNHCR was ready to break new ground when the occasion permitted, as far as it was concerned the occasion was never right if the displaced peoples still resided in their home country. Going global did not include interfering in the internal affairs of a member state. The UNHCR remained an apolitical emergency agency, honoring state sovereignty, waiting on the other side of the border to provide relief, and avoiding any consideration of the causes of refugee flight. So when a delegation from Biafra went to Geneva in November 1967 to plead for the UNHCR's assistance, High Commissioner Sadruddin Aga Khan unequivocally rejected any possible involvement:

> The High Commissioner informed [the representatives of Biafra] that the statute of the Office empowers him to assist in solving problems of refugees

at the request of governments of countries of asylum. A refugee, in this context, is a person who is outside his country and does not, for various specified reasons, wish to avail himself of the protection of his country of origin. Since "Biafra" is not recognized as a separate state, the displaced people from other parts of Nigeria into Eastern [sic] Nigeria do not fall within the mandate of the Office and, therefore, *there is nothing that the Office could do for them.*[26]

The UNHCR was hardly about to enter into the sovereign territory of a member state at the request of a rebel group.

UNICEF was the lone exception to this pattern of indifference. Essentially adopting the military adage that it is better to act and beg for forgiveness than to ask for permission, UNICEF took action before the Nigerian government could make a decision, citing as justification the Nigerian government's proclaimed concern for the needs of the populations on both sides of the conflict; Nigeria's denial that it was blocking aid; Nigeria's failure to reject UNICEF's involvement categorically; and UNICEF's longstanding work with Nigerian children.

The crisis in Biafra shook all aid organizations, though none more than the ICRC, which suffered a significant legitimacy crisis. Certainly the organization had registered various successes, not all of which it could advertise because of its principle of silence. But a growing critique of the organization was that it was not up to contemporary and future challenges, and it was unclear whether this organization, largely made up of patrician, elderly, and ne'er-do-well Swiss lawyers, who, at times, treated humanitarianism as a worthy diversion, would have the ability to undertake the necessary reforms.[27] Its lack of professionalism, or, to put it more bluntly, its amateurish nature, shone through.[28] Biafra and the radical politics of 1968 among Western youth meant that there was greater interest in matters of justice, equality, and solidarity than there was in keeping people alive, so organizations like Oxfam seemed more hip than status quo organizations like the ICRC. International humanitarian law, especially in these "new wars," seemed either irrelevant or dysfunctional. It was not until 1977 that states revised the Geneva Conventions to include two additional protocols, one dealing specifically with internal conflicts.

The delicate task of trying to help the ICRC navigate through the competing interests and reimagine the future was handed to Donald Tansley, a former official of the Canadian International Development Agency who was widely respected for his impartiality and integrity. In 1975 he delivered a report that neither praised nor buried the Red Cross movement but offered some unsettling observations and stark choices that cut fairly close to the bone. There was a wide chasm between the world that was to come and an organization that was starting to seem a relic of the nineteenth century. The world was rapidly changing because of nationalism, economic dislocations, and demography, but these were barely noticed by the rather dowdy, stuffy, scoliotic ICRC. The ICRC, moreover, had so many moving and autonomous parts that it had little oversight and no shared voice on central principles. Because this was an agency that was seemingly unto itself, beyond challenge, and lacking in basic standards of accountability, its errors in judgment and wayward policies repeated themselves. The Red Cross movement had a spirited debate about the report's findings and recommendations, but almost as if to prove the report's point, it acted on few of its suggestions.[29] It was, for the most part, business as usual.

The ICRC also began to face a challenge from an unlikely source that began as a minor and somewhat unremarkable dissent by several disaffected French Red Cross workers. Several veterans of the 1968 student rebellion joined the French Red Cross, hoping to put their medical training to good use while practicing a new style of politics. They were hardly prepared for the combination of the horrors in the field and the personal dangers they confronted, and they were shaken by their experiences. One episode in particular proved particularly upsetting. They were working in a medical clinic when they received wounded villagers fleeing the Nigerian army, which was still in hot pursuit. The French doctors radioed the Red Cross headquarters for advice on what to do, and they were told to leave the clinic and the villagers. They disobeyed and stayed, only to witness the soldiers massacre unarmed and wounded men, women, and children. They were horrified not only by the carnage but also by the Red Cross principle of neutrality, which ruled out any public condemnation. The French doctors responded in a very uncharacteristic way, at least for staff associated with the ICRC. Although they had taken the agency's vow of silence before departing for Biafra, they decided that their private morality trumped organizational loyalty.[30]

One of the leaders of this group was Bernard Kouchner, who was not only shocked by what he witnessed but also appalled by the actions of the ICRC. Referring to the deaths of the French Red Cross workers, Kouchner wrote that "this bruising episode" convinced him and others that they could not in good conscience abide by the ICRC's policy of silence, coming from an organization that had remained mute on the Nazi concentration camps.[31] Fifteen days after the incident, on November 27, 1968, Max Récamier and Kouchner wrote an article in *Le Monde* pleading for international action to aid the imperiled Biafrans.[32] Although critical of the ICRC, they urged those who wanted to support Biafra to use the French Red Cross.[33]

Returning to France, Kouchner violated his vow of silence in the most spectacular manner, organizing marches and media events to raise awareness, lobbying states to condemn the Nigerian government, and rebuking the ICRC's position of neutrality on the grounds that it abated the genocide. He and the other veterans of Biafra, soon to be known as the "Biafris," met regularly to reflect on their experiences and considered creating an "anti–Red Cross."[34] In their first act they formed the Groupe d'Intervention Medical et Chirurgical d'Urgence (GIMCU) to send medical teams to victims of war and natural disasters. Working through the Red Cross, they went to several emergencies, including Peru in August 1970, where they arrived after a six-day journey and cared for two injured people, and East Pakistan later that year, with equally unimpressive results.[35]

Meanwhile Récamier noticed a public call for medical volunteers in the medical journal *Tonus*, which was funded by American pharmaceutical companies and headed by a journalist, Raymond Borel, who had recently worked in East Pakistan. The ad announced the start of a project, Sécours Médical Français (SMF). Launched just before the crisis in East Pakistan in 1971 exploded into violence, fifty doctors and health professionals, including Bernard Kouchner, joined the SMF mission.

Soon thereafter, the Biafris and the Tonusiens, who were mainly journalists, began to discuss whether to unify their forces. The Biafris drew from progressive and Leftist politics, a new philosophy of action, an urge to aid the underdog confronting impossible odds and unimaginable horrors, and a belief that *raison d'état* is the enemy of humanity and that a handful of determined and vocal individuals can save lives.[36] Although sharing many of the same political commitments, the Tonusiens emphasized that doctors can and must serve the underprivileged. The Biafris and the Tonusiens shared more than common values—they also recognized that they could further their individual interests through a strategic collaboration: the latter would gain considerable publicity by associating with the Biafris, and the Biafris, who had been struggling to sustain GIMCU, would get some needed resources.[37] After months of discussions, in December 1971 they agreed to form a new organization, Médecins Sans Frontières (MSF); on January 3, 1972, the group advertised its existence in the pages of *Tonus*, offering its services to national and international organizations.[38] The editorial announced MSF's ICRC-like pledge to "respect the Hippocratic oath as well as the principles of collegiality, material disinterest, and apolitical stance."[39]

MSF represented the conjunction of various historical influences. There was a universalism deriving from both professional medical ethics and human rights. Xavier Emmanuelli, a cofounder of MSF, reflected, "The doctor engages himself in the name of a certain conception of man and of his rights: The right to life, respect of the human being."[40] Professional ethics intersected with human rights, which carries considerable weight in France because it considers itself the birthplace and guardian of the "rights of man." MSF also represented the latest version of a longstanding French ideology that justified foreign intervention for improving human welfare, symbolized by the colonial doctrine of *la mission civilatrice* and personified by Charles Lavigerie, archbishop of Algiers, and the missionary society known as the Pères Blancs (White Fathers).[41] Also influential was the intellectual climate of Paris in the mid to late 1960s, in particular the politics of 1968. A radical spirit enveloped the universities and the youth, spurred by Algeria, Vietnam, and the cause of the Third World and leading to mass protests and calls for sweeping political change.[42] Lastly, there was Europe's recent past—the Holocaust. MSF was a "cultural basin," observed Rony Brauman, comprised of both leftists and rightists, of anticolonialists and humanitarians who imagined protecting and bringing progress to the backward populations.[43]

Kouchner, MSF's famous founder and longtime leader, personified these complicated currents. His grandparents had perished in Auschwitz, and the experience forever haunted him. He came of age surrounded by the cult of the French Resistance and, like many French youths, admired the communists in part because of their unimpeachable anti-fascist credentials. He became deeply involved in radical student politics in the 1960s and in medical school became a leader of the Union des Étudiants Communistes. Yet he was no knee-jerk leftist, ready to excuse the so-called progressive governments that oppressed their populations. In fact, his criticisms of the Soviet Union led the Stalinists to expel him from the party. A chance opportunity allowed him to accompany the first French Red Cross team to Biafra, where he confronted his naïveté while discovering a new platform to develop his political voice. This brash, opinionated, attention-hungry, passionate, and not particularly idealist militant who had a difficult time taking orders and keeping his mouth shut was a product of his times and helped to create a new style of politics that fought for justice not through the old-style politics of protest but instead through direct action on behalf of the victims of the world.

Although MSF resulted from a mishmash of ideological and historical influences, the founding members agreed on a set of principles that were nearly indistinguishable from those of the ICRC, including the right of victims of natural and man-made catastrophes to receive aid; neutrality and independence; abstinence from meddling in the internal affairs of states, governments, and their parties; adherence to medical ethics; and an unwillingness to air publically any opinion regarding the causes of the emergency. Yet one issue proved to be especially divisive: whether and how to denounce publically mass violations of human rights while providing relief.[44] MSF's founding and orienting concept was *témoignage*, which roughly translates as "witnessing."

But could *témoignage* include public denunciations of human rights violations? Initially, the Biafris insisted on it. Deeply affected by the ICRC's policy
of public silence in the face of the Holocaust and the Biafran famine, they
could hardly imagine repeating the errors of the ICRC.[45] The Tonusiens
advocated an ICRC-like position of public silence, arguing that it was impossible to provide relief and at the same time denounce the parties whose
cooperation was needed to get access to victims. As one founding member
put it just days before the creation of MSF: "A doctor does not depart as a
witness. He is not going to write a novel or a newspaper article. He has to
provide relief. The medical secret exists and we have to respect it. Silence is
the condition of our effectiveness." Only if doctors respect the principle of
medical confidentiality, he continued, will a government let them in.[46]

The Tonusien view won the day. As a medical and rights-based organization, MSF would treat civilians and hope that its mere presence might
deter human rights violations and at least call attention to the victims and
the need for political action. MSF's charter stated that it would "maintain
professional discretion and refrain from making judgments or express public opinions—favorable or hostile—with regard to the events, forces and
leaders who accepted their aid."[47] The practice of *témoignage,* according
to the charter, prohibited staff from issuing written or oral declarations
related to its past, present, or future operations without prior approval
of the Comité de Direction Collégiale. Violation of the policy could result
in immediate expulsion (*Titre 2, article 8 des status*).[48] The Biafris went
along with the policy, though probably for tactical reasons. Kouchner, for
instance, later confessed that he had agreed to the compromise in order to
get a new public platform to galvanize international action on behalf of
the world's victims.[49] The contradiction between "witnessing" and "caring" became embedded in the organization and would become a source of
debate for years to come.[50]

The similarity of MSF's founding principles to those of the ICRC prevented nobody from noticing that MSF was a political animal.[51] Bernard
Kouchner defiantly asserted, "I am a political militant. How can one be a
humanitarian militant if one is not political? It is the same thing for me."[52]
In response to their less than spectacular first operations, some in the French
media mocked these "medical hippies," advising them to finish their medical degrees instead of playing altruistic revolutionaries.[53] In 1974 a Kurdish
envoy asked Kouchner for MSF's assistance during the Kurdish rebellion in
northern Iraq. Kouchner and many of the Biafris agreed, but Borel, Bernier,
and others argued against the mission because it was an Iraqi internal matter. Ignoring their objections, Kouchner dispatched a team to Iraq, insisting
that its sole purpose was relief. The dispute continued over the next several months, until Kouchner's position carried the day at the MSF's annual
assembly in February 1975.[54] During the early to mid-1970s, MSF sided

with the Palestinians in Lebanon and with the Sandinistas in Nicaragua, prompting Paul Berman to quip that MSF was "a sort of medical wing to the world guerilla movement."[55]

MSF's remarkably rapid rise was a product of having the right kind of politics and the right kind of internationalist message at the right time.[56] MSF's founders, much like the rest of the French left, were experiencing an ennui because of the left's record in Vietnam, China, the Soviet Union, and Cambodia. While Marxist ideologies were falling out of fashion, the traditional French notions of universality, fraternity, and solidarity were still very much alive.[57] MSF tapped into those lingering sentiments. MSF's coming-out moment occurred in May 1977 when Simone Weil, one of France's most esteemed intellectuals and an icon of French identity, visited MSF, symbolically finalizing its arrival and its privileged place in French politics. By the end of the 1970s, MSF had become a "brand."[58] MSF, the bastard child of the ICRC, was now a rival to be reckoned with.

Vietnam

Vietnam shattered the age of innocence among some of the largest U.S.-based aid agencies. Since World War II American agencies such as CARE and Catholic Relief Services had developed a comfortable arrangement with the United States government—the United States generously funded their activities, and these agencies, in return, acted in ways that furthered U.S. foreign policy. This arrangement, though, hinged on the presumption that their interests coincided and that others did not impugn their motives. Having established a comfortable working relationship for the decade following World War II, CARE and CRS, the leading government-funded aid agencies, followed the United States into the quagmire of Vietnam.[59] CRS got involved early and heavily, driven by a strong anticommunist ideology, a desire to support a Saigon government whose leading officials were Catholics, and financial dependence on the United States. One CRS official acknowledged that the agency worked with the CIA and the American Seventh Fleet in 1954 to help with the flight of seven hundred thousand Catholic refugees to South Vietnam. Although it was "justified as a humanitarian gesture...this relief was actually an integral part of a well-conceived strategy of building support for a reactionary Saigon government in order to avert the widely predicted victory of Ho Chi Minh in the promised elections of 1956." Over the next decade CRS continued to support American policies, including a 1965 food distribution program "for the families of the men who 'joined' the so-called Popular Front."[60] CARE International also lined up behind the United States for similar reasons, minus the religious connection.

In general, both groups "endorsed the government's foreign aid strategy to contain communism and promote American ideas and institutions"; assisted the programs to resettle the nearly one million Catholic refugees who fled North Vietnam after the partition in 1954; viewed security and social and economic policies as intertwined; honored official requests to expand refugee relief, to aid military dependents, and to assist civic actions teams with pacification program; and "explicitly stated their hope that aid would help demonstrate America's sincere concern for the Vietnamese and win political support for Diem's regime."[61] Needless to say, CRS and CARE didn't look very independent at all.[62]

In 1967 CRS's complicity in the war was uncovered by a young Catholic journalist, Michael Novack, in the *National Catholic Reporter*. Exposing the depth and breadth of its programs, he accused CRS of various misdeeds, including diverting food supplies intended for civilian refugees to the Popular Forces militia, a village-level civil defense force created by the government of South Vietnam, and ignoring the needy in North Vietnam and focusing exclusively on South Vietnam. He wrote: "Instead of helping to 'win the hearts and minds of the people,'" the charity caused "moral and physical damage to the Vietnamese culture and its people."[63] CRS, he charged, was an instrument of the American military, which was engaged in an immoral war. Although the agency defended itself by claiming that it had to rely on the United States and South Vietnamese military for protection, Novack's exposé caused the agency such embarrassment that it was forced to close its more controversial programs.[64]

Vietnam ended the cozy relationship between the U.S. government and aid agencies.[65] For practically the first time since World War II, the United States was accused as being the cause of, and not the solution to, a humanitarian emergency.[66] From now on, aid agencies would scrutinize whether and how they were implicated in the foreign policy of the United States. In 1987 Larry Pezzullo, president of CRS, summarized the "loss of innocence" story in the following way:

> It is in many ways remarkable that relative stability among potentially conflicting policy goals should have lasted as long as it did. It was not until Vietnam, I think, that the tensions and conflicts present in the mixture became fully apparent in a public sense. The war in Vietnam produced many casualties at home and in the rice paddies, and one of them was the notion that political and humanitarian goals could be uniformly pursued in harmony. From the sixties onward, we came to see the world and our place in it as substantially different from the post–World War II era. Both the government and the private agencies shed their innocence to one degree or another and often found themselves in opposition as to the goals the country should pursue in the conduct of its international relations. This did not mean that

the humanitarian agenda was removed from the foreign policy debate. It did mean, however, that the close identity of view and purpose that official organizations and the private humanitarian groups had largely shared came into serious question and was not infrequently rejected outright. As a result, there has been a general tendency on the part of official policy makers to attempt to more closely integrate humanitarian programs into conventional areas of political and economic focus. Advocates of humanitarian issues, for their part, have tended to assert for those programs a separate and increasingly independent role relatively free of the political calculus.[67]

With Vietnam a new generation of aid workers began to make their presence felt, many wary of the U.S. government's policies. Although referring to the relationship between faith-based agencies and the government, Bruce Nichols' observation applies equally to the entire relief sector: "the humanitarian coalition in the postwar world had worked as long as no one directly questioned the exercise of international U.S. power. When the legitimacy and humanity of that power fell under suspicion, as it did in the case of humanitarian assistance in Vietnam, the consensus between the church and the state fell apart."[68]

Cambodia

Neighboring both North and South Vietnam, Cambodia became one of Vietnam War's victims. The North Vietnamese were using its heavily jungled eastern territory to channel soldiers and supplies to the front line, and the Americans responded with a ferocious bombing campaign. The war destabilized and inflamed Cambodia's political tensions, eventually leading to a civil war, won by the Khmer Rouge in 1975. Armed with a utopian Marxist ideology, the new regime quickly placed its boots across the necks of the Cambodian people. Reports, frequently carried by those lucky few who had managed to escape to Thailand, told of political purges, forced relocation, mass starvation, systematic torture, and a concerted effort to wipe Cambodia free of the educated and professional classes and all evidence of Western technology. The news went largely ignored in the West. The United States and its allies were still licking their wounds from Vietnam and had little interest, and felt no domestic political pressure, to get involved, while Western intellectuals like Noam Chomsky argued that reports of genocide were Western propaganda.[69]

Cambodia finally grabbed their attention, though, in early 1978, when roughly a hundred thousand Vietnamese troops and twenty thousand Cambodian guerrillas invaded, toppled the Khmer Rouge, occupied Pnomh Penh on January 7, 1979, and established a puppet government.[70] There were two emergencies. Thousands of Cambodians had fled the fighting and the advancing Vietnamese troops, escaping to the Thai border and crowding into large camps controlled by the Khmer Rouge, who treated these camps as sanctuaries where they could confiscate international aid in order to supply its troops, sell food to buy weapons, and "recruit" new soldiers.[71] The Thais, Chinese, and Americans discovered that they had a joint interest in containing the Vietnamese and propping up the Khmer Rouge toward that end. The Thais wanted regional stability and to keep the Vietnamese far away, calculating that proxies were the best way to do that. The Chinese had little interest in seeing its longstanding rival, Vietnam, become a larger regional power. Although the U.S. government took little notice of the genocide in Cambodia, the Vietnamese invasion had finally captured its attention, rekindling fears of dominoes tumbling across the region. Under these circumstances, the genocidal Khmer Rouge could serve a useful purpose.[72]

The second emergency was in Cambodia, where a terrorized, brutalized, and emaciated Cambodian society needed all kinds of aid. Following Vietnam's instructions, Hun Sen, Cambodia's new foreign minister, sent a letter to the ICRC and UNICEF, informing them that three million Cambodians had perished (out of a population of seven million), inviting them to survey the situation and requesting aid to address a growing famine that might claim the lives of half of Cambodia's remaining population. Because the Cambodian government wanted to use the aid for its own military and political objectives, it demanded sole responsibility for its distribution and insisted that any agency working in Cambodia could not work in the camps on the Thai border.

Aid agencies were suddenly in a terrible bind. They were desperate to work in Cambodia as reports now portrayed it as a new Holocaust and comparisons were made between Pol Pot and Hitler. And they were themselves contributing to the pressure to act as they were running advertisements stating "two million more before Christmas," and "If we don't act by Tuesday—come Friday they wont be starving—they'll be dead."[73] Yet relief agencies also were reluctant to violate their principles of neutrality and impartiality and capitulate to the Cambodian government's demands. Leading the negotiations were the ICRC and UNICEF, who were attempting to find a way to provide aid without violating their fundamental principles. Although they were prepared to accept Cambodia's demands that it handle relief distribution, they rejected the government's condition that aid agencies not work in the camps on the Thai border.

While the two leading international agencies were sticking to their principles, Oxfam held separate talks with the Cambodian government. In July 1979 Oxfam, the largest British aid agency, though still quite modest in comparison to the largest American agencies, began sending relief into Cambodia. Oxfam's James Howard accompanied the first shipment of supplies and soon thereafter started separate negotiations with the Cambodian government; eventually he agreed that Oxfam would: hand over the aid to the government, which would then distribute the aid "in co-operation" with Oxfam; not work at the Thai-Cambodian border; and not cooperate with the ICRC or UNICEF.[74] Howard broke with Oxfam's policy of neutrality and impartiality, parted ways with the rest of the NGOs, and undercut the positions of the ICRC and UNICEF for several reasons. There was genuine desire to respond to a situation that had become utterly intolerable. There was considerable pressure from the British public to act. There also were more earthly temptations: Howard imagined that Oxfam would become a leader of a consortium of NGOs in this high-profile event. But, like in many emergency situations, there were no good choices, and the general decision on with whom to work depended heavily on which political situation one found least politically objectionable.[75] Reflecting on the choice of working in Cambodia or in the camps, MSF's Rony Brauman observed: "The choice was…not between a political position and a neutral position, but between two political positions: one active and the other by default."[76] In any event, Oxfam earned the ire of many relief agencies that refused to capitulate to Vietnam's demands, and while at the time Howard could justify the decision based on the tremendous needs of the Cambodian people, later it became known that those on the border were far worse off than those who had remained in Cambodia, as they could forage for food and begin farming the land.[77]

Cambodia had a major impact on MSF. For much of the 1970s, MSF, like many of the relief organizations of the time, was providing temporary assistance. Indeed, Kouchner held that a primary purpose of relief was to generate publicity and international action; that is, MSF's relief operations might save some lives directly, but the real value in the operations was their ability to attract concerted action. The problem was that the circumstances facing refugees were hardly temporary: with nowhere to go, no chance to be resettled elsewhere, and no opportunity to return home, these emergency camps were becoming the basis for semi-permanent cities. One of the implications of this change was that refugees were less in need of emergency relief and more in need of longer-term medical care. In short, the circumstances and needs of the refugees were changing, and MSF doctors that were once used to serving in emergencies were now becoming the refugee camp doctors.[78] Just shy of its tenth anniversary, by the end of the 1970s MSF was experiencing a growing disconnect between its original vision and the challenges it was currently facing in the field. The looming question was: would MSF be an organization that made noise and saved lives in the process, or an organization that saved lives and occasionally made noise?

These tensions came to the fore as a consequence of Cambodia and were played out between Bernard Kouchner, who defended the status quo, and

Claude Malhuret, who was the spokesperson for change.[79] A product of the 1968 revolution, Malhuret worked for MSF in Cambodia in the late 1970s, running a refugee camp virtually on his own for an entire year, struggling to get supplies and to attend to the basic needs of the inhabitants. He returned to Paris with accusations and challenges. MSF was an empty machine, he argued, spending too much time preening for the cameras during high-profile emergencies and failing to realize that the refugee camps were the sites of future dramas, indeed tragedies. Its choices were costing lives. According to Malhuret, MSF staff were "working without a net, diving into the sea without knowing how to swim. We lacked the means, equipment, and financing. We were leaving too late for want of money, and arriving too late."[80] MSF, he challenged, needed to become more professional and bureaucratic. It had to become "a perfect machine, a solid structure, equipped with means, with our materials, and with our emergency logic."[81] It had to create medical teams that were capable of responding to fleeting emergencies and of providing long term-assistance. As opposed to the tendency of MSF to send amateurs to the field to play doctor for a few weeks, it needed trained professionals who would could stay for months at a time. Consequently, MSF needed to rethink the meaning of "volunteers" and consider paying staff. MSF's makeover would not come cheap, and it would have to develop a sophisticated fundraising capacity. He even hinted that perhaps staff should not speak out publicly in order not to jeopardize their ability to stay in the camps.[82]

The Biafris understood that Malhuret was calling not for modest reforms but rather for a fundamental transformation of "their" organization. Many of the accusations rang true. They knew that MSF was far from a well-organized bureaucracy, had a minimal administrative structure, sent physicians into the field without proper training or support, and permitted staff to have a transient lifestyle. They also knew that if MSF was to become more effective on the ground, then it had to become more professional. Indeed, in 1972 they had debated whether to emphasize "urgency medicine," brief interventions in natural catastrophes and war zones, or "developmental medicine," which implied a semi-permanent presence that addressed the lack of medicines, medical assistance, capacity-building, and basic family planning and preventive health.[83] Kouchner successfully argued that while the two styles of medicine could complement each other, MSF does not do "developmental medicine."[84]

Cambodia re-ignited this debate, but now under very different circumstances. Repeating many of their earlier reasons, Kouchner and his allies argued that professionalization and bureaucratization would harm the organization's revolutionary, nimble, and heretical orientation; suffocate its esprit de corps and camaraderie; overwhelm its improvisational tactics; ruin its voluntary ethos; turn MSF staff into bureaucrats of misery and technocrats of charity; and, perhaps the cruelest cut of all, transform MSF into an international development agency.[85]

Slowly but surely, the tide turned against the Biafris.[86] In 1978 the General Assembly of MSF elected a pro-Malhuret slate and handed the Biafris a major defeat.[87] A few months later another development served as the vehicle for the final blow. North Vietnam's victory in 1975 led many Vietnamese to flee the communist government, mostly by boat, which quickly became floating prisons because they lacked adequate water or food and were vulnerable to pirates; neighboring countries refused to allow them to land.[88] The plight of the Vietnamese boat people became a huge event in France. A committee formed to consign a rescue ship, and France's towering intellectual figures Jean-Paul Sartre and Raymond Aron, in a very emotional and media-saturated event, jointly backed the mission.[89] The committee then turned to Kouchner to help organize the action, who accepted the challenge and threw his weight and MSF's name behind *Un Bateau pour le Vietnam—A Boat for Vietnam*.

The Malhuret camp used the planned operation to attack Kouchner and his position. Some members of MSF resented Kouchner's unilateral tendencies and showboating theatrics. This was not about rescuing those stranded at sea, they argued, but feeding Kouchner's ego. Some radical members saw the boat as a swipe at the French communists and questioned its "progressive" character. At this time many Europeans, and particularly MSF, blamed the turmoil in the region on the United States and viewed the Vietnamese as the underdog. Indeed, when President Jimmy Carter deployed the American navy to try to rescue the Vietnamese, suddenly MSF and the American military looked to be in common cause.[90] Lastly, and perhaps most damning, many argued that the boat might do more harm than good because it would encourage people to flee. Emmanuelli, a member of the Malhuret alliance, published an essay ridiculing Kouchner's proposal, suggesting that it was hype without substance, would waste valuable time; would take resources away from where it was really needed (in Cambodia); would save few, if any, lives; and might even cause more suffering if it encouraged more Vietnamese to take to the high seas in search of freedom.[91]

On May 5, 1979, the MSF annual assembly overwhelmingly supported the Malhuret camp, and its opposition to the boat, signaling that MSF was about to enter a new chapter in its development. Emmanuelli's reasons for siding against Kouchner and with the Young Turks nicely captures the forces in favor of change:

At MSF another generation had joined the historic founders at the reigns, and desired to equally share the decision-making: an affair of democracy. These men and these women were our children. They had believed in M.S.F. We had recruited them, they had left on missions in our name. Instructed by our cares, they had worked in the refugee camps in Thailand, discovering with astonishment an original medicine, new situations, and they had learned a lot. They had lived under our banner, in the mud of the rice fields, in trying conditions and in isolation, among the escapees of the Khmer Rouge horror. They had stayed in the field, in sum, more than a single among us had ever done. Coming to maturity in May 1968, they did not have the same values, not the same references, not the same lives of saints nor the same past to exorcise. The Sartre-Aron reconciliation left them unmoved.[92]

The assembly voted to unleash the forces of professionalization and bureaucratization, and, in a dig at Kouchner, proclaimed that "MSF cannot in a single case serve for personal promotion. All MSF members speaking in the name of the organization cannot do it except as mandated by the organization."[93] Kouchner and his allies stormed out of the assembly, forced out of the organization they helped to found. In January 1980 Kouchner built a new platform, Médicins du Monde.

Kouchner's departure hardly ended MSF's taste for guerrilla theater or resolved the tensions relating to a desire to speak out, to provide relief, and to remain outside of political currents.[94] Soon after Kouchner's departure the Malhuret camp tried to bring more attention to the plight of the Cambodian refugees and denounce the Vietnamese-backed Cambodian government's conditions attached to the acceptance of aid, a position that aligned it with the United States and the CIA. Casting aside the possible dangers to its image and any future operation in Cambodia, it joined with the International Rescue Committee, which was rumored to be in cahoots with the State Department, to sponsor a heavily publicized march. On February 6, 1980, fifty people, including MSF doctors, artists, writers, parliamentarians, and actors, staged a march at the border. It was known as "Marche pour la survie au Cambodge" (March for the Survival of Cambodia).[95] Afterward Claude Malhuret and Rony Brauman, two lead organizers of the event, came to regret aspects of the march and became increasingly sensitive to the need to bear witness without being too closely associated with particular states.

Yet the new leaders of MSF were hardly averse to politics, and the ideological crosscurrents that were always present at the agency erupted in part because of the march and in part because of the increasingly anticommunist, pro–human rights position adopted by many of its new leaders.[96] MSF had a reputation for radical politics, partly owing to the fact that many of its original members circulated easily with French communist and Trotskyite parties and supported many newly independent Third World countries. But there was a strong anti-authoritarian and anti-totalitarian streak within the organization, which contributed to an anti–Third Worldist and anticommunist stance. This position, though, emerged less from ideology than from its experiences in the field. Nine out of ten refugees were fleeing communist regimes, which meant that any concern with the causes of refu-gee flight flowed easily into anticommunist views.[97] But MSF was not only anticommunist. It also was "anti–Third Worldist." Brauman, Malhuret, and other MSF leaders resented what they viewed as the left's knee-jerk romance with Third World movements, many of which were causing refu-gee crises and humanitarian emergencies.

In a daring move, MSF's leadership decided, as Brauman put it, to "weaken the white man's bad conscience, dispute the myth that all the mis-ery in the Third World was solely the fault of the West and to consider ways to work against these new forms of totalitarianism." Specifically, in November 1982 Brauman proposed creating an association that would reflect critically and openly on the "Third World," and in January 1985 they created Liberté sans Frontières. Influenced by Hannah Arendt's and Raymond Aron's distinction between human rights and collective rights, Brauman, Malhuret, and others wanted to defend a liberal conception of human rights.[98] Brauman reflected:

> We created this with a clear intention of reaffirming and elaborating on our
> anti-totalitarian position. Between the March [for Cambodia] and this, MSF
> was involved in almost every war zone and refugee camp, gaining a wealth
> of experience. The world before our eyes had a very precise appearance:
> the violence and sometimes ravages of Soviet and communist expansion ap-
> peared to us to be the primordial cause of the misfortune in which we were
> intervening. What we had first noticed in Cambodia was verified elsewhere.
> These were the facts that we wanted to raise in the debate over international
> aid, which was very profoundly impacted by Third Worldism. Although
> some accused us as being of the new right, it was the Third Worldism that
> supported dictators that was the true right.[99]

Intended to bring together the political left and right to combat all forms of totalitarianism, MSF quickly garnered a reputation for being anti-Soviet, pro-American, and pro-Israeli. This development proved to be immensely controversial, especially since many MSF members identified themselves with "Third Worldism" and Liberté sans Frontières's overtly political char-acter violated MSF's charter. It closed its doors in Spring 1989, just as the Cold War was winding down, communism was about to implode, and human rights would become a major force in world politics.

Ethiopia

Ethiopia provided further evidence that when politics and aid clash, the lat-ter will become an instrument of the former. Ethiopia started as a famine that went largely unnoticed by the Western news sources and then, quite suddenly, became the famine that turned aid into a cause. In part because of an early warning system that aid agencies had put into place a decade before and in response to a previous famine, by 1983 they were increasingly aware of the early signs of famine and, accordingly, appealed to their governments to act. However, Cold War dynamics threw cold water on any kind of spur to action by Western governments.[100] Because Ethiopia was allied with the Soviet Union, when U.S. aid agencies appealed to the Reagan administration for aid, they discovered little concern.[101]

When help belatedly arrived, it was accompanied by the sort of media frenzy that must have made Bernard Kouchner envious beyond belief. The media had shown little interest until an unforeseeable episode triggered an international groundswell of interest. On October 23, 1984, BBC ran a story of the famine, and the combination of the commentary by the BBC's Michael Buerk, who spoke in religious terms to describe the horror, and the searing video by cameraman Mohammed Amin, jarred the Western consciousness. Suddenly the famine in Ethiopia became *the* story and *the* cause. Newspapers, newsweeklies, and television stations that previously had been indifferent now rushed to the refugee camps to chronicle what starvation did to the body and the soul. Caught in the media's web, as well, were the images of heroic aid workers persevering against the odds, representing the conscience of the West. Aid now becomes a cause célèbre. Celebrities lined up to demonstrate their compassion. In addition to Bob Geldof's Live Aid concerts in 1985, Michael Jackson and Lionel Richie's song "We Are the World" (recorded by the ad hoc supergroup USA for Africa) became a worldwide hit, raising millions of dollars for famine relief and providing a soundtrack for the dying. Aid had gone wild, and aid agencies began to realize their considerable power when they partnered with the media and celebrities.[102]

All this aid saved lives, but it also had a downside. To put it charitably, not all of this money was being well spent. Ethiopia attracted more aid agencies than any previous emergency, some venerable and some overnight creations by well-meaning volunteers, and the combination of the swirling sums of money and scores of aid agencies working for the first time in a war zone generated considerable waste and duplication.[103] Not only might this aid not have been saving as many lives as it might, but it also might have been, inadvertently, prolonging the suffering. Much like the Cambodian government, the Ethiopian government manipulated aid for its own purposes. At the time Addis Ababa was confronting secessionist rebellions in Tigre and Eritrea, and it began to use aid as an instrument for its military and political campaign, including using the promise of aid to drive out suspect populations, what we now call ethnic cleansing, and to resettle Ethiopians on state-run farms that employed forced labor. Most aid agencies failed to realize, or did their best to ignore, the extent to which they were being manipulated by the Ethiopian government. One former Oxfam employee placed the myopia of his agency squarely on its commitment to radical politics. "The idea was revolution through development. This extraordinarily optimistic ideology...became so strong that aid agencies did not turn away from their developmentalist beliefs, even when poor people were suffering from the effects of famine."[104]

Although it took a while for it to realize the game that was being played, once it did MSF began to object to the Ethiopian government's policies. Reminding him of the Holocaust and the ICRC's policy of silence in the face of mass murder during World War II and Biafra, the forced deportations and labor camps had become unbearable for Brauman.[105] Invited to a press club to speak on humanitarian aid and the difficulties of relief, Brauman spontaneously erupted that "we serve as an alibi, a folding screen. If that continues, we will be obliged to leave."[106] MSF had crossed a line, publically criticizing a government whose cooperation it needed to operate. Not only did Brauman refuse to retract his statements, he repeated the accusation, daring the government to evict MSF. On December 2, 1985, the government granted MSF its wish, ordering the agency out of the country. MSF tried to rally support from the other fifty organizations on the ground, but all refused, preferring to stay quiet and thus being allowed to remain in Ethiopia. For Brauman, Ethiopia offered several lessons regarding the potential negative implications of aid. It signaled "that humanitarianism can serve a murderous political project, and that the interest of victims is not necessarily at the end of humanitarian action."[107] It warned that while neutrality might be seen as the sine qua non of being apolitical, neutrality that breeds silence can serve the powerful, reducing the aid worker to the role of a "ventriloquist" of the powerful.[108] It had to be constantly on guard against the possibility that international solidarity in the name of humanitarianism could buttress a Stalinist approach to modernization, contributing to the destruction of the very people it had come to help.[109]

An episode at the close of the 1980s further exposed some of the fault lines underneath the different agencies when it came to basic questions of humanitarian assistance. In 1988 Kouchner, who at the time was the French secretary of state for humanitarian action, campaigned for a United Nations resolution approving of a "right to intervene," which eventually became United Nations General Assembly Resolution 43/131. Not everyone celebrated. The ICRC's Frederic Maurice wrote that this was the wrong law at the wrong time.[110] Although it is difficult not to detect some jealousy and worry that ICRC's traditional role as the place to regulate all things humanitarian was being usurped, he raised two objections. One was that the UN was the wrong forum to have such discussions because what states created, they could just as easily destroy. Also, humanitarian action was becoming dangerously tied to state action at the possible cost of independence for aid agencies. Referring to the experiences of Biafra, Cambodia, and Ethiopia, Maurice warned of a "permanent failure of those who try to humanize war and attenuate its effects. Developing a humanitarian methodology and project is difficult because of the closeness, within a narrow space, of overweening ambition, crushing historical and individual experience, and political constraints which lies outside the sphere of influence of the humanitarian endeavor. Mysticism, paranoia, and the temptation to assume power have always been the aberrations and canker of humanitarianism."[111] I suspect he took little pleasure in being so prophetic.

PART III

The Age of Liberal Humanitarianism

8

⁓

It's a Humanitarian's World

IN RETROSPECT, the readiness of so many sober politicians and intellectuals to treat the end of the Cold War as a miracle that would usher in a more glorious world seems more than a little bit baffling. But at the time it was understandable. Extrapolating from the history of Great Power competitions during the Cold War, most experts had direly predicted that the balance of terror between the Soviet Union and the United States would end in a major war, perhaps even a nuclear exchange that might presage the end of days. Yet the Soviets and the Americans amazingly ended their rivalry in a fit of cooperation and goodwill. Whereas once the belief was that the best way to prepare for peace was to prepare for war, the new sentiment in security thinking was that preparing for war only made war more likely and that the right mix of security institutions could produce dependable expectations of peaceful change. After decades of worrying about a nuclear Armageddon, the West discovered that it had become a zone of peace.

As the Cold War exited the global stage, international liberalism entered, and a greater contrast could hardly be imagined. Whereas the Cold War coddled authoritarian governments, the rise of international liberalism meant a new day for democracy. The third wave of democratization began in the 1980s, but it became a bona fide fad only with the extraordinary rise in the number of new democracies during the 1990s. Whereas the Cold War had stunted the possibility of truly internationalized markets, international liberalism unleashed the simultaneous process of economic globalization and economic liberalization. Even the world's two major socialist countries, the Soviet Union and China, got market fever. Liberalism worked wonders. It was good for individuals. It was good for societies. Democracies and markets were the touchstones of human freedom, human freedom entailed human rights, human rights included the rule of law, and the rule of law was essential for economic and political liberalization. It was good for global security and prosperity. Liberal states are more peaceful toward their neighbors and their societies, are more trustworthy, and protect the autonomy and liberty of the individual through a culture of law and human rights. Democracy, markets, and the rule of law: if not the holy trinity then at least the troika of the liberal world order.

The Western powers led a campaign to try to extend and deepen international liberalism, and rather like the missionaries of the nineteenth century, they worked with the confidence of believers and the urgency of those who were racing against time. They were enjoying the benefits of liberalism and wanted to share those benefits with the have-nots. And, there was little time to lose, because at the very moment that the world was celebrating their new chapter of peace, it began to catch a glimpse of a darker future.

For all its benefits, the end of the Cold War seemingly unleashed a flurry of pent-up violence. For decades Washington and Moscow had tried to maintain and extend their power by gathering as many allies as possible in the Third World, and they paid handsomely for their support. These Third World governments, in turn, would keep most for themselves and then divide the rest among military and key domestic elites as they created a coalition for the status quo. With the end of the Cold War, the superpowers cut off their clients, leaving these regimes alone to face their long-suffering societies, and the results were deadly. These were not run-of-the-mill wars. These were "new wars." The simultaneous decline of the state's ability to provide security or perform basic governance tasks and the rise of paramilitary organizations led to wars with no "fronts," engulfing cities, towns, and villages. Civilians were no longer a tragic consequence of war but rather war's intended targets. New terminologies were invented to try to capture these obscene developments, including "complex humanitarian emergencies" and "ethnic cleansing," but the categories never did justice to the horrific realities.

These patterns of violence produced a shift in the meaning of international peace and security. Whereas during the Cold War international security implied militarized disputes between states, afterward—and in response to the growing perception that domestic conflicts had produced collapsed states and trigger-happy regions—policymakers and scholars gravitated toward an expanded understanding of security. Traditional military threats still existed, but now there was growing attention to economic security, environmental security, health security, food security, and terrorism. The state was once assumed to be society's protector, but the once-overlooked reality that the state was often a major source of insecurity now became the newfound conventional wisdom. National security gave ground to human security.[1]

The UN became the focal point for discussing how to manage the new security threats. There *were* more civil wars, ethnic conflicts, and domestic meltdowns than ever before. Because neither the United States nor Russia felt that it had proprietary rights over these conflicts in godforsaken places, they now were making it onto the UN Security Council's agenda.[2] In response to a request from the UN Security Council, the secretary-general's office produced *An Agenda for Peace,* an ambitious and forward-thinking blueprint to give the UN the tools for conflict prevention, peacekeeping, and peacebuilding. This document foretold the UN's about face—whereas once it focused on traditional threats to international security and dutifully observed sovereignty and the principle of noninterference, it now focused on violence within states.

There were two general conceptual lines of argument for securing lives at risk: protection and prevention. Whereas once the Security Council ignored the Biafras and the Cambodias on the formal grounds that they were not matters of international security and therefore not its job, it began redefining its mandate and looking into forms of humanitarian intervention. Humanitarian intervention had never been very popular with Third World states, who had frequently been the object of such "humane" gestures during colonialism, and the concept fell into greater disrepute during the Cold War, as the Soviets and Americans claimed that their military actions, by definition, were humanitarian and for the greater global good. But now, with the end of the Cold War and in the face of successive assaults on the human conscience, there was a growing sentiment that the world could and should do something about them. Humanitarian intervention was no longer out of bounds. The first step occurred in response to the plight of the Kurds in northern Iraq following the 1991 Gulf War. In his farewell report to the UN General Assembly, UN Secretary-General Perez de Cuellar referred to the UN's creation of safe havens in northern Iraq for the Kurds as an example of "the collective obligation of States to bring relief and redress in human rights emergencies."[3] The UN's next major step occurred the following year and in response to the famine in Somalia; the UN Security Council, for virtually the first time in its history, cited the famine and the humanitarian emergency—and not its bailiwick of international peace and security.

It was not enough to protect vulnerable populations from the immediate threat of death. The world community also needed to think about preventing conflict, instability, and bloodshed. If those in the humanitarian sector liked to remind everyone about the virtues of teaching a man to fish, those in security studies were equally adamant that an ounce of prevention was worth a pound of cure. As stated in *Agenda for Peace,* the world needed tools to detect crises before they occurred and to stop crises from turning violent, and a veritable cottage industry emerged. In addition to wanting to act before it was too late, there was a growing desire to try to help states make that difficult transition from civil war to civil society. In the new nomenclature of the day, "failed states" needed to be saved.[4] Although most of these states had never worked all that well in the first place, at least not for the governed, there was a growing clamor at the United Nations and elsewhere that the international community had to do more than treat symptoms—it also had to address the "root causes" of conflict.

There were myriad reasons for a turn of events that bore an eerie resemblance to the Age of Imperial Humanitarianism. There were those who wanted to do more than provide the proverbial "bed for the night" or care for the "well-fed dead." As Kofi Annan wrote at the end of his tenure as secretary-general, "If states are fragile, the peoples of the world will not enjoy the security, development, and justice that are their right. Therefore, one of the great challenges of the new millennium is to ensure that all states are strong enough to meet the many challenges that they face."[5] There also were compelling arguments linking failed states to international security. A running theme in many discussions of the post–Cold War order was that a stable international order is premised on a society of stable states.[6] Following up on his claim of an end of history, Francis Fukuyama wrote, "Since the end of the Cold War, weak and failing states have arguably become the single most important problem for international order."[7] Stable states make stable neighborhoods.

The UN, states, and even once state-phobic nongovernmental organizations were now behind state-building. There was no single theory about what created a stable state or what the causes of conflict were, but international state-builders used Western states for their blueprint, as they develop new tools, techniques, and templates for helping states achieve the peace and prosperity enjoyed by those in the West. Humanitarianism and security collapsed under peacebuilding, which became known as "liberal" peacebuilding because of the emphasis on the importance of markets, democracy, and human rights for curing states of their ills and creating more peaceful and progressive societies.[8] Liberals might be identified with extolling the virtues of autonomy, independence, and liberty, but not when it comes to peacebuilding. Liberal peacebuilding is a highly invasive project; the expanded list of factors associated with a stable peace means that nearly all of the features of state and society have become objects of intervention. It would begin with democracy. But democratization cannot exist without a host of other elements, including a free press, an independent judiciary, an educated population, a strong middle class, markets, the rule of law, and basic respect for human rights.[9] Building states for peace and progress, a nineteenth-century motto, now had a late-twentieth-century rendering.

One last development in security affairs deserves mention: terrorism. Many parts of the world did not have to wait until September 11, 2001, to experience firsthand the traumatizing and destructive capacity of terrorism. Just because it had not affected the United States to the same extent did not mean that the threat did not exist. On September 11, the United States unforgettably joined the ranks of the terrorized and in one fell swoop moved terrorism to the top of the global security agenda. Yet the impact of this on humanitarianism is debatable. There are many who write as if humanitarianism was the first casualty of the global war on terror.[10] While there is no denying its effects, my view is that it did not alter but rather accentuated already existing trends. The Bush administration's statement that the "United States today is threatened less by conquering states than we are by weak and failing ones" could almost have been written by the UN secretary-general's office.[11] The view from London and Washington that because failed states bred and coddled terrorist networks, the campaign against terrorism had to include trying to save failed states was simply restating the received view on the relationship between domestic and international order. When Washington began embedding humanitarian assistance in its foreign and military policy, it was continuing a venerable tradition practiced by Democratic and Republican administrations alike. In short, humanitarian organizations, well-intentioned states, and other well-meaning accomplices started a trend, and only when the Bush administration (and other governments) used similar rhetoric to justify their actions did they begin to worry about what they had wrought.

With the end of the Cold War also emerged the orienting concept of globalization. The heated debate over how to define, measure, and assess its benefits and consequences largely assumed that the world was being globalized, like it or not. Globalization, in Thomas Friedman's oft-repeated view, was "flattening" the world. It was creating winners and losers (or, at least in Friedman's view, some who really benefited and some who benefited but just not as much). And because it is better to be a winner than a loser, and because governments have no choice but to play the game of globalization, they needed to compete to be a winner. In order to win, the state that had become supersized after five decades of gluttony would have to become lean and fit. This downsizing was particularly evident in the general assault on the protections afforded society, often won after difficult political struggles. States began shedding their welfare "burden."[12] The state now claimed that basic protections and services were properly the purview of, and more efficiently delivered by, NGOs, faith-based agencies, and even the private sector. At the same moment that states were articulating that the international community had a responsibility to protect when the state failed in its responsibility, states were developing public policies that let their citizens know that in the new "ownership society," they owned their hardship.

In addition to these changes in the forces of destruction and production, there was an equally stunning change in the forces of compassion. It is difficult to know exactly what accounts for the apparent surge of concern for distant strangers. Unlike previous moments that occurred in the aftermath of mass violence and the attempt by the living to atone for the dead, the peaceful end of the Cold War provided no comparable catalyst (although, four years later, Rwanda would). However, states did treat the wondrous end to the Cold War in nearly religious terms, particularly evident when they filed into the international community's church, the United Nations, and spoke of a new global spirit. More tangibly, the revolution in information and transportation technologies created a growing desire and opportunity to help the world's vulnerable. Personified by the "CNN effect," ignorance was no longer an excuse in a world of twenty-four-hour news stations, the World Wide Web, and satellite technology. In addition to knowing facts in real time, it was increasingly possible to act in real time because of radical improvements in transportation technology and logistical capacity. The combination of a growing awareness and capacity contributed to a growing sense of causal responsibility. Some argued that "globalization," namely, activities by the West, was contributing to the breakdown of societies; under these circumstances, its sins of commission compelled it to act. For others, because they possessed both knowledge and ability, the failure to act would constitute a sin of omission. The tremendous leap in the machinery was a consequence of newfound responsibilities and, once the machinery was in place, the pressure to do something increased.

These changes in the boundaries of the community were both a cause and a consequence of new interpretations of sovereignty and the ascendance of human rights. States were increasingly told that sovereignty was not a right but a privilege that depended on how it treated its citizens. In short, there were new standards of civilization. If a state did not live up to those standards, then its sovereignty might be suspended and it might become the object of intervention. There were, as Kofi Annan famously put it, two sovereignties: a sovereignty of peoples and a sovereignty of states.[13] Humanity, he and others were observing, was part of sovereignty.

The ascendance of a human-centered discourse was vividly evident in the area of human rights. For a good deal of the Cold War human rights had a very small following. Third World states disliked the concept because they wanted to keep the West's laws off its body, to protect sovereignty's soft underbelly, and to deal with their internal rivals as they saw fit. And the Americans and the Soviets gave human rights a bad name as they supported violators around the world. Human rights organizations like Amnesty International were novel precisely because there were few of them, and Amnesty focused on political prisoners, a thin sliver of political rights. The human rights agenda got a shot in the arm in the mid-1970s from the Helsinki Process, which identified a basket of values that included human rights, and a further boost from President Ronald Reagan, who championed human rights not simply because of a self-interested desire to whip the "evil empire" but also because he genuinely believed that liberty, American-style, was a fundamental human value.

In the 1990s, however, rights talk seeped into every nook and cranny of world affairs. The UN Security Council began to articulate the importance of human rights, to link human rights and security, to invest peacekeeping operations units with human rights units, and to ensure that human rights were part of postconflict endeavors. Already existing humanitarian organizations more fully linked their areas of relief and protection to discourses of rights. Development organizations like United Nations Development Programme (UNDP) began to reformulate development as a "right." Once limited to political rights, human rights expanded to include women's rights, civil rights, religious rights, and even economic rights. Genuine security was redefined to include human rights. Human rights required both negative and positive liberty. The state had to be restrained from violating the liberty and life of its citizens, but individuals also needed capabilities to realize their potential as they defined it.[14] In general, the discourse of human rights was promoting the idea of universality, empowering individuals who could help to dilute the power and politics of states, creating a human-centered approach that dissolved traditional left-right divisions, and helping invest the international community with objective, universal, values.[15]

These changes in the forces of destruction, production, and compassion ushered in a new chapter of humanitarianism. A strong word of caution, however. Biographers writing the recent history of humanitarianism and today's aid workers give the impression that the convulsive changes that rocked the world beginning in the 1990s forced aid agencies to confront, for nearly the first time, a series of questions, dilemmas, and controversies. There was, in this view, life before and after the end of the Cold War. The previous chapters have, with any luck, ended such sentimentality and historical amnesia. Yet the end of the Cold War *was* a turning point, as the intensification of many already existing trends reshaped the governance of humanitarianism in two significant ways.

There was a shift in the purpose of humanitarianism, expanding from symptoms to root causes and becoming avowedly political in the process. Although certain branches of humanitarianism had always included a desire to do more than treat symptoms, ever since the ICRC's birth in 1863 humanitarian action became closely associated with life-saving relief owing to natural and humanly created disasters, and those who wanted to treat causes adopted other banners, such as development. But now the concept of humanitarianism was becoming associated with these grander goals. As early as 1992, UN Secretary-General Boutros Boutros-Ghali argued that there was a link between relief and development, and that relief must feed into development and the crisis of development caused the need for relief.[16] Aid agencies that were once oriented around a single goal were now becoming multidimensional, and these multidimensional agencies were searching to improve their coordination and coherence. Whereas once fields of activity such as emergency aid, development, human rights, and conflict prevention operated independently, beginning in the 1990s organizations and think tanks were making new connections between them and proposing new ways to integrate them, most famously the relief-development continuum. Then there came postconflict peacebuilding, which made it even more difficult to separate humanitarianism from other areas of life. Humanitarianism had always struggled to police the boundaries between itself and the world of politics and power, but beginning in the 1990s many aid agencies developed something akin to an open borders policy, operating with the assumption that they could humanize the world before the world politicized them.[17]

Given this rapidly changing world, it is no surprise that humanitarianism went through an identity crisis. Acting as the high priest of the community, the ICRC tried to keep the label of humanitarianism for emergency relief and fought against reformers who wanted to expand the concept to include all kinds of activities that might improve the world. The emergency and alchemical camps entered into a debate over the fundamental meaning of humanitarianism—including its basic purpose, its guiding principles, and its relationship to politics.

A humanitarian governance that was previously defined by a relatively loose association of organizations that occasionally coordinated their activities and was bankrolled by shadow states yielded to a more centralized network of states, international organizations, nongovernmental organizations, and part-time members such as foundations and corporations. A century of growing involvement by states and international organizations in the delivery of assistance now came fully into view. Until World War I nongovernmental organizations virtually monopolized relief activity. Between the wars states exhibited some interest, though the demise of the High Commissioner for Refugees and the International Relief Union were proof of their lackluster support. After World War II, states became silent partners, prepared to provide funding but not much else and always trying to ensure that aid did not violate their interests. States had established an array of emergency and reconstruction agencies after World War II to tend to Europe, and these had all gone global over the next several decades. But there were certain lines these organizations would not cross, namely, the internal affairs of states, most notably when they refused to get involved in Biafra. There were momentary exceptions. In 1971 the UNHCR became a center of action during the Indo-Pakistani conflict, and that same year the UN General Assembly created the UN Disaster Relief Organization.[18] However, in a report delivered around this time, the UN confessed that "the United Nations system is not geared for action of this kind, nor is it realistic to suppose that given its structure, it could become so."[19] Recoiling from new opportunities, the UN made it clear that while it would be willing to use its good offices during times of crises and to help negotiate access to victims during emergencies, the Red Cross movement and nongovernmental organizations remained the workhorses.[20]

With the end of the Cold War, the UN system and regional organizations became more deeply involved in all aspects of humanitarianism. In 1992 the UN passed Resolution 46/182, which pledged to strengthen the UN's humanitarian capacities and created a Department of Humanitarian Affairs. Already existing international humanitarian organizations such as the UNHCR became increasingly visible, as they were working in emergency areas and bringing relief to people rather than waiting for people to cross a border to get to relief. International organizations that once limited themselves to development, including the UNDP and the World Bank, now joined the cause. Regional organizations became players as well, including the European Community Humanitarian Aid Office (ECHO), created in 1992. As the world became fonder of humanitarianism, it became too important to be left to the initiatives of loosely networked nongovernmental organizations and had to be centralized.

The trends in humanitarian governance toward a more ambitious agenda and a willingness to work more closely with states inflamed the tensions between humanitarian organizations and the powerful, on the one hand, and the powerless, on the other. Emergency organizations had always been concerned about their association with states, and so, too, had alchemical organizations, though to a much lesser extent; in both cases they huddled around the principles of impartiality, neutrality, and independence to ensure that they were not mistaken for states or others with political interests. However, the tumult of the 1990s and the growing willingness of states to support various forms of humanitarian action caused relief agencies to reconsider what kind of relationship they might and should have. The debates were particularly pronounced over the use of force. Because of the (apparent) growth in the number of possible candidates for an intervention, the growing willingness of states to use their troops to do the right thing, and the grudging acceptance by relief agencies that force might be a necessary evil to fight a greater evil, relief agencies found themselves trying to find a principled formula for deciding when and how to support humanitarian intervention. The problem was that states expected something in return for their kindness, and it was not always clear to aid agencies whether the cost to the victims (and to themselves) would be too high. Many aid agencies began to feel suffocated, and began crying "humanitarian space" to extricate themselves from this deathly embrace.

Yet humanitarian agencies appeared to be rather oblivious to the fact that while states were encroaching on their space, they were doing much the same thing with respect to their recipients. As they were becoming more "political," they were attempting to change more areas of life—and thus accumulating more power over the vulnerable. Yet this breach of politics also was accompanied by a form of anti-politics. After a series of horrendous experiences, most importantly the failure in Rwanda, aid agencies undertook an inventory of all that had gone wrong and began to introduce a series of reforms that were intended to improve their capacity to protect and prevent. But these reforms were largely driven by the international experts and rarely included the views of the "victims." To be sure, aid agencies knew that there were various normative and practical reasons to include local populations in decisions that were supposed to be for their benefit; the discourse of stakeholders, local knowledge, and participation were reactions to the belief that the failure to be inclusive was besmirching their democratic credentials and had become a primary reason for program failure. Yet, even the forgiving members of the sector acknowledged that there was a major gap between what they said and what they did. Or, to put it in slightly more worrying terms, the paternalism became buried in the machinery of humanitarianism.

9

⤲

Armed for Humanity

VIOLENCE IS part of humanitarianism's history. The violence we usually associate with humanitarianism is the violence that causes humanitarian action. But there also is the violence deployed in the name of humanitarianism. As famously observed by Hannah Arendt, the first signs that humanitarianism could legitimate bloodshed occurred with the French Revolution, when proclamations of humanity, fraternity, and liberty inspired beheadings, riotous behavior, and mass killings. Some of the greatest crimes of the last few centuries have been carried out in the name of alleviating suffering and improving human welfare. Violence also has been justified for protecting those whose lives are at immediate risk from malevolent forces, a notion closely associated with humanitarian intervention. Not everyone who claims to be a humanitarian shares the same views regarding the use of force for protecting lives. Some see humanitarian intervention as a necessary possibility. Others ridicule the idea of humanitarian war as an oxymoron or insist that if war must be waged in the defense of human rights, it should be called anything but humanitarian.

These debates regarding the relationship between humanitarian action and the use of force are as old as humanitarianism itself, but in the last decade of the last century they became a point of controversy among humanitarian organizations. This is not the place to review the legal, political, and ethical debate about the legitimacy of humanitarian intervention, but the growing acceptance of humanitarian intervention brings to the surface various tensions inherent in the relationship between states and humanitarian organizations as well as other dilemmas that aid agencies confront when they feel that they cannot live with and cannot live without states.[1]

There was no single position among the aid agencies, or even much consistency within an agency as it moved from one emergency to another. Instead, their reaction depended on the specifics of the situation, how they defined "humanitarian" and whether they viewed the principles of neutrality and independence as commandments or guidelines; whether they believed military force for the protection of human rights was an oxymoron; and whether they thought that force might produce a good outcome.[2] For emergency agencies of the old school, military force might sometimes be needed, but it was probably wrong-headed to classify any use of force as humanitarian and it was probably best to disassociate humanitarianism from any act of war.[3] For other agencies, mainly in the alchemical camp, the fundamental goal was to deliver relief and protect civilians, and the application of force might be both expedient and principled. Although various events over the 1990s reflected the meandering and momentary reactions of aid agencies to the use of force during emergencies, Somalia, Bosnia, Rwanda, and Kosovo were the most consequential. Over the course of the decade, a silent pattern developed: whereas at the beginning of the decade aid agencies tried to recruit states for their cause, by the beginning of the next decade they had discovered that states had already co-opted humanitarianism for their interests.

Somalia and Armed Protection

Beginning in the late 1980s a power struggle erupted in Somalia. At the outset, the contest was between the Ethiopian-funded Somali National Movement (SNM) and the Somali government of Siad Barre, but it took a violent turn in 1988 when the SNM launched a guerrilla war against Siad. An increasingly unpopular Siad began to retaliate severely and indiscriminately, and soon thereafter it seemed as if every clan had its own militia and was vying for political power. The greatest military threat, however, came from General Mohamed Farah Aideed, and he successfully defeated Siad in 1991, resulting not in his coronation but rather in an increase in clan-on-clan violence. Their war destroyed most urban centers, political institutions, and the economy, and left upward of twenty thousand civilian casualties, a million displaced people, and the specter of mass starvation.[4]

NGOs wandered into a situation unlike anything previously encountered. There was no central government, not even in name only. There were dozens of militias, each answering only to themselves. Nor were they fighting the familiar ideological goals of the Cold War. Instead, they seemed to be motivated by a strange mixture of longstanding grudges, new power plays for political power, turf protection, and revenge. Aid organizations confronted a bewildering maze of violence and politics as they attempted to negotiate access to the hundreds of thousands of Somalis who were on the verge of starvation. In order to have the privilege of delivering assistance, the militias extorted food aid from the relief agencies. If they did not comply, then either they would not be allowed to pass or they would be attacked.[5]

Aid agencies had several alternatives, none of them good. They could decide to withdraw, but with fatal consequences for those in the camps. Or, they could hire "protection" from the local clans. MSF's James Orbinski captures the moment well: "The needs were overwhelming. Some of the old humanitarian rules of neutrality and independence seemed to be falling apart, and it wasn't clear what the new rules would be. For the first time ever, the Red Cross, MSF, and other aid agencies were paying armed guards from various clans to protect aid workers and food supplies."[6] But, still, the militias were able to make out like the bandits that they were, confiscating, according to various estimates, anywhere from 20 to 80 percent of the food, depending on the time and place.[7] The only way to secure aid from the poachers was to be protected by a local clan. Once a group did that, though, its neutrality became suspect. Nevertheless, aid workers could operate in relative safety, captured by the following exchange. One worker asked another whether they were at risk of being shot. No, the other replied. "Because if we get shot, then the NGOs leave, and there's nobody left to pay protection money or salaries. They want us afraid and alive. So you should be afraid and happy, because it means you can work. It's a little fucked up, isn't it?"[8] In any event, the aid agencies quickly realized that they were contributing to the famine because the militias had every intention of keeping it alive in order to keep the aid flowing. Given the unprecedented nature of the challenge—or, at any rate, the belief that Somalia had no precedents—aid agencies had no ready-made answers for how to provide relief without also fueling the war.

One possible escape from this nightmare was an international force. Various NGOs, alongside a growing number of UN officials and human rights activists, began campaigning for a humanitarian intervention. After a gun battle ensued when a CARE convoy refused to give a pay-out to the militias, killing five relief workers, CARE's president Philip Johnston began to call for armed protection, appealing to the United States, the UN, and anyone else who would listen; in his judgment, this was the only way to save starving Somalis. Unlike years before when no one would have bothered to listen, in this early post–Cold War moment the UN was beginning to consider various forms of armed intervention in the defense of human life. In 1991 the United Nations established Operation Provide Comfort to provide aid to the Kurds who were fleeing Saddam Hussein, and the following year it began playing a role in Bosnia. For a mixture of reasons, including a desire to demonstrate that the UN also cared about emergencies in Africa, the UN Security Council decided to provide armed protection for the relief convoys, which proved to be the first step on a slippery slope toward an all-out war between UN forces and Mohammed Farah Aideed. Not only did most aid agencies go along with a new arrangement that they helped to create, which some later sarcastically dubbed "Operation Shoot to Feed," but many American NGOs, operating under their umbrella organization, Interaction, began pushing Washington and New York to up the ante.[9] But not everyone was thrilled by this; the European NGOs in particular were generally unified that this was a bad idea.[10] MSF had reluctantly agreed to seek the protection of local militias, but the situation became intolerable when the UN began doing "peace enforcement." As Rony Brauman reflected, it became impossible to contemplate humanitarian neutrality when licensed defenders were firing into crowds and delivering aid directly to the very people who were the executioners of the population. "For the first time in Somalia, they killed under the banner of humanitarianism."[11] MSF closed the mission and walked away, leaving other agencies to deal with the dilemmas. Asked whether he has any regrets, Johnston said, "Hell no. Hell no."[12] While armed force might now be possible, aid agencies relied on their instincts, often fueled more by passions than by well-honed ideas.

Bosnia, the Humanitarian Alibi, and Indifference

The war in the former Yugoslavia lasted four bloody years, from 1991 through November 1995, leading to the deaths of over one hundred thousand civilians; the displacement of millions of people; the destruction of towns, villages, and communities; and war crimes, including rape, ethnic cleansing, and genocide. Although the Western response to the gravest humanitarian crisis in Europe since World War II was half-hearted until the very end, it nevertheless looked impressive on paper—the UNHCR led the world's largest relief operation, the UN had thirty thousand peacekeepers, and NATO engaged in active military operations for the first time in its nearly fifty-year history. Yet humanitarianism was less of an answer to the conflict than its alibi. As David Rieff, in his characteristically provocative way, suggested: "The deeper question is whether Bosnia was a major humanitarian crisis at all."[13] Whether it was or was not, it forced aid agencies to choose between competing principles. By the end the UN and the UNHCR had their principles turned inside-out until it was rarely clear whether they were bending their principles because they had no choice or because they believed it was the right thing to do, bouncing between victims of a situation not of their own making and willing participants.[14]

Various factors contributed to the eventual dissolution of Yugoslavia, though many mark 1988, when President Slobodan Milošević introduced constitutional reforms that tipped the delicate balance of power among the federations toward Serbia, as the point of no return. This action encouraged the growth of nationalist sentiments and separatist movements, leading to the quick succession of declarations of independence by Slovenia and Croatia in 1991. A war soon broke out between Croatia and Serbia, causing sectarian violence, massive displacement of the Serbian minority in Croatia, and the arrival of the UNHCR to provide relief for the refugee populations, with the added hope that it might deter future flight. In September 1991 the UN Security Council declared an arms embargo, and in February 1992 it created the United Nations Protection Force, which was mandated to deploy to those parts of Croatia that had a significant Serbian minority and to monitor the ceasefire between Serb and Croat forces.

In April 1992 Bosnia-Herzegovina proclaimed its independence, leading to clashes between its three principal communities, Muslims, Serbians, and Croats. Immediately thereafter, the Serbian forces initiated a campaign of ethnic cleansing, rape, and terrorism, leading to tens of thousands of dead and the displacement of nearly 2.6 million Bosnians. The West's claim to care was betrayed by its anemic response, and the gap between its words and its deeds widened to the point that it had to do something. Perhaps the tipping point came when *Newsday*'s Roy Guttman published a series of articles in July and August 1993, complete with chilling pictures of emaciated Bosnians cowering behind barbed wire fences, all too reminiscent of the Nazi concentration camps. Guttman, who eventually won a Pulitzer Prize for his reporting, was working on a lead given to him by the ICRC's Patrick Glasser, who had stumbled onto the camps weeks before and then debated with others at the agency about how to get the news out without compromising the ICRC's neutrality. Apparently, though, the Serbs were using the ICRC and then the journalists. They allowed them to visit the camps, anticipating that it would stir memories of the Holocaust and cause the Europeans to accept the Bosnians—thus playing directly into Serbia's plan to cleanse Bosnia.[15]

From this point on, the UN and the West wanted to do something, but not too much—and humanitarianism became the perfect vehicle.[16] After watching helplessly as the UNHCR and the aid community struggled to deliver supplies while being shelled by Serbian forces, on July 13, 1992, the Security Council, operating under Chapter VII, mandated the UN force "to ensure the security and functioning of Sarajevo airport and the delivery of humanitarian assistance."[17] A few months later and in response to ethnic cleansing and further attacks on civilian populations, the UN created six "safe areas," which might be more accurately called penal colonies. The UN responded to every violation with another resolution, which only increased the gap between what it had pledged to do and what it was actually doing. Eventually the UN's mandate included various actions, including instituting no-fly zones, defending the safe areas, delivering humanitarian assistance, making Sarajevo free from heavy weapons, and much more, in the over one hundred Security Council resolutions over four years. Although the UN could use "all necessary means" to enforce these resolutions, they rarely did, as Serbian forces carried out ethnic cleansing and other atrocities in full view of the UN. While the Bosnian leaders explicitly preferred military assistance to humanitarian assistance, arguing that they needed a fighting chance to stay alive, the UN Security Council and Western states "decided for them that they should be fed and not armed."[18]

Neither the UN nor the UNHCR were prepared to handle the demands of a civil war they knew had been tossed into their laps. Indeed, UN Secretary-General Boutros-Ghali's first response was to oppose the UN's involvement, a position that not only was based on a sensible reading of the situation but also was consistent with a UN that had avoided all civil wars ever since the operation in the Congo in the early 1960s. Ignoring his objections, the Security Council established the UN Protection Force in Yugoslavia, best known as UNPROFOR. Now the UN had the impossible task, in the words of one former UN senior political adviser, of "trying to hold back the tide with a spoon."[19]

Although the UN operated under a Chapter VII mandate, allowing it to use force and operate without the consent of the parties, it clung to peacekeeping's principles of consent, impartiality, and neutrality, preferring negotiation to saber-rattling. The UN's position, in fact, represented a return to the traditional interpretation of its principles after a brief period of experimentation. With the end of the Cold War and in response to the new kinds of security conflicts and protection demands, Boutros-Ghali and other UN officials championed a more muscular UN that would use force to discharge its responsibilities and keep the peace. Somalia and other peacekeeping setbacks sent UN officials back to basics.[20] After watching the Somalia operation descend into a war between the UN and U.S. forces and the Somali militias, UNPROFOR Commander Michael Rose vowed not to cross the "Mogadishu Line" and become "helpless."[21] A few months later, and in response to President William J. Clinton's suggestion that the UN enforce the peace and battle the Bosnian Serbs, Rose said, "If someone wants to fight a war here on moral or political grounds, fine, great, but count us [the UN] out. Hitting one tank is peacekeeping. Hitting infrastructure command and control, logistics, that is war, and I'm not going to fight a war with painted tanks."[22]

The UN's well-known preference for avoiding a fight meant that the Bosnians Serbs had the upper hand, could frustrate the UN's basic activities, obstructing its use of the Sarajevo airport and the delivery of food to the safe havens, seemingly enjoying every opportunity to increase the hardship and pile on the humiliation. At stake, though, was more than the UN's pride—lives were hanging in the balance. One MSF worker summarized it well: "The UN troops were instructed to protect the aid supplies—but they were prevented from using force to protect people."[23] The predictable, violent, and sad conclusion of this culture of impartiality was the passivity of the Dutch peacekeepers in response to the genocide committed by the Bosnian Serb forces in Srebrenica in July 1995. Years later Secretary-General Kofi Annan bravely acknowledged that the United Nations was suffering from "an institutional ideology of impartiality even when confronted with attempted genocide."[24]

The UN's desire to cling to its principles owed not only to creed but also to self-interest. To become more fully involved in Bosnia, particularly when it doubted the diplomatic and military backing of the Security Council and NATO, might leave the UN vulnerable politically and militarily. By insisting on these principles, the UN could avoid further involvement and—it hoped—provide some cover from future criticism. When the media and the international aid community castigated the UN for failing to defend civilians, Boutros-Ghali and others responded by emphasizing the centrality of the humanitarian mission, transforming a moral failure into something of an organizational victory: if UNPROFOR was judged according to how well it protected civilians, then its activities were a failure; if, however, it was judged by its delivery of humanitarian relief, then it could be judged a qualified success. And by emphasizing the delivery of humanitarian relief rather than the protection of civilians, UN officials could shift responsibility from themselves to the participants of the conflict. The UN could not be blamed for what the parties brought on themselves.

There were occasional instances when the UN and NATO backed up their threats with force, but such instances typically occurred when their bluff had already been called many times or when peacekeepers were in danger. For instance, the UN rejected NATO's recommendation for air strikes in response to the Serb assault on the safe haven of Goražde in the spring of 1994. In defending its decision, Kofi Annan, at the time the undersecretary-general for peacekeeping operations, argued that air strikes are "to protect lives—not just of the handful of UN soldiers who might be threatened by a given attack but the thousands of lightly armed peacekeepers and hundreds of unarmed relief workers, military observers and police monitors whose lives could be threatened by precipitous military action."[25] Missing from Annan's list of groups to be protected were the residents of the safe havens. NATO was not much better, as it declared that the aim of the air strikes was to protect UN personnel, not the sixty-five thousand residents of Goražde.[26] The UN and NATO disagreed on whether force should be used to protect peacekeepers; the Bosnians apparently were not part of the moral calculus.

The UN designated the UNHCR the "lead agency," a logical choice given the centrality of the refugee crisis, a title that gave it responsibility for overseeing humanitarian activities. Although the UNHCR had been in the limelight over the years, it was now the centerpiece of the largest relief operation in the world, coordinating over 250 aid agencies.[27] More spectacularly, it was now delivering relief during a civil war and trying to bring relief to people so that they did not have to wait until they crossed a border. Unlike the High Commissioner's response to the prospect of getting involved in Biafra, there was very little hesitation; the times had changed, the refugees needed protecting, and Bosnia represented a platform for the UNHCR to demonstrate its continuing relevance at a time when some states were asking whether the refugee agency was a luxury.[28] The UNHCR's move into areas once defined as taboo caused it to become even more emphatic about its neutrality and impartiality.[29] However, it had a harder time maintaining the appearance of independence because it was widely understood to be acting on behalf of a UN Security Council under the control of the West. The UNHCR found itself squarely in the middle of several dilemmas.[30]

Although the UNHCR initially saw its presence as buying time for a political solution, not as a substitute for it, it became the de facto substitute for a political response.[31] An incident in February 1993 captures the situation. Serbian forces had little incentive to cooperate with the UN operation or the delivery of relief, so they began a policy of harassing, obstructing, and attacking the aid convoys. High Commissioner Sadako Ogata had been bitterly complaining about the agency being placed in an impossible situation. The UNHCR was expected to negotiate with Serbian militias that were making the delivery of aid a highly dangerous game, and whenever the Serbs did allow the convoys through it was always after they had "lightened" the load. Nor did the Bosnian government necessarily appreciate a "humanitarian" policy that seemed to be guaranteeing a slow death for its people. The UN peacekeepers were supposed to facilitate the delivery of aid, but they seemed more interested in protecting themselves than the aid shipments. Feeling pressure from all sides, Ogata began threatening to withdraw the operation unless she got more cooperation from the Serbs, the Muslims, and the peacekeepers. Then in February 1993 Serbian forces stopped the UNHCR from delivering aid to eastern Bosnia, with Serbian President Radovan Karadžić who has since been convicted of war crimes at the Hague, graciously offering to let the Muslims leave their enclaves in Serbian territory. In response to a proposal that was ethnic cleansing in the guise of humanitarianism, the Bosnian government banned all aid deliveries to Sarajevo, hoping to pressure the UN to use force against the Serbs.

Ogata had had enough. She suspended the UNHCR's operations until the parties stopped making a "mockery" of the UNHCR's efforts and honored their pledge to permit the deliver of relief. "No decision that I took in my ten years as high commissioner," she reflected, "caused as much havoc."[32] She was blasting the Serbs for their cruelty. She was insinuating that the Bosnian Muslim leadership was aggravating the situation for its own political advantage. And, most alarming from the standpoint of the UN, she was threatening to withdraw the international community's symbol of concern. If the UNHCR departed, it would trigger a humanitarian and political chain reaction: the departure of the UNHCR would increase the pain and suffering of the Bosnian population; UNPROFOR's primary mandate would be null and void because there were no aid convoys to protect, thus potentially encouraging its departure; and the West's strategy of using humanitarianism as a substitute for concerted political and military action would be exposed. Boutros-Ghali overruled Ogata the following day, forcing the UNHCR to remain.[33]

Bosnia was a humanitarian crisis not only because individuals were forced to flee their homes but also because neighboring countries refused to let them cross their borders to safety. Under international refugee law, individuals are allowed to seek asylum, but European states refused entry to thousands, preferring to ask the UNHCR to bring relief to the people trapped in Bosnia. The UNHCR agreed, moving beyond its traditional mandate for "bona fide" refugees to help "internally displaced peoples" and others in "refugee-like" circumstances, including those who did not want to flee but were nevertheless affected by the war. Putting the best face on an ugly situation, the UNHCR stated that it was giving the Bosnians a "choice." But it was not much of a choice, and there was not much that the UNHCR could do about it. Occasionally the UNHCR protested to European governments, but they were unmoved. There is no evidence that if the UNHCR had upped the ante and threatened to withdraw, it would have caused Europe to comply with existing international refugee law. So, in the words of one UN official, the UNHCR was reduced to helping the Europeans with their policy of "containment through charity."[34]

The UNHCR called this policy "preventive protection," which, according to the UNHCR's Working Group on International Protection, operated on the "overriding principle in Bosnia and Herzegovina [that UNHCR] should be to bring safety to the people, rather than to bring people to safety."[35] Yet this policy of preventive protection exposed the Bosnians to danger. The UNHCR and UNPROFOR were not necessarily bringing safety to the Bosnians. They were bringing supplies—not protection. The false equation between aid and protection was well understood by many UNHCR officials, who privately acknowledged that preventive protection was not protecting refugees but rather exposing them to harm.[36] This policy also became implicated in the Serbian campaign of ethnic cleansing. If they helped populations flee to "safe areas" and other "protected zones," then they were facilitating ethnic cleansing. If they did not, then Bosnians might die. Ogata summarized the moral dilemma in the following way: "If you take these people you are an accomplice to ethnic cleansing. If you don't you are an accomplice to murder."[37]

Humanitarianism, many aid agencies concluded, had become an alibi for the West's inaction in Bosnia. The initial position of many humanitarians was that providing assistance was a reasonable response until a solution could be found, only to discover that the more effective humanitarianism became, the less pressure the West felt to do what needed to be done. In the context of French President François Mitterrand's lightening-quick visit to Sarajevo, MSF's Rony Brauman wrote an incendiary article in *Libération*. Under the title "Humanitarianism, Modern Name for Cowardice," he castigated France's inaction and Mitterrand's theatrics. Comparing Europe's response to Bosnia to Europe's capitulation to Hitler in 1938, he wrote that "behind our medicines and our humanitarian convoys, the first racial State in Europe since the Third Reich is in the process of forming itself, now that a planned, announced, then realized 'ethnic cleansing' is nearly achieved."[38] Writing with Bosnia at his back, Alain Destexhe, the former secretary-general of MSF, wrote:

> All over the world, there is unprecedented enthusiasm for humanitarian work. It is far from certain that this is always in the victims' best interests....In dealing with countries in ongoing wars of a local nature, humanitarian aid has acquired a near monopoly of morality and international action. It is this monopoly we seek to denounce. Humanitarian action is noble when coupled with political action and justice. Without them, it is doomed to failure and especially in the emergencies covered by the media, becomes little more than a play thing of international politics, a conscience-solving gimmick.[39]

If humanitarianism was an alibi—and therefore prolonged suffering—then what good was humanitarianism? Perhaps humanitarianism needed to give war a chance.

Rwanda

The genesis of this tragic chapter of Rwanda's history can be briefly told. Until Rwandan independence in 1962, the minority Tutsis ruled, favored by the Belgian colonialists. Rwandan independence catapulted the majority Hutus to the top and reduced the Tutsis to an intermittently tolerated minority population. A wave of Hutu-on-Tutsi violence from 1959 to 1963 led to the flight of hundreds of thousands of Tutsis to various neighboring countries, though mainly to Uganda, situated directly to the north. Beginning in the late 1980s, refugees who had fled Rwanda to neighboring Uganda in the 1960s, mainly Tutsis, established an independence movement, the Rwanda Patriotic Front (RPF). From Uganda they launched a civil war in 1990 against the Hutu-led Rwandan government; in response to the RPF's battlefield successes, a French-led force intervened to support its longtime Hutu allies, which led to a temporary lull in the civil war, but the fighting never ended. After intense negotiations between the government and the RPF in the summer of 1993, they concluded the Arusha Accords, which pledged to end the civil war and usher in a new chapter of national reconciliation, inter-ethnic cooperation, and democracy.

On October 5, 1993, the Security Council, albeit with some concerns over whether peace was possible, authorized a peacekeeping operation, the United Nations Assistance Mission in Rwanda (UNAMIR), to oversee the Arusha Accords. The pessimists turned out to be prophetic. The parties were unable to implement the basic elements of the agreement, and violence increased as a consequence of this stagnation. UNAMIR Force Commander Roméo Dallaire was the most clear-eyed of the UN command, as he predicted widespread bloodshed if the UNAMIR force was unable to demonstrate some muscle to back up the mandate and give the political moderates the ability to compromise.

On April 6, 1994, hell came to Rwanda. The plane carrying Rwandan President Juvénal Habyarimana, who was returning from Tanzania, where he was rumored to have agreed to the transitional government, was shot down as it approached Kigali International Airport. Although there remains considerable debate about who downed the plane, with evidence pointing to both the RPF and Hutu extremists, the plane crash immediately led to the extremist forces spreading out across Kigali, erecting road blocks and executing moderate Hutu and Tutsi politicians. With only 2,500 lightly-armed peacekeepers scattered throughout Rwanda, UNAMIR was ill-prepared to confront the wave of terror unleashed by Hutu extremists against Tutsis and Hutu moderates. Any question regarding the ability of the UN peacekeepers to protect Rwandans, or even themselves, was answered on April 7 when extremist forces brutally murdered ten Belgian peacekeepers.

There has been considerable debate over why the UN decided to do nothing in the face of the genocide; my previously published conclusion is that states and UN officials largely followed their principles and their interests to the exit. Several points, though, are particularly germane here. There was a growing belief at the UN that its survival and the effectiveness of peacekeeping depended on honoring the principles of consent, neutrality, and impartiality, which fed directly into a policy of non-use of force, even in the face of civilian killings. Peacekeeping was only effective when there was a peace to keep, and if there was no peace to keep, then there was no reason for the UN to be there.

The juxtaposition of the UN Security Council voting to withdraw nearly all of the UN peacekeepers at the same time that the rate of killing appeared to accelerate led a surge of states, international agencies, and world leaders to call for a military intervention to stop what was now widely recognized as a genocide.[40] Even MSF, which had once refused to take an official position on the question of humanitarian intervention either in principle or in any single instance, supported the use of force. Its decision to act was driven not only by the daily images of carnage but also by a fear that humanitarianism might become, just like in Bosnia, a "fig leaf" for action—and MSF wanted to avoid resembling the ICRC during the Holocaust. MSF-France launched a campaign proclaiming, "You don't treat a genocide with doctors; you don't respond to a humanitarian crisis with a stethoscope." By early May the UN appeared to be the only opponent of intervention. Finally the UN did authorize two interventions, the first with considerable trepidation and the second with considerable insincerity. In the first instance, in late June, after weeks of endless debate on whether there should be an intervention and who should lead it, France proposed to enter Rwanda and create a "safe zone" for civilians. The UN reluctantly gave its blessing to a state that had a history of giving support to the very same rogues now accused of perpetrating genocide. The results were decidedly mixed, with some crediting "Operation Turquoise" with saving thousands of lives and others for saving thousands of genocidaires. The second intervention was, in fact, authorized in May—before Operation Turquoise. Specifically, the UN authorized UNAMIR II, which was to provide an additional 5,500 troops for Rwanda; the problem was that no government was willing to send its troops into a theater of killing; the UN troops rolled into Kigali only once they were in no danger of having to do anything.

After having sat out the genocide, the UN and the international community leapt into action when the next humanitarian emergency unfolded. Beginning on July 1, 1994, nearly two million Hutus began emptying out of the country, fearful of the approaching Rwandan Patriotic Front and the possibility that the Tutsis would give as good as they got. They settled into makeshift camps the size of small cities but without shelter, water, or medical assistance—cameras captured images of suffering and the spectacle of widespread disease. These were some of the first sustained images Western populations had of the genocide. Until this moment, the few Western media outlets that covered Africa were in South Africa to report on the expected election of Nelson Mandela in late April, and when the election ended and they discovered what was happening in Rwanda, they trekked thousands of miles north, only to find that it was unsafe to enter the country and that they were reduced to waiting on the Rwandan border for pictures and stories. At this point, the horrors of the refugee movement tumbled into view. Seemingly tapping into the mounting guilt for having done nothing during the genocide, those countries that were unavailable to stop the killers unleashed an impressive relief operation. It did not matter that the killers were among the refugees. In the media's coverage, all were victims, though the Hutu refugees got preferential treatment.

As the UN, the UNHCR, hundreds of relief agencies, and a supporting cast of thousands, including the American military, began to distribute relief, they soon discovered that they were doing more than feeding innocent refugees—they also were feeding the genocidaires. The camps were quickly controlled by the Hutu extremists and the remnants of the Rwandan army who took control of the camps that offered protection, fresh recruits, and international aid. The aid workers were, once again, in a moral no man's land. When they threatened to remove the genocidaires from the distribution network, they were physically threatened. When they began encouraging refugees to leave these camps for the new camps being prepared in Rwanda, they discovered that the refugees who thought about leaving were threatened with death if they did. Aid agencies, including the UNHCR, began appealing to the UN and states to provide a military force to give them protection and evict the criminal elements from the camp, but states were no more keen for this task than they were for intervening to stop the genocide. This left aid agencies with a stark choice: stay or get out. Most chose to stay, though a few, including MSF-France, left because they could not accept the price of doing business.

The genocide in Rwanda in 1994 has been extensively covered in books, memoirs, documentaries, and even an Academy Award–nominated feature film. That it has found a place in the world's ranking among the great crimes of the twentieth century, arguably second only to the Holocaust, is certainly an outcome that the few who saw what was happening in Rwanda at the time could have predicted. Its place in our collective memory is nearly as much of a surprise as the actual genocide. Why it should rank so highly is, on first blush, something of a mystery. Unlike the Holocaust, which occurred in "civilized" Europe, Rwanda happened in a place few Westerners knew anything about (except for maybe the mountain gorillas), even fewer have met someone from Rwanda, and only a tiny handful have visited. It happened in Africa, where violence on this scale, at least from the perspective of many in the West, is part of its tidal rhythms. Indeed, a few years later, in neighboring Congo even more people died, and it is difficult to find anyone, outside of a few NGOs, who seems to care or is troubled by the lack of a response. Yet Rwanda haunts.

If so, it is because "our" complicity is undeniable. It was not only the killing that was shocking. So, too, was the West's apparent indifference. There certainly have been many other moments when the West has chosen to ignore mass killings, but never before when there were 2,500 UN troops on the ground. The Security Council knew of the spiraling violence and it decided to do the unthinkable—it first ordered its UN troops to not take risks to save or protect Rwandans and then decided to reduce its presence from 2,500 to 200 troops with a mandate restricted to helping the parties try to negotiate an end to the killing. In other words, the West had blood on its hands. Choosing not to act when it had knowledge and opportunity to stop a genocide, according to many, was tantamount to contributing to the genocide itself. It was not only outside critics of the UN who leveled this charge, eventually many who were responsible for making life-and-death decisions harbored similar thoughts.

Atonement cannot begin until there has been an admission of having sinned, and it took a while for anyone in the West in a position of responsibility to place the blame on themselves. At first the international community blamed the United States, a reasonable conclusion given that it had spent most of the genocide adopting the position of "see no evil, hear no evil, speak no evil." Soon the U.S. claim to not knowing what was happening, as Bill Clinton insisted after the fact, became exposed for the fabrication it was. A few years later it became more widely known that others in positions of responsibility could get medals for moral cowardice. Other Security Council members also had been cautious about recommending an intervention, scared away by the deadly anarchy on the ground and the recent experiences in Somalia. And then the UN Secretariat's equivocation came to light; neither Boutros-Ghali nor Annan had recommended an intervention during the first, critical weeks and, in fact, did their best to muzzle those UN officials, including Dallaire, who did.[41]

It took a while, and considerable outside pressure, before those who had reason to know and the power to end the genocide began to acknowledge how little they had done. Once they did, though, they frequently found themselves overcome with grief. Nearly everyone I have talked to that was even remotely involved has expressed a profound sense of loss and has wondered what they might have done differently. Those who refused to abandon their posts, the Rwandans, or their conscience, including Dallaire and a handful of relief workers, remain haunted by what they saw and what the international community failed to do. Also disturbed were those who either could or should have known better. If it was possible to feel justified in ignoring a genocide that left eight hundred thousand dead and a whole country traumatized, an event that happened while there were troops on the ground, then what did that say about one's humanity?

The acts of atonement by states and UN officials took various forms. Having been absent during the genocide, the UN was quick to establish an international tribunal in Arusha, Tanzania, to try the architects and executors of the genocide. Only after a few years were the bystanders made to answer for their lack of action. Although there were various factors that caused Western leaders to act in Kosovo in 1999, certainly the memories of having done little to stop genocide in Bosnia and Rwanda supplied emotional fuel. Later that same year, Annan's UN General Assembly speech on the need for a doctrine of humanitarian intervention was widely interpreted as part of his public confession for having done too little, too late in Rwanda. And, memories of Rwanda are widely credited with having motivated the eventual principle of a "responsibility to protect." The living were atoning for their sins and trying to keep the dead among the living.

The aid community proved more willing to look critically at itself, and the result was a sustained reform effort. An immediate issue was how to reduce the negative consequences of aid. Mary Anderson's appropriation of the Hippocratic oath, "do no harm," proved to be easier said than done—or measured.[42] Still, it reframed the terms of the debate, creating a greater willingness to examine how aid becomes sandwiched between underlying causes and political outcomes. Many questioned how they could not have seen the genocide coming and indicted a technocratic orientation that had seemingly blinded them to the politics of the place. Rwanda had been something of a darling of the aid world, routinely touted as the Switzerland of Central Africa. Aid agencies had rushed into Rwanda, engaging in various forms of community development, providing technical assistance, building schools, and organizing coffee cooperatives. As they did, they willfully ignored politics.[43] It seemed, recalled a high-ranking official of Catholic Relief Services who had served in Rwanda, that they were fixated on technical aspects of development at the expense of everything else, including ethnicity. And when the genocide erupted, it took them a while to see it for what it was. MSF's initial reaction, for instance, was to interpret the violence as a return to civil war, with the horrific but quite expected casualties. As MSF legal adviser Françoise Bouchet-Saulnier put it, "Sometimes there are those at MSF who think it normal that people die without our knowing why. In Burundi [which saw ethnic killings in October 1993], a lot of people were dying, but it was as if the MSF people thought it was normal because there was a war."[44] Moreover, MSF's medical and emergency room mentality led it to concentrate exclusively on effects to the neglect of causes, which, once again, obscured the politics of the place. For those agencies, mainly in the alchemical camp, already moving in a more political direction, Rwanda provided genocidal proof of the necessity of their direction. For those who had not yet gone through the debate, Rwanda demonstrated the need to recover from the past and to insert the language of human rights and social justice into their humanitarianism.

Kosovo and Humanitarian War

Kosovo was an autonomous province of the Yugoslav Republic until 1990, when Yugoslav President Slobodan Milošević formally abolished its autonomy.[45] From here on out, Belgrade steadily took control of its political, economic, and cultural affairs, and the Albanian population, which formed the vast majority of Kosovo's population, began to see their lives diminished. In response, Ibrahim Rugova, a well-known Albanian writer, advised passive resistance and established the Democratic League of Kosovo; soon thereafter, in September 1991 an underground plebiscite voted overwhelmingly for independence.

The situation in Kosovo remained fairly stable during the Yugoslavian wars, but once they ended, it deteriorated. In response to continuing repression by the Federal Republic of Yugoslavia, a previously unknown organization, the Kosovo Liberation Army (KLA), carried out a series of attacks in April 1996. In response to a deteriorating and violent situation, international involvement increased beginning in late 1997. In March 1998 the Security Council adopted Resolution 1160, which called on the KLA and Belgrade to negotiate a political settlement, imposed an arms embargo on both parties, and warned of the "consideration of additional measures" in the absence of progress toward a peaceful solution. In response to further violence, including many civilian deaths and the displacement of hundreds of thousands of individuals, in April 1998 the Contact Group for the Former Yugoslavia agreed to impose new sanctions on Belgrade (Russia, a member of the group, objected). In June, UN Secretary-General Annan informed NATO of the possible need for the Security Council to authorize military action. In September the Security Council adopted Resolution 1199 declaring that Kosovo was a "threat to peace and security in the region." Although Russia permitted this resolution, it served notice that it would oppose any authorization of military force by the Security Council.

Because of the Russian impediment, the Western states shifted their attention to NATO. Citing "humanitarian intervention" as the legal justification for any possible use of force, on October 9, 1998, NATO Secretary-General Javier Solana warned of future military action if Belgrade did not comply with international demands.[46] Apparently because of this warning, on October 25 Belgrade agreed to a ceasefire to be monitored by NATO from the air and by unarmed peace monitors from the Organization of Security and Cooperation in Europe on the ground. The humanitarian and security situation improved, but only temporarily; in the absence of a political agreement, the KLA and the Serbian authorities continued to maneuver for war. A particularly grisly incident in January 1999, when Serbian troops killed forty-five civilians in the city of Račak, led NATO to threaten air strikes. Indeed, at this point NATO became more fully committed to coercive diplomacy to force Belgrade to accept various principles about Kosovo's future status, including the restoration of its autonomy and international protection by NATO.[47] Against the backdrop of the threat of force if there was no negotiated settlement, beginning on February 6, 1999, the combatants and outside parties held a series of talks at Rambouillet, France, but they collapsed on March 19.

Following through on its threat, NATO launched air strikes on March 24, its first active military encounter in its fifty-year history. Many world leaders, from Czech President Václav Havel to U.S. President Bill Clinton, offered the decision to bomb Kosovo as evidence of cosmopolitanism and a growing sense of international community. Among the many statements, perhaps most famous was British Prime Minister Tony Blair's "doctrine for the international community," which argued that a more interconnected world requires a more interconnected set of foreign policies that consider not just interests but also values.[48] Although it is easy to dismiss the thoughts of politicians, who are hard-wired to invest all military action with a higher meaning, that some of these statesmen, including Václav Havel, had never before taken such a position gives some credence to the claim that world leaders were making a direct connection between the possibility of global solidarity and the need to defend the lives of the weakest members of the community.

That said, President Clinton might have provided a more accurate set of reasons for this unprecedented action: prevent a humanitarian emergency, preserve European stability, and maintain NATO's credibility.[49] Given the Bosnian precedent and Serbian violations of the basic human rights of Kosovar Albanians, Western officials had good reason to fear the worst, both in the immediate and the medium-term future. As Michael Reisman observed: "The facts were alarming. As always, information was imperfect, but enough was available to indicate that bad things were happening, things chillingly reminiscent of some earlier as well as, lamentably, more recent events in this century; and it was reasonable to assume (and, to some, irresponsibly naive not to assume) that, given the people involved, worse things were in store."[50] And the West's inaction in Bosnia and Rwanda cast a long shadow of shame.[51] Consequently, NATO proclaimed Kosovo to be a "humanitarian war" that would protect the Kosovar Albanians.[52] There also were security considerations. The Bosnian conflict always threatened to expand beyond the Yugoslavian borders, and while the violence was quarantined, the political and security effects were not. Kosovo's implosion might invite intervention by Greece, Italy, Turkey, and other European countries. Finally, NATO was concerned about its own future. As NATO debated its response to Kosovo, others were using the occasion of NATO's upcoming fiftieth anniversary to debate NATO's relevance and future. Kosovo potentially gave NATO an opportunity to answer its critics and demonstrate its continued relevance.

NATO's bombing campaign, however, seemed to trigger the very humanitarian emergency it was designed to prevent. Milošević responded by unleashing a torrent of ethnic cleansing, causing hundreds of thousands of Kosovar Albanians to flee. Within two weeks, a half-million Kosovars had crossed into Albania and gathered at the Macedonian border, producing the largest refugee flight in Europe since World War II. This spectacle—mass displacement caused by a humanitarian war—was quickly becoming a major public relations disaster for an organization that had initially seen this operation as a public relations savior. Although few charged NATO with being directly responsible for this turn of events, it was heavily criticized for its failure to anticipate Milošević's move. But NATO was not the only organization overwhelmed by the flood of refugees. So, too, were the UNHCR, the lead humanitarian agency, and most relief agencies. In any event, it was NATO that was accused of creating the situation, and it was NATO that was expected to do something about it. Given all of this, NATO decided that relief was too important to be left to the relief agencies.[53] It began holding immediate discussions with the UNHCR.

On April 3, 1999, one day before NATO's fiftieth anniversary, UNHCR High Commissioner Ogata requested NATO's assistance. This was an unprecedented and highly controversial decision because never before had the UNHCR approached a combatant for direct assistance. Many at the UNHCR objected on the grounds that whatever temporary benefit the UNHCR might receive from NATO's assistance would be outweighed by the cost to its independence and ability to work in the field. Ogata overruled these objections on the grounds that the UNHCR needed NATO to help overcome Macedonia's unwillingness to permit entry of refugees (the government feared destabilizing the ethnic balance) and logistical problems in Albania.[54] NATO stepped in and acted as a "surge protector."[55]

NATO made a critical contribution at the outset of the refugee crisis but then transformed what was supposed to be a temporary and supporting role into a permanent and commandeering role throughout the war and long after its assistance ceased to be needed.[56] The agreement between NATO and the UNHCR, as one evaluator observed, was a "Trojan Horse that allowed NATO to effectively take over the humanitarian operation from the inside."[57] NATO became a "full-service" relief agency, helping to build camps, distribute relief, ensure security, coordinate the actions of relief agencies—and set the agenda.[58] Its decision to overstay its welcome and extend its activities into unauthorized areas had relatively little to do with the needs of the refugees and everything to do with NATO's need to maintain support for the air campaign.[59] By continuing to play a coordinating role, NATO was able to cast its actions as humanitarian and thus continue to legitimate the war. For instance, the leaders of AFOR, NATO's Albanian force dedicated to relief, commanded: "All activities undertaken by AFOR should contribute to the enhancement of NATO's public image and the undermining of critics of the NATO air campaign."[60]

Although most agencies resented the hit to their autonomy, the surprise was that there was little outrage or outright rebellion. After all, the same agencies that had strenuously guarded their humanitarian space—their independence, impartiality, and neutrality—in places like the Congo and Sudan were now working alongside, getting assistance from, and being directed by a combatant—and doing so with relative ease.[61] MSF was one of the few organizations that refused to participate on the grounds that doing so violated basic principles of humanitarian action and placed refugees at risk.[62] In general, while some NGOs attempted to distinguish themselves from governments, one observer concluded that "most were happy to go along with these arrangements."[63]

Why? Certainly some relief organizations believed that they had little choice. MSF's financial independence might allow it to walk away, but those agencies that relied on Western funders could not be so high-minded. To criticize NATO's heavy-handed presence in the humanitarian operation overtly or to refuse to work in camps run by their own governments would have cut against their short- and the long-term interests.[64] And, Kosovo was not some forgotten emergency in the middle of Africa; instead, it was a media-saturated crisis in Europe, providing a showcase for many agencies to demonstrate to the world and their donors what they could do.

Yet their willingness to ally themselves with NATO also owed to their perception that they were on the same side. Many openly supported NATO action because they had watched the lack of a response to Bosnia and now were desperately worried they were about to see indifference redux.[65] In the months leading up to the war, many agencies had continuously reminded Western powers of what their impotence had wrought in Bosnia and how the end game required the threat and use of military force, urging the West to apply these lessons learned to Kosovo. InterAction, the association of American NGOs, wrote to the U.S. National Security Council as early as June 1998 to encourage a military intervention to protect Kosovar Albanians.[66] As the violence continued with no political settlement in sight, more agencies made increasingly urgent appeals for a more forceful response. Accordingly, once the diplomatic talks collapsed and the bombing began, they saw themselves as allied with NATO as part of a humanitarian operation designed to protect civilians.[67] Oxfam appeared so enthralled with the idea of a NATO intervention that one journalist called the British army "a bit like Oxfam's military wing."[68] In general, human rights organizations and relief agencies that had integrated a rights discourse into their operations turned out to be humanitarian warriors.

NATO's commandeering of the relief effort, the alliance between aid agencies and NATO, and the general politicization of humanitarianism had several consequences for the provision of relief and protection of civilians. It contributed to a bilateralization of the relief effort. Once NATO took charge of the relief effort, it quickly delegated different zones to different governments and their militaries, bypassing the UNHCR, which was increasingly starved for funds, and favoring their "national" NGOs to work in their "national" camps.[69] Although NATO insisted that this organization would improve the efficiency of the relief effort, it also would allow them to take credit for the relief effort.[70] As one aid worker reflected, "NGOs from particular countries were often selected to work in particular camps where 'their' army was in control—not necessarily because that NGO was the most competent."[71]

More problematic, the bilateralization of relief by NATO did not necessarily benefit the refugees. Notwithstanding NATO's boast that it was more efficient than NGOs, its lack of experience showed, as it made various mistakes, including choosing sites that had been previously rejected by NGOs because of their unsuitability.[72] Bilateralism also led to varying standards, inequalities across camps, the failure of NATO's troop-contributing countries to meet the basic needs of the populations, and the attempt by beneficiaries to play one national authority off of another in order to get the best aid package.[73]

Now that humanitarian agencies and NATO were on the same side, many agencies felt the need to censor their views regarding its conduct of the war. They had lobbied NATO to use force, if needed, and thus implicitly or explicitly viewed the start of hostilities as an unfortunate but necessary development. Consequently, once the war began and they began to fear that NATO's wartime conduct might be increasing civilian casualties and violating international humanitarian law, the aid agencies did not feel free to speak their minds.[74] NATO's decision to avoid ground troops and to fight the war from the air made it easier for Milošević to execute ethnic cleansing; that is, how NATO fought the war in the name of protection actually led to a protection crisis. MSF had a pointed debate over whether or not to call for ground troops, and while there was considerable sympathy for the need, ultimately it refused to say one way or another, because it was worried about giving sanction to a "humanitarian war."[75] Accordingly, when the consequences unfolded, MSF felt poorly positioned to criticize NATO for delivering exactly what it had wanted.[76] Aid agencies also were remarkably quiet when rumors began circulating that NATO was dropping cluster bombs; Human Rights Watch was one of the few rights-based agencies to speak out against their purported use. Although some agencies protested NATO's bombing of Belgrade and targeting of non-military facilities, again, the decibel level was noticeably low. Oxfam, for instance, muted its concerns in order to avoid confronting Western governments at a critical moment during the war.[77]

This politicized humanitarianism also shattered the sacrosanct principle of impartiality.[78] Indeed, it revealed the extent to which these principles rested on a functionalist and interest-based logic. Relief agencies developed and defended these principles because they facilitated their access to populations at risk, gave them a measure of security and operational freedom, enhanced their legitimacy and funding, and enabled them to work virtually anywhere in the world.[79] Yet in Kosovo, impartiality served no immediate purpose, as these goals were already assured. Indeed, in Kosovo the traditional incentives for impartiality reversed course. As Nicholas Stockton wrote, "There were neither security concerns nor difficulties negotiating access to the refugee populations with parties to the conflict. There were no donors insisting on strategies to minimize the incorporation of aid into the dynamics of the conflict. On the contrary, working in the camps actually required agencies to set aside impartiality. That they were prepared to do so with such dispatch creates the strong suspicion that the value of humanitarian principles for many agencies is a means more than an end."[80]

The willingness to forgo impartiality, however, was not without costs. From Serbia's perspective, NATO's humanitarian and military activities were one and the same.[81] Indeed, because NATO had militarized the camps, it became a legitimate target in Serbia's eyes. And because relief agencies were allied with NATO, they also could be treated as combatants.[82] There also was relatively little attention to the humanitarian situation in Serbia. Serbia had been hosting a very large refugee community, many of whom had fled the Croatian province of Krajina in the last stages of ethnic cleansing during the Bosnian war. It then experienced civilian casualties as a result of the NATO bombing. In response to these perceived humanitarian needs, in May 1999 a UN interagency needs assessment mission called for more assistance to Serbia, but none came. Although impartiality-guided aid agencies should have shown up on both sides of the border and attempted to treat all those in need according to the same allocation principles, "political considerations seem to have given rise both to humanitarian excesses on one side of the conflict, and a equally dramatic shortfall on the other."[83]

Kosovo offered no conclusions, only further uncertainties, about the legitimacy of humanitarian intervention, and the UN-sanctioned intervention in East Timor a few months later only added to the confusion. In an attempt to prod further debate, in 1999 Annan delivered a speech at the UN General Assembly outlining two sovereignties, one defined by the sovereignty of states and the other by the sovereignty of peoples, and calling for the UN to debate how it should respond when states violated the sovereignty of their peoples.[84] Recognizing that the UN has a remarkable capacity for talking to death all good ideas, the Canadian government helped to create the International Commission on Intervention and State Sovereignty. As fate would have it, the commission delivered its report just days after September 11, 2001, ensuring that one of the year's most anticipated reports received a minimum of media attention.

The process that led up to the "responsibility to protect" has been much discussed, but several features capture some broader trends regarding the relationship between humanitarianism and international community.[85] Perhaps most famous was the very idea of a "responsibility to protect," which suggested that if states fail to honor their responsibilities to their peoples, then the international community inherits that responsibility. In many respects, this statement was both revolutionary and evolutionary: it was revolutionary in terms of its crystallization of the claim that sovereignty is not sacrosanct but instead is conditional on how states treat their people, and evolutionary because it was a logical outcome of decades of statements regarding a right to relief. In short, it represented a concise articulation of the longstanding claim about the relationship between the sense of international community and the obligations of that community to protect its weakest members. But a responsibility to protect was not limited to using military force to protect lives. The international community also had a responsibility to act before the crisis erupted into violence. And it also had a "responsibility to rebuild," tying protection to prevention, and humanitarianism to state-building, in a rebuilding exercise opening the door to forms of Western intervention to an extent that would make the nineteenth-century imperial humanitarians blush.[86]

The responsibility to protect represented a logical conclusion of a series of important developments about the relationship between humanitarianism and the international community, and the U.S.-led invasions of Afghanistan and Iraq represented the logical conclusion of decades of transforming humanitarianism from the private into the public. Although U.S. officials did not initially justify the campaigns on humanitarian grounds, preferring to anchor their actions in more traditional national security discourse, humanitarianism colored these invasions in various ways. While the United States did not read these interventions through the language of a responsibility to protect, others did, including Michael Ignatieff, a prominent member of the International Commission on Intervention and State Sovereignty; both the Taliban and Saddam Hussein had bludgeoned their peoples, and Hussein had committed genocide against the Kurdish minority, thus offering fairly persuasive arguments that they were not worthy of sovereignty.

After the invasion, the United States turned to humanitarianism for justifying the war. The United States tied the language of failed states to international security, running with the claim that domestic stability (namely, democracy), markets, and the rule of law are critical for international stability.[87] From the U.S. perspective, humanitarianism was now part of military strategy, integral to winning over "hearts and minds" and thus instrumental for furthering American goals. Much to the horror of aid agencies, Colin Powell called NGOs "force multipliers" and part of the U.S. combat operations.[88] Rumors ran wild among the aid community that if American NGOs did not get on board in Iraq, then they would have their funding cut. The United States engaged in various actions that blurred the roles of the military and humanitarian organizations, including parachuting relief boxes in packages that resembled those that carried ordinance, and having combat troops shed their uniforms in favor of civilian clothing as they delivered relief. Perhaps most controversially, the United States assembled Provincial Reconstruction Teams (PRTs), units that combined military and humanitarian objectives.[89]

But this blurring was not a consequence of the American military strategy to appropriate humanitarianism only; it also occurred because humanitarianism had become more clearly political in its objectives. Although one aid worker recalls many agencies complaining bitterly about the "mixing of military and humanitarian mandates," the simple fact was that the two were becoming indistinguishable. Both sides wanted to strengthen law and order, weaken the warlords, combat corruption, and support human rights. These were all worthy objectives, and it is difficult to see how Afghanistan can attain a reasonable future without them "but they were also clearly political, which meant that we were taking sides in what was turning into a bitter conflict."[90] Agencies, the aid worker continued, had become "part of the front line in what the liberal interventionists now regard as a global war to bring a radical transformation to these conservative and traditional societies."[91] Whereas in the beginning of the 1990s the controversy was whether aid agencies should seek military assistance, a decade later it was the military that sought aid workers for their objectives.[92]

According to many aid agencies, this blurring of boundaries jeopardized the ability of aid agencies to reach those in need and endangered the lives of aid workers, who might now be mistaken as enemy combatants.[93] Although there remains considerable controversy regarding the motives of those who attack aid workers, few suggest that the merger of humanitarianism and combat operations makes life easier for them.[94] After the brutal killing of five MSF workers in northern Afghanistan in the summer of 2004, MSF announced its withdrawal after twenty-four years in Afghanistan and blamed the U.S. government for politicizing aid and thus making aid workers part of the U.S. coalition. And in another war also being fought in the name of humanitarianism, on October 27, 2003, the ICRC headquarters in Baghdad was bombed, killing two ICRC staff and wounding many others outside the gates of the compound. Although the causes of these attacks are still debated, most aid agencies concluded that a primary reason was because of the mixing of aid and war.[95]

Humanitarian organizations are used to being vulnerable, it is an oc-cupational hazard, but they want that vulnerability on their own terms. It should be a vulnerability that owes not to the assumption that they have a unity of purpose with armed forces but rather a vulnerability that owes to their lack of armed protection. It is a vulnerability that is rooted in their being armed with nothing other than good intentions and solely interested in the needs of the population. It is this form of vulnerability, according to many, that provides the basis of trust and their ability to work where they are needed.[96]

10

꧁

Politics and Anti-Politics, or the New Paternalism

OVER THE decades alchemical and emergency agencies differed in many ways, but there was little disagreement on the importance of being apolitical. They knew that their actions had political effects, a point forthrightly accepted by alchemical agencies and sheepishly conceded by emergency agencies. And they had different understandings of what it meant to be apolitical: for those on the emergency side, it meant limiting themselves to saving lives at immediate risk, and for those on the alchemical side, it could include other goals such as development so long as they portrayed such goals as part of universal values and did not intentionally upset the political status quo. But they knew that their moral authority, their ability to work in deeply political waters and get access to those in need, even their ability to raise money, depended on keeping up apolitical appearances. And they did—until the 1990s.

The world-changing events of the 1990s caused all humanitarian agencies to rethink their relationship to politics and, in the process, their humanitarian identity. Remarkably, the emerging consensus was that humanitarianism could and should engage in politics, if by politics it meant explicitly recognizing that the goals of justice, peace, and equality required changing politics as usual. Some who favored this move insinuated that because their politics was a politics of humanity, it should not be mistaken with a contemptible form of politics of the state. But accepting this view required considerable nuance. Nor did this more accepting view of politics sit well with everyone, especially those on the emergency side. But the times were changing, and humanitarianism was changing with them.

Yet there was a counterreformation coming from a different direction. In the process of enlarging the space and goals of humanitarianism, humanitarian organizations shifted their focus from the ends of humanitarianism to the means. Becoming better at what they did was hardly a sin and, in most respects, long overdue. Humanitarianism was too big and too important to be left to amateurs, and the victims deserved better. This machinery, built in the name of the victims, though, increasingly removed decisionmaking power from them. In other words, both politics and anti-politics swelled the power of those whose intentions were always good over those who could not be assumed to know any better or act in their own best interests.

Becoming Political

Over the 1990s, aid agencies were increasingly practicing their own version of creative destruction—moments of destruction also became opportunities for acts of creation that potentially created a more just, secure, and peaceful world. Such sentiments became realized and then exercised in the context of postconflict reconstruction and peacebuilding, when those who once focused on keeping people alive now began to wonder how to help people put their lives and their societies back together. But few imagined a return to a status quo that contributed to the suffering and killing. Instead, they reimagined what life might be like, and they envisioned uplifting possibility. They would dismantle the instruments of violence by disarming warring factions, separating armed groups, decommissioning weapons, reintegrating soldiers into civilian life, and professionalizing militaries, civilian police, and the entire public security apparatus. They would help those who had fled during the violence return to their homes and become reintegrated in society. They would assemble the foundations for economic development by privatizing the marketplace, creating stock markets, introducing new tax codes, promoting more efficient property rights, enacting land reform, and (re)building the basic infrastructure required for commerce. They would promote democracy by monitoring elections, giving technical advice to candidates on how to organize political parties and campaign in competitive elections, promoting institutions of representation, and rebuilding the administrative apparatus and the judicial system. They would advance human rights and the rule of law by developing an independent media, civil society organizations, and a culture of tolerance.

What led humanitarian agencies down this political path? The notion of a "herd mentality" suggests that changes in the global environment were responsible. As recounted in the previous chapter, the global forces of destruction, production, and compassion created new opportunities and pressures for aid agencies to go where they once failed or refused to go. But were they pushed or did they jump? The heart of the question is: how are we to understand the simultaneous increase in generosity by major powers for postconflict and peacebuilding activities that had a decidedly liberal hue and the growing willingness of Western aid agencies to undertake programs that pointed in the same direction? Perhaps major donors used their power of the purse to get aid agencies either to do what they would otherwise not do or to rearrange their priorities in ways that matched what donors were willing to fund. How much coercion was involved, or how much aid agencies were willing to change their policies, depends on whether one believes that aid agencies and major donors had coinciding or contending interests. If the latter, aid agencies were ready to do what it took to satisfy what their big donors wanted. If the former, aid agencies were simply capitalizing on new opportunities and picking low-hanging money.[1]

The story of aid agencies finding politics, I argue, has less to do with money and more to do with identity. The major donors were ready to put up more money for more activities at precisely the same time that many alchemical agencies wanted to do more than provide a "bed for the night" or keep alive the "well-fed dead." Ethics creep as mission creep. This was hardly a new development. After World War II in Europe many relief agencies turned to reconstruction, moving from "help to self-help." Relief and development agencies were tunneling toward each other: relief agencies were increasingly contemplating how to tie relief to postconflict reconstruction, and development agencies were increasingly trying to use relief operations as a springboard for development. Both relief and development agencies were interacting more and more with human rights activists, and the three sectors began discovering areas of common concern and wondering how integrating their activities might create synergies for progress and peace.[2] Yet moving toward politics was not a simple transition for a humanitarian identity that had long defined itself in opposition to politics. In addition to pockets of resistance within particular agencies that eventually moved toward politics, the emergency humanitarians argued that principles that served them well for over a century would see them through the current challenges, too.

This debate over the humanitarian identity was shaped by its relationship to human rights. For many aid agencies, human rights was a four-letter word, so to speak. Human rights activists named and shamed, championed reform movements, badgered states to respect the rule of law. Humanitarian organizations, on the other hand, attended the needs of the population and believed that passing judgment on the government would risk sacrificing their principal responsibility. Yet this new liberal international order was organized around a rights discourse, and human rights activists, often unaware that many in the relief sector distinguished between humanitarianism and human rights, began to wander onto humanitarian soil. Many in the relief sector returned the interest in human rights, as they began exploring the relationship between their traditional activities and the practices of human rights and, increasingly, accepting the world of politics. Yet not everyone was thrilled with this turn of events, a point communicated clearly to me by an aid worker who exclaimed that he would have an easier time having a beer with a soldier than having a cup of coffee with a human rights activist. The coming-of-age stories of CARE International, Catholic Relief Services, World Vision International, the UNHCR, and MSF illustrate how the same global forces were filtered through distinctive humanitarian identities to produce different positions regarding politics.

CARE

Over the 1990s CARE underwent a dramatic process of organizational change that led it, at first grudgingly and then willingly, into politics. It became a "rights-based," antipoverty agency that sought to transform societies and reform international and national public policies. As one high-level CARE official put it, "We used to say we were 'non non non' but now we are political and we see this."[3] What accounts for this change of mind? The organization did not appear to be chasing the money. At the same time that CARE was revisiting its organizational culture, it also was striving to diversify its funding base and reduce its dependence on the United States. Also, CARE was focusing on social and economic rights, whereas the U.S. government preferred its rights political and civil. Its advocacy work frequently led it to oppose American foreign policy. Nor is there evidence that CARE adopted the rights language with the expectation that it would be rewarded for doing so. In fact, many CARE officials asserted that the general view at the time was that embracing rights might cost them. An organization that had built its reputation and generated much of its income based on service delivery might be mortgaging its future. Former CARE president Peter Bell, who oversaw the change, insisted that moving toward rights was not a marketing device. Indeed, he continued, "We would do infomercials for RBA [rights-based approach] on TV, and it was a complete loser. We were told by consultants to go back to the starving baby and emergencies. We decided to swallow the lost dollars."[4] In general, CARE's attempt to placate its donors revolved around improving the quality of its programs, reducing their cost, and locating additional sources of support—not changing its priorities.[5]

CARE gravitated toward rights and politics because of considerable reflection over shortcomings in the field, a leadership change that stimulated, organized, and channeled these internal discussions toward a rights framework, and a belief that the inclusion of politics would address chronic issues of deprivation, poverty, and violence. By the late 1980s, staff had become profoundly dissatisfied with the status quo, and events of the 1990s would not make them any happier. Development had fallen on hard times in the 1980s, development assistance was harder to come by, and there was mounting evidence that CARE's policies were not effective. CARE staff can easily narrate the progression of their unease and their proposed solution. In the 1970s there was the African food crisis, which led to a consideration of the multiple causes of food scarcity, including the argument, associated with Amartya Sen, regarding the relationship between authoritarianism and famine. Staff also began to research how individuals and families cope and survive during famines and severe food shortages, which, in turn, led to a greater interest in household decisions. Importantly, as they searched for the causes of the programs' failures, they circled around the omitted variables of rights and politics.

These considerations led to the Household Livelihood Security (HLS) in 1994.[6] Before the HLS, CARE, like many development agencies, typically treated households as distinct and relatively independent units that required more inputs in order to put food on the table and escape chronic poverty; reducing poverty, therefore, amounted to generating more income and then, with any luck, investing that income wisely so that it could improve the family's circumstances. A major problem with this orientation, CARE staff concluded, was that it extracted the household from its environment and thus ignored the structural causes of poverty. This conclusion challenged CARE's service delivery mentality. Delivering more services was not the answer, changing the environment was. CARE was now stepping outside of the friendly confines of its technical and managerial world and into the world of politics and power.[7] Accordingly, as it developed the HLS, it also dissected the "the relative power relationships within and among households and authority structures."[8] It now began to think "holistically," that is, to integrate politics into its operations. Soon thereafter, CARE began to use the language of rights, to see individuals as rights-bearers and governments and others as rights-protectors and to tie rights to poverty and development. In 1999 CARE pulled together these threads into the "Unifying Framework for Poverty Eradication and Social Justice," in which it highlighted the need to alter social positions, in order to improve social equity; human conditions, in order to improve economic security; and the enabling environment, in order to improve governance.[9] Politics and rights were part of the antipoverty equation.

Relief workers also were struggling over how to improve their policies, though they were doing so in a context of humanitarian emergencies. For the most part, CARE workers, like relief workers everywhere, were consumed with the immediate challenge of saving people. Once conflict gave way to a postconflict process, though, they began to explore the relationship between relief and reconstruction. Rights became a natural bridge between the two—especially once rights were framed to include both relief and livelihoods. At this point CARE staff joined the chorus of others in the field who were speaking of a "relief-rights-development continuum." Additionally, relief workers began to tire of treating symptoms and began to explore the causes of vulnerability and use the language of mitigation. Such reflections immediately led relief workers to draw a straight line connecting rights, politics, and causes of suffering.[10]

The executive office at CARE played an important role in organizing and channeling these discussions. Philip Johnston, a longtime member of CARE, resigned as president in 1992 and was replaced by Peter Bell. A former chair of Americas Watch (the precursor of Human Rights Watch) and a member of the boards of both HRW and CARE, Bell embodied the very split between the humanitarian and the human rights communities. Bell came to the office convinced that CARE had to get beyond technique and consider rights and empowerment, a position that CARE staff feared would transform their relief and development organization, which worked quietly behind the scenes and sought the cooperation of governments, into a rights-oriented organization that shouts at governments, stomps its feet, makes noise, and names and shames.

Fearing a backlash, the executive office moved cautiously. At first it distinguished between needs and rights. A rights-based perspective presumes that people have claims to "minimum levels of treatment, services, and opportunities," simply because of their humanity. Consequently, individuals are entitled to these items, not because they need them to survive or live a life with dignity but merely because they are entitled to them. Its starting point was the Universal Declaration of Human Rights, because of its broad support from the NGO community and its orienting concepts like dignity, justice, and empowerment, which were part of CARE's values. This exercise was followed by a discussion that focused on how rights are understood at the local level. CARE also held a conversation on its core values, ultimately creating a vision statement that employed the language of rights, dignity, and empowerment.[11]

In November 1996 CARE's International Board launched a formal examination of the relationship between its activities and human rights. Working with the Ford Foundation, it sponsored a series of field-based studies that used a "human rights lens" to examine CARE's activities. These cases led CARE to explore the possibility of a more systematic appraisal of the benefits and risks of such an approach, but with "remarkable consensus" among senior staff from eighteen field and home offices on the need to integrate a human rights perspective into CARE's relief and development programs.

By the end of the 1990s, CARE had gravitated toward a rights-based approach (RBA). According to CARE, RBA focuses on "people achieving the minimal conditions for living with dignity. They are not only civil and political rights, but also social, cultural, and economic rights. At a basic level, we focus on the rights related to livelihood security—such as nutrition, education, and economic opportunity. But we also consider other conditions influencing livelihood security and, more broadly, life with dignity—such as personal security and participation in public affairs."[12] In other words, a right-based approach conceivably includes nearly all kinds of cultural, religious, social, economic, and political activities.

An organization that once rejected "politics" now embraced it—and the only question left was how political should it be. Bell, who once worried that the mere mention of politics might cause major institutional turmoil, now used the concept without fear. Nearing the end of his tenure, Bell reflected on these changes. In the early 1990s CARE had been a "service delivery" organization that prided itself on its "ability to control...complex logistical systems [and its] technical and apolitical" character. Not anymore. Although it knows that as "humanitarian agency" it must be "independent, impartial, and nonpartisan," it also "must understand and grapple with power relations. We have come to realize that our commitment to reducing—and ultimately ending—extreme poverty is, by its very nature, political. This is not the CARE that our parents would have known!" Previous definitions of neutrality, Bell continued, no longer made sense. Whereas once neutrality meant a "commitment to be apolitical," [that is, to avoid any contact with or input into public affairs or matters of governance]," now neutrality allows CARE to stand in favor of principles even as it avoids partisanship. In sum, whereas humanitarianism once was viewed as the opposite of politics, now politics and humanitarianism share the same space and are opposed to "partisanship."

CRS

A remarkably similar story occurred at Catholic Relief Services, though its Catholic identity shaped the answers they gave to the questions that were being asked at CARE and other relief agencies. CRS entered the late 1980s in something of a malaise, and the end of the Cold War only added to its worries. CRS had become one of the world's premier development agencies, which was hardly gratifying given that there was mounting evidence that the billions of dollars in assistance were not translating into development for the world's poor. CRS fell into a "funk," as one former official recalled. Moreover, the end of the Cold War translated into a decline in development assistance, which had a devastating effect on CRS, which was already reeling from a drop in private giving. There was a palpable shortage of money, but there was no shortage of metaphors. CRS, according to one official, was like a "sponge going dry"; according to another, "like air going out of a balloon."[13] These financial worries were very poorly timed: the post–Cold

War spike in humanitarian emergencies increased the pressure on CRS to provide more and different kinds of services. One senior executive recalled that, at the time, they feared that they were three years away from bankruptcy. The combination of an already demoralized organization, declining financial support, and growing needs created a looming existential angst.[14]

During the early 1990s, CRS coped with the rising demands as best it could, but everything came apart with the Rwandan genocide. Many staff had worked in Rwanda and had close Rwandan friends, many of whom had worked for the agency. The Rwandan genocide was not an abstraction but an intimate and emotionally felt event. The bloodshed washed away communities in which they had worked, destroyed years of programming, and claimed the lives of their friends and their families. In addition to the shock, grief, and sense of loss, many questioned how they could have lived and worked in Rwanda and not have seen the possibility of a genocide. They knew of the animosity between the Hutus and the Tutsis, but never did they imagine that such divisions might evolve into one of the century's great crimes. They wondered whether their programs were partially to blame for their myopia, technical programs that were designed to improve the welfare of communities but were purposefully oblivious to the politics of ethnicity.[15] What James Orbinski wrote about MSF was true of many agencies, including many with whom I spoke at CRS: "In retrospect, the response of MSF was technically near perfect, but politically uninformed. Although three of MSF's five operational centres had been working in the country since 1990, there had been no systematic effort to develop a coherent political analysis. Now a reactive response to the chaos on the ground was the best MSF could do, and this meant that no one knew or was able to infer just what was going on."[16]

The genocide forced CRS to confront a set of fundamental, identity-defining questions that had lingered for several years but had been postponed in deference to the momentary emergency. Its journey included a reconsideration of its Catholic identity. As many staff recall, Catholic Relief Services had always been Catholic, but over the years its professional and technocratic ethos had crowded out any religious overtones. There was no "Catholic" way to development—instead, there were methods underpinned by technical, objective knowledge learned from development manuals and economics departments. Also, emphasizing their technocratic character helped CRS avoid charges that it was operating in the grand tradition of colonialism and furthering the political interests of the United States. But after Rwanda, as one senior staff recalled, "We decided that if we were going to survive, then we had to return to our Catholic identity." Staff turned to Catholic Social Teaching as their guide, drawing from the theological orientation laid down by Vatican II and its emphasis on social engagement and justice. Thus began the movement toward a "justice lens." Following these religious tenets, in 1995 CRS launched a strategic planning process designed to integrate "justice" into its identity and programming.[17] "Justice," for CRS, included human rights. But its definition of human rights went beyond the conventional definition adopted by many rights agencies, for it also incorporated "the active promotion of transformations within societies that would prevent further human rights abuses by cultivating a culture of peace, respect, and dignity."[18]

There is little evidence that CRS sought to recover its Catholic identity for financial reasons. In fact, at the time some worried that this direction might cost the agency at a moment when it could not afford to jeopardize any source of support. Becoming more avowedly Catholic might hurt its ability to raise money from non-Catholic sources, including the U.S. government. Adopting a more radical position on issues such as social justice and human rights might put it on the outs with American officials; this was not just speculation, for during the 1980s CRS's opposition to American policy toward Latin America had complicated its relations with donors. So, as one senior staff summarized, "We might be biting the hand that feeds us." Also, the American Catholic population is politically diverse, and CRS, which had been drifting leftward ever since Vietnam, might now find itself out of step with the increasingly conservative Catholic base. Lastly, some CRS staff worried about the reaction of American Catholic Bishops, though they were pleasantly surprised when the response seemed to be, "What took you so long?" During the 1980s they had wondered where the Catholic was in their name, and so were delighted to see a concerted effort to reconnect with Catholic Social Teaching.

CRS was now moving toward considerations of justice and trying to promote the "right relationship"—the "right ordering of relationships between and among individuals, groups, communities, nations, and the wider human community." Although "justice" and the "right relationship" cannot be precisely defined, it includes the dignity and equality of the individual, the rights and responsibilities individuals have to one another, the common good, solidarity, preferential treatment for the poor, and subsidiarity and stewardship.[19] An essay written for CRS's 2000 World Summit Conference summarized the emerging view that Catholic Social Teaching and CRS's guiding principles demand that CRS examine "*systems and structures* and...support the appropriate role of the State in promoting the common good." CRS needs to become engaged in peacebuilding, not at the expense of justice but in its name. It put the challenge squarely: "We can choose to address one piece at a time and have individuals peppered throughout the agency working on particular pieces of a pie that may or may not form a whole, or we can make a conscious decision to support a transformative approach that changes hearts and minds while creating the necessary structures to support such a shift in conceptual understanding."[20] In short, CRS began to move toward a position that involved tackling the root causes of injustice and the violation of human rights that are essential for human dignity, which required that it interrogate the fundamental structures of society. In general, CRS, as one staffer summarized, was trying to bring together the sacred and the social.

A striking feature of the "justice lens" was the way it treated the relationship between the haves and the have-nots. "Solidarity" took on a new meaning. Solidarity had traditionally meant identifying with the struggles of others to help them overcome oppression. In other words, "we" help "them" try to upend systems of inequality that are produced and sustained by local forces. Americans need do nothing more than write a check. But what if "we" and our actions are part of these systems of inequality, however unintended? To be in genuine solidarity demanded that Americans ask tough questions about how their conduct sustains injustice. As the Reverend J. Bryan Hehir observed, "Solidarity is the conviction that we are born into a fabric of relationships, that our humanity ties us to others, that gospel consecrates those ties and that the prophets tell us that those ties are the test by which our very holiness will be judged."[21] Americans need to ask themselves how they consume, how they vote, how they trade, how they spend, and how the sum total of those activities contributes to the enrichment or impoverishment of others. What would Jesus drive?

Various constituencies within CRS supported this change in orientation. In 1993 Ken Heck was named executive director, and one of his platforms was the need to reconnect the organization to its Catholic roots, by which he meant not the justice lens but rather a closer connection to local churches around the world. There were, as already mentioned, those who had worked in Rwanda. Others wanted to address the causes of suffering. There were staff who had worked in Latin America and who were deeply influenced by a Catholic Church that frequently was preaching liberation theology, was on the front lines of social justice and progressive politics, and was insisting that it was necessary to delve beneath the symptoms of injustice to get to the causes. Not everyone was ready for this sort of change; particularly anxious were those who were not Catholics or who had not seen themselves as working in a faith-based agency that wore its religion on its sleeve. As part of this process of change, all four thousand CRS employees went through a series of discussions, known as a "justice reflection," organized around the justice lens. As one high-ranking staff person reflected, this process "changed our DNA."[22]

World Vision International

World Vision International turned in a more political direction around the time of the end of the Cold War.[23] Until the 1990s, WVI kept its vow to abstain from working with and accepting contracts from states and multilateral organizations in any significant way, but beginning in that decade it relaxed its position for several reasons. It wanted to diversify its funding base and reduce its reliance on sponsorship in order to increase its flexibility. Emergencies, postconflict reconstruction processes, and state agendas created new funding opportunities. It believed that capitalizing on official assistance could further its private fundraising, and vice versa. WVI did not go down this path lightly. As WVI President Graeme Irvine wrote: "We must be fully aware of the implications of becoming what has been called a 'public service contractor,' with consequent pressure to conform to the requirements of major funding sources in contradiction with our essential character."[24] In order to guard against that possibility, WVI pledged to limit its revenue from official sources to 20 percent, and it has held to that.

WVI's decision to turn toward politics, with an explicit consideration of social justice, inequality, access to power, and poor people's movements, resulted from disappointments with its programs' effectiveness, a concern that its programs needed to reclaim their spiritual and religious character, and religious debates. As already noted, at its creation WVI emphasized relief and religious conversion, all the while following a traditional line regarding the separation of church and state, and then in the 1980s it became more technocratic. But as soon as WVI began drifting in a more technocratic direction, there was a concerted conversation in the agency over the relationship between religion and development. After much debate, WVI adopted the language of "transformational development," understood as incorporating the material *and* spiritual aspects of development. Several factors account for its rise and significance. There was growing dissatisfaction with a "modernist" approach to development that assumed that material inputs were separate from spirituality. In addition, those in the agency were periodically taking their "temperature" to see if they were "Christian enough" and began to try to identify a Christian perspective on development.[25] This had been an ongoing concern, and beginning in the 1990s the conversation turned to the connection between Christianity and social justice, and fundamental rights.[26] Furthermore, like much of the aid community, WVI began to consider the relationship between relief and reconstruction and how to tackle the causes of violence, injustice, and hardship. In general, WVI broke away from its traditional religious confines and into the political world, as it addressed explicitly issues of power, governance, and justice. Although it avoided the language of politics because of its longstanding discomfort, favoring euphemisms like "advocacy," WVI's humanitarianism now occupied some of the same ground it once conceded to Caesar.

The UNHCR

Even the UNHCR was getting into politics. According to its mandate, the UNHCR is a humanitarian and apolitical organization, which largely meant that it would not involve itself in the causes of refugee flight. For its first three decades, the UNHCR was true to its mandate and tried to expand in every direction but politics. Yet beginning in the 1980s it confronted a set of external pressures that forced it to reexamine the dividing line between humanitarianism and politics. The primary catalyst was the UNHCR's need to shift its position on solutions to refugee crises from asylum and third-country resettlement to repatriation.[27] All three possible solutions to refugee flight are mentioned in the UNHCR's statute, but it quickly developed a belief that the permanent solution for a refugee was relocation outside her home country. This orientation derived less from principles than from the circumstances confronted by the UNHCR during its first three decades. Specifically, most of the refugees the UNHCR encountered came from communist countries. They did not want to return home and the West could not imagine sending them back. These factors led the UNHCR to develop an "exilic bias," which matched its desire to steer clear of politics.[28] As the executive committee reflected on its humanitarian clause, "From the time of its establishment in 1951 until the early 1980s, there was a broad international consensus that UNHCR could only respect its 'humanitarian and non-political' status by confining its activities to countries of asylum and by responding to refugee movements once they had taken place. Any effort to address the conditions giving rise to forced populations displacements within countries of origin…would have involved the Office in functions which fell beyond the scope of its Statute, and were therefore impermissible."[29]

By the late 1970s, however, Western and Third World states began to resent the heavy demands placed on them by the refugee regime, especially the growing refugee populations in their own countries, at times violently forcing them to go home; such states were now adopting, according to the High Commissioner, a policy of "deterrence."[30] States expected the UNHCR to do its part, and the UNHCR had very little choice but to go along—refusing would not help the refugees, many of whom were in immediate danger, and it would certainly complicate the UNHCR's relationship with powerful patrons. Moreover, the growing refugee population residing in semi-permanent cities was a fiscal sinkhole for the UNHCR, leading it to look for ways to reduce their numbers and alleviate some of the financial pressures.[31] This emerging position on repatriation was driven not only by expediency and budgets but also by principles. The refugee agency was committed to helping refugees, many of whom wanted to go home and were "spontaneously repatriating."[32]

Because it would be difficult to determine when it was safe to repatriate refugees without some sense of whether the situation at home had improved, the UNHCR had to begin to look at the conditions of refugee-producing countries—in other words, politics. The UNHCR's repatriation practices included a commitment that refugees return home with "safety and dignity," which invariably necessitated examining the political and human rights climate that would affect their reintegration. The UNHCR also began to consider the relationship between refugee repatriation and economic assistance.[33] By the 1980s the UNHCR was monitoring the politics of refugee-producing countries and the factors that would affect repatriation, a development given further support by the arrival of the new High Commissioner, Jean-Pierre Hocke.[34] Soon thereafter the UNHCR began proposing concepts such as "state responsibility" and "root causes," stating that refugee flows are caused by "violations of human rights and, increasingly, by military or armed activities" and exploring how these factors prevented the successful repatriation of refugees.[35] These developments were blurring the UNHCR's distinction between humanitarianism and politics. As Hocke mused, while UNHCR is mandated to be humanitarian and apolitical,

> where does one draw the line between the "humanitarian" and the "political"? Sometimes a facile distinction is made by referring to all action addressed to the situation in the country of asylum as "humanitarian" and any action addressed to the causes of the situation in the country of origin as "political." I reject this distinction. To me, any action which is addressed to and motivated by the concern and well-being of human beings is "humanitarian".... UNHCR must be concerned with the question of root causes.[36]

Acutely aware that it was treading into sensitive waters, each step of the way was carefully monitored for the first signs of pushback from states.

The 1990s and its new security environment created new pressures and opportunities for the UNHCR to become more deeply involved in the affairs of states. Civil wars and collapsed states were producing massive refugee flows, destabilizing neighboring countries and entire regions; in many instances population displacement was not simply a tragic byproduct of war but rather its intended effect. Beginning with the 1991 Iraq War, the UNHCR was becoming increasingly involved in bringing relief to displaced peoples instead of waiting for displaced peoples to receive relief on the other side of an international border. Also, there were more refugees repatriating than ever before. Between 1985 and 1990, roughly 1.2 million refugees went home, but in the following five years, often in the context of peace agreements, that number exploded to 9 million. The UNHCR was the obvious candidate to help with the repatriation and reintegration, which meant that it had to become more deeply involved in domestic politics.[37] Repatriation, in turn, led to in-country assistance, internal protection, development, human rights, and peacebuilding.[38] By 1997 the agency redefined reintegration such that it was virtually synonymous with "sustainable" return, that is, a harmonious relationship among returnees, civil society, and the consolidated state.[39] Lastly, like many international humanitarian agencies, the UNHCR distinguished itself as apolitical by disavowing human rights work, which was inherently political because it was impossible to monitor and report on human rights violations without challenging the state in some capacity. Accordingly, the UNHCR followed tradition and tried to avoid any whisper of human rights.[40] The general movement to connect refugee rights to human rights simply blurred the distinction between the humanitarian and the political.

A 1991 document captured the emerging spirit of the times and provided a window on future developments. The UNHCR's Working Group on International Protection explored the viability of its apolitical credentials given its growing involvement in refugee-producing countries. It made four observations. First, "The evolution of UNHCR's role over the last forty years has demonstrated that the mandate is resilient enough to allow, or indeed require, adaptation by UNHCR to new, unprecedented challenges through new approaches, including in the areas of prevention and in-country protection." Refugee rights, the document noted, are part and parcel of human rights; thus, the UNHCR's role as protector of refugee law legitimates its growing concern for the violations of human rights that cause refugee flows. Second, the UN General Assembly recognized the UNHCR's humanitarian expertise and experience for justifying its expansion into activities not traditionally defined within the office's mandate.[41] Third, "the High Commissioner's non-political mandate requires neutrality," but "neutrality must be coupled with a thorough understanding of prevailing political and other realities." Fourth, whereas once humanitarianism meant avoiding the "political" circumstances within the home country and honoring the principle of noninterference, it soon began to include aspects of the state's internal affairs.

These developments elevated the UNHCR's profile and international relevance, a welcome relief to an organization that had spent the previous decade worried about its future.[42] During the 1980s states had increasingly questioned the UNHCR's existence and effectiveness, and by decade's end it was experiencing a major financial crisis.[43] The 1990s presented not only new challenges for the organization but also new opportunities to demonstrate its continued importance. As High Commissioner Sadako Ogata wrote, "We have gone the extra mile to carry out our mission, and sometimes we had to do what others were not ready or not prepared to do.... [W]e should not give up on a project just because it does not fit into traditional schemes.... *In order to be financed, in a highly competitive environment*, UNHCR must develop new, *interesting* approaches to fulfill its core mission."[44] Developing "interesting" approaches was good for refugees and their agency. In general, states were signaling to the UNHCR that it could become more involved in political areas once kept under lock and key, a situation that many in the UNHCR believed rewarded the organization for what it should be doing anyway.

Yet UNHCR staff was divided over how far they could go down the political road without jeopardizing the agency's "humanitarian" and "apolitical" character.[45] The principal division in the UNHCR on these matters was between the "fundamentalists" and the "pragmatists." Fundamentalists maintained a more legalistic approach to refugee matters, emphasizing law, the mandate, and various mechanisms that would ensure their impartiality, neutrality, and independence, and were likely to reside in the legal and protection divisions of the organization. The "pragmatists" argued for a more flexible interpretation of refugee law and the UNHCR's mandate, for becoming involved in broader international peace and security issues, especially as they pertained to helping create and sustain a more stable and democratic home country that would not threaten repatriating refugees. In other words, the UNHCR could maintain its principles while satisfying its patrons. Importantly, the pragmatists were represented by Ogata herself.[46] Although Ogata claimed to want to find a middle ground between those who embraced and those who rejected politics, she clearly favored the former, defining "humanitarian" as any action that increased the well-being of the individual while avoiding those controversies that were highly political and best handled by states.[47] The UNHCR now defined humanitarian assistance to include prevention, which was always preferable to the cure, and the attempt to foster respect for human rights in order to curtail refugee flows. It insisted that this development did not imply that it was political, because it was operating with the consent of the state (except in those circumstances where there was no state to give consent), but its humanitarianism now included practices it once decried as politics.[48]

MSF

Not all aid agencies were ready to embrace politics. In keeping with its well-earned reputation for speaking its mind, MSF became the standard-bearer of the emergency humanitarianism's fundamentalist position. Indeed, it seemed that the more political humanitarianism became, the more that MSF wanted to defend a "pure" humanitarianism that never really existed, at least not at MSF. It had already backpedaled away from the notion of humanitarian intervention, taking even positions that appeared to cut against its founding spirit of making noise to bring international action to protect populations at risk. While all other agencies were drifting into peacebuilding and postconflict reconstruction, MSF put on the brakes. As one member emphasized: "A lot of other NGOs talk about the need for reconstruction—well, I don't want to be engaged in reconstruction, because I don't want Mr. Taliban to think I'm trying to rebuild his country as part of the U.S. strategy. I want to be able to go to him honestly and say, 'All we're trying to do is keep people alive, to provide medical care for people who are wound or sick. We're not trying to build your country at all, that's not our job.'"

Strikingly, MSF began to separate itself from the human rights agenda and even voiced second thoughts about its founding principle of *témoignage*. As one MSF staffer recalled, when MSF created the practice of *témoignage*, it was radically new because it "broke with the long tradition of silence attached to humanitarian action.... The overthrow of this taboo has become a sort of identity mark for MSF."[49] But in the subsequent three decades, MSF had gone from being a trend-setter to being part of a pack of rights-bearing agencies—and it was not always thrilled about the company it was keeping. States were draping themselves in a human rights discourse. There were scores of rights-based agencies who believed that human rights and humanitarianism were the same thing, as they privileged "rights" over "need" and were occasionally willing to use food to promote human rights.[50] Human rights increasingly became something of a dirty word at MSF. In countless interviews, I was told by MSF workers that MSF is *not* a human rights agency. Yes, they would concede, rights is part of its mandate, but it is not a rights-based organization, meaning an agency that is more interested in promoting freedom than basic needs, more interested in building legal and moral cases against governments than creating a space in which humanitarian agencies can operate.[51] They began to have debates over the meaning of *témoignage* to ensure that it did not look like concepts adopted by rights agencies.[52]

Yet even this medical emergency agency felt the pressure to put down roots in an unexpected way. Over its three decades it was increasingly working in non-emergency settings, especially as once temporary refugee camps became semipermanent entities. In fact, more and more of its budget was dedicated to providing medical care in non-emergency settings. And, because it seemed unjust that refugees should be treated better than the surrounding population, it opened its clinics to the local communities. Soon MSF had become the principal public health provider in various locales, a position that made many MSF staff uneasy, even as they saw no acceptable alternative, given that the resource-challenged government was probably not going to take its place if it departed. Although MSF had drifted into the position of becoming a permanent health provider in various communities, it had steered clear of formally declaring any interest in broader public health issues, in part because these were deemed to be matters of governance. In 2000, though, it departed from tradition when it launched the "access to medicines" campaign. Using the money (and prestige) it received after winning the Nobel Peace Prize in 1999, MSF decided to see whether it could drum up support for more research on "Third World diseases" and lower the cost of life-saving medicines that were prohibitively expensive for local populations (as well as for medical agencies such as MSF that were playing a greater role in the long-term care of populations). It was now applying the concept of *témoignage* to situations other than emergencies and crises, using its considerable expertise and status to push for a new public health regime.[53]

The decision to start this campaign was hotly debated within the organization. Some worried that MSF was about to experience its own version of mission creep. It would be impossible to create greater access to life-saving medicines without working with governments, international organizations, and the pharmaceutical companies that controlled the patents—in other words, without becoming deeply involved in politics. Many felt that MSF should not involve itself in lobbying.[54] Yet MSF ultimately decided to take the plunge. In many respects, they were being pushed by their field offices, who were watching their patients die because they were poor and did not have access to medicines that were widely available to those in wealthy countries with working public health systems. However, MSF was being shaped not only by the local but also by the global, in this case, a particular sort of globalization. Many MSF staff worried that globalization was turning the ordinary into the extraordinary, that is, encouraging a mentality in which structural inequalities were diagnosed as episodic outbursts that could be treated in a piecemeal fashion. By deciding to move beyond an emergency mentality, MSF wanted to avoid "being reduced to the role of symbolic actor in the globalization process, even becoming its 'good conscience.'"[55]

At stake, from MSF's perspective, was not only its identity but also the species of humanitarianism in general. Humanitarianism, as MSF kept insisting in its texts, documents, and public events, concerned the impartial, neutral, and independent relief to victims of conflict and natural disasters. It was the opposite of politics. States might use military force to protect civilians, but this was not humanitarianism. NGOs might be engaged in various kinds of postconflict reconstruction projects, but this was not humanitarianism. In a speech to NATO in December 2009, MSF International President Christophe Fournier tried to set the record straight between MSF's version of humanitarianism and the long list of activities that might be worthwhile but do not merit the term:

> All these other activities [reconstructing the country, promoting democracy, and so on] might be worthy of praise. They may be even exactly the sort of activities that NATO and NATO countries should be promoting in Afghanistan. But they are goals and activities which fall outside of humanitarian ones. Related? Yes. But outside. More importantly, when humanitarian goals and activities are lumped together with this larger, broader, and

more future-oriented agenda, the direct result is confusion and even contradiction. The indirect result is that civilians in conflict do not receive the
assistance to which they have a right.[56]

These might all be worthwhile activities, but are political and are not
humanitarian.

What was occurring, according to many MSF staff, was not simply the
expansion of the concept or its wrong-headed appropriation. Instead, it
was the transfiguration of humanitarianism beyond all recognition.[57] And,
once humanitarianism became political and included all these other activities, then it would become increasingly difficult for humanitarian agencies
to do what they were supposed to do: save lives at risk. By moving away
from any hint of politics in public, even as many staff conceded in private
that they were political in various ways, MSF was attempting to maintain
a space for humanitarianism. MSF's response to the changing and increasingly politicized times was to try to save humanitarianism from itself. Yet
the ICRC, MSF, and others that held onto the ancient "tongue" of humanitarianism increasingly resembled the aged people in an isolated village who
cling desperately to the hearth language.

As the language of humanitarianism broadened to include new forms of
intervention for the purpose of removing the causes of suffering, injustice,
and war, the people behind this shift were necessarily suggesting that they
had a fairly good idea about what kinds of states and societies should be
created after destruction. Whether they were correct or misguided regarding their plans or not, they were justifying their accumulation of considerable decisionmaking authority on the grounds that they knew what was in
the best interest of local populations, not only in the short term but also
in the long term; that they had divine or quasi-divine sources of knowledge
that gave them confidence in their templates; and that local voices mattered
only to the extent that they helped to implement these existing plans, not
in deciding what the good life was or how to get there. In short, they were
acting in ways not far removed from the actions of liberals and missionaries
during the Age of Imperial Humanitarianism. And they seemed to be every
bit as confident.

Anti-Politics

Humanitarian organizations were fearfully watching states and international organizations gather more power in humanitarian action, but they
seemed blissfully oblivious to their accumulation of power over those in
need. In many respects, their (in)sensitivities were a reflection of their
hard-wired assumptions that states were self-interested beings, international

organizations were not much better, and only they were genuinely interested in the welfare of others. Far from exercising power *over* the weak, they were trying to *em*power them by leveling inequalities. Their good intentions said it all.

Rwanda shattered their comforting self-image. For the aid world, there is before Rwanda and after Rwanda. Rwanda prompted humanitarian agencies to take a long, hard look at themselves and their emerging sector—and they did not like what they saw. Humanitarian agencies might have better intentions than states and international organizations, but good intentions alone were not going to save lives. The Joint Evaluation of Emergency Assistance to Rwanda, one of the first truly independent, bare-knuckled investigations of a relief effort, indicted the response. In one of the report's most oft-quoted passages, "Whilst many NGOs performed impressively, providing a high quality of care and services, a number performed in an unprofessional and irresponsible manner that resulted not only in duplication of wasted resources but may also have contributed to an unnecessary loss of life."[58] This was more than a kick in the pants—this was a blow between the eyes. However diplomatically stated, the charge was that humanitarianism had *contributed to an unnecessary loss of life*. The shortcomings of the humanitarian sector were not limited to Rwanda; its criticisms could have been written about every single large-scale operation.

While aid agencies might have politely received the recommendations and moved on, to their credit they took them seriously and began an impressive process of reforming the entire sector.[59] In almost all respects, these reforms had a visible payoff. Yet their actions, designed to perfect the machinery, also seemed to be building a proverbial "iron cage" that placed more physical, psychological, and moral distance between themselves and those they wanted to help. There was something of an irony here. At the very moment that humanitarianism was becoming more keen to become political, the movement to become more rule-governed and professional had a depoliticizing effect, removing from the equation the history and the power that produced the suffering, thus treating politics as technique.[60] In other words, humanitarianism was becoming obsessed with the means to the neglect of the ends. Modernization was having its chilling effect on humanitarianism, just as it had on other professions of care.

One of the damning critiques of the humanitarian response in Rwanda and of other operations was the absence of uniform standards of care. Although this had always been true, the consequences became especially troubling with more aid agencies than ever before, some quite professional but others quite amateurish.[61] In response, several of the leading aid agencies initiated what became Sphere, a process designed to "improve the quality of the assistance provided to people affected by disasters, and to enhance the accountability of the humanitarian system and its response."[62] In pursuit of these dual goals, Sphere created two documents. The accurately named "Minimum Standards in Disaster Response" established minimal standards in the areas of water, sanitation, nutrition, shelter, site planning, and health.[63] The Humanitarian Charter articulated a concept of responsibility and the principle of a right to assistance.[64] At times their ambitions became audacity. Initial versions of the Charter commanded that "when states are unable to respond they are *obliged* to allow the intervention of humanitarian organizations."[65] Although this passage was dropped from a subsequent version, it reflected how a sense of urgency can lead to overwrought claims. In any event, Sphere represented a highly self-conscious and important effort by aid agencies to link technical standards to human rights.

Although widely applauded, the exercise was not without its critics. Some wondered whether Sphere was placing too much responsibility on NGOs for handling the welfare of populations in need and for achieving these standards. After all, states are responsible for their citizens.[66] Also, now that victims had rights, others had duties, suggesting that humanitarianism was not an act of kindness but rather the fulfillment of an obligation.[67] These "rights" owed not only to the discourse of human rights but also to business ethics. Following the increasingly popular service models developed by the business sector during the 1980s and 1990s, the architects of Sphere imagined beneficiaries as consumers, with consumer rights akin to business contracts with the supplier of a service.[68] To some extent, asking consumers to insist on their rights was a step toward empowering the "citizens," but it was not exactly clear who the parties to the contract were or to whom these citizens would appeal when a supplier failed.

The move by aid agencies to articulate the rights of the beleaguered provided an opening to incorporate local voices, but their role was minimal, both in its creation and in its implementation. While those who ran Sphere were keenly sensitive to the need to involve the major aid agencies, there is little evidence that they were anywhere near as worried about including the beneficiaries.[69] Sphere's emphasis on trying to develop technical standards and basic needs contributed to this neglect. The presumption is that because basic bodily needs vary little from place to place, the most important people to have around the table are the experts and the professionals, not the end users. However understandable and defensible, it did translate into a general orientation that exhibited little urgency in soliciting the views of the populations in need. Moreover, once the aid community had identified these standards, then local populations were expected to participate whenever their rights were not met. In general, as one critique observed, Sphere revealed a highly truncated notion of participation, in which participation did not mean "being open to local perspectives, priorities, and concerns, which may differ significantly from the objective of technical experts," but instead meant asking recipients to present "shopping lists" whereby "people state what they know aid agencies will provide (clinics, medicine, food, wells), even if other types of aid would support them."[70]

Sphere *was* an important innovation, because it articulated a template for the basic needs of populations at risk, but aid agencies still needed to figure out how to measure their effectiveness and whether they were doing more harm than good. Rwanda was most certainly not the first time that aid might have prolonged a war (Biafra) or contributed to further suffering (Ethiopia), but it was the first time that aid agencies collectively and systematically puzzled over how they might determine their impact. This was not a simple methodological task. Humanitarian organizations must define "impact," specify their goals and translate them into measurable indicators, gather data in highly fluid emergency settings, establish baseline data in order to generate a "before and after" snapshot, control for alternative explanations and variables, construct reasonable counterfactual scenarios, and incorporate the traditional practices of survival among local populations during times of hardship.[71] Initially they turned to the health sciences field, with its epidemiological models, and to the development field, with its program evaluation tools, and in many instances added a rights-based perspective.[72]

Donor governments also were demanding that aid agencies provide evidence of their impact. Although many officials were equally affected by scenes of aid feeding insurgents, bandits, and criminal elements, their interest in evaluation also emerged from the adoption of "new public management" principles. These principles originated with the neoliberal orthodoxy of the 1980s. One of neoliberalism's goals was to reduce the state's role in the delivery of public services and instead rely on commercial and voluntary organizations, which were assumed to be more efficient. As the public sector contracted out services, it also introduced new reporting requirements and monitoring mechanisms to make sure that these for-profit and nonprofit agencies were doing what they said they would do and using the public's money wisely.[73] Until the 1990s states felt little motivation to extend these expensive administrative controls to the humanitarian sector because humanitarian assistance was a minor part of the foreign aid budget; states did not view humanitarianism as central to their foreign policy goals; and states trusted that humanitarian agencies were efficient and effective. However, once humanitarian funding increased and humanitarianism became more central to security goals, states began to question the effectiveness of humanitarian organizations.[74] Toward that end, states began introducing new contracts that demanded more reporting requirements and introduced more monitoring mechanisms.

This hard look at effectiveness had a subtle but significant effect on the ethical metrics agencies used to calculate their actions.[75] For much of their history, aid agencies instinctively used deontological or duty-based ethics to guide their practices. Some actions are simply good in and of themselves, regardless of their consequences. For humanitarian actors, there is a duty to heal the wounds and reduce the suffering of distant strangers. The growing concern with unintended consequences, however, fed into an ethic of consequentialism—whether, on balance, aid does more harm than good.[76]

This shift from duties to consequences had four important implications for the relationship between the giver and the recipient. To begin with, aid workers are nearly solely responsible for deciding what the consequences are and how to measure them. For instance, MSF's controversial and generally applauded decisions to withdraw from Ethiopia in 1985 and Goma, Zaire, in 1994 on the grounds that aid was doing more harm than good did not incorporate the views of the recipients.[77] Second, while aid agencies have introduced innovations to try to incorporate perspectives from the local populations, including needs assessments and participatory action methods, their actual impact on the decisionmaking process is debatable in part because how these needs assessments are used appears to be ad hoc and highly dependent on the individuals in the agency assigned responsibility for incorporating them into future decisions.[78]

Third, the desire to measure places a premium on numbers—for instance, lives lost and saved, people fed, children inoculated—to the neglect of nonquantifiable goals such as witnessing, being present, conferring dignity, and demonstrating solidarity. Is it possible to quantify, for instance, the reuniting of families, the providing of burial shrouds, or the reducing of fear and anxiety in individuals who are in desperate situations?[79] If these activities and their impacts cannot be operationalized, will they be left outside of the model? And, if so, will humanitarian agencies privilege those activities and outcomes that can be measured, thus altering the basic ethical calculations that underpin their interventions? And further, if the measurable variables are no longer dependent on the subjective needs of the "beneficiaries," why and how will they be consulted? The "commodification" of humanitarian values, Hugo Slim observed, was undermining wider humanitarian values.[80] This commodification might very well have important, indirect effects that further displace fundamental values. For instance, staff will have to spend more of their time making calculations, designing spreadsheets, putting together impressive PowerPoints, and, because these are increasingly important techniques, staff will be hired who have these skills. Although "science" and "values" can co-exist, in recent history they are not equal partners.

Lastly, the "do no harm" approach, most closely associated with Mary Anderson's pathbreaking work, begins with the observation that because all aid has consequences, including prolonging conflicts and contributing to systems of injustice, it behooves aid agencies to determine what are those consequences and adjust accordingly. The consequence of this insight, according to Anderson, is for aid agencies to try to determine how aid can be linked to broader systems of "justice, peace, and reconciliation."[81] But invariably this has meant that aid workers determine how and when to link aid to these broader objectives—and how to define and operationalize woolly concepts such as justice, peace, and reconciliation. In other words, the pledge to do no harm meant that aid agencies now were involved in influencing the very life and meaning of the community.

Developing standards, articulating codes of conduct, and assessing impacts would have little practical meaning without new systems of accountability.[82] For much of their history, aid agencies have felt little pressure to be accountable to either their donors or their recipients. But now accountability became a pressing issue. There were various innovations, including, most prominently, ALNAP, the Active Learning Network for Accountability and Performance in Humanitarian Action.[83] In 1999 various NGOs initiated the Ombudsman for Humanitarian Assistance to address their accountability to their "clients," and when they were unable to create a position, they founded the Humanitarian Accountability Project.[84]

Yet, so far, the consensus is that these accountability projects have spent more time demonstrating their accountability to their donors than to their beneficiaries.[85] One systematic review of the accountability experiments and initiatives concluded that "while non-governmental organizations...have to respond to a wide range of interested bodies to whom they are accountable in some way, the current system is in no way accountable directly to beneficiaries or 'claimants'—the very people it purports to assist."[86] In a similarly critical spirit, another review concluded, "There appears to be much less experimentation, implementation, and documentation of beneficiary participation than would be expected on the basis of the widely proclaimed importance of this issue."[87] Why? The principal excuse is that the emergency situation makes it impossible. Yet because most assistance occurs after the emergency, this justification falls short.[88] Indeed, rather than the situation, it is apparently the demand for accountability by donors that makes up the driving force. The pressure to look to donors to the neglect of local actors is accentuated by competition between aid agencies for funding.[89] In general, many in-house critics of humanitarianism worry that the discourse of accountability is masking a drift in power to the donors at the expense of the recipients.[90]

Rwanda also forced aid workers to acknowledge that a humanitarian emergency was no place for amateurs. Individuals do not need a license to be parents—and aid workers generally do not need a license to practice relief. A legacy of the nineteenth-century charitable societies, aid workers wore their "volunteer" badge with pride, with the implication that they were not paid professionals. It was not that agencies wanted to act like amateurs or had no interest in improving their skills, but the last thing they wanted was to become, in Bernard Kouchner's memorable phrase, "technocrats of misery." But the news from Rwanda and other sites of humanitarian action was that their lack of professionalism was costing lives. In response, they began to professionalize, developing specific knowledge derived from disciplines such as health sciences and engineering, from established manuals, and from specialized training programs run by private firms, nongovernmental organizations, states, and academic institutions. There emerged "lead agencies" who were responsible for establishing the credentials of those who wanted to set up camps. These developments were absolutely necessary to improve the quality of humanitarian assistance.

Yet the professionalization of the humanitarian sector also increased the distance between aid workers and recipients. As professionals relying on expert, objective, and generalized knowledge, they had less need to learn about nuances of the local conditions before developing and implementing their policies. Professionalism, observed Rony Brauman, had the effect of reducing proximity to technique and creating greater distance between the giver and the receiver.[91] As one MSF worker reflected about the noticeable lack of informal interactions with local populations, "We have less time to drink tea. Most of us avoid interacting on a one-to-one basis with the people. We don't have time. We like being on the internet. We don't think that much can be gained that will help us do our job."[92] Another similarly worried, "Few people are really close and in touch with people. The possible exception is the medical examination, but this is still open to the critique [that it is] a highly ritualized affair with power firmly on one side." At times their professional training included methodologies that explicitly attempted to incorporate the views of local populations, but in the end, expert knowledge nearly always trumped local knowledge. The pressure to professionalize and to demonstrate technocratic prowess, at the expense of other kinds of commitments, such as witnessing, solidarity, or religious duty, was resonant.[93]

Aid agencies *were* aware that they were becoming dangerously distant from the very people they wanted to help, and, much like the response to the failures of Rwanda, they tried to introduce reforms that mandated contact. The key buzzword was "participation." In the 1980s the development sector spearheaded the push for "participation," a reaction to the conclusion that one reason for the failures of development and the structural adjustment reforms of the 1980s was neglect of the views of marginal populations. The revolutionary conclusion was that people should be the authors of their change.

Although the discourse of participation had radical roots, perhaps most closely associated with the liberation theology of Paulo Freire, it soon went mainstream. Everyone in the development sector was now talking about "participation" and "empowerment." But unlike radical interpretations of participation that imagined a radical reworking of state-society relations, the general view of participation, especially at entities like the World Bank, was that individuals needed to be liberated from the state and be able to enter into markets, the ultimate empowering institution. Participation also was important for getting stakeholders to buy into programs they were expected to implement. It also became part of the means and not part of the ends of politics; participation was intended not to improve values such as equality, fairness, and dignity but rather to improve the efficiency and effectiveness of decisions. According to some critics, participation did little more than legitimate projects that had fallen on hard times.[94] In this respect, the discourse of participation functioned much like the appearance of the discourse of development after colonialism had been discredited. Indeed, the recent popularity of the concept of partnership perhaps says more about existing anxieties among aid workers who worry about the distance between themselves and local populations than about the provision of remedies for the maladies. In a similar spirit, MSF has made much of the importance of the principle of proximity, though several staff intimated that this insistence on proximity is probably an indicator of its growing absence.[95]

The modernization, standardization, and professionalization of the humanitarian sector was a necessary and understandable reaction to the events of the 1990s. After decades of asking the international community to recognize a right to assistance, states and international organizations were now fully engaged. In many respects, they got what they were asking for. States did not give them everything they requested or everything populations needed, and what was given came with strings attached, but the end result ventured into a dimension perhaps never imagined by Henry Dunant, the Jebbs, Herbert Hoover, or even Bernard Kouchner. With more resources and opportunities than ever before, on a grander stage than ever before, their shortcomings were now more grievous and conspicuous. The response was to rationalize, a necessary development in many respects in keeping with the twentieth century's traditional response to failure. If the machine does not work, then the machine must get bigger, stronger, and more technically adept. This machinery, moreover, might potentially do more than save people from imminent death. It might also be able to remove the causes of suffering, an admirable response—and also entirely in keeping with the twentieth century's modernist instincts. Although aid agencies did not inflict nearly the same kind of damage, nor introduce the same kind of authoritarian tendencies, as the state had in James Scott's *Seeing Like a State,* that magnificent archeology of a defining feature of the modernist legacy, their grand schemes of improving life also brought new forms of power—which could be abused like any other.[96] Humanitarianism's syllogistic and paternalistic tendencies were increasingly trapped in its own iron cage of compassion.

Conclusion

Empire of Humanity

H
UMANITY HAS come a long way in the last two centuries. Over two hundred years ago post-Enlightenment thinkers embraced the "man of feeling" because he was morally superior to, and truer to life than, the coldly mechanical and self-absorbed human imagined by earlier rationalists. Although such thoughts were relatively unorthodox at the time, they are positively commonplace today. We accuse those who appear unmoved by tragedy of lacking humanity. Compassion is seen as a virtue, so much so that it has become a status symbol, and individuals, organizations, and states compete to be recognized for their generosity. Moreover, there has been a dramatically wider definition of the populations whose suffering we narrate and the kinds of obligations we feel as a consequence of these stories.[1] The significance of this development goes beyond mere sentimentality and storytelling, for it has fueled the rise of an international humanitarian order, a cosmopolis of morally minded militias supported by international law, norms, and institutions that reach out to suffering strangers around the world. Is this progress? If benevolence to distant strangers is a sign, then we can affirm that there is progress. We can justly celebrate the ascendance of a humanitarian governance dedicated to humanity's highest moral principle—the alleviation of human suffering.[2]

Yet however high and far humanitarianism has journeyed, it was never otherworldly and has always been inescapably part of this world. Humanitarianism's earthly and heavenly qualities, as I noted in the introduction and have traced over its history, have produced an ensemble of contrapuntal melodies. Humanitarianism is a creature of the very world it aspires to civilize; from the days of the abolitionists to today's peacebuilders, humanitarian action has been lodged somewhere between the present day and the utopian. Humanitarianism is not one of a kind but rather has a diversity of meanings, principles, and practices; all humanitarians share a desire to relieve unnecessary suffering, but agreement ends there. The ethics of humanitarianism are simultaneously circumstantial and universal; humanitarians are a product of their times even as they illuminate their actions with the transcendent. Humanitarianism is a mixture of care and control; to make the world a better place requires power. Its relationship to moral progress can be both revolutionary and counterrevolutionary. Humanitarianism ministers to the needs of others and to those of the deliverer; acts of compassion lift the givers toward the sacred.

A humanitarian governance that contains these tensions has expanded to the point that it can be mistaken for an empire of humanity. How can a cosmopolis dedicated to improving human welfare be likened to an empire? Empires are renowned for three defining characteristics: they involve long-distance rule by one people over another; they lack legitimacy because they rule without the blessing or participation of the people; and power radiates downward and for the purpose of advancing the empire's interests. Empires and humanitarian governance both cross borders, but doesn't the resemblance end there? Humanitarian governance looks more like a rival to empire, because it is dedicated to the emancipation and empowerment, not the oppression and subservience, of those who are hanging on for dear life. But a second, more discerning look suggests that although humanitarian governance is not an empire in sheep's clothing, it does bear some of its markings.[3]

Empires are branded as illegitimate because of their authoritarian qualities, but humanitarian governance is hardly a paragon of democratic rule. It is only over the last few decades that humanitarian governance has incorporated the views of the local populations—and it is debatable how much energy humanitarians have put into these efforts or how receptive they are to redirection.[4] Humanitarians offer many reasons why it is difficult to adhere to modern standards of participation, but the implication is that the legitimacy of humanitarian governance does not depend on a process of deliberation, dialogue, or even consent.

Humanitarian governance stakes its legitimacy on its purpose, which, as stated, presumably distinguishes it from empires. We revile empires because they advance the power and interests of the privileged few to the detriment of the vast majority; humanitarian governance is sanctified precisely because it helps the marginalized peoples of the world. Yet empires are not without their charms, at least according to their defenders. As the British and French empires helped themselves to the world, it was often said that they were helping the world, by spreading civilization and emancipating backward populations. Edmund Burke's criticism of the British Empire was not that empire itself was necessarily illegitimate but rather that its legitimacy depended on acting as a public trustee and for the benefit of the ruled. Over two hundred years later, Michael Ignatieff, one of the world's leading voices on human rights and a principal author of "Responsibility to Protect," defended the American empire on similar grounds.[5] Critics of empire dismiss these claims as fantastical and self-serving ideologies of the powerful. In contrast, similar assertions by humanitarian organizations are typically accepted because of the perceived virtue of those organizations. In humanitarianism we trust.

Yet various commentators question humanitarianism's innocence. Humanitarian governance occasionally has a chummy relationship with the very empires that it supposedly resists.[6] Powerful states generously fund humanitarian organizations, and the agendas of Great Powers and humanitarian groups have overlapped over the decades. The line between the governmental and the nongovernmental has always been blurred, perhaps never more so than today.[7] States have become increasingly important to all aspects of humanitarianism, and humanitarian organizations have taken on state-like functions such as providing public goods and serving as de facto government ministries. Humanitarianism has become a big business, and increasingly aid agencies are administered by executive offices that focus on the bottom line and market share. As humanitarian governance has grown, it has become more centralized, more distant from those it wants to help. Although humanitarians do not have a capital city (true, Geneva often presents itself as the capital of the humanitarian world) and their operations could benefit from more coordination, decisionmaking power is hardly pluralistic. In the typical humanitarian case, the ruling class is made up of well-to-do foreigners, and local populations largely provide security, support, and menial labor in a way that is reminiscent of earlier empires.[8] In fact, aid agencies have even developed a "remote control" system that allows headquarters to direct field operations carried out by locals. It is an understandable reaction to the growing threats to aid workers, but the development raises chilling comparisons to imperial rule. Lastly, virtue is not enough. Consequences matter. In the pursuit of effectiveness, humanitarian governance has become more professionalized and bureaucratic, probably improving its efficiency but potentially at the cost of expanding local participation. Although many might accept the trade-off on the grounds that it improves welfare, it raises the issue of whether technocrats are truly best able to determine what others want and whether there is a way to hold them accountable when they go too far.

Although humanitarian governance has the characteristics of empire, it differs in at least one critical way: it is dedicated to its own destruction. It is an empire of humanity, and humanity matters. In contrast to empires that fight for their immortality and whose decline we attribute to misadventure and self-defeating miscalculation, humanitarian governance hopes to put itself out of business. Empires might not mind—and might even enjoy—helping others as they help themselves, but the fundamental purpose of empire is to further the interests of the core, not the periphery. Domestic debates over the costs of empire typically revolve around whether too much is being spent overseas and whether the nation's power might be protected more efficiently. Humanitarian organizations may need to get bigger in order to do their job, but their basic purpose is to further the needs and interests of others. Debates about the costs of humanitarian governance revolve around whether there might be more effective ways to help others—not whether there might be a better path for furthering the interests of headquarters.

The label "empire" may or may not be warranted, but humanitarian governance relentlessly favors the views, values, and interests of the compassionate. This prejudice restages the tensions of humanitarianism. The tensions do not tug in opposite directions and result in a standoff. They produce outcomes that consistently favor the humanitarians over its subjects. In this concluding chapter I explore four themes related to this self-referential quality of humanitarianism. I open with the observation that humanitarianism is first and foremost about ministering to the emotional and spiritual needs of the giver. Good things can happen for others when we pursue our spiritual needs, but it is striking how the level of organized compassion increases at the very moment when death and destruction indict the humanity of the compassionate.

If acts of compassion originate from the giver's emotional and spiritual needs, then it will be nearly impossible for humanitarianism to be practiced as it is preached—in a morally flat world in which assistance is given based on objective material needs. In the introduction I asserted that humanitarianism provides evidence of the existence of international community, and in earlier chapters I suggested how they have nourished each other. Yet the history of humanitarianism also provides discomfiting evidence that a community based on suffering has several limitations. Suffering is not a solid basis for creating a shared humanity and, in fact, can (re)create difference. We live in multiple communities that have varying claims on us. When humanitarians intervene to reduce suffering, they often pursue those reforms that they believe will enable individuals to achieve their humanity. Because we live in a world of diverse communities, we also live in a world of diverse humanitarianisms. Suffering strangers might not be the optimal means for their reconciliation.

The practice of compassion involves politics and privileges the power of the passionate. Paternalism is the concept that best captures the nature of power in the ethics of care, and paternalism has been present since humanitarianism's beginning. The humanitarianism of today is and is not the humanitarianism of yesteryear, and much the same can be said of paternalism. Paternalists always believe that they know best, but in modern times expertise has replaced God and explicitly civilizational references. Expert knowledge does more than provide a basis for intervening—it also provides a mechanism for keeping power concentrated at the top. Lastly, humanitarian governance is sustained by a holy alliance uniting humanitarianism, moral progress, and faith. Faith underwrites both humanitarianism and progress, and I doubt that either could exist without it. But humanitarianism and progress require more than a faith that is self-referentially sustaining. They require a faith that accommodates a form of doubt, one that opens space for the objects of compassion to interject their own beliefs, views, and visions into the practice of humanitarianism.

The Life You Save

To understand the spectacular growth of humanitarianism requires us to pay attention to the forces of compassion. But this is not a compassion that pulses evenly and steadily. Instead, it surges at particular moments, typically at the very same moment that the givers question their own humanity, experience spiritual desolation, wonder if they are as good as they believe themselves to be. Moments of mortal and spiritual destruction are precursors to the flood of compassion. Compassion may be the oxygen of humanitarianism, but destruction runs through its veins.

The dead have been part of humanitarianism's past, and they will be part of its future—and without the dead, humanitarianism would have no future. We are comfortable thinking of the past as influencing the present and the future, but the dead barely register. They should. In the concluding notes to their masterpiece, *Dialectic of Enlightenment*, Max Horkheimer and Theodor Adorno offer a "Theory of Ghosts." Their frustratingly brief commentary hints at the connection between how the living relate to the dead and the overall health of a society. They memorably write, "Only the conscious horror of destruction creates the correct relationship with the dead: unity with them because we, like them, are the victims of the same condition and the same disappointed hope."[9] Using Paul Klee's *Angelus Novus*, Walter Benjamin wrote in his *Theses on the Philosophy of History* of an "angel of history" that is entrapped between hope and destruction (see figure 11). Some of history's most moving and memorable speeches are eulogies that speak of the sacrifices of the dead and pledge the living to honor their memory. Consider Abraham Lincoln's fabled oration following the Battle of Gettysburg, which claimed roughly fifty thousand casualties in three short, grisly days:

> The world will little note, nor long remember what we say here, but it can never forget what they did here. It is for us the living, rather, to be dedicated here to the unfinished work which they who fought here have thus far nobly advanced. It is rather for us to be here dedicated to the great task

Walter Benjamin wrote in his *Theses on the Philosophy of History:*

> A Klee painting named "Angelus Novus" shows an angel looking as though he is about to move away from something he is fixedly contemplating. His eyes are staring, his mouth is open, his wings are spread. This is how one pictures the angel of history. His face is turned toward the past. Where we perceive a chain of events, he sees one single catastrophe which keeps piling wreckage upon wreckage and hurls it in front of his feet. The angel would like to stay, awaken the dead, and make whole what has been smashed. But a storm is blowing from Paradise; it has got caught in his wings with such violence that the angel can no longer close them. The storm irresistibly propels him into the future to which his back is turned, while the pile of debris before him grows skyward. This storm is what we call progress.

Figure 11 Paul Klee, *Angelus Novus.* © 2010 Artists Rights Society (ARS), New York / VG Bild-Kunst, Bonn.

remaining before us—that from these honored dead we take increased devotion ...—that we here highly resolve that these dead shall not have died in vain—that this nation, under God, shall have a new birth of freedom—and that government of the people, by the people, for the people, shall not perish from the earth.

It is through the dead and the recognition of their pain, suffering, and sacrifice that the living embrace their own humanity. Humanity is necrotic.[10]

Disaster, paradoxically, can catalyze human improvement. For the religiously minded it can be interpreted as "an act of God," revealing God's anger and his command for acts of redemption.[11] The Bible contains many episodes wherein episodes of destruction—including, most famously, Noah's Ark—which leads to new covenants (in this case, quite literally, a rainbow). Throughout American history religious leaders and sects have interpreted cataclysms as messages from God, punishing sinners and warning onlookers to make amends and get right with their maker.[12] Nor is it only the religious that have the capacity to see the bright side of devastation. "The most potent philosophies of the last two centuries," observes Kevin Rozario, "have insisted that improvement or 'progress' unavoidably moves through catastrophic rhythms of destruction and reconstruction, ruin and renewal."[13]

Humanitarianism helps the living come to terms with their ghosts. It is a form of theodicy, providing a means by which survivors can reconcile their belief in the possibility of a more perfect world with cruelty, suffering, and evil. Through rites of compassion the survivors seek salvation and deliver proof of the possibility of progress. The American Civil War, according to the historian Drew Gilpin Faust, created a "republic of suffering," and the tremendous intellectual ferment, soul-searching, and religious and philosophical experimentation after the Civil War owed much to those who tried to transform their haunting into a better world.[14] The impact of the Civil War helps explain the almost self-destructive dedication of A. T. Pierson, the great late-nineteenth-century American evangelical, to causes of social justice for the urban poor and then to his discovery, late in life, of world missions as he became a leading figure of the student missionary movement.[15] Across the Atlantic a follower of the spiritualist tradition of the day, Eglantyne Jebb, the founder of Save the Children, noted that she felt an "unusually close connection with the dead," and it was in part because of this connection that she dedicated herself to social reform. As she wrote elsewhere, "To be united with God you must be united with life....Power of life must manifest itself in action...work...is the purposeful manifestation of the Divine Will."[16] Bernard Kouchner tells of the powerful effect of his grandparents' deaths in the concentration camps on his commitment to humanitarian action and social justice. It was not Ralph Lemkin's invention of a new category called genocide that produced the Genocide Convention but rather the six million Jews who perished in the Holocaust. It was not the members of the International Commission on Intervention and State Sovereignty who advanced a "responsibility to protect," but instead the eight hundred thousand Tutsis who were systematically massacred in just one hundred days as the international community chose to do nothing. It is the millions of dead that haunt the surviving generations, who believe that the only way they can atone for their sins and the sins of others is by creating moral institutions of care. Communities of memory are forced to become communities of caring.[17]

Humanitarianism has its own version of creative destruction. Humanitarians certainly do not pray for destruction, but their hope for human improvement can be parasitic with respect to it.[18] Devastation invites reformers to imagine new arrangements that can peel away the causes of suffering and create the spiritual and material foundations for a better world. Few humanitarians enter a world of ruin with the goal of putting the pieces back together the way they were; instead, they treat the ruin as an opportunity to seek justice and human improvement. In the aftermath of the immensely destructive earthquake in Haiti in January 2010, the appeal campaigns often declared that relief was not enough, that assistance must make Haiti better than it was. Steven Van Zandt, a guitarist for Bruce Springsteen's E Street Band and recognized by the UN for his work for human rights in South Africa, offered a familiar call to alms. "Let's not rebuild Haiti; let's reimagine it."[19] He was only saying what had been said in countless other episodes. Suspended between a past defined by suffering and a possible future in which those who might otherwise be sacrificed receive a stay of execution, humanitarianism is torn between a narrative of eternal darkness and the constant promise that the living might build a more perfect world.

Those who experience unnecessary suffering need the compassion of the others, but the compassionate also depend on suffering strangers. Humanitarianism has flourished at the very moment that nations worry about losing a sense of mission and people seek to restore their humanity. The timing of the British campaign against the slave trade arguably stemmed from religiously inspired coalitions less interested in the welfare of slaves than in advancing their religious cause at home and abroad, and they tied the campaign to the British Empire's need for a new sense of purpose after the loss of the American colonies.[20] There are many reasons why the "Save Darfur" coalition came together in the United States in early 2004, but it was no coincidence that it occurred at precisely the same moment that many Americans were doubting their country's moral compass as a consequence of the U.S. government's invasion of Iraq. Humanitarianism is the answer when the devout worry about the moral character of society.

Dunant hoped that Christians who joined voluntary medical teams would become more religious as a consequence of tending to soldiers; while Christianity was supposed to save the world, humanitarianism would help save Christianity. Today, many join religiously based humanitarian organizations not only to do good but also to express their identity through the practice of compassion. Over the twentieth century the West looked to humanitarianism as mind-numbing events damaged its self-image.[21]

If people continue to turn to humanitarianism to maintain their sense of self and humanity, humanitarianism will have a healthy future. A humanitarianism that depends on a mounting body count and a subsequent search for meaning by the survivors will have a long life span. Humanitarian organizations paint a near-apocalyptic picture of the future, spinning visions of ethnic cleansing and mass murder, of climate change causing more tsunami-like disasters, of a steady barrage of public health emergencies and pandemics, of failed states that unleash domestic chaos and regional havoc, of growing levels of international inequality and poverty that fuel misery and violence.[22] The next few decades, if these predictions are even partially met, may not lead to the end of days, but they certainly will create plenty of opportunities to imagine rebirth.

The Loneliness of Long-Distance Humanitarianism

Many—and I include myself in this—have claimed that the growth of humanitarianism is a sign of the development of international community. It is the recognition of our shared humanity through the common experience of suffering that breaks down barriers and creates the bonds of community. It is the existence of compassion across borders that provides evidence of extended obligations constituted by diffuse feelings of belonging. Although humanitarianism may have originated with the Enlightenment and may have been sparked by Christianity, it has achieved a universal status. All the major religions have traditions of compassion and charity, and humanitarianism has become genuinely ecumenical. Humanitarianism has outgrown its parochial religious origins and become part of a secularized humanity. Humanitarianism belongs to everyone and no one.

Yet to what extent does the mitigation of suffering provide a fulfilling expression of one's humanity or the basis for meaningful community? Humanity can be lonely and alienating. The discourse of humanity, once it spreads to cover all human beings, can reduce individuals to superficial qualities, stripping them of the very cultural, historical, and social processes that make them human and confer genuine dignity on them. To be fully human, and to recognize the humanity of others, requires intimacy and a genuine appreciation of difference.[23] Social psychology studies suggest that we are happiest when giving to others and feeling as if we are part of something larger than ourselves, but it is unclear whether the effects are the same when we use PayPal to send money to a charity in a distant country on the recommendation of websites such as "Global Giving" as they are when we donate our money to those who are culturally or geographically close.

More worrisome, the very technologies that expand compassion and a sense of community can create new forms of difference and indifference. Witnessing the pain of others can inspire feats of compassion, but it also can lead to feelings of superiority and a politics of pity, pleasure, prurient arousal, even sadism.[24] Sympathy can create social distance as well as dissolve it. The very images that humanitarians use to mobilize action can prompt revulsion. As one historian noted, those who want to "arouse popular opposition to evil practices" must display those practices in all their horror: "'civilized' virtue required a shocked spectatoral sympathy in response to pain scenarios both real and willfully imagined. But...viewing the spectacle of suffering could inflict terrible moral damage on the spectator, turning him or her into a 'savage.'"[25] Suffering here becomes a spectator sport. Over the decades many aid agencies have worried that their attempt to communicate the pain of others might lead to the dehumanization of those they want to help, reducing them to nothing more than stick figures of misery. The visual technologies that shrink moral and physical distance and generate sympathy may also have the opposite effect.[26]

It is very likely that we cannot build a thick sense of community on the sufferings of others, so humanitarianism as practiced will never achieve its prized impartiality. Peter Singer may be right that, from a strictly utilitarian perspective, there are no grounds for privileging the needs of one over the comparable needs of another.[27] But if our desire to give depends on our search for meaning and belonging, then principles of impartiality and culturally neutered notions of humanity are unlikely to satisfy. To put the matter more starkly: discourses of humanity imply nondiscrimination, but discrimination might be the natural order of things—and some forms of discrimination might be necessary to realize our humanity. "Many people genuinely do not wish to be saints," wrote George Orwell in his famous essay on Mohandas Gandhi, "and it is probable that some who achieve or aspire to sainthood have never felt much temptation to be human beings....To an ordinary human being, love means nothing if it does not mean loving some people more than others."[28]

Yet we cannot easily divide the world into two groups, those who are part of the community and those who are outside. The world cannot be carved neatly into mutually exclusive communities. Instead, we reside in multiple communities.[29] Concentric circles of community produce concentric circles of obligation; as our sense of community thins, so too does our sense of responsibility. We have responsibilities to our children and our parents, and we are willing to make extraordinary sacrifices for them. We have responsibilities to our neighbors and fellow citizens, and being a good citizen can demand sacrifice—but it is not nearly as constant or intense a demand as we feel for those who are kin. Religious, ethnic, and national identities influence who gets our attention. Diaspora groups give to the homeland during a famine but may be indifferent where they have no national or ethnic allegiance. American Jews give more to Jews in need than to non-Jews in similar circumstances. Egyptians have been relatively generous toward Palestinians but palpably indifferent to the plight of Darfuris in neighboring Sudan. Islam has a rich heritage of charitable activity—to fellow Muslims. The search for a full and emotionally satisfying life involves selectivity.

These acts of discrimination occur routinely among aid agencies that otherwise pledge allegiance to principles of impartiality. Although they claim to give based on need, rarely do aid agencies undertake a systematic assessment of needs. Instead, existing attachments play an important role.[30] Lutheran World Relief accepted the principle of impartiality but then justified its focus on Lutherans in Austria and Germany after World War II based on "family" concerns. Catholic Relief Services pledged impartiality, but in its early years gave primarily to Catholics, especially to those in Eastern Europe. Many Islamic agencies insist that they operate according to needs but typically work only in Islamic societies—a practice many defend on the grounds of existing demand, ease of access, and cultural proximity to the populations in need. But religious loyalty on the part of staff is not far beneath the surface; it is a reason many Muslims join Islamic aid agencies rather than secular agencies such as Oxfam. Although humanitarianism's principles of humanity and impartiality are designed to defeat such selectivity, humanitarians who are culturally closest to a population may be best able to meet its material and spiritual needs. There are universal baselines covering what people need to stay alive physically, but no such baselines exist for what heals the human heart.[31] In theory humanitarians insist that only principles of impartiality reflect a robust conception of humanity. Their practices suggest not a failure of aid agencies to live up to their principles but rather the inability of strict impartiality to generate a sustained sense of community.[32]

These observations regarding thick and thin communities, multiple communities, and material and spiritual necessities suggest that humanitarianism is as much about values as it is about needs. The values I have in mind are not impartiality, humanity, and the like but rather ideas regarding what people need to develop their humanity and what societies require to mitigate human suffering. Emergency humanitarians typically insist that they have little interest in such things. They care about needs, not values. The humanitarian version of the Latin injunction "Kill them all. Let God sort them out" would appear to be "Save them all. Let God sort them out."

Emergency humanitarians aspire to reduce the quota of victims.[33] Yet even many who leave home with no greater ambition than to save lives find it impossible, after they reach the site of an emergency, to not want to do more. And, as we have seen, this is only one version of humanitarianism, and others have grander ambitions, aspiring to remove the causes of oppression and suffering. It seems no more possible to maintain a stripped-down version of humanitarianism than a bare-bones version of liberalism—no easier to restrain aid workers from thinking about confronting the causes of suffering than to keep liberals from wondering how to increase the world's quotient of freedom. Humanitarianism's needs-based commitments, much like liberalism's defense of freedom, are chronically vulnerable to ideologies and systems of meaning that promise to be spiritually and emotionally fulfilling.[34]

More to the point, much of humanitarianism involves crossing boundaries and injecting values that are presumed to do a better job of improving well-being. When humanitarians dream of changing the world, they do so in their own language. In the nineteenth century, humanitarians favored the language of civilization, believing that commerce, Christianity, and colonialism would save lives and societies. Today many humanitarians (and others) aspire to create the conditions for positive liberty, to enable individuals to live a life of dignity and realize their aspirations, but they often assume that the holy trinity of democracy, markets, and the rule of law will enable individuals to do so. Although many humanitarians claim to be more modest than the missionaries of the nineteenth century, it would be difficult to prove that claim from their programs, which are impressively wide-ranging and leave no economic, cultural, political, or social possibility unexamined. To listen to local voices, in fact, reminds us that one person's universal is another person's contingent.[35] There are many reasons why local populations might reject those who come bearing gifts, but one is surely the fear that humanitarians are not content to truck, dump, and run but instead seek permanent revolution.

If we live in a world of overlapping communities and real, practicing humanitarianism reflects their existence, then we should expect a future filled with humanitarianisms. Although my history of humanitarianism has recognized this diversity, my decision to divide the world between emergency and alchemical humanitarianism has reduced the key point of difference to whether humanitarians limit themselves to saving lives or aspire to do more. In a globalizing, Western-based humanitarianism these were important fault lines, and the categorization makes sense. While the same distinction could be applied to the organizations emerging from the global South, and particularly from the Islamic world, there may be other, more consequential marks of difference. More colloquially, other "civilizational" qualities may have more relevance. The ICRC and World Vision International have been on opposing sides of a debate regarding humanitarianism, but they may bond over their "Western heritage" once they begin coordinating with non-Western aid agencies. Or World Vision International, a religious organization that recognizes that people have spiritual as well as material needs, may discover that it has more in common with Islamic aid agencies than it does with the ICRC. More generally, though, for humanitarian organizations that want to do more than relieve suffering in the here and now and hold different visions of the good society, suffering is unlikely to break down cultural divides. Wherever the dialogue leads, it will reflect the shifting relationship between humanitarianism and international community. Tracing the twists and turns of humanitarianism illuminates the ever-changing politics of international communities.

The Power of Compassion

Any form of rule, even rule in the name of humanity, requires power and politics. Yet humanitarianism presents itself as having accomplished the impossible—a form of governance that has ethical purity. There are many reasons why humanitarians have had difficulty acknowledging that they are mere mortals. They see themselves as the voice of those who otherwise would not be heard; in solidarity with the vulnerable and in opposition to systems of oppression; and connected to universal values that lift them from domain of politics and into the realm of ethics. It is not only a sense of entitlement that inspires humanitarians to imagine that they are affiliated with the sacred. They work hard at it because they believe that their ability to act is dependent on appearing apolitical to those who, in many cases, are the very sources of distress.

Yet keeping power and politics separate from humanitarianism requires a struggle of Sisyphean magnitude. The idea of humanitarianism without politics was always a contrivance maintained by those who wanted to practice their particular kind of politics in a world of states. Many join humanitarian organizations because they want to make a difference and engage in a politics of resistance. They travel to sites of suffering to bear witness and to protest an international sacrificial order that demands its quota of victims. They lobby governments to respect international humanitarian law. Politics, and lots of it, is required if humanitarians are to remove the causes of suffering. And even if they intend to stay out of politics, their actions have political effects. Humanitarians complain about politics and states encroaching on their turf, but humanitarians have always defined their turf in political terms.

Humanitarians are highly sensitive to the power that states have over them, but they have been amazingly insensitive to the power they have over those they want to help. Paternalism is the form of power most familiar to humanitarians. Humanitarianism is the desire to relieve the suffering of distant strangers. Paternalism is the act of interfering in the lives of others, often without their permission, on the grounds that such interventions are for their own good. Paternalism and humanitarianism are not twins, but the family resemblance is often uncanny. Humanitarians frequently act first and ask questions later—and at times, not at all. There are often good reasons why it is not possible for local populations to form committees to help design humanitarian assistance. Emergencies require urgent action and to seek the consent of the victims would cost lives. Aid agencies often work in situations where there is no functioning or legitimate government, so it is not obvious who can grant consent, and sometimes those who claim to be representatives of the people owe their position to brute force and not popular will. These are powerful explanations, and they can be convincing justifications for paternalism. Still, as MSF's Rony Brauman put it, paternalism is the "slope on which we are constantly sliding."[36] Some humanitarian organizations slide faster than others, and some do not even realize the ground beneath them is uneven.

Although paternalism has been present since humanitarianism's beginning, its character has altered with the changing times in much the same way that humanitarianism has changed in relationship to an evolving global order. I cannot here attempt to survey the many different kinds of international paternalism, but the history of humanitarianism provides insight into why and how the paternalism of the nineteenth century is not the same as the paternalism of today. A good place to start is the obvious claim that whereas in the nineteenth century being called a paternalist was not necessarily an insult, today it is. During their Imperial Age, humanitarians had a confidence in their superiority, a belief in their duty to help others, and a conviction that local populations needed to be educated and liberated from backward traditions before they could participate in their own rule. These paternalist attitudes were not reserved for people thousands of miles away and of a different skin color; elites held similar views of the domestic lower classes and distinguished between the deserving and undeserving poor, believing that the poor needed moral education before they could become responsible, vote-bearing citizens.

These attitudes are now thoroughly stigmatized. Colonialism's dismal record delivering on its promise of progress did not help, but its record is less relevant than the ascendance of international liberalism's discourse of equality, autonomy, and liberty. Beginning with World War I and the principles of nationalism and self-determination, continuing through World War II and the demand for immediate decolonization and sovereign equality, right up in the present day with the blossoming of a human rights discourse, these values associated with liberalism guide how people should and do treat each other. In keeping with these developments, humanitarians are supposed to operate with the explicit or implicit consent of the recipients, expectations that are evident in the various rhetorics of partnership, participation, and local knowledge. As Nancy Lindborg, president of Mercy Corps, put it, the goal is to give people "voice and choice." To act otherwise is to run the risk of landing on a paternalist watch list.

Although humanitarians might legitimate their presence and activities by seeking the explicit consent and active participation of local peoples, arguably more often they look to universal values. In other words, the roles they represent are not from the West and they are not from the locale, instead they are from the international community. To hook its wagon to values associated with a particular time and place is to give humanitarian governance a personality, when in fact it requires a customary quality to generate its moral standing. Humanitarian governance, to be successful, achieves a moral authority that derives not from any special place but rather from a shared humanity. It must be existentially thin, not thick.[37] It is a moral authority contingent on the presumption of universal values that gives humanitarians the power to act. It is what allows them to go where mere laypersons, and certainly not partisans, cannot.

It is not enough to be good; humanitarians also must do good. It was not always this way. For most of its history humanitarians acted as if showing up was enough. In the good old days of humanitarian action, many aid agencies barely registered as organizations; they were seemingly temporary structures assembled with a minimum of planning and staffed by volunteers who had big hearts but little training. In many respects, those who ran these organizations enjoyed their seat-of-the-pants, jerry-built lifestyle because it reflected their idea of what a voluntary organization looks like. However, those days are history. Over the last several decades, as described in chapter 10, humanitarianism modernized in every conceivable way, in response both to donors who wanted assurance that their money was being spent wisely and to agencies who were increasingly convinced that emergency relief was no place for amateurs.

No longer able to rely exclusively on its moral authority, humanitarianism now had to demonstrate its competence. Accordingly, it began developing specialized knowledge, advanced training, bureaucracies with standard operating procedures, and rule books with guidelines. These developments had several consequences directly related to the power and politics of humanitarian governance. Like moral authority, expert authority denies its own politics by presenting itself as objective and impartial. Experts rely on rules, technical knowledge, evidence, and science to generate their perceived detachment. Moreover, the expert justifies action in relation to specialized knowledge that is available to everyone—if everyone had the same knowledge, they would act in roughly the same way. Experts are not inherently better than others, just more knowledgeable. And in fact, they would love nothing better than to share that knowledge with others—to teach others how to fish. Expertise is similar to moral authority in another way as well: it claims nothing for itself but everything for others. An expert knowledge that has these self-effacing qualities provides firm ground for paternalism.

The growing importance of expert knowledge has helped preserve and extend the rule of humanitarian governance. A culture of liberalism that values an inclusive process of participation and a culture of expertise that values specialized knowledge pull in opposite directions, but the centralizing forces have the upper hand. Over the last several decades the automatic answer to any problem on the ground was more coordination, more standardization, more integration, and more centralization. Along these lines, Alex de Waal writes: "Each step was taken for specific reasons, with particular problems in mind. None was simply imposed by the international bureaucracy, rather they were negotiated between different governments and institutions. Some were adopted reluctantly. But each step represented a transfer of power to international institutions. Two aspects of these initiatives stand out. One, each has been technical or bureaucratic.... Two, each attempt has failed."[38] I am less certain than de Waal of the chronic failure of these reforms to improve the quality of assistance. But if we judge these reforms in terms of their ability to preserve the power of humanitarians, then they have been an unqualified success. Knowledge is the trump card. There is, of course, a growing respect for "local knowledge," but since local knowledge is contrasted with expert knowledge and local knowledge therefore can never be expert knowledge, experts usually get the first—and last—word.

A related effect of the growing importance of expert knowledge for humanitarian governance is that it potentially undermines its sacred status. Experts, if they are good, deliver results and are judged on that basis. Virtue matters less than consequences. If the ultimate measure of success is the outcome, then who cares whether the blankets, medicine, and food are delivered by Oxfam, Walmart, Halliburton, or the U.S. military?[39] Many humanitarian organizations concede the general point that results matter, but they fight back on several counts. They insist that they are just as efficient as, if not more efficient than, states or corporations, in part because they have a pool of cheap labor. They show up when needs are great, not only when there are profits to be made or power to be grabbed. Humanitarian organizations are defending their turf not because of self-interest but rather because the focus on consequence may be bad for those in need. They might be right about that. But it is worth noting that win, lose, or draw, power remains at the top.

Expertise and the overall modernization of the sector not only helps maintain and expand the rule of humanitarian governance, it also has the potential to expand the physical and emotional distance between humanitarians and those in need. The lifestyle of the humanitarian, especially in conflict and postconflict situations, is increasingly a world apart from those on the street. Many of these changes are associated with understandable security precautions. But they also stem from a growing machinery that organizes action from the top down and rotates individuals from place to place depending on their skill set. Although it is dangerous to romanticize the missionaries, the missionary tended to stay in one place for years at a time, which compelled them to learn local languages and customs, which in turn could foster a genuine appreciation of local ways of knowing and doing. Compare that lifestyle with the professional humanitarian, whose expertise is not a place but rather a method, whose presence is always temporary, whose qualifications prioritize technique at the expense of knowledge of local cultures and languages, and whose orientation is always home base, many thousands of miles away.

One last point. All this talk of moral and expert authority can obscure the very real presence of brute power. All authority is related to power, and although power does not require force, force frequently appears. Humanitarianism, like paternalism, also can justify the use of power. Force need not be violent, but the history of humanitarianism is littered with violent actions in the name of humanity. When Hannah Arendt wrote about a "passion of compassion," she was not singing its praises but offering a warning: "The most powerful and perhaps the most devastating passion motivating revolutionaries . . . [is] the passion of compassion."[40] Arendt traced this passion of compassion from a revolutionary France that justified a reign of terror in the name of fraternity, equality, and humanity to various twentieth-century quasi-utopian movements that justified violence in the name of "the people."[41] Her thoughts cast a dark cloud over the following statement by the first UN undersecretary for humanitarian affairs, Jan Eliasson: "And, finally, let us in the humanitarian community always remember these two words: 'passion and compassion.' Nothing happens in life without passion, but without compassion the wrong things happen."[42]

Today humanitarian intervention valorizes military force to protect the "people," intimating that such violence is "responsible" and that failure to use violence to protect the weak is an "irresponsible" or immoral act that creates something close to a moral equivalence between the perpetrator and the bystander. My point is not to reproach humanitarian intervention—I find it impossible to contemplate the killings in Rwanda, Darfur, and the Congo without demanding the deployment of all necessary means—but rather to point out that doctrines of humanity have always demanded their share of violence. Given humanitarianism's history, there is no reason to bet on a different future.

Faith-Based Humanitarianism

Humanitarianism provides no moral high ground. At best it offers equal shares of possibility and disappointment in the continuing quest to improve the conditions experienced by the majority of the world. It offers tangible expression of one of the most important of human emotions—compassion—and it warns against the excesses committed in the name of compassion. The universe of stories of suffering has expanded, which has created more opportunities for intervention, some welcome and others less so. Humanitarianism may have become an outlet for those looking for a place to express their politics in a place of purity, but it offers no such refuge. Its growth can be interpreted as confirming that humans are as cruel as ever—or as confirming that they have developed a greater sense of humanity.[43] How can we seriously contemplate the notion of progress after the Holocaust, Rwanda, and other displays of depravity over the last century? Yet barbarism is as old as human history, whereas humanitarianism is relatively young, perhaps indicating the belief that the world can be made better.

Debate about whether humanitarianism is capable of progress or is a sign of progress cannot be settled by mere evidence. Instead, one's answer is a matter of faith. Humanitarianism begins and ends with faith, it sustains and is sustained by faith. But faith is not one of a kind. There is a faith associated with religion, as in faith-based organizations. However, faith is more than religion, faith is a belief in the transcendental. Religion entails a belief in the transcendental but so too do movements that aspire to spread "human flourishing."[44] Whatever their motives, many who work in the humanitarian community situate their actions in relation to the transcendental, to the existence of something bigger than themselves. But many in the humanitarian community express a second type of faith—a belief in the absence of evidence.

In many respects, and appropriately enough, the conversation among humanitarians regarding the possibility of progress in the absence of proof resembles the irresolvable debate about the existence of God. If we cannot look to evidence to decide, then what should we do? In *The Will to Believe*, William James offered one response. There are those who insist that in the absence of evidence, we should withhold belief. If we withhold belief, there is no logical ground for acting. But, James countered, this would merely create a self-fulfilling prophecy: we do not believe that God exists, we act as if he does not exist, and so we have outcomes that confirm our belief that there is no God. In order for God to exist, James continues, we must act as if God exists. He writes that "there are cases when a fact cannot come at all unless a preliminary faith exists in its coming."[45] James is not arguing that people should chase after windmills or be captured by their fantasies. "The talk of believing by our volition seems...from one point of view, simply silly. From another point of view it is worse than silly, it is vile."[46] Instead, he is counseling that until we have actual evidence to conclude that God does not exist, we are better off assuming that she does. And if we act on the belief of God's existence, then we might very well produce evidence that confirms our initial faith. As Immanuel Kant wrote, he had to "deny knowledge to make room for faith."[47] By making room for faith, we make room for what otherwise would have been impossible. There is always, of course, the chance that we will bet wrong. "For my own part," James asserted, "I have also a horror of being duped; but I can believe that worse things than being duped may happen to a man in this world."[48]

This is the kind of argument I have heard over the years from those in the humanitarian community. If they do not believe that it is possible to improve the humanitarian sector, if they do not credit the possibility of moral progress, then nothing will happen. As Brauman reflected, "I am not sure if progress exists, but it is good to act as if I believe it exists."[49] Progress cannot occur unless we believe it is possible and act on that belief. Because we do not have sufficient evidence that humanitarianism does harm, we should continue to act as if it does good. In the meantime, we will continue to search for evidence of progress, and, with any luck, acting as if it is possible will eventually produce evidence of its existence.

Several years ago I attended a workshop on the effectiveness of the humanitarian sector. After a bit of hemming and hawing, one participant confessed that while he could point to times where he had made a difference, he also lived with uncertainty and remorse about other times when his actions may have made things worse. Several other participants made similar admissions. And then another aid worker added, for good measure, that if Darfur was any example, then it was not clear that the humanitarian sector had learned anything in the last two decades. After listening quietly, a veteran of the Sudan, Somalia, and East Timor, erupted: "I do not care if we can or cannot show that humanitarianism has improved the lives of others in need. *I know that I must act.*" I thought at the time that his comment captured much of what was wrong with the humanitarian ethic—acting without thinking. But later I developed a more forgiving interpretation: he was summoning the spirit of William James—not a decision to disregard evidence, but a will to believe until convinced otherwise. These are equal possibilities that can be equally true.

James and other defenders of the reasonableness of religious belief are using pragmatic arguments, which are appropriate since, ultimately, humanitarianism is a pragmatic activity. It might look to the transcendental, but its work is on the ground. Yet many pragmatic arguments also are prudential arguments, judging action and beliefs on the basis of self-interest. If somehow I manage to produce moral progress, then we are all better off.

But even if I fall short, I am still a better person because I have developed my moral character. I might as well bet that there is a God, because there are few costs for betting wrong and lots of benefits for betting right. The costs of betting wrong include the very lives of those who otherwise would have been saved and spared unnecessary suffering.

Although it is the presence of faith that sustains humanitarianism and the possibility of progress, blind faith can be its downfall. Humanitarianism does not need true believers. Herein lies one last contradiction of humanitarianism. Faith is required to imagine an always elusive humanity, to persevere despite the onslaught of disappointment and the cascade of evidence of humanity's failings. Yet frequently it is a *crisis* of faith that has bent the path toward realizing progress in humanitarianism and humanitarianism as progress. Humanitarianism has made its greatest strides when humanitarians questioned the consequences of their actions, examined the complexity of their motives, fretted over the development of a machinery that might build a stronger wall between themselves and those in need, discovered ways in which those who come to emancipate also bear new mechanisms of domination, and began collecting evidence to understand what does and does not work. Eventually, though, the progress of humanitarianism cannot be achieved by humanitarians acting alone. Instead, it depends on creating a space for the objects of humanitarianism to express their own will to believe and the opportunity to act on those beliefs.

Notes

INTRODUCTION

1. The numbers come from the following sources: for Rwanda, Borton, et al., *The International Response to Conflict and Genocide*; for Kosovo, Tanguy, "Foreign and Humanitarian Aid"; for Aceh, Indonesia, Cosgrove, *Synthesis Report*, 16; for Haiti, Waldie, "Good Intentions Gone Wrong."

2. ALNAP, *State of the Humanitarian System*, 18.

3. The last figure comes from ibid., 19, 22. While it does not break down official and private giving, this is a reliable observation based on historical patterns and other data provided.

4. ALNAP, *State of the Humanitarian System*, 22.

5. Slim, "Relief Agencies and Moral Standing in War."

6. Chomsky, "Humanitarian Imperialism."

7. Chimni, "International Institutions Today"; Horkheimer and Adorno, *Dialectic of Enlightenment*, p. 93.

8. See, for instance, de Waal, *Famine Crimes*; Donini, "Through a Glass Darkly"; Terry, *Condemned to Repeat?*; Vaux, *Selfish Altruist*; Barnett and Weiss, eds., *Humanitarianism in Question*; Kennedy, *Dark Sides of Virtue*; Rieff, *Bed for the Night*; Chandler, *From Kosovo to Kabul and Beyond*; Duffield, *Global Governance and the New Wars*; Bradol, "Sacrificial International Order"; Fassin, "Humanitarianism as a Politics of Life"; Taithe, "Reinventing (French) Universalism"; Dawes, *That the World May Know*; Brauman, *Humanitaire*; Lischer, *Dangerous Sanctuaries*; Moore, *Hard Choices*; Fassin, "Noli Me Tangere"; Fassin and Pandolfi, *Contemporary States of Emergency*; and Redfield, "Doctors, Border, and Life in Crisis."

9. Bender, ed., *Antislavery Debate*.

10. McLisky, "Due Observance of Justice." Gill, "Calculating Compassion in War"; Taithe, "The Red Cross Flag in the Franco-Prussian War," 25.

11. Singer, "Famine, Affluence, and Morality" and *One World*; Chatterjee, *Ethics of Assistance*; Shapcott, "Anti-Cosmopolitanism"; Linklater, "Towards a Sociology of Global Morals."; and MacCunn, "Cosmopolitan Duties."

12. Brauman, "From Philanthropy to Humanitarianism," 400–401.

13. Fassin, "Humanitarianism," 151.

14. Fassin and Reichtman, *Empire of Trauma*, 153.

15. Twain, *On the Damned Human Race*.

16. Hutchinson, *Champions of Charity*.

17. Rorty, "Who Are We?" 13. See also Rorty, "Human Rights, Rationality, and Sentimentality." For another argument regarding the possibility of developing universal moral codes around human suffering, see Linklater, "Towards a Sociology of Global Morals."

18. For the relationship between responsibility and community, see Smiley, *Moral Responsibility*.

19. Cited in Gorgé, *International Relief Union*, 10–11.

20. Immanuel Kant, *Perpetual Peace*, 34; translation based on Berlin, *Crooked Timber of Humanity*, v.

21. On Islam and humanitarianism, see Benthall and Bellion-Jourdan, *Charitable Crescent;* de Cordier, "Faith-based Aid, Globalization, and the Humanitarian Front Line"; Bellion-Jourdan, "Islamic Relief Organizations"; Benthall, "Humanitarianism and Islam after 11 September"; Singer, *Charity in Islamic Societies;* Clarence-Smith, *Islam and the Abolition of Slavery;* Bornstein and Redfield, "Genealogies of Suffering"; Habito and Inabaa, eds., *Practice of Altruism;* and Duriez, Mabille, and Rousselet, eds., *Les ONG confessionnelles.*

22. For discussions regarding whether and how they differ, see Wilson and Brown, "Introduction," in *Humanitarianism and Suffering*, ed. Wilson and Brown, 4–18; Bouchet-Saulnier, "Between Humanitarian Law and Principles"; Chandler, *From Kosovo to Kabul,* ch. 1; Minear, *Humanitarian Enterprise,* ch. 3; and Leebaw, "The Politics of Impartial Activism."

23. ALNAP, *State of the Humanitarian System,* 20.

24. Slim, "Military Intervention to Protect Human Rights."

25. The six largest international nongovernmental aid agencies are CARE, Médecins Sans Frontiéres, Catholic Relief Services, Save the Children, World Vision, and Oxfam, and these six account for the vast majority of expenditures and programming in the sector. ALNAP, *State of the Humanitarian System,* 20.

CHAPTER 1

1. Scott, *Moral Economy of the Peasant.*

2. Dewey, *Common Faith,* 19. Also see Taylor, *Secular Age.*

3. This tripartite distinction was first used in Barnett and Weiss, "Humanitarianism." However, I depart from the original formulation as I have replaced "forces of salvation" with "forces of compassion," a label used in Bornstein and Redfield, eds., *Forces of Compassion.*

4. Slim, *Call to Alms.*

5. In his commentary on "Conservative, or Bourgeois Socialism," *The Communist Manifesto,* ch. 3, cited in Roberts, *Making English Morals,* 5.

6. For a review of this literature, see Haskell, "Capitalism and the Origins of the Humanitarian Sensibility," parts 1 and 2.

7. Duffield, "Governing the Borderlands."

8. For statements of this sort, see Donini, "Far Side"; Duffield, *Global Governance and the New Wars; Development, Security, and Unending War;* and "Getting Savages to Fight Barbarians"; Gunewardena and Shuller, eds., *Capitalizing on Catastrophe.*

9. See Himmelfarb, *Poverty and Compassion* and *Idea of Poverty.*

10. Landis, "Fate, Responsibility, and 'Natural' Disaster Relief."

11. Macrae et al., "Uncertain Power," 18–21.

12. On the Enlightenment and Kantian categories, see Rorty, "Human Rights, Rationality, and Sentimentality," 133–34; and Baier, *Progress of Sentiments.*

13. Kant, "On the Common Saying," 188.

14. Slim, "Médecins Sans Frontières: Some Personal Reflections on the La Mancha Process," *My Sweet La Mancha,* July–October, 2005, 92.

15. Bogaev, Interview with Medical Anthropologist Dr. Paul Farmer.

16. Brauman, "MSF and the Limits of Humanitarian Action," 143.

17. Cited in Finkielkraut, *In the Name of Humanity.*

18. Blustein, *Moral Demands of Memory,* 35.

19. Finkielkraut, *Imaginary Jew,* cited in ibid., 39.

20. For a moving statement on the presence of the dead, see Harrison, *Dominion of the Dead*.

21. Kant, "On the Common Saying."

22. Rozario, *Culture of Calamity*, 21.

23. Borgwart, *New Deal for the World*, 9

24. There is a considerable literature on the relationship between the representation of suffering and forms of action. See, for example, Kleinman and Kleinman, "Appeal of Experience"; Boltanski, *Distant Suffering*. Relatedly, Margaret Keck and Kathryn Sikkink argue that those claims that involve the bodily integrity of "innocent" populations, particularly when the relationship between cause and effect is perceived as immediate and direct, will have greater resonance. Keck and Sikkink, *Activists Beyond Borders*.

25. Cited in Grant, *Civilised Savagery*, 42.

26. For discussions, see Pictet, *Fundamental Principles*; Forsythe 2001; Terry, *Condemned to Repeat?*; Weiss, "Principles, Politics, and Humanitarian Action"; Duffield, "Governing the Borderlands: Decoding the Power of Aid"; Minear, *Humanitarian Enterprise*; Ramsbotham and Woodhouse, *Humanitarian Intervention*, 14–18.

27. Fournier, "Our Purpose Is to Limit."

28. MSF's Rony Brauman is credited with introducing the concept in the early 1990s. See Brauman, "Introduction," 3–9. For recent debates, see Grombach-Wagner, "An IHL/ICRC perspective"; Pilar, "Humanitarian Space Under Siege."

29. Fassin, "Humanitarianism as a Politics of Life," 507.

30. Spellman, *Fruits of Sorrow*, 7, 64.

31. Chandler, *From Kosovo to Kabul and Beyond*.

32. Mauss, *Gift*.

33. Arendt, *On Revolution*; and Butt, "Suffering Stranger."

34. Dworkin, "Paternalism," 65; see also 70–76. For a sampling of the definitional debate, see Archard, "Paternalism Defined"; Garren, "Paternalism, Part I" and Paternalism, Part II"; Sartorius, ed., *Paternalism*; Gert and Culver, "Paternalistic Behavior"; VanDeVeer, *Paternalistic Intervention*; Lawrence Mead, "The Rise of Paternalism" in *New Paternalism*, ed. Mead, 1–38; Husak, "Legal Paternalism"; Young, "John Stuart Mill, Ronald Dworkin, and Paternalism"; and Dworkin, *Sovereign Virtue*.

35. Margalit, *Ethics of Memory*, 36.

36. Maskalyk, *Six Months in Sudan*, 80–81.

37. Mehta, *Liberalism and Empire*, 89–90.

38. Mead, ed., *New Paternalism*.

39. Cited in Finkielkraut, *In the Name of Humanity*, 5–6. For other discussions on the changing conception of the human, see Todorov, *Conquest of America*; Crawford, *Argument and Change*; and Finnemore, *Purpose of Intervention*.

40. Gilroy, *Postcolonial Melancholia*, 66.

41. In a related observation, Rony Brauman argues that contemporary humanitarianism has two currents that date back to the nineteenth century: the Red Cross model and the "department (service) of colonial health" model. The first model suggests no to politics and to moral judgments (though even the Founding Fathers believed in a civilizing mission). The second model is bound up with colonialism, evident in the Colonial Health Corps and the Indigenous Medical Assistance in the early twentieth century in West Africa; these public health projects introduced new systems of colonial control over populations. Brauman further observes that while these two paradigms overlap, they are not coterminous: the first is "inscribed in power" while the other "positions itself in front of it." Brauman, *Penser dans l'urgence*, 45–47.

42. Fournier, "Our Purpose Is to Limit."

43. For discussions of these principles, see Pictet, *Fundamental Principles of the Red Cross*; Forsythe, *Humanitarians*; Terry, *Condemned to Repeat?*; Weiss, "Principles, Politics, and Humanitarian Action"; Minear, *Humanitarian Enterprise*; and Plattner, "ICRC Neutrality." How rules are translated into practice on the ground, though, is another matter. See Hilhorst and Schmiemann, "Humanitarian Principles and Organizational Culture."

44. Nyers, "Emergency or Emerging Identities?"; Cutts, "Politics and Humanitarianism"; Mallki, "Refugees and Exile"; Minear, *Humanitarian Enterprise*, 76; Warner, "Politics of the Political/Humanitarian Divide."

45. Cited in Fassin, "Humanitarianism as a Politics of Life," 509.

46. Michel Foucault, *Dits et ecrits* (Paris: Gallimard, 1994), vol. 4, 708, cited in Finkiel-kraut, *In the Name of Humanity*, 88.

47. Forsythe, *Humanitarians*, 172; and Ignatieff, *Warrior's Honor*, 119.

48. Fassin, "Humanitarianism as a Politics of Life," 516.

49. Ibid.

50. I thank Rony Brauman for this point. Interview with the author, Paris, France, February 10, 2009.

51. Buxton and Fuller, *White Flame*, 15.

52. Smillie, *Alms Bazaar*; and Smillie and Minear, *Charity of Nations*; Quelch and Laidler-Kylander, *The New Global Brands*.

53. Campbell, *History of CARE*, 113.

54. Black, *Cause for Our Times*, 33.

55. This period is well captured in Gehman, *Let My Heart Be Broken*.

56. Kouchner, *Charité Business*; also see Kent, *Anatomy of Disaster Relief*, 41.

57. Campbell, *History of CARE*, 115, 117.

58. Bachman, *Together in Hope*, 68–69; funding Issue Paper, Lutheran World Relief, March 10, 1990, Exhibit E.

59. Black, *Cause for Our Times*, 35–36, 163–65.

60. Ibid., 63, emphasis in original; and Jones, *In Famine's Shadow*, 40.

61. Ibid., 56; and Jones, *In Famine's Shadow*, 35.

62. de Waal, *Famine Crimes*; Smillie and Minear, *Charity of Nations*; Simeant, "What is Going Global?"; Cooley and Ron, "NGO Scramble."; de Waal, "Humanitarianism Unbound," 10; Stirrat, "Competitive Humanitarianism"; Hulme and Edwards, *NGOs, States, and Donors*; and Polman, *The Crisis Caravan*. There is potentially an upside to this competition between aid agencies for money. According to Neil Wright, former head of the Yugoslav liaison unit at the UNHCR, "NGOs don't want to be coordinated. They depend on being able to sell, to market the performance of their activities in order to get more donors. And that is positive, the more NGOs doing that, the wider the net is trawled to bring in resources to carry out humanitarian activity." Wright, "UNHCR and International Humanitarian Cooperation in the Former Yugoslavia," 53.

63. Pfeffer and Salancik, *External Control of Organizations*, 2; Alford, *Organizations Evolving*, 49; and Powell and DiMaggio, *New Institutionalism*. I sketched the nature of this model, while taking into account individual variation, in Barnett, "Humanitarianism Transformed." Also see Heins, "Democratic States, Aid Agencies, and World Society"; and Lissner, *The Politics of Altruism*.

64. See Barnett, "Evolution without Progress?"

65. Spellman, *Fruits of Sorrow*; Feldman, "Quaker Way."

CHAPTER 2

1. Sznaider, "Sociology of Compassion," 124–25; and Halttunen, "Humanitarianism and the Pornography of Pain."

2. Crane, "Suggestions towards a Genealogy," 206–7. See also Halttunen, "Humanitarianism and the Pornography of Pain"; Laqueur, "Bodies, Details, and the Humanitarian Narrative."

3. McLoy, *Humanitarian Movement*, 1.

4. Cited in Gorgé, *International Relief Union*, 10.

5. Arendt, *On Revolution*, 70–71. For similar claims on the burst of sympathy and activity, see Haskell, "Capitalism and the Origins of the Humanitarian Sensibility, Part 1," 360; Hunt, *Inventing Human Rights*; Smillie, *Alms Bazaar*, 37–39; Richard Wilson and Richard Brown, "Introduction," *Humanitarianism and Suffering*, ed. Wilson and Brown, 1–9; Moyn, "Empathy in History, Empathizing with Humanity," 399–400.

6. Arendt, *On Revolution*, 72.

7. Cartwright, "Kant, Schopenhauer, and Nietzsche."; Moyn, "Empathy in History, Empathizing with Humanity," 413–14.

8. Nietzsche, *On the Genealogy of Morality*, 7, cited from Moyn, "The Last Utopia." On modernity and loss, see Pippin, "Nietzsche and the Melancholy of Modernity." For an insightful discussion of the historical meanings and origins of the related but not coterminous concepts of sympathy and empathy, see Moyn, "Empathy in History."

9. Fiering, "Irresistible Compassion," 195. Also see A. R. Humphreys, "'The Friend of Mankind'"; and Hunt, *Inventing Human Rights,* 64–65.

10. Hunt, *Inventing Human Rights,* 150.

11. Ibid., introduction.

12. Roberts, *Making English Morals,* 4; and Haskell, "Capitalism and the Origins of Humanitarian Sensibility, Part 1," 357–60.

13. Fiering, "Irresistible Compassion," 212.

14. Roberts, *Making English Morals,* p. 4. Also see Laqueur, "Bodies, Details, and the Humanitarian Narrative," p. 178.

15. Klingberg, "Evolution of the Humanitarian Spirit," 260.

16. Stedman-Jones, *End to Poverty?*

17. Roberts, *Making English Morals,* 65.

18. Ibid., 3.

19. On humanitarianism's multilayered origins, see Klingberg, "Evolution of the Humanitarian Sprit," 260; Lewis and Williams, *Private Charity in England, 1747–1757.* According to Roberts, three lines of inquiry dominate the debate regarding the causes of moral reform in England: capitalism and industrialization are the structure and reformers are the superstructure helping to stabilize a class-ridden society undergoing tremendous strain; moral reform resolved societal conflict, but unlike the first perspective does not reduce conflict to an economic base; and an emerging civil society and public sphere becomes developed and used by reformers. Roberts, *Making English Morals,* 4–14.

20. Tronto, *Moral Boundaries,* 36.

21. Hochschild, *Bury the Chains,* 73–74; Roberts, *Making English Morals;* Cowherd, *Politics of English Dissent,* 47.

22. Randall, "Churches and the Liberal Tradition"; Roberts, *Making English Morals,* 46–48; Smith, "Historic Waves of Religious Interest in America"; and Fiering, "Irresistible Compassion." As far as the general role of religion in humanitarianism, Lyons asserts that "there is scarcely any great humanitarian crusade of the nineteenth century, from the abolition of slavery to the abolition of war, in which various churches of Christendom, either as institutions or through their individual members, did not play a prominent role." *Internationalism in Europe,* 245.

23. Although forms of evangelicalism existed throughout Europe and wherever there was Protestantism, the most concentrated and intensive activity occurred in the United States and England. For overviews of this period of evangelicalism, see Marsden, *Understanding Fundamentalism and Evangelicalism;* and Noll, *Rise of Evangelicalism.*

24. In the United States there were several awakenings; the first was closely associated with the eighteenth-century movement of Jonathan Edwards and George Whitfield; the second, at the turn of the nineteenth century, helped to institutionalize the very idea of social reform in the United States. In Britain a moral crisis emerged in the late eighteenth century because of the loss of the American colonies, tremendous population flows, urbanization, and other structural changes, leading to what appeared to be a "moral breakdown." Roberts, *Making English Morals,* 31–38.

25. Thomas, *Revivalism and Cultural Change,* 67.

26. Ibid.

27. Porterfield, "Protestant Missionaries," 54–55.

28. Alongside the expansion of Protestant evangelism was Catholic missionary work. From the beginning of the first explorations, the Jesuits established outposts among the indigenous peoples. In the United States, unlike the Protestants who used the public school systems, print media, and public policy to try to convert citizens, American Catholics developed an extensive network of charitable organizations, schools, hospitals, and assorted programs, often linked by the Catholic Church. Although evolving partly as a counterbalance to Protestant evangelism, the influence of Protestant culture on the evolution of Catholic charitable and welfare societies also was evident in the development of a relationship between personal piety and social service, especially those branches that had a liberal, progressive orientation. Ibid., 54.

29. The Calvinist idea of social responsibility and reform had a lingering effect. The idea of social responsibility existed among the prophets of ancient Israel, and then Christianity fused the traditional Judaic concern with the idea of resurrection and Jesus as the Messiah; notably, concerns about social decay became linked to an apocalyptic view in which the

Kingdom of God would create a new social order. This apocalyptic vision lay dormant after the establishment of the Roman Church, became popular once again with the Protestant Reformation, most famously with Calvinist thought, and then reemerged with the rapid changes of the late eighteenth century. Ibid., 54–55.

30. For broad commentaries on the link connecting structural change, religious reform, and humanitarianism, see Carlton, "Humanitarianism, Past and Present"; and Curti, "Changing Pattern."

31. Renwald, *Humanitarianism and British Colonial Policy.*

32. Ibid., 25–26.

33. Zabriskie, "Rise and Main Characteristics," 8, cited in Bellot, "Evangelicals and the Defense of Slavery," 19.

34. Carlton, "Humanitarianism, Past and Present," 50.

35. Roberts, *Making English Morals,* 2.

36. Quoted in Hochschild, *Breaking the Chains,* 144.

37. Ibid., 144.

38. Link, "Samuel Taylor Coleridge and the Economic and Political Crisis." For this development over the nineteenth century, see Himmelfarb, *Poverty and Compassion;* Agnew, *From Charity to Social Work;* and Reamer, *Social World Values and Ethics.*

39. Young, *Bearing against Sin;* and West, *Politics of Revelation and Reason.*

40. Stanley, *Bible and the Flag,* 63, 161; Noll, "Evangelical Identity, Power, and Culture," 33–34.

41. Thomas, *Revivalism and Cultural Change,* 77; Gamber, "Antebellum Reform," in *Charity, Philanthropy, and Civility in American History,* 129–33; and Shah, "For the Sake of Conscience."

42. Thomas, *Revivalism and Cultural Change,* 78–79.

43. Cowherd, *Politics of English Dissent,* 46–47; see also Renwald, *Humanitarianism and British Colonial Policy,* 25–26.

44. Carlton, "Humanitarianism, Past and Present," 54; see also Parmelee, "Rise of Modern Humanitarianism"; Griffin, "Religious Benevolence as Social Control"; Gamber, "Antebellum Reform," 132–34; Banner, "Religious Benevolence as Social Control: A Critique"; Piven and Cloward, "Humanitarianism in History"; Cohen and Scull, eds., *Social Control and the State;* Roberts, *Making English Morals,* ch. 4; Rozario, *Culture of Calamity;* and Walker, "Crisis and Normality," 2.

CHAPTER 3

1. For studies of the development of abolitionist thought and mobilization against the slave trade in Britain, see Brown, *Moral Capital;* Hochschild, *Bury the Chains;* Drescher, *Capitalism and Antislavery;* Oldfield, *Popular Politics and British Anti-Slavery;* and Klingberg, *Anti-Slavery Movement in England.*

2. Hochschild, *Break the Chains,* 5.

3. Ibid., 45, 87.

4. Cowherd, *Politics of English Dissent,* 47. A religious commitment did not necessarily lead to an enlightened view on slavery. There were clergy, evangelicals, and religious folks who favored slavery. See Bellot, "Evangelicals and the Defense of Slavery."

5. There is, of course, tremendous debate over how to understand the motives of the abolitionists and their relationship to capitalism. See Donald, "Toward a Reconsideration of Abolitionists"; Thomas Haskell, "Capitalism and the Origins of the Humanitarian Sensibility," parts 1 and 2; and Ashworth, "Relationship between Capitalism and Humanitarianism."

6. Brown, *Moral Capital,* 57.

7. Stanley, *World Missionary Conference* and "Christianity and Civilization," 172.

8. Quoted in Festa, *Sentimental Figures of Empire,* 188, 201.

9. Hochschild, *Bury the Chains,* 222–25; Klingberg, *Anti-Slavery Movement in England,* vii; and Brown, *Moral Capital.*

10. Brown, *Moral Capital,* 25–26.

11. Cowherd, *Politics of English Dissent,* 46; Fage, *History of West Africa,* 117–18; Renwald, *Humanitarianism and British Colonial Policy;* and Festa, *Sentimental Figures of Empire,* 64–65, 203.

12. Hochschild, *Bury the Chains,* 134.

13. Ibid., 227. Pressed to imagine what would replace slavery and what a British empire free of slavery would look like, some of the early abolitionists argued that a diversified

trading system from western African would help local populations and lead to more prosperity for the empire. Toward that end, in the late eighteenth century the British government supported a scheme in Sierra Leone, which, in effect, tied the abolitionists to a new push for imperialism. Brown, *Moral Capital,* 322, 328.

14. Hochschild, *Bury the Chains,* 314.

15. Porter, "Trusteeship, Anti-Slavery, and Humanitarianism," 204.

16. Porter, *Religion versus Empire?* 139, and "Trusteeship, Anti-Slavery, and Humanitarianism," 207.

17. Fage, *History of West Africa,* 117–18. See also Renwald, *Humanitarianism and British Colonial Policy.*

18. Porter, "Trusteeship, Anti-Slavery, and Humanitarianism," 209. See also Boyd Hilton's magisterial cultural history of the period, *The Age of Atonement.*

19. Quoted in Porter, "Trusteeship, Anti-Slavery, and Humanitarianism," 199.

20. Grant, *Civilised Savagery.*

21. Dirks, *Scandal of Empire.*

22. Festa, *Sentimental Figures of Empire,* 236–37.

23. Pitts, *Turn to Empire,* 14–16.

24. Grant, *Civilised Savagery.*

25. For three excellent intellectual histories of the leading thinkers on the subject of the relationship between liberalism and imperialism, see Muthu, *Enlightenment against Empire;* Pitts, *Turn to Empire;* and Mehta, *Liberalism and Empire.*

26. Conklin, *Mission to Civilize;* Taithe, "Religious Responses, Humanitarianism, and Colonialism," "Algerian Orphans and Colonial Christianity," and "Reinventing (French) Universalism"; and Shorter, *Cross and Flag in Africa.*

27. Pitts, *Turn to Empire;* Mehta, *Liberalism and Empire;* and Muthu, *Enlightenment against Empire.*

28. This account draws entirely from Sharma, *Famine Philanthropy and the Colonial State.* See also Davis, *Late Victorian Holocausts.*

29. Porter, "Trusteeship, Anti-Slavery, and Humanitarianism," 209.

30. Stanley, "Welcoming Lecture," 2.

31. For this periodization, see Noll, "Evangelical Identity, Power, and Culture," 33–34. For the argument that missionary activity dominated the humanitarian scene, see Williams, *Ideal of the Self-Governing Church.* For general overviews of missionary movements, see Porter, *Religion versus Empire?;* Stanley, *Bible and the Flag;* Renwald, *Humanitarianism and British Colonial Policy,* esp. chs. 2–4.

32. Stanley, "Christian Missions and the Enlightenment," 8, 11.

33. Stanley, "Christianity and Civilization," 170–71.

34. Ibid., 172; Porter, "Trusteeship, Anti-Slavery, and Humanitarianism," 229.

35. Porter, *Religion versus Empire?* 32–38; Stanley, *Bible and the Flag,* 63, 161; and Renwald, *Humanitarianism and British Colonial Policy,* 49.

36. Stanley, *Bible and the Flag,* 63–64.

37. Porter, "Trusteeship, Anti-Slavery, and Humanitarianism," 209.

38. Although dwarfed in terms of numbers and notoriety, the American missionary movement also made a mark. It differed from its European co-religionists in several ways. Because there was no established or state church in the United States, American missionaries tended to rely more on voluntary contributions. (However, many of the most important European missionaries and missionary societies—like the Baptist William Carey and the Moravians—were also voluntary and separate from state-established churches.) Moreover, because the United States was expanding westward and not overseas, except in the case of the Hawaiian Islands, it was less clearly associated with commercial or strategic ambitions. Indeed, many missionaries had difficulty getting the attention and protection of American officials. Curti, *American Philanthropy Abroad,* 138–39. That said, American missionaries resembled their European co-religionists in several ways. They had similar origins; bolstered by evangelicalism, shades of millenarianism, and the belief that even savages were children of God and could be saved, they descended on the unsuspecting armed with the Bible and the conviction that conversion was the path to salvation. Of course, missionaries got considerable help from a United States government that desired to "civilize" the Native American populations. See Sandos, *Converting California;* and Hoxie, *Final Promise.*

39. Wilberforce, *Appeal to the Religion, Justice, and Humanity,* 64–65.

40. "As the original Victorian anti-slavery organizations receded to the political margins, the leadership of the British anti-slavery movement passed to the Protestant missionary

societies, which embraced abolition as a central cause in their civilizing mission, especially in Africa." Grant, *Civilized Savagery,* 26.

41. Hiney, *On the Missionary Trail,* 22–23.

42. Carson, "The British Raj," 67.

43. Porter, *Religion versus Empire?* 39–44.

44. Stanley, *Bible and the Flag,* 68–69.

45. Porter, *Religion versus Empire?* 32–38; and Varg, "Motives in Protestant Missions," 75–78.

46. Boddy, *Civilizing Women,* 31, 41.

47. Bashford, *Imperial Hygiene;* and Haynes, *Imperial Medicine.*

48. Grant, *Civilised Savagery,* 19; see also Stanley, *Bible and the Flag,* 70–74.

49. "The African Slave Trade and Its Remedy," quoted in Noll, "Evangelical Identity, Power, and Culture," 47.

50. Boddy, *Civilizing Women,* 17–18.

51. Porter, "Trusteeship, Anti-Slavery, and Humanitarianism," 229, and, Porter, *Religion versus Empire?* 283. For an innovative examination of the role of missionary protestants in sowing the seeds for potential anti-colonial unrest and democratic development, see Woodbury, "Dividing Elites."

52. Hiney, *On the Missionary Trail,* 30.

53. Porter, "Religion, Missionary Enthusiasm, and Empire," 222. A classic case is how the British population's desire to stamp out the slave trade led to the ill-fated British expedition to the Sudan in 1882, opposed on strategic grounds by Prime Minister William Gladstone. See Holt, *Mahdist State in the Sudan,* 32–44; and Neilands, *Dervish Wars,* 23–34.

54. Boddy, *Civilizing Women,* 4. See also Spurr, *Rhetoric of Empire.*

55. Cassels, "Bentinck"; van der Veer, *Imperial Encounters,* 41–43; and Pitts, *Turn to Empire,* 13.

56. De Gruchy, "Who Did They Think They Were?" 213–15.

57. Renwald, *Humanitarianism and British Colonial Policy,* ch. 6; Stanley, *Bible and the Flag,* 90; Hall, *Civilizing Subjects;* McLisky, "'Due Observance of Justice.'"

58. Varg, "Motives in Protestant Missions," 73; Stanley, *Bible and the Flag,* 73, 78–83; Renwald, *Humanitarianism and British Colonial Policy,* ch. 6.

59. Darch, "Missionaries as Humanitarians?"

60. Stanley, "Christianity and Civilization," 173.

61. Stanley, "Welcoming Lecture," 1–2.

62. Sjoblom, "Missionary Image of Africa," 12.

63. Porter, "Trusteeship, Anti-Slavery, and Humanitarianism," 216–17; Cooper and Stoler, *Tensions of Empire;* Lester, "Reformulating Identities," "Settlers, the State and Colonial Power," and *Imperial Networks;* and Lambert and Lester, "Geographies of Colonial Philanthropy."

64. Cited in Porter, *Religion versus Empire?* 328.

65. Hochschild, *King Leopold's Ghost.* Henry Morton Stanley was originally given the name *Bula Matadi,* the "rock buryer," and then Swedish missionaries applied the name to the Congo state, signifying its double connotation of opening up the Congo and the brutality that made it a subject of eventual censure. What initially worried the Swedish missionaries, though, was not the treatment of the labor force but rather that the Congo state was putting up various obstacles in their way. Sjoblom, "Missionary Image of Africa," 9.

66. Porterfield, "Protestant Missionaries," 64–65; see also Rosenberg, "Missions to the World," 245.

67. Cooper and Stoler, *Tensions of Empire;* Lester, "Reformulating Identities," "Settlers, the State, and Colonial Power," and *Imperial Networks;* and Lambert, "Geographies of Colonial Philanthropy."

68. Curti, *American Philanthropy Abroad,* ch. 6; and Porterfield, "Protestant Missionaries," 69.

69. See the work by Brian Stanley: "Defining the Boundaries of Christendom," "Africa through European Christian Eyes," "Twentieth-Century World Christianity," "Church, State, and the Hierarchy of 'Civilization,'" and "Edinburgh 1910 and the Oikoumene." See also Gairdner, *Echoes from Edinburgh 1910;* Morrison, "World Missionary Conference"; and Malueke, "Mission and Political Power."

70. Robert, *Occupy Until I Come.*

71. World Missionary Conference, Report of the Commission VII: Missions and Governments, 96–97.

72. Ibid., 96–97.

73. Grant, *Civilised Savagery,* 8.

74. Ibid., 32.

75. Ibid., 63.

76. Weitz, "From the Vienna to the Paris System," 1339. See also Anghie, "Colonialism and the Birth of International Institutions."

77. Grant, *Civilized Savagery,* ch. 5.

78. Watenpaugh, "The League of Nations' Rescue."

CHAPTER 4

1. Ignatieff, "Warrior's Honor," 110.

2. For overviews of the origins of the laws of war, see Best, *War and Law Since 1945;* Macalister-Smith, *International Humanitarian Assistance;* and Reisman, *Laws of War.*

3. Forsythe, *Humanitarians,* 15; and Boissier, *From Solferino to Tsushima,* 20.

4. For a review of pre-1864 movements toward the idea of relief and the laws of war, see Boissier, *From Solferino to Tsushima,* 125–63.

5. For statements regarding the ICRC's religious roots, see André Durand, *History of the International Committee of the Red Cross,* 48; and Boissier, "Henry Dunant," 411.

6. Forsythe, *Humanitarians,* 28; and Guillermand, "Historical Foundations."

7. Ignatieff, *Warrior's Honor,* 112.

8. Some of the stiffest opposition to Dunant's proposal came from those who might have been expected to support it—those who also were campaigning for greater medical relief. Florence Nightingale, for instance, refused to support the proposals on the grounds that the job of saving soldiers was too important to be left to amateurs and that military organizations had both the responsibility and the potential capacity to improve their medical relief. Consequently, if Dunant's proposals became reality, it might harm the goal of medical relief because it would displace energy into creating volunteer bands that did not have the professional training to help soldiers. See Hutchinson, *Champions of Charity,* 39–41. Eventually the real successes in helping the wounded came from innovations in medical technology and military organization, stirred in part by the realization that those armies that gave their soldiers top medical care were the armies that could patch up their soldiers and get them back to the front—and win.

9. Hutchinson, *Champions of Charity,* 30. Maunoir's study of the U.S. Sanitary Commission led him to conclude that the absence of neutrality meant that physicians had a more difficult time tending to the wounded. Boissier, *From Solferino to Tsushima,* 102.

10. For an invaluable study of how humanitarianism can become co-opted by and central to war mobilization, see Taithe, "Red Cross Flag."

11. Hutchinson, *Champions of Charity,* ch. 4.

12. Ibid., 203.

13. Importantly, there was no discussion of how international humanitarian law might apply to the rapidly colonized world.

14. Ibid., 143.

15. Ibid., 204; see also Moorehead, *Dunant's Dream,* 122.

16. Brauman, *Penser dans l'urgence,* 45–47; Taithe, "The Red Cross Flag in the Franco-Prussian War," 30.

17. For instance, there was an outpouring of support in the U.S. and Europe in response to the Russian famine of 1891. Rosenberg, "Missions to the World," 248. For an overview of American philanthropic activities in the pre–World War I period, with particular emphasis on the role of ethnic groups in mobilizing assistance, see Curti, *American Philanthropy Abroad,* chs. 1–7.

18. Curti, *American Philanthropy Abroad,* 270–76.

19. Mulley, *Woman Who Saved the World,* 63. See also Mahood, *Feminism and Voluntary Action,* which focuses more on the social and cultural context of her life.

20. Mulley, *Woman Who Saved the World,* 154.

21. Her husband was a close relation of Thomas Fowell Buxton, who had succeeded Wilberforce as the leader of the abolitionists in the British Parliament, and whose strategy for ending slavery through commerce and a "Charter of Rights for the Natives" made him one of the leading humanitarians of his day.

22. Mulley, *Woman Who Saved the World*, 48–49, 170–75.

23. Quoted in ibid., 66.

24. Ibid., 204.

25. Quoted in ibid., 274.

26. Ibid., 208.

27. Ibid., 295.

28. For a detailed account of Hoover's participation and the bluffing and bravado that he used to establish the CRB and then keep it running, see Nash, *Life of Herbert Hoover*. After the war Hoover headed the American Relief Administration (ARA), which was initially organized to help with the famine in Russia. Like future efforts, though, it connected charity to political ambitions and economic interests: Hoover and others saw relief as a way to gain influence in Russia and possibly undermine the Bolsheviks, and many in Congress and farmers were hoping to find markets for American agriculture. Rosenberg, *Spreading the American Dream*, 75–77, 117–18.

29. A similar trend toward institutionalization also was evident in the League of Nations. See Watenpaugh, "Pious Wish."

30. Curti, *American Philanthropy Abroad*, 279–93. See also Rosenberg, "Missions to the World," 249; and Patenaude, *Big Show in Bololand*.

31. Nichols, *Uneasy Alliance*, 38.

32. Holborn, *Refugees;* and Sugino, "'Non-Political and Humanitarian Clause,'" 35.

33. Coles, *Voluntary Repatriation*, 43.

34. League of Nations, Official Journal, Special Supplement No. 115, Records of the Fourteenth Assembly, Text, 1933, 48, cited in Sugino, "'Non-Political and Humanitarian Clause,'" 36.

35. See John Hutchinson, "Disasters and the International Order" and "Disasters and the International Order II"; Macalister-Smith, "International Relief Union of 1932," and "International Relief Union."

36. Gorgé, *International Relief Union*, 25.

37. Ibid., 51.

38. Ibid., 12.

39. Ibid., 13.

40. However, the swing toward pacifism during the interwar years placed the ICRC slightly out of favor because it was viewed as working to humanize and not abolish war. For a survey of the first fifty years of the ICRC, see Forsythe, *Humanitarians*, 29–33.

41. Hutchinson, *Champions of Charity*, 288–303; see also Moorehead, *Dunant's Dream*, ch. 10.

42. Hutchinson, *Champions of Charity*, 97–102.

43. Ibid., 339.

44. Forsythe, *Humanitarians*, 38–41.

45. Ibid., 34.

46. This summary draws exclusively from Baudendistel, *Between Bombs and Good Intentions*.

47. Ibid., 213.

48. For a study of the attempted extension of the rights of children in a colonial context, see Dominique Marshall, "Children's Rights in Imperial Political Cultures."

49. K. P. Grant, *Civilizing Savages*, cited in Marshall, "Children's Rights in Imperial Political Cultures," 286.

50. For an interesting argument regarding the growing tendency of missionaries to operate under the secularized banner of "internationalism," see Robert, "The First Globalization."

CHAPTER 5

1. Plesch, *America, Hitler, and the United Nations*, 202.

2. Morgenthau, "Human Rights and Foreign Policy," 345.

3. Cited in Rozario, *Culture of Calamity*, 127.

4. Borgwardt, *New Deal for the World*, 78.

5. Ibid., 78.

6. Ruggie, "International Regimes, Transactions, and Change"; and Polanyi, *Great Transformation*.

7. Borgwardt, *New Deal for the World*.

8. Cooper, "Modernizing Bureaucrats"; Duffield, *Development, Security, and Unending War*; and Cowen and Shenton, *Doctrines of Development*.

9. Albert Hirschman, "The Rise and Decline of Development Economics," in Hirschman, *Essays in Trespassing*.

10. For an inventory of causes for the rise of development aid, see Kent, *Anatomy of Disaster Relief*, 40–41.

11. Quoted in George Creel, "Food for a Ravaged World," *Colliers*, vol. 112, July 17, 1943, 21, cited in Curti, *American Philanthropy Abroad*, 503.

12. Cited from Curti, *American Philanthropy Abroad*, 503.

13. See Escobar, *Encountering Development*; and Rist, *History of Development*.

14. Quoted in Black, *Cause for Our Times*, 68.

15. Rostow, *Stages of Economic Growth*.

16. Morris, *The Fog of War*.

17. Althusser, "International of Decent Feelings," 22–23.

18. Gong, *Standard of Civilization in International Society*.

19. Rabinow, *French DNA*; Kritsiotis, "Imagining the International Community"; Malkki, "Citizens of Humanity"; Young, *Postcolonialism*, esp. part 3.

20. Ignatieff, *Human Rights as Political Idolatry*.

21. Borgwardt, *New Deal for the World*, 66.

22. Morefield, *Covenants without Swords*, 3.

23. Iriye, *Global Community*, ch. 2; and Borgwardt, *New Deal for the World*, 71.

24. Black, *Cause For Our Time*, 68.

25. Quoted in Smillie, *Alms Bazaar*, 119.

26. Pergande, *Private Voluntary Aid in Vietnam*, 40. See also Sullivan, "Politics of Altruism."

27. Campbell, *History of CARE*, 155. The growing role of the U.S. government presaged a shift not merely from private to public but also from religious to secular. In the United States between 1939 and 1941, over 80 percent of all voluntary contributions came from ethnically and religiously oriented organizations; during the war this percentage was cut in half; and then from 1946 to 1953 it fell to just over 10 percent. Although there were various causes of this shift, most important was the U.S. government's preference for secular organizations such as CARE and the growing role of organized labor. Curti, *American Philanthropy Abroad*, 508–12.

CHAPTER 6

1. Cohen, "Between Relief and Politics," 438.

2. Shephard, "'Becoming Planning Minded.'"

3. Shephard observes that Churchill's speech of August 20, 1940, in which he linked relief to a hearts and minds campaign, is usually regarded as the moment when politics began to steer relief. Ibid., 408.

4. Memorandum to Secretary of State Hull from A. A. Berle et al., in Berle Collection, cited in Nichols, *Uneasy Alliance*, 55.

5. Egan, *Catholic Relief Services*, 15.

6. There are wildly different estimates of how many aid agencies existed at the time of America's entry into the war. Curti cites three hundred, Bloomstein twice that many. Curti, *American Philanthropy Abroad*, 452–56; Bloomstein, *History of CARE*, Box 2, 6.

7. Pergande, *Private Voluntary Aid in Vietnam*, 29.

8. Nichols, *Uneasy Alliance*, 61–62.

9. Curti, *American Philanthropy Abroad*, 458–60, 480–85.

10. Cohen, "Between Relief and Politics," 439.

11. Ibid., 438.

12. Reinisch, "We Shall Rebuild Anew," 455.

13. Boudreau, "The Problem of World Health," in *Winning the Peace* (St. Louis, Mo., 1944), 69, cited in ibid., 452.

14. Shephard, "'Becoming Planning Minded,'" 406.

15. Cohen, "Between Relief and Politics," 439.

16. Wilson, *In the Margins of Chaos,* 269, emphasis added.

17. Kent, *Anatomy of Disaster Relief,* 37–38.

18. Bachman, *Together in Hope,* 35, 45.

19. Ibid., 22–25.

20. Egan, *Catholic Relief Services.*

21. Ibid., 6; and Nichols, *Uneasy Alliance,* 58–59.

22. Egan, *Catholic Relief Services,* 3.

23. Pergande, *Private Voluntary Aid in Vietnam,* 28.

24. Memo on the origins of Catholic charity at the beginning of World War II, April 18, 1939, Bishop Edward E. Swanstrom Collection, XX–1, Box 1.

25. Curti, *American Philanthropy Abroad,* 491–93.

26. Campbell, *History of CARE,* 5–19.

27. Bloomstein, *History of CARE,* box 2, 43.

28. Although some on the board wondered why a "temporary" organization required such impressive facilities, apocryphally, one staff member observed at the time that the American Jewish Joint Distribution Committee had begun as a temporary outfit after World War I but was now thirty years old.

29. Campbell, *History of CARE,* 53.

30. By June 1948 CARE was the largest shipper of food aid, accounting for roughly 25% of the total. The three major religious agencies, the AJJDC, the WRS, and CRS had 21%, 17% and 12%, respectively, with twelve other agencies making up the balance. Bloomstein, *History of CARE,* box 2, 264.

31. Curti, *American Philanthropy Abroad,* 498–99.

32. Campbell, *History of CARE,* 46.

33. Ibid., 53.

34. Bloomstein, *History of CARE,* Box 2, 202.

35. Ibid., Box 2, 28.

36. Ibid., Box 2, 207.

37. Black, *Cause for Our Times.*

38. Ibid., 26–27.

39. Lutheran World Relief 1958 annual report; archives 1954–58, 167.

40. Interview at CARE headquarters, Atlanta, Georgia, November 2, 2006. See also Campbell, *History of CARE,* 66. Not everyone welcomed CARE's offerings, though. CARE tried but failed to establish operations in the Middle East. The Israeli government, probably because of pressure from the United Jewish Appeal, which was worried about competition, ultimately refused assistance. Various Arab governments also said no, assuming that an agency closely associated with the United States could not be entirely trusted. CARE did, however, conclude an agreement to send technical materials to Jordan. Bloomstein, *History of CARE,* box 2, 290.

41. Black, *Cause for Our Time,* 28–29, 32, 81. See also Kent, *Anatomy of Disaster Relief,* 38–39; and Jones, *In Famine's Shadow,* 31–32.

42. Empie and Whiting, "Lutheran World Relief."

43. This version is derived from material in Rohrer, *Open Arms,* 39–50, quotation 47. See also Bornstein, *Spirit of Development,* 17–23.

44. Irvine, "New Partnership."

45. Bob Pierce, "Too Late for America?" *Eternity Magazine,* May 1958, cited in Whaites, "Pursuing Partnership," 413.

46. Borgwardt, *New Deal for the World,* 119.

47. Reinisch, "We Shall Rebuild Anew."

48. Borgwardt, *New Deal for the World,* 119.

49. Smillie, *Alms Bazaar,* 39.

50. Black, *Cause for Our Times.*

51. Interview, Monrovia, California,

52. Catholic Relief Services, Bishop Edward Swanstrom Archives, XX–1A, Box 5.

53. Lutheran World Relief, "Lutheran World Relief." A decade later it returned to the same question, and this time the board voted to recommend at the next board meeting to change the name to Lutheran World Response. November 10, 1989. More traditionally minded heads prevailed.

54. Nichols, *Uneasy Alliance.*

55. Bloomstein, *History of CARE*, box 2, 414. Not surprisingly, given this underlying connection, the Soviets refused to cooperate with CARE and viewed it as an arm of American foreign policy and looked suspiciously on those in communist countries who wanted to have friendly relations with CARE.

56. Harold Miner, Address, March 31, 1960, CARE Archives, cited in Curti, *American Philanthropy Abroad*, 499.

57. P.L. 480 revealed differences between aid agencies regarding how comfortable they were with a partnership with the U.S. government. Sullivan, "Politics of Altruism," 765–66.

58. Bachman, *Together in Hope*, 51.

59. Statement to the Senate Foreign Relations Committee by Dr. Paul C. Empie on behalf of Lutheran World Relief, July 8, 1959, archives 1954–58, emphasis added. For another account of the questionable ties between the United States and LWR, see Nichols, *Uneasy Alliance*, 93.

60. Ibid., 13–17.

61. Flipse, "Latest Casualty of War," 248.

62. Nichols, *Uneasy Alliance*, 97.

63. Catholic Relief Services, Bishop Edward E. Swanstrom Collection, XX–1, Box 12.

64. Catholic Relief Services, "Memo from consulting team," July 14, 1978, Bishop Edward E. Swanstrom Collection, XX–1, Box 22.

65. Pergande, *Private Voluntary Aid in Vietnam*, 39.

66. Bachman, *Together in Hope*, 68–69.

67. In 1958 a controversy erupted among religious agencies over whether they were using P.L. 480 shipments to proselytize, and there was compelling evidence that they were. Nichols, *Uneasy Alliance*, 93.

68. For more on this depoliticized and philanthropic form of humanitarianism, see Slim, "Not Philanthropy but Rights," 9–12.

69. Catholic Relief Services, office memorandum, "Restatement of Basic Motivation and Philosophy of Catholic Relief Services—USCC," April 18, 1975, Bishop Edward E. Swanstrom Collection, XX–1, Box 11 emphasis added.

70. "Proposal for a Strategy to Deal with World Hunger," Lutheran World Relief, December 1974, 10, LWR Archives, September–December 1974.

71. Quoted in Black, *Cause for Our Times*, 86.

72. Ibid., 156, 172–73.

73. Ibid., 162. See also Burnell, "Charity Law and Pressure Politics."

74. World Vision International Council. *World Vision's Ministry of Mission Challenge*, 1–2.

75. Ibid.

76. Ibid.

77. World Vision's Evangelism Ministry; Directions for the Future. Discussion Paper for World Vision International Council, September 16–19, 1986; World Vision International. International Council. May 31, 1978; A Declaration of Internationalization; Graeme Irvine, "Presentation of Internationalization Report"; World Vision International, Commission on Internationalization, 1978–1983. Interim Report, September 1984; Report of the Internationalization Study Committee, For Submission to the meeting of the Combined Boards, World Vision International, Honolulu, Hawaii, April 19–24, 1976. These documents are in the author's possession.

78. Interview with former WVI staff.

79. Albert Hirschman, "The Rise and Decline of Development Economics," in Hirschman, *Essays in Trespassing*.

80. Quoted in Grant, *Civilised Savagery*, 7.

CHAPTER 7

1. Wiseberg, *International Politics of Relief*, 32, 111–13, 129, and ch. 7; Brauman, *Penser dans l'urgence*, 85; Waters, "Influencing the Message," 697–718.

2. Wiseberg, *Politics of International Relief*, 475, 512.

3. Moorhead, *Dunant's Dream*, 623–24; Foley, *Thin Blue Line*, 16–19.

4. Black, *Cause for Our Times*, 122–23.

5. Forsythe, *Humanitarians*, 52–54.

6. Shawcross, *The Quality of Mercy,* 48, cited in Keen, *Complex Emergencies,* 131.

7. For what it might have been able to do, see Brauman, "From Philanthropy to Humanitarianism," 402–4.

8. Delorenzi, *ICRC Policy Since the End of the Cold War,* 17.

9. Davis, "International Committee of the Red Cross and Its Practice of Self-Restraint."

10. Wiseberg, *Politics of International Relief,* 150.

11. Ibid., 344–56. See also Goetz, "Humanitarian Issues in the Biafra Conflict."

12. Holborn, *Refugees,* 59–60; and Loescher, *Beyond Charity,* 53.

13. Kennedy, "International Refugee Protection," 4. See also Holborn, *Problem of Our Time,* ch. 4; UNHCR, *State of the World's Refugees,* 83.

14. Kennedy, "International Refugee Protection," 5. See also Sztucki, "Conclusions on the International Protection of Refugees," 290–92; Holborn, *Refugees,* 156; and Jaeger, "Status and the Protection of Refugees," 2, 38–39.

15. Ogata, "World Order, Internal Conflict, and Refugees"; also see Ogata, "Challenges on the Front Line of Refugee Assistance, 202–4.

16. For discussions of the UNHCR's extreme dependence, see Loescher, *Beyond Charity,* 137, and *UNHCR in Global Politics,* 349–50.

17. Kennedy, "International Refugee Protection," 14–15; Skran, "International Refugee Regime," 25, 28; and Holborn, *Refugees,* 89–90.

18. Loescher, *Beyond Charity,* 64–66, and *UNHCR in World Politics.*

19. Skran, "International Refugee Regime," 16; and Holborn, *Refugees,* 387.

20. Importantly, these high-profile operations also made it easier for U.S. State Department officials to argue that the UNHCR was furthering U.S. national interests, thus leading to an increase in U.S. appropriations for the organization. Loescher, *Beyond Charity,* 67.

21. Barnett and Finnemore, *Rules for the World,* ch. 5; and Jaeger, "Status and the Protection of Refugees," 48. According to High Commissioner Felix Schnyder, these resolutions "allowed potentially for flexibility which was indispensable to the action of my Office. Those resolutions, together with the mandate, formed a coherent whole into which it should in future be possible to integrate divergent situations as those concerning the 'old' and new refugee problems." Schnyder, "Les Aspects Juridiques Actuel du Probleme des Refugies," 18.

22. Khan, "Legal Problems Relating to Refugee Problems in Africa," 56.

23. Schnyder, "Les aspects juridiques actuels du problème des réfugiés." 16–17.

24. Ibid., 8.

25. Coles, "Approaching the Refugee Problem Today," 131.

26. Notes of a confidential UNHCR meeting with Mr. Udo Affia, Commissioner of Health of breakaway Eastern Nigeria "Biafra," November 9, 1967, cited in Goetz, "Humanitarian Issues in the Biafra Conflict," 6.

27. Shawcross, *Quality of Mercy,* 103.

28. Forsythe, *Humanitarians,* 63.

29. Moorehead, *Dunant's Dream,* 630–34; and Forsythe, *Humanitarians,* 88–92.

30. Vallaeys, *Médecins Sans Frontières,* 72. For a detailed examination of their experiences in and reactions to Biafra, see Weber, *French Doctors,* chs. 1–2.

31. Vallaeys, *Médecins Sans Frontières,* 73.

32. Parts of the essay, interestingly enough, were published in the ICRC's journal, *International Review of the Red Cross,* in January 1969.

33. Vallaeys, *Médecins Sans Frontières,* 74;

34. Weber, *French Doctors,* ch. 3.

35. Ibid., 76–80.

36. Taithe, "Reinventing (French) Universalism," 149.

37. Weber, *French Doctors,* 95–105.

38. Vallaeys, *Médecins Sans Frontières,* 114–20.

39. Kerleroux, "Dossier: Associated for Action," 1–2.

40. Ninin and Deldique, *Globe Doctors,* 33.

41. Taithe, "Reinventing (French) Universalism," 147–58.

42. Bortolotti, *Hope in Hell,* 45. Emmanuelli, *Les prédateurs,* 144, 151, 155–56, 163.

43. Brauman, *Penser dans l'urgence,* 58–59.

44. On contradictions, see Ninin and Deldique, *Globe Doctors,* 101–15.

45. Their positions certainly could not have been predicted from their professions. After all, "the men of the press were calling for discretion and silence, while those who took

the Hippocratic Oath—admitted inside houses, my eyes will not see what happens there; my tongue will be quite to the secrets confided in me—invoked the right to bear witness." Weber, *French Doctors*, 108. For a general discussion of the meaning of witnessing at MSF, see Redfield, "A Less Modest Witness."

46. Vallaeys, *Médecins Sans Frontières*, 126; and Bernier, *Des medecins sans frontières*, 50.

47. Bortolotti, *Hope in Hell*, 47–48.

48. Bernier, *Des medecins sans frontieres*, 51.

49. Vallaeys, *Médecins Sans Frontières*, 123; Brauman, "From Philanthropy to Humanitarianism," 407–9.

50. Ninin and Deldique, *Globe Doctors*, 88–89; Brauman, "Forward," xxi.

51. Weber, *French Doctors*, 114–22; and Ninin and Deldique, *Globe Doctors*, ch. 8.

52. Vallaeys, *Médecins Sans Frontières*, 46, 64.

53. Weber, *French Doctors*, ch. 8

54. Bortolotti, *Hope in Hell*, 49; and Weber, *French Doctors*, 122–28, 134.

55. Berman, *Power and the Idealists*, 232.

56. Vallaeys, *Médecins Sans Frontières*, 188–95, 198–99; and Weber, *Globe Doctors*, 178–79.

57. Taithe, "Reinventing (French) Universalism," 149.

58. Ibid., 149.

59. Pergande, *Private Voluntary Aid in Vietnam*, vi.

60. Interview with Rocco Sacci, director of information, Catholic Relief Services, September 13, 1972, New York, cited in Wiseberg, *Politics of International Relief*, 514.

61. Pergande, "Private Voluntary Aid and Nation Building in South Vietnam" and *Private Voluntary Aid in Vietnam*, vii.

62. Pergande, *Private Voluntary Aid in Vietnam*, xii.

63. Flipse, "Latest Casualty of War," 245; Kauffman, "Politics, Programs, and Protests." World Vision also found itself co-opted, albeit not as intentionally so. Alan Whaites, "Pursuing Partnership," 413.

64. Flipse, "Latest Casualty of War," 263.

65. Nichols, *Uneasy Alliance*, 105.

66. Ibid., 105.

67. Pezzullo, "Cooperation in Humanitarian Efforts," 5–6. See also Whaites, "Pursuing Partnership," 413.

68. Nichols, *Uneasy Alliance*, 101.

69. Shawcross, *Quality of Mercy*, ch. 3.

70. Nichols, *Uneasy Alliance*, 176–77.

71. For a good overview of the camps as a humanitarian sanctuary, see Terry, *Condemned to Repeat?* ch. 4.

72. Shawcross, *Quality of Mercy*, 70–71.

73. Terry, *Condemned to Repeat?* 146.

74. Shawcross, *Quality of Mercy*, 148–54. WVI's Stan Mooneyham refused to be blackmailed. "There is no way politics can stop us helping people anywhere. I won't violate your borders, but I *will* help your people in Thailand." He got his way. Ibid., 168.

75. Terry, *Condemned to Repeat?* 148–49.

76. Brauman, "Refugee Camps, Population Transfers, and NGOs," 181.

77. Black, *Cause for Our Times*, 222–32.

78. Bortolotti, *Hope in Hell*, 51.

79. Brauman, *Humanitaire, le dilemme*, 65; Ninin and Deldique, *Globe Doctors*, 125–30; and Weber, *French Doctors*, ch. 9.

80. Kerleroux, "Dossier: Associated for Action," 2. See also Taithe, "Reinventing (French) Universalism," 150.

81. Vallaeys, *Médecins Sans Frontières*, 246, 248.

82. Bortolotti, *Hope in Hell*, 51.

83. Vallaeys, *Médecins Sans Frontières*, 134–35.

84. Ibid., 146.

85. Brauman, *Penser dans l'urgence*, 72–80.

86. Vallaeys, *Médecins Sans Frontières*, 205.

87. Ibid., 251–52.

88. Weber, *French Doctors*, 210.

89. Ninin, and Deldique, *Globe Doctors*, 132.

90. Vallaeys, *Médecins Sans Frontières*, 294; and Berman, *Power and the Idealists*, 238–44.

91. Taithe, "Reinventing (French) Universalism," 150.

92. Emmanuelli, *Les prédateurs*, 131.

93. Weber, *French Doctors*, 239.

94. Ibid., ch. 12.

95. Vallaeys, *Médecins Sans Frontières*, 355; and Brauman, *Penser dans l'urgence*, 98–99.

96. Brauman, *Penser dans l'urgence*, 99.

97. Vallaeys, *Médecins Sans Frontières*, 323.

98. Brauman, "Learning from Dilemmas," 136.

99. Vallaeys, *Médecins Sans Frontières*, 423. See also Brauman, "Forward," xxii–xxiii.

100. Shawcross, *Quality of Mercy*, ch. 21.

101. Smith, "Ethiopia and the Politics of Famine Relief," 32; Duffield and Prendergast, "Sovereignty and Intervention after the Cold War"; Kissi, "Beneath International Famine Relief in Ethiopia."

102. Brauman, *Humanitaire, le dilemme*.

103. Black, *Cause for Our Times*, 260.

104. Vaux, *Selfish Altruist*, cited in Rieff, *Bed for the Night*, 104.

105. Weber, *French Doctors*, 400.

106. Ibid., 410. Also interview with the author, Paris, France, February 10, 2009.

107. Brauman, *Penser dans l'urgence*, 131–33.

108. Médecins Sans Frontiéres, "Interview with Rony Brauman (II): The Humanitarian Movement," MSF Internal Newsletter, September-October 2002, 73.

109. Brauman, "Learning from Dilemmas," 138.

110. Maurice, "Humanitarian Ambition," 289, 363–72.

111. Ibid., 365. See also Yves Sandoz, "'Droit' or 'Devoir d'Ingerence'"; and Torrelli, "From Humanitarian Assistance to 'Intervention on Humanitarian Grounds'?"

CHAPTER 8

1. Chandler, *From Kosovo to Kabul and Beyond*; and Paris, "Human Security."

2. Slim, "Protecting Civilians," 155–56.

3. *Report of the Secretary-General on the Work of the Organization*, UN General Assembly Official Records, 46th session, Supp. No. 1, 5, UN Doc A/46/1, 1991, cited in Foley, *Thin Blue Line*, 47.

4. See Halman and Ratner, "Saving Failed States"; Krasner and Pasqual, "Addressing State Failure"; Herbst, "Let Them Fail"; Ghani and Lockhart, *Fixing Fragile States*; Fukuyama, *State-Building*; Chesterman, Ignatieff, and Thakur, eds., *Making States Work*; and Rice, "Promise of Democratic Peace."

5. Annan, *In Larger Freedom*. See also Cooper, *Breaking of Nations*; Rotberg, "New Nature of Nation-State Failure"; White House, *National Security Strategy*; and Dobbins et al., *Beginner's Guide to Nation-Building*. In addition, *Foreign Policy*'s annual ranking of weak states is invaluable.

6. Barnett, "New United Nations Politics of Peace."

7. Fukuyama, *State-Building*, 92.

8. On liberal peacebuilding see, Paris, *At War's End* and "International Peacebuilding and the 'Mission Civilisatrice.'"

9. United Nations, *Agenda for Peace*, para. 21.

10. Minear, *Humanitarian Enterprise*, conclusion; and Macrae and Harmer, eds., "Humanitarian Action."

11. White House, *National Security Strategy*.

12. Walker, "Chaos and Caring," 4.

13. Annan, *Question of Intervention*. For earlier statements, see Commission on Global Governance, *Our Global Neighborhood*.

14. Sen, *Development as Freedom*; and Commission on Human Security, *Human Security Now*.

15. Chandler, *From Kosovo to Kabul and Beyond*, 3; and Rieff, *Bed for the Night*, 79.

16. Tsui and Myint-U, "Institutional Response."

17. Slim, "Relief Agencies and Moral Standing"; Sugino, "'Non-Political and Humanitarian Clause,'" 46.
18. Tsui and Myint-U, "Institutional Response."
19. Cited in ibid.
20. Ibid., 2, 3; Kent, *Anatomy of Disaster Relief,* 52–54.

CHAPTER 9

1. For debates on humanitarian intervention, see Weiss, *Humanitarian Intervention: Ideas in Action;* and Holzgrefe and Keohane, eds., *Humanitarian Intervention;* and Allen and Styan, "A Right to Interfere?"
2. Slim, "Military Intervention to Protect Human Rights"; "Military Humanitarianism and the New Peacekeeping"; and "Relief Agencies and Moral Standing in War." For a good discussion of the extension of the ICRC's identity to these issues during and after the Cold War, see Delorenzi, *ICRC Policy Since the end of the Cold War.*
3. Slim, "Military Intervention to Protect Human Rights," 5.
4. For a good overview of the historical setting and a detailed account of the intervention, see Rutherford, *Humanitarianism under Fire.*
5. De Waal, *Famine Crimes,* 168–79.
6. Orbinski, *Imperfect Offering,* 77. See also Rutherford, *Humanitarianism under Fire,* 50, 95.
7. Foley, *Thin Blue Line,* 54–55.
8. Orbinski, *Imperfect Offering,* 81.
9. Quoted in Foley, *Thin Blue Line,* 55. The description of InterAction is from Rutherford, *Humanitarianism under Fire,* 72–73. See also de Waal, "Humanitarianism Unbound," 18–19.
10. Rutherford, *Humanitarianism under Fire,* 96.
11. Vallaeys, *Médecins Sans Frontières,* 509–10.
12. Interview with the author.
13. Rieff, *Bed for the Night,* 130.
14. Ibid., 143.
15. Ignatieff, "The Warrior's Honor," in Ignatieff, *Warrior's Honor: Ethnic War and Modern Conscience,* 135–37.
16. Kenney, "See No Evil, Make No Policy," 33; Roberts, "Humanitarian War," 442; and Urquhart, "Who Can Police the World?" 33.
17. Roberts, "Humanitarian War," 442.
18. Destexhe, "Holding Humanitarianism Hostage," 141.
19. Thornberry, "Saving the War Crimes Tribunal," 75, cited in Pasic and Weiss, "Politics of Rescue," 108.
20. Preston, "U.N. Officials Scale Back," A40; and Ledgerwood, "UN Peacekeeping Missions: The Lessons from Cambodia," *Asia Pacific Issues,* Analysis from the East-West Center, no. 11, March 1994, 5.
21. Interview by Renaud Girard, *Le Figaro,* February 28, 1994, cited in Cigar, *Genocide in Bosnia,* 189.
22. Cohen, "U.N. General Opposes More Bosnia Force," *New York Times,* September 29, 1994, A7.
23. Quoted in Rieff, *Bed for the Night,* 136.
24. "Report of the Secretary-General pursuant to General Assembly resolution 53/35: the fall of Srebrenica," A/54/549, presented November 15, 1999.
25. Annan, "The UN's Power in Bosnia."
26. Clark, "UN Exposed by Debacle in Gorazde," *Financial Times,* April 18, 1994, 2; and Pomfret, "UN Finds Good Intentions Don't Feed," A1.
27. Cutts, "Humanitarian Operation in Bosnia, 1992–95."
28. Weiss and Pasic, "Reinventing UNHCR," 47.
29. Sugino, "'Non-Political and Humanitarian Clause,'" 49, 56–58.
30. Young, "UNHCR and ICRC," 788.
31. Ibid., 788.
32. Ogata, *Turbulent Decade,* 83.
33. Pasic and Weiss, "Politics of Rescue," 114–15.
34. Quoted in Rieff, *Bed for the Night,* 131.

35. Peterson, "Statement to the Security Council."

36. Mooney, "Presence, Ergo Protection?"; Barutciski, "Critical View"; Ogata, *Turbulent Decade,* 90; and Cunliffe and Pugh, "Politicization of the UNHCR."

37. Cited in Young, "UNHCR and ICRC," 796. See also Ogata, *Turbulent Decade,* 55

38. Vallaeys, *Médecins Sans Frontières,* 526.

39. Destexhe, "Forward," 13–14, cited in Pasic and Weiss, "Politics of Rescue," 110. See also de Waal, "Humanitarianism Unbound," 22.

40. De Waal, "Humanitarianism Unbound," 28–33.

41. On the indifference of the United States, see Power, *Problem from Hell;* on the indifference of the UN, see Barnett, *Eyewitness to a Genocide.*

42. Anderson, *Do No Harm.*

43. Uvin, *Aiding Violence.*

44. Binet, "Genocide of the Rwandan Tutsis, 1994," 14.

45. The background is informed by Malcolm, *Kosovo: A Short History;* Mertus, *Kosovo: How Myths and Truths Started a War;* and Judah, *Kosovo.*

46. Annan apparently approved of this tactic. See "Letter from Secretary-General Solana to Permanent Representatives of North Atlantic Council," October 9, 1998, cited in Simma, "NATO, The UN and the Use of Force," 7.

47. Simma, "NATO, The UN and the Use of Force," 7.

48. Blair, "Doctrine of the International Community."

49. Statement by President Bill Clinton Confirming NATO Air Strikes on Serb Military Targets, Federal News Service, March 24, 1999. See also Press Statement of Javier Solana, Secretary-General of NATO, NATO Press release (1999) 040, March 24, 1999.

50. Reisman, "Kosovo's Antimonies," 860.

51. Roberts, "NATO's 'Humanitarian War.'"

52. Ibid.

53. Suhrke, Barutciski, Sandison, and Garlock, *Kosovo Refugee Crisis;* and Orbinski, "Kosovo: Aid Under Siege Once Again."

54. Morris, "UNHCR and Kosovo," 14–17; Ogata, *Turbulent Decade,* 144–48. For a general discussion of the military's role in the Kosovo conflict, see Minear, van Baarda, and Sommers, "NATO and Humanitarian Action." On NATO's initial contribution, see Krahenbuhl, "Conflict in the Balkans."

55. Minear, van Baarda, and Sommers, "NATO and Humanitarian Action," 76.

56. Porter, "Partiality of Humanitarian Assistance," 5.

57. Ibid., 5. Ogata negatively reflects on the experience when she writes, "NATO had decided to engage in humanitarian assistance even before the NATO-UNHCR agreement of April 3 and had gone beyond the defined areas of cooperation." Ogata, *Turbulent Decade,* 149.

58. Rieff, *Bed for the Night,* 204.

59. Porter, "Partiality of Humanitarian Assistance," 5.

60. Quoted in Minear, van Baarda, and Sommers, "NATO and Humanitarian Action," 64. The authors also note that NATO's working definition of CIMIC [civilian military coordination] as it applies to Kosovo and elsewhere is, "A military operation, the primary intention and effect of which is to support a civilian authority, population, international or non-governmental organization, the effect of which to assist in the pursuit of a military objective." Ibid., 64.

61. Vaux, *Selfish Altruist,* 66–67; Roggo, "After the Kosovo Conflict"; and Porter, "Partiality of Humanitarian Assistance."

62. Roggo, "After the Kosovo Conflict."

63. Porter, "Partiality of Humanitarian Assistance," 5. See also Vaux, *Selfish Altruist,* 27, 28.

64. Porter, "Partiality of Humanitarian Assistance," 5.

65. Orbinski, *Imperfect Offering,* 326.

66. Minear, van Baarda, and Sommers, "NATO and Humanitarian Action," 63.

67. While international lawyers and commentators focused on whether the NATO action was legal because it had not received Security Council approval, aid agencies exhibited little concern with such legal niceties, preferring to judge the legitimacy of the action not on whether it followed the proper legal procedures but on whether its ends were consistent with human rights goals.

68. Norton-Taylor, "From Killing to Cuddling," cited in Foley, *Thin Blue Line,* 36.

69. Morris, "Humanitarian Interventions in Macedonia," 5–6. Porter, "Coordination in the Midst of Chaos," 21, 22; and Minear, van Baarda, and Sommers, "NATO and Humanitarian Action."

70. Roggo, "After the Kosovo Conflict," 3; and Porter, "Coordination in the Midst of Chaos," 19, 21.

71. Porter, "Coordination in the Midst of Chaos," 21.

72. Ibid., 21.

73. Ogata, *Turbulent Decade,* 149–50.

74. Wiles, "Kosovo Emergency"; and Vaux, *Selfish Altruist,* 20, 22.

75. Orbinski, *Imperfect Offering,* 330.

76. Vaux, *Selfish Altruist,* 20, 22.

77. Ibid., 23.

78. Porter, "Partiality of Humanitarian Assistance," 4.

79. Leader, *Politics of Principle,* 2.

80. Stockton, "In Defence of Humanitarianism."

81. Curtis, "Politics and Humanitarian Aid," 10.

82. Krahenbuhl, "Conflict in the Balkans," 4.

83. Porter, "Partiality of Humanitarian Assistance," 6; and Wiles et al., "Independent Evaluation," 78.

84. Annan, "Two Concepts of Sovereignty."

85. For a detailed history, see Bellamy, *Responsibility to Protect.*

86. International Commission on Intervention and State Sovereignty." For a statement where responsibilities generate ongoing intervention, see Evans, *Responsibility to Protect.*

87. White House, *National Security Strategy.*

88. Powell, "Remarks." See also Lischer, "U.S. Military Interventions."

89. Rocha, "Afghanistan."

90. Foley, *Thin Blue Line,* 111.

91. Ibid., 115.

92. Ibid., 119.

93. Dziedzic and Seidl, *Provincial Reconstruction Teams;* and Save the Children, *Provincial Reconstruction Teams and Humanitarian-Military Relations in Afghanistan.*

94. De Torrente, "Humanitarian Action under Attack."

95. Tanguy, "When Intervening in the Name of Humanity," cited in Slim, "Military Intervention to Protect Human Rights," 5; Buisonnière, "La Mancha, Here We Come!" 2; and Coquoz, "The Involvement of the Military in Humanitarian Activities," cited in Slim, "Military Intervention to Protect Human Rights," 5. See also Scheizer, "Moral Dilemmas for Humanitarianism."

96. Fournier, "Our Purpose Is to Limit."

CHAPTER 10

1. Barnett, "Evolution without Progress?"

2. ActionAid, "Peacebuilding and Reconciliation," 2002.

3. Interviews with CARE officials, Atlanta, Georgia, November 1–2, 2006.

4. Interview with the author, Atlanta, Georgia, November 2, 2006.

5. Henry, "CARE International," 115, 116.

6. Frakenberger, Drinkwater, and Maxwell, *Operationalizing Household Livelihood Security,* 1–4.

7. Interview with CARE staff, Atlanta, Georgia, November 2, 2006.

8. "Frequently Asked Questions about RBA," 3.

9. McCaston, *Moving CARE's Programming Forward;* and McCaston and Rewald, *Conceptual Overview.*

10. Interview at CARE headquarters, November 6, 2006.

11. Interview with Peter Bell and other senior staff, Atlanta, November, 2006.

12. Bell, "Presentation on Rights-Based Approaches."

13. Interview, CRS headquarters, Baltimore, Maryland, October 18, 2005.

14. Wiest, "Remarks."

15. In this respect, it recalls Uvin, *Aiding Violence.*

16. Orbinski, *Imperfect Offering,* 173.

17. For a general statement regarding CRS's connections to Catholic debates, both at the Vatican and in the United States, see Pezzullo, "Church's Servant Mission and Social Teaching." In the address, Pezzullo depicts CRS as a reflection of the emergence of the United States into a position of world leadership, a role that has had a broadening effect on the Catholic Church in America.

18. Ibid.

19. Reilly, "Beyond the 'Protection' of Human Rights."

20. The first quotation is from Gary, "Bringing the State Back In," 11, emphasis in original; the second is from Reilly and Cilliers, "Champions for Peace," 9.

21. Wiest, "Remarks."

22. Ibid.

23. Irvine, *Strategic Directions,* 7; and World Vision International, "New Vision Journey Findings—Executive Summary," 2002.

24. Irvine, *Best Things in the Worst Times,* 6–7.

25. Interview with former WVI official, June 12, 2008.

26. Much of the intellectual history and theological foundations for the move toward transformational development is covered in Myers, *Walking with the Poor.*

27. An additional development was the growing number of attacks by home governments against militarized refugee camps on their borders. Sugino, "'Non-Political and Humanitarian Clause,'" 49, 52–53.

28. Coles, *Voluntary Repatriation* and "Approaching the Refugee Problem Today."

29. EXCOM Standing Committee, Follow-Up to ECOSOC Resolution 1995/56, *UNHCR Activities in Relation to Prevention,* EC/46/SC/CRP.33, May 28, 1996, cited in Sugino, "'Non-Political and Humanitarian Clause,'" 54.

30. Skran, "International Refugee Regime," 8; and UNHCR, Executive Committee of the High Commissioner's Programme, "Note on International Protection," 3.

31. Pitterman, "International Responses to Refugee Situations," 51–54.

32. Warner, "Voluntary Repatriation."

33. Crisp, "Mind the Gap!" 3.

34. Loescher, *UNHCR and World Politics,* 248.

35. Ibid., 249. On prevention, see Chimni, "Meaning of Words," 444. On root causes, see Coles, "Approaching the Refugee Problem Today," 203; and UNHCR, Executive Committee of the High Commissioner's Programme, "Note on International Protection," 2; on "state responsibility," see "Note on International Protection," 8.

36. Hocke, "Beyond Humanitarianism," cited in Sugino, "'Non-Political and Humanitarian Clause,'" 55.

37. Crisp, "Mind the Gap!" 9.

38. Macrae, "Aiding Peace," 2–3; and Crisp, "Mind the Gap!"

39. UNHCR, Executive Committee of the High Commissioner's Programme, "Forty-Eighth Session Annual Theme: Repatriation Challenges," cited in Macrae, "Aiding Peace," 3.

40. Sugino, "'Non-Political and Humanitarian Clause,'" 47–48.

41. UNHCR, Executive Committee of the High Commissioner's Programme, "Note on International Protection."

42. Crisp, "Mind the Gap!" 7; Cunliffe and Pugh, "Politicization of UNHCR."

43. Loescher, *UNHCR and Global Politics,* 262–63.

44. Ogata, *Turbulent Decade,* 347, emphasis added.

45. Coles, "Approaching the Refugee Problem Today," 211.

46. Barnett, "Humanitarianism with a Sovereign Face."

47. Coles, "Approaching the Refugee Problem Today," 244–45.

48. Also see Ogata, "World Order, Internal Conflict, and Refugees"; Forsythe, "UNHCR's Mandate"; and Loescher, *UNHCR and Global Politics,* 363.

49. Bouchet-Saulnier, "Humanitarian Responsibility and Humility," 135.

50. Brauman, "MSF and the Limits of Humanitarian Action," 144; Bouchet-Saulnier, "Humanitarian Responsibility and Humility," 133; and de Torrente, "Humanitarian Action under Attack."

51. Brauman, "Learning from Dilemmas," 137.

52. Bouchet-Saulnier, "Humanitarian Responsibility and Humility"; and Brauman, "MSF and the Limits of Humanitarian Action," 144.

53. Parisel, "Evolution in the Role of MSF," 8–9. For a detailed overview of the campaign, see Orbinski, *Imperfect Offering*, ch. 9

54. Bortolotti, *Hope in Hell*, 161–62.

55. Parisel, "Evolution in the Role of MSF," 8–9.

56. Fournier, "Our Purpose Is to Limit."

57. Brauman, "Learning from Dilemmas," 136.

58. Borton et al., *International Response to Conflict*, 161.

59. Mitchell, "La Mancha Process," 83. For a recent example of the focus on the machinery of the humanitarian sector, see Adinolfi, et al., *Humanitarian Response Review*.

60. This definition of depoliticization comes from Brown, *Regulating Aversion*, 15. See also Ferguson, *Anti-Politics Machine*; Fisher, "Doing Good?", 446.

61. Leader, *Politics of Principle*.

62. Sphere Project, 1.

63. Gostelow, "Sphere Project."

64. Darcy, "Locating Responsibility."

65. Cited in Foley, *Thin Blue Line*, 163, emphasis added.

66. Darcy, "Locating Responsibility," 113.

67. M. Van Dyke and R. Waldman, "The Sphere Project Evaluation Report, Mailman School of Public Health, Columbia University, 2004, 4, cited in Darfour, de Geoffroy, Maury, and Grunewald, "Rights, Standards and Quality," 126. See also Darcy, "Locating Responsibility," 118.

68. Darcy, "Locating Responsibility," 116.

69. For the story of Sphere, see Buchanan-Smith, "How the Sphere Project Came into Being."

70. Darfour, de Geoffroy, Maury, and Grunewald, "Rights, Standards and Quality" 137.

71. Humanitarian Policy Group, "Measuring the Impact of Humanitarian Aid"; Fearon, "Measuring Humanitarian Impact"; and Darcy, "Acts of Faith?"

72. O'Brien, "Benefits-Harms Analysis"; O'Brien "Politicized Humanitarianism"; Frerks and Hilhorst, "Evaluation of Humanitarian Assistance"; and Humanitarian Policy Group, "Measuring the Impact of Humanitarian Aid."

73. Macrae et al., *Uncertain Power*, 18–21.

74. De Waal, *Famine Crimes*, 78–79.

75. There also were growing calls to "measure need," to replace subjective and emotional assessments with cooler and more objective criteria as a way to reinforce the impartiality principle and bring more attention to the forgotten emergencies. In short, objective indicators are the best way to reestablish values and principles. Oxley, "Measuring Humanitarian Need."

76. Slim, "Doing the Right Thing"; Duffield, *Global Governance;* and Des Gasper, "'Drawing a Line.'"

77. Stockton, "Accountable Humanitarianism and MSF," 95.

78. Darcy and Hofmann, *According to Need?*

79. Darcy, "Acts of Faith?" 8.

80. Slim, "Relief Agencies and Moral Standing," 345.

81. Anderson, *Do No Harm*, 1, cited in Foley, *Thin Blue Line*, 40.

82. Smillie and Minear, *Charity of Nations*, 215–24; Slim, "By What Authority?"; and Stein, "Humanitarian Organizations: Accountable—Why, to Whom, for What, and How?"

83. Slim, "By What Authority?"

84. Mitchell and Doane, "Ombudsman for Humanitarian Assistance?"; and Christoplos, "Humanitarianism, Pluralism, and Ombudsmen."

85. Mitchell and Doane, "An Ombudsman for Humanitarian Assistance?"

86. Slim, "By What Authority?"

87. Hilhorst, "Being Good at Doing Good?" 205.

88. Hilhorst, "Being Good at Doing Good?"

89. Stirrat, "Competitive Humanitarianism."

90. Nicholas Stockton, "The Accountable Humanitarian," The Luce Lecture, 2005, cited in Davis, "Concerning Accountability," 11; and Foley, *The Thin Blue Line*, 204; Hudson, "Making the Connection."

91. Médecins Sans Frontiéres, "Interview with Rony Brauman (II)." Also see Brauman, "From Philanthropy to Humanitarianism," 414–15, on additional dangers of professionalization and "mechanization."

92. Grombach-Wagner, "La'art de boire du thé," 48–49.
93. Macrae and Harmer, eds., "Humanitarian Action," 9.
94. Cornwall and Brock, "What Do Buzzwords Do?"
95. Pompetti, "Proximity."
96. Moore, "Humanitarian Agendas."

CONCLUSION

1. Laqueur, "Mourning, Pity," 54–55.
2. Fassin, "Humanitarianism," 153.
3. For discussions of the relationship between humanitarianism and empire, see Chimni, "Globalization, Humanitarianism"; Duffield, *Global Governance*; Chandler, *Empire in Denial*; Donini, "Through a Glass Darkly."
4. ALNAP, "State of the Humanitarian System."
5. Ignatieff, *Empire Lite*.
6. Donini, "Through a Glass Darkly."
7. Fassin, "Humanitarianism," 151.
8. Thanks to Peter Walker for offering empirical support for this observation.
9. Horkheimer and Adorno, *Dialectic of Enlightenment*, 215.
10. Pogue Harrison, *Dominion of the Dead*, ix–xi.
11. Halttunen, "Humanitarianism and the Pornography of Pain," 304.
12. Rozario, *Culture of Calamity*. For a general discussion on the relationship between bodies, death, and humanitarianism, see Laqueur, "Bodies, Details, and the Humanitarian Narrative." On the relationship between disaster and God in the context of the 2010 Haitian earthquake, see Wood, "Between God and a Hard Place," 11.
13. Rozario, *Culture of Calamity*, 3.
14. Faust, *This Republic of Suffering*; Menand, *The Metaphysical Club*.
15. Robert, *Occupy until I Come*.
16. Quoted in Mulley, *Woman Who Saved the Children*, 185.
17. Margalit, *Ethics of Memory*, 206–7.
18. For an interesting compatible argument that develops the concept of the "technologies of care," see Ophir, "The Sovereign, the Humanitarian, and the Terrorist." Many relief agencies treat disasters as a chance to get their "foot in the door," to address root causes, and to remove chronic vulnerabilities. Kent, *Anatomy of Disaster Relief*, 20.
19. Van Zandt, "Don't Rebuild Haiti: Reimagine It."
20. Brown, *Moral Capital*. See also Festa, *Sentimental Figures*, 171.
21. Orford, *Reading Humanitarian Intervention*.
22. See Borrel et al., *Ambiguity and Change*; and the publications associated with the Humanitarian Futures Programme.
23. Arendt, *Origins of Totalitarianism*, 336, cited in Katznelson, *Desolation and Enlightenment*, 109; and Mehta, *Liberalism and Empire*, 25.
24. Halttunen, "Humanitarianism and the Pornography of Pain," 308, 309; Laqueur, "Mourning, Pity," 33; and Festa, "Sentimental Figures," 5, 51.
25. Halttunen, "Humanitarianism and the Pornography of Pain," 330. For a beautifully crafted text on the aesthetics and poetics of how aid workers understand the suffering of others, see Dawes, *That the World May Know*.
26. Korf, "Antinomies of Geography"; Ginzburg, "Killing a Chinese Mandarin"; and Boltanski, *Distant Suffering*.
27. Singer, *Life You Save*.
28. Orwell, "Reflections on Gandhi," 85–92.
29. O'Neill, *Bounds of Justice*.
30. Rubenstein, "Distributive Commitments," 215–34.
31. Benthall, "Have Islamic Aid Agencies?"
32. Hopgood, "Moral Authority, Modernity," 238.
33. Bradol, "Sacrificial International Order."
34. On this feature of liberalism, see Mehta, *Liberalism and Empire*, 79.
35. Donini, Minear, and Walker, "Future of Humanitarian Action," 190–204.
36. Interview with the author, Paris, France, February 10, 2009.
37. Stephen Hopgood makes a similar point regarding authority. Hopgood, "Moral Authority, Modernity," 238.

38. de Waal, *Famine Crimes,* 69–70. See also Ferguson, *Anti-Politics Machine;* and Scott, *Seeing Like a State.*

39. Hopgood, "Saying 'No' to Walmart?" 98–123; Davis, "Concerning Accountability in Humanitarian Action," 7.

40. Arendt, *On Revolution,* 72.

41. Natsios, "NGOs and the Humanitarian Impulse," 136.

42. Jan Eliasson, "Ten Years of Humanitarian Action," 13.

43. On this debate, Festa, *Sentimental Figures,* ch. 1; Dean, *Fragility of Empathy;* and Moyn, "Empathy in History."

44. Taylor, *A Secular Age.*

45. James, *Will to Believe,* 25.

46. Ibid., 7.

47. Kant, *Critique of Pure Reason,* 29.

48. James, *Will to Believe,* 19.

49. Interview with the author, Paris, France, February 10, 2009.

References

Aaltola, Mika. *Western Spectacle and the Emergence of Humanitarian World Politics*. New York: Palgrave, 2009.

Abrahamson, Rita. "The Power of Partnerships in Global Governance." *Third World Quarterly* 26, no. 7 (2005): 1453–67.

ActionAid. "Peacebuilding and Reconciliation." 2002. http://www.actionaid.org/ourpriorities/peacebuilding/peacebuilding.shtml.

Agnew, Elizabeth. *From Charity to Social Work: Mary E. Richmond and the Creation of an American Profession*. Urbana: University of Illinois Press, 2003.

Alford, Howard. *Organizations Evolving*. New York: Sage Press, 1999.

Allen, Tim and David Styan. "A Right to Interfere: Bernard Kouchner and the New Humanitarianism." *Journal of International Development* 12 (2000): 825–42.

ALNAP. "The State of the Humanitarian System: Assessing Performance and Progress." Overseas Development Institute, London, 2010. Available at www.alnap.org/pool/files/alnap-sohs-final.pdf, accessed July 12, 2010.

Althusser, Louis. "The International of Decent Feelings." In *The Spectre of Hegel: Early Writings,* 21–35. London: Verso, 1946.

Anderson, Mary. *Do No Harm: How Aid Can Support Peace—or War*. Boulder, CO: Lynne Rienner, 1999.

Anghie, Antony. "Colonialism and the Birth of International Institutions: Sovereignty, Economy, and the Mandate System of the League of Nations." *International Law and Politics* 34 (Spring 2002): 513–633.

Annan, Kofi. *In Larger Freedom: Toward Development, Security, and Human Rights for All*. New York: United Nations Press, 2005.

——. *The Question of Intervention: Statements by the Secretary-General*. New York: United Nations, 1999.

——. "Two Concepts of Sovereignty." *Economist*, September 18, 1999, 49–50.

——. "The UN's Power in Bosnia." *Washington Post*, March 28, 1994.

Archard, David. "Paternalism Defined." *Analysis* 50, no. 1 (January 1990).

Arendt, Hannah. *On Revolution*. New York: Penguin Books, 1994.

——. *Origins of Totalitarianism*. New York: Penguin Books, 1973.

Ashworth, John. "The Relationship between Capitalism and Humanitarianism." *American Historical Review* 92, no. 4 (1987): 813–28.

Bachman, John. *Together in Hope: Fifty Years of Lutheran World Relief.* New York: Lutheran World Relief, 1995.

Baier, Annette. *A Progress of Sentiments: Reflections on Hume's Treatise.* Cambridge: Harvard University Press, 1991.

Banner, Lois. "Religious Benevolence as Social Control: A Critique of an Interpretation." *Journal of American History* 60, no. 1 (June 1973): 23–41.

Barnett, Michael. "Evolution without Progress? Humanitarianism in a World of Hurt." *International Organization* 63, no. 4 (2009): 621–64.

——. *Eyewitness to a Genocide: The United Nations and Rwanda.* Ithaca: Cornell University Press, 2002.

——. "Humanitarianism with a Sovereign Face: UNHCR in the Global Undertow." *International Migration Review* 35, no. 1 (2001): 244–76.

——. "The New United Nations Politics of Peace: From Juridical Sovereignty to Empirical Sovereignty." *Global Governance* 1, no. 1 (1995): 79–97.

Barnett, Michael, and Martha Finnemore. *Rules for the World: International Organizations in Global Politics.* Ithaca: Cornell University Press, 2004.

Barnett, Michael, and Tom Weiss. "Humanitarianism: A Brief History of the Present." In *Humanitarianism in Question: Politics, Power, and Ethics,* ed. Michael Barnett and Tom Weiss, 1–48. Ithaca: Cornell University Press, 2008.

Barutciski, Michael. "A Critical View on UNHCR's Mandate Dilemmas." *International Journal of Refugee Law* 14, nos. 2/3 (2002): 365–81.

Bashford, Alison. *Imperial Hygiene: A Critical History of Colonialism, Nationalism, and Public Health.* New York: Palgrave Press, 2005.

Baudendistel, Rainer. *Between Bombs and Good Intentions: The Red Cross and the Italo-Ethiopian War, 1935–1936.* New York: Berghahn Books, 2006.

Bell, Peter. "Presentation on Rights-Based Approaches." InterAction, Washington, D.C., November 7, 2001.

Bellamy, Alex. *Responsibility to Protect.* London: Polity Press, 2009.

Bellion-Jourdan, J. "Islamic Relief Organizations: Between 'Islamism' and 'Humanitarianism.'" *International Institute for the Study of Islam in the Modern World (ISIM) Newsletter* 5, no. 15 (2000).

Bellot, Leland. "Evangelicals and the Defense of Slavery in Britain's Old Colonial Empire." *Journal of Southern History* 37, no. 1 (1971): 19–40.

Bender, Thomas, ed. *The Antislavery Debate: Capitalism and Abolitionism as a Problem in Historical Interpretation.* Berkeley: University of California Press, 1992.

Benthall, Jonathan. "Have Islamic Aid Agencies a Privileged Relationship in Majority Muslim Areas? The Case of Post-Tsunami Reconstructions in Aceh." *Journal of Humanitarian Assistance,* June 26, 2008. available at http://jha.ac/2008/06/26/have-islamic-aid-agencies-a-privileged-relationship-in-majority-muslim-areas-the-case-of-post-tsunami-reconstruction-in-aceh/, accessed July 12, 2010.

——. "Humanitarianism and Islam after 11 September." In *Humanitarian Action and the "Global War on Terror": A Review of Trends and Issues,* ed. J. McRae and A. Harmer, 37–47. London: HPG Report, ODI, 2003.

Benthall, Jonathan, and Jerome Bellion-Jourdan. *The Charitable Crescent: Politics of Aid in the Muslim World.* London: I. B. Tauris, 2003.

Berlin, Isaiah. *The Crooked Timber of Humanity.* Princeton, NJ: Princeton University Press, 1990.

Berman, Paul. *Power and the Idealists.* New York: Soft Skull Press, 2005.

Bernier, Philippe. *Des Médecins Sans Frontières.* Paris: Albin Michel, 1980.

Bloomstein, Charles. *History of CARE,* Charles Bloomstein Collected Papers, 1938–2002, Swarthmore College Peace Collection, Swarthmore College.

Blustein, Jeffrey. *The Moral Demands of Memory.* New York: Cambridge University Press, 2008.

Boddy, Janice. *Civilizing Women: British Crusades in Colonial Sudan.* Princeton, NJ: Princeton University Press, 2007.

Bogaev, Barbara. Interview with Medical Anthropologist Dr. Paul Farmer. *Fresh Air,* National Public Radio September 25, 2003.

Boissier, Pierre. *From Solferino to Tsushima: History of the International Committee of the Red Cross.* Geneva: Henry Dunant Institute, 1985.

——. "Henry Dunant." *International Review of the Red Cross* 161 (August 1974): 411.

Boltanski, Luc. *Distant Suffering: Morality, Media, and Politics.* New York: Cambridge University Press, 1999.

Borgwardt, Elizabeth. *A New Deal for the World: America's Vision for Human Rights.* Cambridge: Harvard University Press, 2005.

Bornstein, Erica. *The Spirit of Development: Protestant NGOs, Morality, and Economics in. Zimbabwe.* Stanford: Stanford University Press, 2005.

Bornstein, Erica, and Peter Redfield, eds. *Forces of Compassion: Humanitarianism between Ethics and Politics.* Santa Fe: SAR Press, 2011.

Borrel, Annalies, et al. *Ambiguity and Change: Humanitarian NGOs Prepare for the Future.* Feinstein International Center: Tufts University. August 2004.

Bortolotti, Dan. *Hope in Hell: Inside the World of Doctors Without Borders.* Canada: Firefly Books, 2004.

Borton, John, et al. *The International Response to Conflict and Genocide: Lessons from the Rwanda Experience. Joint Evaluation of Emergency Assistance to Rwanda. Study 3: Humanitarian Aid and Effects.* Copenhagen: Steering Committee of the Joint Evaluation of Emergency Assistance to Rwanda. March 1996.

Bouchet-Saulnier, Françoise. "Between Humanitarian Law and Principles: The Principles and Practices of 'Rebellious Humanitarianism.'" 2000 MSF International Activity Report.

——. "Humanitarian Responsibility and Humility—Or How to Relate our Actions to our Principles, to Relate What We Do to What We Say." In *Médecins Sans Frontières, My Sweet La Mancha,* 132–39. Geneva: Médecins Sans Frontières International, 2005.

Bradol, Jean-Herve. "The Sacrificial International Order and Humanitarian Action." In *In the Shadow of "'Just Wars'": Violence, Politics, and Humanitarian Action,* ed. Fabrice Weissman, 1–22. Ithaca: Cornell University Press, 2004.

Brauman, Rony. "Forward." In Médecins Sans Frontières, *World in Crisis: The Politics of Survival at the End of the Twentieth Century.* New York: Routledge, 1997.

——. "From Philanthropy to Humanitarianism: Remarks and an Interview." *South Atlantic Quarterly,* 103, 2/3, Spring/Summer, 2004, 397–417.

——. *Humanitaire: Le dilemme, avec Philippe Petit.* Paris: Editions Textuel, 1996.

——. "Introduction." In *Populations in Danger: Médecins Sans Frontières,* ed. Francois Jean, 3–9. London: John Libbey, 1992.

——. "Learning from Dilemmas." In *Nongovernmental Politics,* ed. Michael Feher, 131–48. New York: Zone Books, 2007.

——. "MSF and the Limits of Humanitarian Action." In *Médecins Sans Frontières, My Sweet La Mancha,* 140–46, Geneva: Médecins Sans Frontières International, 2005.

——. *Penser dans l'urgence: Parcours critique d'un humanitaire.* Paris: Seuil, 2006.

——. "Refugee Camps, Population Transfers, and NGOs." In *Hard Choices: Moral Dilemmas in Humanitarian Intervention,* ed. Jonathan Moore, 177–94. Lanham, MD: Rowman and Littlefield, 1998.

Brown, Christopher. *Moral Capital: Foundations of British Abolitionism.* Chapel Hill: University of North Carolina, 2006.

Brown, Wendy. *Regulating Aversion: Tolerance in the Age of Identity and Empire.* Princeton, NJ: Princeton University Press, 2006.

Buchanan-Smith, Margie. *How the Sphere Project Came into Being: A Case Study of Policy-Making in the Humanitarian Aid Sector and the Relative Influence of Research.* Working Paper 215. London, UK: Overseas Development Institute, 2003.

Buisonnière, Marine. "La Mancha, Here We Come!" *La Mancha Gazette,* May 2006, MSF Internal Newsletter, 2.

Burnell, Peter. "Charity Law and Pressure Politics in Britain: After the Oxfam Inquiry." *Voluntas* 3, no. 3 (1992): 311–334.

Butt, Leslie. "The Suffering Stranger: Medical Anthropology and International Morality." *Medical Anthropology* 21 (2002): 1–24.

Buxton, Dorothy, and Edward Fuller. *The White Flame: The Story of the Save the Children Fund.* New York: Longmans, Freen, and Co., 1931.

Campbell, Wallace. *The History of CARE: A Personal Account.* New York: Praeger, 1990.

Carlton, Frank. "Humanitarianism, Past and Present." *International Journal of Ethics* 17, no. 1 (1906): 48–55.

Carson, Penny. "The British Raj and the Awakening of the Evangelical Conscience: The Ambiguities of Religious Establishment and Toleration." In *Christian Missions and the Enlightenment*, ed. Brian Stanley, 45–70. Grand Rapids, MI: William Eerdmans, 2001.

CARE. "Frequently Asked Questions about RBA." Atlanta: CARE International, 2002.

Cartwright, David. "Kant, Schopenhauer, and Nietzsche on the Morality of Pity." *Journal of the History of Ideas* 45, no. 1 (1984): 83–98.

Cassels, Nancy. "Bentinck: Humanitarian and Imperialist- The Abolition of Suttee." *Journal of British Studies* 5, no. 1 (1965): 77–87.

Catholic Relief Services. Bishop Edward Swanstrom Collection, Baltimore, MD: Catholic Relief Services.

Chandler, David. *Empire in Denial: The Politics of State-Building*. New York: Pluto Press, 2006.

——. *From Kosovo to Kabul and Beyond: Human Rights and International Intervention*. London: Pluto Press, 2006.

Chatterjee, Deen K., ed. *The Ethics of Assistance: Morality and the Distant Needy*. New York: Cambridge University Press, 2004.

Chesterman, Simon, M. Ignatieff, and R. Thakur, eds. *Making States Work: State Failure and the Crisis of Governance*. Tokyo: United Nations University, 2005.

Chimni, B. S. "Globalization, Humanitarianism, and the Erosion of Refugee Protection." Refugee Studies Centre Working Paper. Oxford: Oxford University, 2000.

——. "International Institutions Today: An Imperial Global State in the Making." *European Journal of International Law* 15, no. 1 (2004): 1–37.

——. "The Meaning of Words and the Role of UNHCR in Voluntary Repatriation." *International Journal of Refugee Law* 5, no. 3 (1993).

Chomsky, Noam. "Humanitarian Imperialism: The New Doctrine of the Imperial Right." *Monthly Review* 60, no. 4 (2008): 22–50.

Christoplos, Ian. "Humanitarianism, Pluralism, and Ombudsmen: Do the Pieces Fit?" *Disasters* 23, no. 2 (1999): 125–38.

Cigar, Norman. *Genocide in Bosnia*. College Station: Texas A & M Press, 1995.

Clarence-Smith, William Gervase. *Islam and the Abolition of Slavery*. New York: Oxford University Press, 2006.

Clark, Bruce. "UN Exposed by Debacle in Gorazde." *Financial Times*, April 18, 1994, 2.

Clinton, William. "Confirming NATO Air Strikes on Serb Military Targets." Federal News Service, March 24, 1999.

Cohen, G. Daniel. "Between Relief and Politics: Refugee Humanitarianism in Occupied Germany, 1945–1946." *Journal of Contemporary History* 43, no. 3 (2008): 437–49.

Cohen, Roger. "U.N. General Opposes More Bosnia Force." *New York Times*, September 29, 1994, A7.

Cohen, Stanley, and Andrew Scull, eds. *Social Control and the State*. New York: St. Martin's Press, 1983.

Coles, Gervase. "Approaching the Refugee Problem Today." In *The Question of Refugees and International Relations*, ed. Gil Loescher and Laila Monahan, 373–410. New York: Oxford University Press, 1989.

——. *Voluntary Repatriation*. Geneva: UNHCR, 1985.

Commission on Global Governance. *Our Global Neighborhood: The Report on the Commission on Global Governance*. NEW YORK: Oxford University Press, 1995.

Commission on Human Security. *Human Security Now*. New York: United Nations, 2003.

Conklin, Alice. *A Mission to Civilize: The Republican Idea of Empire in France and West Africa, 1895–1930*. Stanford: Stanford University Press, 1997.

Cooley, Alex, and James Ron. "The NGO Scramble." *International Security* 27, no. 1 (2002): 5–39.

Cooper, Frederick. "Modernizing Bureaucrats, Backward Africans, and the Development Concept." In *International Development and the Social Sciences: Essays on the History and Politics of Knowledge*, ed. Cooper Frederick and Randall Packer, 64–92. Berkeley: University of California Press, 1998.

Cooper, Frederick, and Ann Stoler, eds. *Tensions of Empire: Colonial Cultures in a Bourgeois World*. Berkeley: University of California Press, 1997.

Cooper, Robert. *The Breaking of Nations: Order and Chaos in the Twenty-First Century*. London: Atlantic Books, 2003.

Cornwall, Andrea, and Karen Brock. "What Do Buzzwords Do for Development Policy? A Critical Look at 'Participation,' 'Empowerment,' and 'Poverty Reduction.'" *Third World Quarterly* 26, no. 7 (2005) 1043–60.

Cosgrove, John. *Synthesis Report: Expanded Summary. Joint Evaluation of the International Response to the Indian Ocean Tsunami.* London: Tsunami Evaluation Coalition, 2007. Available at www.alnap.org/pool/files/Syn_Report_Sum.pdf, accessed July 12, 2010.

Costanza Adinolfi, David Bassiouini, Halver Fossum Lauritzsen, and Howard Roy Williams. *Humanitarian Response Review: An Independent report commissioned by the United Nations Emergency Relief Coordinator for Humanitarian Affairs.* New York: Office for the Coordination of Humanitarian Affairs (OCHA), August 2005.

Cowen M. P., and R. W. Shenton. *Doctrines of Development.* New York: Routledge, 1996.

Cowherd, Raymond. *The Politics of English Dissent.* New York: New York University Press, 1956.

Crane, R. S. "Suggestions Towards a Genealogy of the 'Man of Feeling.'" *English Literary History* 1, no. 3 (December 1934): 205–30.

Crawford, Neta. *Argument and Change in World Politics: Ethics, Decolonization, and Humanitarian Intervention.* New York: Cambridge University Press, 2002.

Crisp, Jeff. "Mind the Gap! UNHCR, Humanitarian Assistance, and the Development Process." *New Issues in Refugee Research,* Working Paper No. 43 (2001).

Cunliffe, S. Alex, and Michael Pugh. "The Politicization of the UNHCR in the Former Yugoslavia." *Journal of Refugee Studies* 10, no. 2 (1997): 134–53.

Curti, Merle. *American Philanthropy Abroad.* New Brunswick, NJ: Transaction Books, 1988.

——. "The Changing Pattern of Certain Humanitarian Organizations." *Annals of the American Academy of Political and Social Science* 179 (May 1935): 135–59.

Curtis, Devon. "Politics and Humanitarian Aid: Debates, Dilemmas, and Dissension." *Humanitarian Policy Group Report 10.* London: Overseas Development Institute, 2001.

Cutts, Mark. "The Humanitarian Operation in Bosnia, 1992–95: Dilemmas of Negotiating Humanitarian Access." *New Issues in Refugee Research,* Working Paper 8. Geneva: UNHCR, 1999.

——. "Politics and Humanitarianism." *Refugee Survey Quarterly* 17, no. 1 (1998): 1–15.

Darch, John. "Missionaries as Humanitarians? Opposition to the Recruitment of Indentured Labour for Queensland in the 1860s and 70s." Available at www.martymission.cam. ac.uk/cjDarch.html, accessed January 28, 2008.

Darcy, James. "Acts of Faith? Thoughts on the Effectiveness of Humanitarian Action." Paper presented to the SSRC Seminar Series, "Transformation of Humanitarian Action." New York. New York, April 12, 2005.

——. "Locating Responsibility: The Sphere Humanitarian Charter and its Rationale." *Disasters* 28, no. 2 (2004): 112–23.

Darcy, James, and Charles Antoine-Hofmann. *According to Need? Needs Assessment and Decision-Making in the Humanitarian Sector.* Humanitarian Policy Group, Report 15, September 2003.

Darfour, C., V. de Geoffroy, H. Maury, and F. Grunewald. "Rights, Standards, and Quality in a Complex Humanitarian Space: Is Sphere the Right Tool?" *Disasters* 28, no. 2 (2004): 124–41.

Davis, Austen. "Concerning Accountability in Humanitarian Action." London: Network Paper 58, Humanitarian Practice Network. London: Overseas Development Institute, March 2007.

Davis, Mike. *Late Victorian Holocausts.* New York: Verso Press, 2002.

Davis, Morris. "The International Committee of the Red Cross and Its Practice of Self-Restraint." *Nonprofit and Voluntary Sector Quarterly* 4 (January 1975): 63–68.

Dawes, James. *That the World May Know: Bearing Witness to Atrocity.* Cambridge: Harvard University Press, 2007.

de Cordier, Bruno. "Faith-Based Aid, Globalization, and the Humanitarian Front Line: An Analysis of Western-Based Muslim Islamic Aid Organizations." *Overseas Development Institute,* 2009.

De Gruchy, John W. "Who Did They Think They Were?" In *The Imperial Missions of the British Protestant Missions, 1880–1914,* ed. Andrew Porter, 213–225. Grand Rapids, MI: William Eerdmans, 2003.

de Torrente, Nicholas. "Humanitarian Action under Attack: Reflections on the Iraq War." *Harvard Human Rights Journal* 17 (Spring 2004): 1–30.

de Waal, Alex. *Famine Crimes: Politics and the Disaster Relief Industry in Africa.* Bloomington: Indiana University Press, 1998.

——. *Humanitarianism Unbound: Current Dilemmas Facing Multi-Mandate Relief Operations in Political Emergencies.* London: African Rights.

Dean, Carolyn. *The Fragility of Empathy after the Holocaust.* Ithaca: Cornell University Press, 2004.

Deorenzi, Simone. *ICRC Policy since the End of the Cold War: Contending with the Impasse in International Humanitarian Action.* Geneva: International Committee of the Red Cross, 1999.

Destexhe, Alain. "Forward." In *Populations in Danger,* ed. Francois Jean, London: Médecins Sans Frontiéres, 1995.

——. "Holding Humanitarianism Hostage: The Politics of Rescue." *Ethics and International Affairs* 11 (1997).

Dewey, John. *A Common Faith.* New Haven: Yale University Press, 1934.

Dirks, Nicholas. *The Scandal of Empire.* Cambridge: Harvard University Press, 2004.

Dobbins, James, et al. *The Beginner's Guide to Nation-Building.* Santa Monica, CA: RAND, 2007.

Donald, David. "Toward a Reconsideration of Abolitionists." In *Lincoln Reconsidered,* 3rd ed., 31–43. New York: Random House, 2001.

Donini, Antonio. "The Far Side: The Meta-Functions of Humanitarianism in a Globalized World." *Disasters* 34, no. 2 (2010): 220–37.

——. "Through a Glass Darkly: Humanitarianism and Empire." In *Capitalizing on Catastrophe: Neoliberal Strategies in Disaster Reduction,* ed. N. Gunewardana and M. Shuller, 29–46. Plymouth, UK: AltaMira Press, 2008.

Donini, Antonio, Larry Minear, and Peter Walker. "The Future of Humanitarian Action: Mapping the Implications of Iraq and Other Recent Crises." *Disasters* 28, no. 2 (2004): 190–204.

Douzinas, Costas. "The Many Faces of Humanitarianism." *Parrhesia* 2 (2007): 1–28.

Drescher, Seymour. *Capitalism and Antislavery: British Mobilization in Comparative Perspective.* New York: Oxford University Press, 1987.

Duffield, Mark. *Development, Security, and Unending War: Governing the World of Peoples.* Malden, MA: Polity Press, 2007.

——. "Getting Savages to Fight Barbarians: Development, Security, and the Colonial Present." *Conflict, Security, and Development* 5, no. 2 (2005): 141–60.

——. *Global Governance and the New Wars: The Merging of Development and Security.* New York: Zed Press, 2001.

——. "Governing the Borderlands: Decoding the Power of Aid." *Disasters* 25, no. 4 (2002): 308–20.

Duffield, Mark and John Prendergast. "Sovereignty and Intervention after the Cold War: Lessons from the Emergency Relief Desk." *Middle East Report* (March–June 1994): 9–15.

Dufour, Charlotte, et al., "Rights, Standards, and Quality in a Complex Humanitarian Space: Is Sphere the Right Tool?" *Disasters,* 28, no. 2 (2004): 124–41.

Durand, André. *From Sarajevo to Hiroshima: History of the International Committee of the Red Cross.* Geneva: Henry Dunant Institute, 1984.

Duriez, B., François Mabille, and Kathy Rousselet, eds. *Les ONG Confessionnelles: Religions et Action Internationale.* Paris: L'Harmatta, 2007.

Dworkin, Gerald. "Paternalism." *Monist* 56 (1972): 64–84.

Dworkin, Ronald. *Sovereign Virtue: The Theory and Practice of Equality.* Cambridge: Harvard University Press, 2000.

Dynes, Russell. "The Dialogue Between Voltaire and Rousseau on the Lisbon Earthquake: The Emergence of a Social Science View." *International Journal of Mass Emergencies and Disasters* 18, no. 1 (2000): 97–115.

Dziedzic, Michael, and Colonel Michael K. Seidl. *Provincial Reconstruction Teams: Military Relations with International and Nongovernmental Organizations in Afghanistan.* USIP Special Report No. 147. August 2005.

Egan, Eileen. *Catholic Relief Services: The Beginning Years: For the Life of the World.* New York: Catholic Relief Services, 1988.

Egeland, Jan. *A Billion Lives: An Eyewitness Report from the Frontlines of Humanity.* New York: Simon and Shuster, 2008.

Eliasson, Jan. "Ten Years of Humanitarian Action." *The Humanitarian Decade: Challenges for Humanitarian Assistance in the Last Decade and into the Future*, vol. I, 7–16, New York: UN Office for the Coordination of Humanitarian Affairs, 2002.

Emmanuelli, Xavier. *Les prédateurs de l'action humanitaire*. Paris: Albin Michel, 1991.

Empie, Paul, and Henry Whiting. "Lutheran World Relief and Programs in Countries of Endemic Need." November 1958. Lutheran World Relief Archives, *Archives, 1954–1958*.

Escobar, Arturo. *Encountering Development*. Princeton, NJ: Princeton University Press, 1995.

Evans, Gareth. *Responsibility to Protect: Ending Mass Atrocities Once and For All*. Washington, DC: Brookings Press, 2009.

Fage, J. D. *A History of West Africa: An Introductory Survey*. 4th ed. New York: Cambridge University Press, 1969.

Fassin, Didier. "Humanitarianism: A Nongovernment Government." In *Nongovernmental Politics*, ed. Michael Feher, 149–60. New York: Zone Books, 2007.

——. "Humanitarianism as a Politics of Life." *Public Culture* 19, no. 3 (2007): 499–520.

——. "*Noli Me Tangere*: The Moral Untouchability of Humanitarianism." In *The Forces of Compassion*, ed. Erica Bornstein and Peter Redfield. Santa Fe: School of Advanced Research, 2011.

Fassin, Didier, and Mariella Pandolfi, eds. *Contemporary States of Emergency: The Politics of Military and Humanitarian Interventions*. New York: Zone Books, 2010.

Fassin, Didier, and Robert Rechtman. *The Empire of Trauma: An Inquiry into the Conditions of Victimhood*. Princeton, NJ: Princeton University Press, 2009.

Faust, Drew Gilpin. *This Republic of Suffering: Death and the American Civil War*. Cambridge: Harvard University Press, 2008.

Fearon, James. "Measuring Humanitarian Impact." Paper presented to the SSRC seminar series "Transformation of Humanitarian Action." New York City, December 5, 2004.

Feher, Michael, ed. *Nongovernmental Politics*. New York: Zone Books, 2007.

Feldman, Ilana. "The Quaker Way: Ethical Labor and Humanitarian Relief." *American Ethnologist* 34, no. 4 (2007): 689–705.

Ferguson, James. *The Anti-Politics Machine: "Development," Depoliticization, and Bureaucratic Power in Lesotho*. Minneapolis: University of Minnesota Press, 1994.

Festa, Lynn. *Sentimental Figures of Empire in Eighteenth-Century Britain and France*. Baltimore: Johns Hopkins University Press, 2006.

Fiering, Norman. "Irresistible Compassion: An Aspect of Eighteenth Century Sympathy and Humanitarianism." *Journal of the History of Ideas* 37, 2 (1976): 195–218.

Finkielkraut, Alain. *In the Name of Humanity: Reflections on the Twentieth Century*. Judith Friedlander, trans. New York: Columbia University Press, 2000.

——. *The Imaginary Jew*. Lincoln: University of Nebraska Press, 1997.

Finnemore, Martha. *The Purpose of Intervention*. Ithaca: Cornell University Press, 2004.

Fisher, William. "Doing Good? The Politics and Antipolitics of NGO Practices." *Annual Review of Anthropology* 26 (1997): 439–64.

Flipse, Scott. "The Latest Casualty of War: Catholic Relief Services, Humanitarianism, and the War in Vietnam, 1967–1968." *Peace and Change* 27, 2 (April 2002): 245–70.

Foley, Conor. *The Thin Blue Line: How Humanitarianism Went to War*. New York: Verso Press, 2008.

Forsythe, David. *The Humanitarians*. New York: Cambridge University Press, 2005.

——. "UNHCR's Mandate: The Politics of Being Non-Political." *New Issues in Refugee Research*, no. 33 (2001).

Fournier, Christophe. "Our Purpose Is to Limit the Devastations of War." Speech at a conference in Rheindahlen, Germany, organized by NATO's Allied Rapid Reaction Corps. December 7–8, 2009. Available at www.doctorswithoutborders.org/press/release_print.cfm?id=4307, accessed July 12, 2010.

Fox, Renee. "Medical Humanitarianism and Human Rights: Reflections on Doctors without Borders and Doctors of the World." *Social Sciences and Medicine* 41, no. 12 (1995): 1607–16.

Frakenberger, Timothy, Michael Drinkwater, and Daniel Maxwell. *Operationalizing Household Livelihood Security: A Holistic Approach for Addressing Poverty and Vulnerability*. Atlanta: CARE, 2000.

Frerks, Georg, and Dorothea Hilhorst. "Evaluation of Humanitarian Assistance in Emergency Situations." *New Issues in Refugee Research,* Working Paper no. 56. Geneva: UNHCR, February 2002.

Fukuyama, Francis. *State-Building: Governance and World Order in the Twenty-First Century.* Ithaca: Cornell University Press, 2004.

Gairdner, W. H. T. *Echoes from Edinburgh 1910: An Account and Interpretation of the World Missionary Conference.* Layman's Missionary Movement, 1910.

Gamber, Wendy. "Antebellum Reform: Salvation, Self-Control, and Social Transformation." In *Charity, Philanthropy, and Civility in American History,* ed. Lawrence Friedman and Mark McGarvie, 129–54. New York: Cambridge University Press, 2003.

Garren, David. "Paternalism, Part I." *Philosophical Books* 47, no. 4 (2006): 334–41.

——. "Paternalism, Part II." *Philosophical Books* 48, 1 (2007): 50–59.

Gary, Ian. "Bringing the State Back In: Implications for CRS and Its Partners." Catholic Relief Services—USCC, World Summit Conference, September 2000.

Gasper, Des. "'Drawing a Line': Ethical and Political Strategies in Complex Emergency Assistance." *European Journal of Development Research* 11, no. 2 (1999): 87–114.

Gehman, Richard. *Let My Heart Be Broken with the Things That Break the Heart of God.* New York: McGraw-Hill, 1960.

Gert, Bernard, and Charles Culver. "Paternalistic Behavior." *Philosophy and Public Affairs* 6, no. 1 (1976): 45–57.

Ghani, Ashraf, and Claire Lockhart. *Fixing Fragile States.* New York: Oxford University Press, 2008.

Gill, Rebecca. "Calculating Compassion in War: The 'New Humanitarian' Ethos in Britain 1870–1918." Ph.D. Dissertation, University of Manchester, 2005.

Gilroy, Paul. *Postcolonial Melancholia.* New York: Columbia University Press, 2005.

Ginzburg, Carlo. "Killing a Chinese Mandarin: The Moral Implications of Distance." *Critical Inquiry* 21, no. 1 (1994): 46–60.

Goetz, Nathaniel. "Humanitarian Issues in the Biafra Conflict." *New Issues in Refugee Research.* Working Paper no. 36. April 2001.

Gong, Gerritt. *The Standard of Civilization in International Society.* New York: Oxford University Press, 1984.

Gorgé, Camille. *The International Relief Union: Its Origins, Aims, Means, and Future.* Geneva: International Relief Union, 1938.

Gostelow, L. "The Sphere Project: The Implications of Making Humanitarian Principles and Codes Work." *Disasters* 23, 4 (1999): 316–25.

Grant, Kevin. *A Civilised Savagery: Britain and the New Slaveries in Africa, 1884–1926.* New York: Routledge, 2005.

Griffin, Clifford. "Religious Benevolence as Social Control, 1815–1860." *Mississippi Valley Historical Review* 44 (December 1957): 423–44.

Grombach-Wagner, Johanna. "An IHL/ICRC perspective on humanitarian space." *Humanitarian Exchange Magazine* 32 (December 2005). http://www.odihpn.org/report.asp?ID=2765.

——. "La'art de Boire du thé." In *Médecins Sans Frontières, My Sweet La Mancha:* 48–49, Geneva: Médecins Sans Frontières International, 2005.

Guillermand, Jean. "The Historical Foundations of Humanitarian Action." *International Review of the Red Cross* 34 (1994): 42–55.

Gunewardana, N., and M. Shuller, eds. *Capitalizing on Catastrophe: Neoliberal Strategies in Disaster Reduction.* Plymouth, U.K.: AltaMira Press, 2008.

Habito, Ruben L. F., and Keishin Inabaa, eds. *The Practice of Altruism, Caring, and Religion in Global Perspective.* Cambridge: Cambridge Scholars Press, 2006.

Hall, Catherine. *Civilizing Subjects: Metropole and Colony in the English Imagination, 1830–1867.* Chicago: University of Chicago Press, 2002.

Halman, Gerald, and Steven Ratner. "Saving Failed States." *Foreign Policy* 89 (Winter 1992/93): 3–20.

Halttunen, Karen. "Humanitarianism and the Pornography of Pain." *American Historical Review* 304 (April 1995): 303–34.

Harrison, Robert Pogue. *The Dominion of the Dead.* Chicago: University of Chicago Press, 2003.

Haskell, Thomas. "Capitalism and the Origins of the Humanitarian Sensibility, Part 1." *American Historical Review* 90, 2 (1985): 339–61.

——. "Capitalism and the Origins of the Humanitarian Sensibility, Part 2." *American Historical Review* 90, 3 (1985): 547–66.

Haynes, Douglas. *Imperial Medicine: Patrick Monson and the Conquest of Tropical Disease.* Philadelphia: University of Pennsylvania Press, 2001.

Heins, Volker. "Democratic States, Aid Agencies, and World Society: What's the Name of the Game?" *Global Society* 19, no. 4 (October 2005), 361–84.

Henry, Kevin. "CARE International: Evolving to Meet the Challenges of the 21st Century." *Nonprofit and Voluntary Sector Quarterly* 28, no. 4 (1999): 109–20.

Herbst, Jeffry. "Let Them Fail: State Failure in Theory and Practice: Implications for Policy." In *When States Fail: Causes and Consequences,* ed. Robert I. Rotberg, 302–18. Princeton, NJ: Princeton University Press, 2003.

Hilhorst, Dorothea. "Being Good at Doing Good? Quality and Accountability of Humanitarian NGOs." *Disasters* 26, no. 3 (2005): 193–212.

Hilhorst, Dorothea, and Nadja Schmiemann. "Humanitarian Principles and Organizational Culture: Everyday Practice in Médecins Sans Frontiéres-Holland." *Development in Practice* 12, nos. 3/4 (2002): 490–500.

Hilton, Boyd. *Age of Atonement: The Influence of Evangelicalism on Social and Economic Thought.* New York: Oxford University Press, 1992.

Himmelfarb, Gertrude. *The Idea of Poverty: England in the Early Industrial Age.* New York: Alfred Knopf, 1984.

——. *Poverty and Compassion: The Moral Imagination of the Late Victorians.* New York: Vintage Press, 1992.

Hiney, Tom. *On the Missionary Trail: A Journey through Polynesia, Asia, and Africa with the London Missionary Society.* Boston: Atlantic Monthly Press, 2000.

Hirschman, Albert. *Essays in Trespassing: Economics to Politics and Beyond.* New York: Oxford University Press, 1981.

Hochschild, Adam. *Bury the Chains: Prophets and Rebels in the Fight to Free an Empire's Slaves.* New York: Houghton Mifflin, 2005.

——. *King Leopold's Ghost: A Story of Greed, Terror, and Heroism in Colonial Africa.* New York: Mariner Books, 1999.

Hocke, Jean-Pierre. "Beyond Humanitarianism and the Need for Political Will to Resolve Today's Refuge Problem." Joyce Pearce Memorial Lecture, Oxford University, October 1986.

Holborn, Louise. *Refugees: A Problem of Our Time: The Work of the United Nations High Commissioner for Refugees, 1951–72.* Lanham, MD: Scarecrow Press, 1975.

Holt, P. M. *The Mahdist State in the Sudan.* Oxford: Clarendon Press, 1970.

Holzgrefe, J. L., and Robert Keohane, eds. *Humanitarian Intervention: Ethical, Legal, and Political Dilemmas.* New York: Cambridge University Press, 2003.

Hopgood, Stephen. "Moral Authority, Modernity, and the Politics of the Sacred." *European Journal of International Relations* 15, no. 2 (2009): 229–55.

——. "Saying 'No' to Walmart? Money and Morality in Professional Humanitarianism." In *Humanitarianism in Question: Politics, Power, Ethics,* ed. Michael Barnett and Tom Weiss, 98–123. Ithaca: Cornell University Press, 2008.

Horkheimer, Max, and Theodor Adorno. *Dialectic of Enlightenment.* New York: Continuum Books, 1976.

Hoxie, Frederick. *A Final Promise: The Campaign to Assimilate the Indians, 1880–1920.* Lincoln: University of Nebraska Press, 2001.

Hudson, Alan. "Making the Connection: Legitimacy Claims, Legitimacy Chains, and Northern NGOs' International Advocacy." In *New Roles and Relevance: Development NGOs and the Challenge of Change,* ed. D. Lewis and T. Wallace. 89–97. Bloomfield, CT: Kumarian Press, 2000.

Hulme, David, and Michael Edwards, eds. *NGOs, States, and Donors: Too Close for Comfort?* New York: MacMillan Press, 1997.

Humanitarian Policy Group. "Measuring the Impact of Humanitarian Aid: A Review of Current Practice." *HPG Research Report* no. 17, Overseas Development Institute, June 2004.

Humphreys, A. R. "'The Friend of Mankind,' 1700–60: An Aspect of Eighteenth-Century Sensibility." *Review of English Studies* 24, 95 (1948): 203–18.

Hunt, Lynn. *Inventing Human Rights.* New York: Norton Press, 2007.

Husak, Douglas N. "Legal Paternalism." In *The Oxford Handbook of Practical Ethics,* ed. Hugh LaFollette, 387–412. New York: Oxford University Press, 2003.

Hutchinson, John. *Champions of Charity: War and the Rise of the Red Cross*. Boulder, CO: Westview Press, 1997.

——. "Disasters and the International Order: Earthquakes, Humanitarians, and the Ciraolo Project." *International History Review* 22, 1 (2000): 1–36.

——. "Disasters and the International Order II: The International Relief Union." *International History Review* 23, 2 (2001): 253–98.

Ignatieff, Michael. *Empire Lite: Nation Building in Bosnia, Kosovo, Afghanistan*. New York: Vintage, 2003.

——. *Human Rights as Political Idolatry*, Princeton: Princeton University Press, 2001.

——. *The Warrior's Honor: Ethnic War and Modern Conscience*. New York: Henry Holt, 1997.

International Commission on Intervention and State Sovereignty. *The Responsibility to Protect*. Ottawa: IDRC, 2001.

Iriye, Akira. *Global Community: The Role of International Organizations in the Making of the Contemporary World*. Berkeley: University of California Press, 2002.

Irvine, Graeme. *Best Things in the Worst of Times: An Insider's View of World Vision*. Wilsonville, OR: Bookpartners, 1996.

——. "A New Partnership." An Address by Acting President, Graeme Irvine, at a combined WVUS/WVI Chapel, February 22, 1989.

——. "Presentation of Internationalization Report." Interim Report, World Vision International, Commission on Internationalization, 1978–1983. September 1984.

——. *Strategic Directions for World Vision International, 1990–92*. Monrovia, CA: World Vision International, 1992.

Jaeger, Gilbert. "Status and the Protection of Refugees." International Institute of Human Rights, Ninth Study Session. July 1978.

James, William. *The Will to Believe*. New York: Dover Publications, 1956.

Jessen Peterson, Soren. "Statement to the Security Council." *Refugee Survey Quarterly* 17, no. 1 (1998): 65–68.

Jones, Mervyrn. *In Famine's Shadow: A Private War on Hunger*. Boston: Beacon Press, 1965.

Judah, Tim. *Kosovo: War and Revenge*. New Haven: Yale University Press, 2002.

Kant, Immanuel. *The Critique of Pure Reason*. Norman Kemp Smith, trans. London: Macmillan, 1929.

——. "On the Common Saying: This Might be True in Theory, But It Does Not Apply in Practice." In *Kant: Political Writings*, ed. Hans Reiss, 61–92. New York: Cambridge University Press, 1970.

——. *Perpetual Peace and Other Essays on Politics, History, and Morals*. Ted Humphrey, trans. Indianapolis: Hackett Publishing, 1983.

Katznelson, Ira. *Desolation and Enlightenment: Political Knowledge after Total War, Totalitarianism, and the Holocaust*. New York: Columbia University Press, 2001.

Kauffman, Christopher. "Politics, Programs, and Protests: Catholic Relief Services in Vietnam, 1954–1975." *Catholic Historical Review* 91, no. 2 (April 2005): 223–50.

Keck, Margaret, and Kathryn Sikkink. *Activists Beyond Borders*. Ithaca: Cornell University Press, 1998.

Keen, David. *Complex Emergencies*. Boston: Polity Press, 2008.

Kennedy, David. *The Dark Sides of Virtue: Reassessing International Humanitarianism*. Princeton, NJ: Princeton University Press, 2005.

——. "International Refugee Protection." *Human Rights Quarterly* 8 (1986): 1–69.

Kenney, George. "See No Evil, Make No Policy." *Washington Monthly*, November 22, 1992, 33.

Kent, Randolph. *Anatomy of Disaster Relief: The International Network in Action*. London: Pinter, 1987.

Kerleroux, Julie. "Dossier: Associated for Action." *Messages*. MSF Internal Newsletter, no. 128. March 2004.

Khan, Sadruddin Aga. 1976. "Legal Problems Relating to Refugees and Displaced Persons." Paper delivered at the Hague Academy of International Law, August 2–4, 1976.

Kissi, Edward. "Beneath International Famine Relief in Ethiopia: The United States, Ethiopia, and the Debate over Relief Aid, Development Assistance, and Human Rights." *African Studies Review* 48, no. 2 (September 2005): 111–32.

Kleinman, Arthur, and Joan Kleinman. "The Appeal of Experience, the Dismay of Images: Cultural Appropriations of Suffering in Our Time." In *Social Suffering*, ed. A. Kleinman, V. Das, and M. Lock, 1–24. Berkeley: University of California Press, 1997.

Klingberg, Frank. *The Anti-Slavery Movement in England: A Study in English Humanitarianism.* New Haven: Yale University Press, 1968.

——. "The Evolution of the Humanitarian Spirit in Eighteenth-Century England." *Pennsylvania Magazine of History and Biography* 66, no. 3 (July 1942): 260–78.

Korf, Benedikt. "Antinomies of Geography: Moral Geographies and Post-Tsunami Aid in Southeast Asia." *Geoforum* 38, no. 2 (2007): 366–78.

Kouchner, Bernard. *Charité Business.* Paris: Le Pre aux Clercs, 1986.

Krahenbuhl, P. "Conflict in the Balkans: Human Tragedies and the Challenge to Independent Humanitarian Action." *International Review of the Red Cross* 837 (2000): 11–29.

Krasner, Stephen, and Carlos Pasqual. "Addressing State Failure." *Foreign Affairs* 84, no. 4 (2005): 153–63.

Kritsiotis, Dino. "Imagining the International Community." *European Journal of International Law* 13, no. 4 (2002): 961–92.

Lambert, David, and Alan Lester. "Geographies of Colonial Philanthropy." *Progress in Human Geography* 28, no. 3 (2004): 320–41.

Landis, Michele. "Fate, Responsibility, and the 'Natural' Disaster Relief: Narrating the American Welfare State." *Law and Society Review* 33, no. 2 (1999): 257–318.

Laqueur, Thomas. "Bodies, Details, and the Humanitarian Narrative." In *The New Cultural History,* ed. Lynn Hunt. 176–204. Berkeley: University of California Press.

——. "Mourning, Pity, and the Work of Narrative in the Making of 'Humanity.'" In *Humanitarianism and Suffering: The Mobilization of Empathy,* ed. Richard Ashby Wilson and Richard Brown, 31–57. New York: Cambridge University Press, 2009.

Leader, Nicholas. *The Politics of Principle: The Principles of Humanitarian Action in Practice.* London: Overseas Development Institute, 2000.

Leal, Pablo Alejandro. "Participation: The Ascendancy of a Buzzword in the New-Liberal Era." *Development in Practice* 17 (August 2007): 4–5, 539–48.

Ledgerwood, Judy. "UN Peacekeeping Missions: The Lessons from Cambodia." *Asia Pacific Issues,* Analysis from the East-West Center, no. 11, March 1994.

Leebaw, Bronwyn. "The Politics of Impartial Activism: Humanitarianism and Human Rights." *Perspectives on Politics* 5, no. 2 (June 2007): 223–40.

Lester, A. *Imperial Networks: Creating Identities in Nineteenth Century South Africa and Britain.* London, Routledge, 1991.

——. "Reformulating Identities: British Settlers in Early Nineteenth-century South Africa." *Transactions of the Institute of British Geographers* 23 (1998): 515–31.

——. "Settlers, the State, and Colonial Power: The Colonization of Queen Adelaide Province, 1834–37." *Journal of African History* 39 (1998): 221–46.

Lewis, W. S., and Ralph Williams. *Private Charity in England, 1747–1757.* New Haven: Yale University Press, 1938.

Link, Arthur. "Samuel Taylor Coleridge and the Economic and Political Crisis in Great Britain, 1816–1820." *Journal of the History of Ideas* 9, no. 3 (1948): 323–38.

Linklater, Andrew. "Towards a Sociology of Global Morals with an Emancipatory Intent." *Review of International Studies* 21, no. 1 (2007): 135–50.

Lischer, Sarah. *Dangerous Sanctuaries: Refugee Camps, Civil War, and the Dilemmas of Humanitarian Aid.* Ithaca: Cornell University Press, 2003.

——. "U.S. Military Interventions and the Humanitarian Force Multiplier." Paper presented at the annual meeting of the International Studies Association, Montreal, Quebec, Canada, March 17, 2004.

Lissner, Jorgen. *The Politics of Altruism: A Study of the Political Behavior of Voluntary Development Agencies.* Geneva: Lutheran World Federation, February 1977.

Loescher, Gil. *Beyond Charity: International Cooperation and the Global Refugee Crisis* New York: Twentieth Century Fund, 1993.

——. *The UNHCR and World Politics: A Perilous Path.* New York: Oxford University Press, 2001.

Lutheran World Relief. "Lutheran World Relief: Another Look at the Name." Lutheran World Relief, Baltimore, Maryland, May 16, 1979.

——. Proposal for a Strategy to Deal with World Hunger." December 1974, 1o, LWR Archives, September–December 1974.

Lyons, F. S. L. *Internationalism in Europe, 1815–1914.* Amsterdam: A.W. Sythoff-Leyden, 1963.

Macalister-Smith, Peter. *International Humanitarian Assistance: Disaster Relief Actions in International Law and Organizations.* Boston: Martinus Nijhoff Publishers, 1985.

——. "The International Relief Union: Reflections on Establishing an International Relief Union of July 12, 1927." *Legal History Review* 54 (1986): 363–74.

——. "The International Relief Union of 1932." *Disasters* 5, no. 2 (1981): 147–54.

MacCunn, John. "Cosmopolitan Duties." *International Journal of Ethics* 9, no. 2 (1899): 152–68.

Macrae, Joanne. "Aiding Peace...and War: UNHCR Returnee Reintegration, and the Relief-Development Debate." *New Issues in Refugee Research*. Geneva: UNHCR, 1999.

Macrae, Joanna, et al. *Uncertain Power: The Changing Role of Official Donors in Humanitarian Action, Humanitarian Policy Group*. London: Overseas Development Institute, no. 12, December 2002.

Macrae, Joanna, and Adele Harmer, eds. "Humanitarian Action and the 'Global War on Terror.'" *HPG Report*, Overseas Development Institute, London, July 2003.

Mahood, Linda. *Feminism and Voluntary Action: Eglantyne Jebb and Save the Children, 1879–1928*. New York: Palgrave Macmillan, 2009.

Malcolm, Noel. *Kosovo: A Short History*. New York: Harper Perennial, 1999.

Malhuret, Claude. "Report from Aghanistan." *Foreign Affairs* 62 (Winter 1983): 426–35.

Malkki, Liisa. "Citizens of Humanity: Internationalism and the Imagined Community of Nations." *Diaspora* 3, no. 1 (1994): 41–68.

——. "Refugees and Exile: From 'Refugee Studies' to the National Order of Things." *Annual Review of Anthropology* 24 (1995): 495–523.

Maluleke, Tinyiko Sam. "Mission and Political Power: Edinburgh 2010, Commission VII Reconsidered." Paper presented at the Towards 2010 conference. Edinburgh, Scotland.

Margalit, Avishai. *The Ethics of Memory*. Cambridge, MA: Harvard University Press, 2002.

Marsden, George. *Understanding Fundamentalism and Evangelicalism*. Grand Rapids, MI: William Eerdmans, 1991.

Marshall, Dominique. "Children's Rights in Imperial Political Cultures: Missionary and Humanitarian Contributions to the Conference on the African Child of 1931." *International Journal of Children's Rights* 12, no. 3 (2004): 273–318.

Maskalyk, James. *Six Months in Sudan: A Young Doctor in a War-Torn Village*. New York: Spiegel and Grau, 2009.

Maurice, Frédéric. "Humanitarian Ambition." *International Review of the Red Cross* 32 (July–August 1992): 289, 363–72.

Mauss, Marcel. *The Gift: The Form and Reason for Exchange in Archaic Societies*. New York: Norton Press, 2000.

McCaston, M. Katherine. *Moving CARE's Programming Forward: Unifying Framework for Poverty Eradication and Social Justice and Underlying Causes of Poverty*. Atlanta: CARE, 2005.

McCaston, M. Katherine, and Michael Rewald. *A Conceptual Overview of Underlying Causes of Poverty*. Atlanta: CARE, 2005.

McLisky, Claire. "'Due Observance of Justice, and the Protection of their Rights': Philanthropy, Humanitarianism, and Moral Purpose in the Aborigines Protection Society circa 1837 and its Portrayal in Australian Historiography, 1883–2003." *Limina: A Journal of Historical and Cultural Studies* 11 (2005): 57–66.

McLoy, Shelby. *The Humanitarian Movement in Eighteenth-Century France*. Lexington: University of Kentucky Press, 1957.

Mead, Lawrence, ed. *The New Paternalism: Supervisory Approaches to Poverty*. Washington, DC: Brookings Institution, 1997.

Médecins Sans Frontières. *My Sweet La Mancha*. Geneva: Médecins Sans Frontières International, 2005.

——. "Interview with Rony Brauman (II): The Humanitarian Movement." *MSF Internal Newsletter*, September–October 2002, 72–75.

Mehta, Uday Singh. *Liberalism and Empire: A Study in Nineteenth-Century British Liberal Thought*. Chicago: University of Chicago Press, 1999.

Menand, Louis. *The Metaphysical Club: A Story of Ideas in America*. New York: Farrar, Straus, and Giroux, 2002.

Mertus, Julie. *Kosovo: How Myths and Truths Started a War*. Berkeley: University of California Press, 1999.

Minear, Larry. *The Humanitarian Enterprise: Dilemmas and Discoveries*. Bloomfield, CT: Kumarian Press, 2002.

Minear, Larry, T. van Baarda, and M. Sommers. "NATO and Humanitarian Action in the Kosovo Crisis." *Occasional Papers*, Institute for International Studies, Brown University, Providence, R.I., 2000.

Mitchell, John. "The La Mancha Process: A Comment." In *Médecins Sans Frontières, My Sweet La Mancha*, 83–84. Geneva: Médecins Sans Frontières International, 2005.

Mitchell, John, and Deborah Doane. "An Ombudsman for Humanitarian Assistance?" *Disasters* 23, no. 2 (1999): 115–24.

Mooney, Erin. "Presence, Ergo Protection? UNPROFOR, UNHCR, and the ICRC in Croatia and Bosnia-Herzegovina." *International Journal of Refugee Law* 7, no. 3 (1995): 407–35.

Moore, David. "Humanitarian Agendas, State Reconstruction, and Democratization Processes in War-Torn Societies." *New Issues in Refugee Research*, Working Paper 24, July 2000.

Moore, Jonathan, ed. *Hard Choices: Moral Dilemmas in Humanitarian Intervention*. Lanham, MD: Rowman and Littlefeld, 1999.

Moorhead, Caroline. *Dunant's Dream: War, Memory, and the History of the Red Cross*. New York: Harper Collins, 1998.

Morefield, Jeanne. *Covenants without Swords: Idealist Liberalism and the Spirit of Empire*. Princeton, NJ: Princeton University Press, 2005.

Morgenthau, Hans J. "Human Rights and Foreign Policy." In *Moral Dimensions of American Foreign Policy*, ed. K. Thompson, 341–48, New Brunswick, NJ: Transaction Books, 1984.

Morris, Errol. *The Fog of War: Eleven Lessons from the Life of Robert McNamara*, Directed by Errol Morris. Los Angeles, CA: Sony Pictures Classics, 2003.

Morris, Nicholas. "UNHCR and Kosovo: A Personal View from Within UNHCR." *Forced Migration Review* 5 (1999): 14–17.

Morris, Peter. "Humanitarian Interventions in Macedonia: An NGO Perspective." *Forced Migration Review* 5 (August 1999): 5–6.

Morrison, Charles Clayton. "The World Missionary Conference." *Christian Century*, July 7, 1910.

Moyn, Samuel. "Empathy in History, Empathizing with Humanity." *History and Theory* 45, no. 3 (2006): 397–415.

——. *The Last Utopia: Human Rights in History*. Cambridge: Harvard University Press, 2010.

Mulley, Clare. *The Woman Who Saved the World: A Biography of Eglantyne Jebb Founder of Save the Children*. Oxford: One World, 2009.

Muthu, Sankar. *Enlightenment against Empire*. Princeton, NJ: Princeton University Press, 2003.

Myers, Bryant. "Humanitarian Response: Christians in Response to Uprooted People." *Missology: An International Review* 35, no. 2 (April 2007): 195–214.

——. *Walking with the Poor: Principles and Practices of Transformational Development*. New York: Orbis Books, 1999.

Nash, George. *The Life of Herbert Hoover: The Humanitarian, 1914–17*. New York: Norton, 1988.

Natsios, Andrew. "NGOs and the Humanitarian Impulse: Some Have it Right." *Ethics and International Affairs* 11, no. 1 (1997): 133–36.

Neilands, Robin. *The Dervish Wars: Gordon and Kitchner in the Sudan*. London: John Murray Publishers, 1996.

Nichols, Bruce. *The Uneasy Alliance: Religion, Refugee Work, and U.S. Foreign Policy*. New York: Oxford University Press, 1988.

Nietzsche, Friedrich. *On the Genealogy of Morality*. Carol Diethe, trans., and Keith Ansell-Pearson, ed. Cambridge: Cambridge University Press, 1996.

Ninin, Catherine, and Pierre-Edouard Deldique. *Globe Doctors: 20 ans d'Aventure Humanitaire*. Paris: Pierre Belfond, 1991.

Noll, Mark. "Evangelical Identity, Power, and Culture in the Great Nineteenth Century." In *Christianity Reborn: The Global Expansion of Evangelicalism in the Twentieth Century*. ed. Donald Lewis, 31–51. Grand Rapids, MI: William Eerdmans, 2004.

——. *The Rise of Evangelicalism: The Age of Edwards, Whitefield, and the Wesleys*. Westmont, IL: InterVarsity Press, 2004.

Norton-Taylor, Richard. "From Killing to Cuddling." *Guardian*, August 17, 2000.

Nyers, Peter. "Emergency or Emerging Identities? Refugees and Transformations in World Order." *Millennium* 28, no. 1 (1999): 1–26.

Obiaga, Ndubisi. *The Politics of Humanitarian Organizations Intervention.* New York: University Press of America, 2004.

O'Brien, Paul. "Benefits-Harms Analysis: A Rights-Based Tool Developed by CARE International." *Humanitarian Exchange Magazine.* Humanitarian Practice Network, London: Overseas Development Institute, March 20, 2002.

——. "Politicized Humanitarianism: A Response to Nicholas de Torrente." *Harvard Human Rights Journal* 17 (Spring 2004): 31–39.

Ogata, Sadako. "Challenges on the Frontline of Refugee Assistance." Lecture delivered at Harvard University, November 10, 1999.

——. *The Turbulent Decade.* New York: Norton, 2005.

——. "World Order, Internal Conflict, and Refugees." Lecture delivered at Harvard University, October 28, 1996.

Oldfield, J. R. *Popular Politics and British Anti-Slavery: The Mobilization of Public Opinion against the Slave Trade, 1787–1807.* Manchester: Manchester University Press, 1995.

O'Neill, Onara. *Bounds of Justice.* New York: Cambridge University Press, 2000.

Ophir, Adi. "The Sovereign, the Humanitarian, and the Terrorist." In *Nongovernmental Politics,* ed. Michael Feher, 161–81. New York: Zone Books, 2007.

Orbinski, James. *An Imperfect Offering: Humanitarian Action for the Twenty-First Century.* Toronto: Walker and Company, 2009.

Orford, Ann. *Reading Humanitarian Intervention: Human Rights and the Use of Force in International Law.* New York: Cambridge University Press, 2003.

Orwell, George. "Reflections on Gandhi." *Partisan Review* 6, no. 1 (January 1949): 85–92.

Oxley, Marcus. "Measuring Humanitarian Need." *Humanitarian Exchange* (September 2001): 28–30.

Paris, Roland. *At War's End: Building Peace after Civil Conflict.* Cambridge: Cambridge University Press, 2004.

——. "Human Security: Paradigm Shift or Hot Air." *International Security* 26, no. 2 (2001): 87–102.

——. "International Peacebuilding and the 'Mission Civilisatrice.'" *Review of International Studies* 28, no. 4 (2002): 637–656.

Parisel, Alex. "Evolution in the Role of MSF." *MSF Newsletter,* April 2001, 8–9.

Parmelee, Maurice. "The Rise of Modern Humanitarianism." *American Journal of Sociology* 21, no. 3 (1915): 345–59.

Pasic, Amir, and Thomas Weiss. "The Politics of Rescue: Yugoslavia Wars and the Humanitarian Impulse." *Ethics and International Affairs* 11 (1997): 105–31.

Patenaude, Bertrand M. *The Big Show in Bololand: The American Relief Expedition to Soviet Russia in the Famine of 1921.* Stanford: Stanford University Press, 2002.

Pergande, Delia. "Private Voluntary Aid and Nation Building in South Vietnam: The Humanitarian Politics CARE." *Peace and Change* 27, no. 2 (2002): 165–97.

——. *Private Voluntary Aid in Vietnam: The Humanitarian Politics of Catholic Relief Services and CARE, 1954–1965.* Ph.D. dissertation, Lexington, University of Kentucky, 1999.

Pezzullo, Lawrence. "The Church's Servant Mission and Social Teaching: The Response and the Challenge of the Church in the U.S." Speech delivered at Pontifical North American College. Rome, Italy, 1990.

——. "Cooperation in Humanitarian Efforts: A Case Study Response in Ethiopia." *Executive Office/I-C Box 13, Lawrence Pezzullo—Speaking Engagement,* 1987, 5–6.

Pfeffer, Jeffrey, and Gerald Salancik. *The External Control of Organizational Analysis.* Chicago: University of Chicago Press, 1991.

Pictet, Jean. *The Fundamental Principles of the Red Cross.* Geneva: Henry Dunant Institute, 1979.

Pilar, Ulrike von. "Humanitarian Space under Siege: Some Remarks from an Aid Agency's Perspective." Background paper prepared for the symposium, "Europe and Humanitarian Aid: What Future? Learning from Crisis." April 22–23, 1999, Bad Neuenahr, Germany.

Pippin, Robert. "Nietzsche and the Melancholy of Modernity." *Social Research* 66, no. 2 (Summer 1999): 495–520.

Pitterman, Shelly. "International Responses to Refugee Situations: The United Nations High Commissioner for Refugees." In *Refugees in World Politics,* ed. E. Ferris, 43–81. New York: Praeger Press, 1985.

Pitts, Jennifer. *A Turn to Empire: The Rise of Imperial Liberalism in Britain and France.* Princeton, NJ: Princeton University Press, 2005.

Piven, Francis Fox, and Richard Cloward. "Humanitarianism in History: A Response to the Critics." In *Social Welfare or Social Control? Some Historical Reflections on Regulating the Poor,* ed. Walter Trattner, 115–47. Knoxville: University of Tennessee Press, 1983.

Plattner, Denise. "ICRC Neutrality and Neutrality in Humanitarian Assistance." *International Review of the Red Cross* 311 (March–April 1996): 161–79.

Plesch, Dan. *America, Hitler, and the United Nations: How the Allies Won World War II and Forged a Peace.* London: I.B. Tauris, forthcoming.

Pogue Harrison, Robert. *The Dominion of the Dead.* Chicago: University of Chicago Press, 2003.

Polanyi, Karl. *The Great Transformation.* New York: Beacon Press, 2001.

Polman, Linda. *The Crisis Caravan.* New York: Metropolitan Books, 2010.

Pomfret, John. "UN Finds Good Intentions Don't Feed Beset Bosnians." *Washington Post,* January 21, 1994, A1.

Pompetti, Fabio. "Proximity: A Lapsed Illusion or a Necessary Way of Behaving?" In *Médecins Sans Frontières, My Sweet la Mancha,* 194–95, Geneva: Médecins Sans Frontières International, 2005.

Porter, Andrew. "Religion, Missionary Enthusiasm, and Empire." In *The Oxford History of the British Empire, Volume III: The Nineteenth Century,* ed. Andrew Porter, 222–46. New York: Oxford University Press, 2001.

——. *Religion versus Empire? British Protestant Missionaries and Overseas Expansion, 1700–1914.* Leicester, U.K.: Apollos Press, 1990.

——. "Trusteeship, Anti-Slavery, and Humanitarianism." In *The Oxford History of the British Empire,* Vol. 3: *The Nineteenth Century,* ed. Andrew Porter, 198–221. New York: Oxford University Press, 2001.

Porter, Toby. "Coordination in the Midst of Chaos: The Refugee Crisis in Albania." *Forced Migration Review* 5 (August 1999): 20–23.

——. "The Partiality of Humanitarian Assistance: Kosovo in Comparative Perspective." *Journal of Humanitarian Assistance* (June 2000). Available at www.jha.ac/articles/a057. htm, accessed July 12, 2010.

Porterfield, Amanda. "Protestant Missionaries: Pioneers of American Philanthropy." In *Charity, Philanthropy, and Civility in American History,* ed. Lawrence Friedman and Mark McGarvie, 49–70. New York: Cambridge University Press, 2003.

Powell, Colin. "Remarks to the National Foreign Policy Conference for Leaders of Nongovernmental Organizations." October 26, 2001. http://usinfo.state.gov/topical/pol/ terror/01102606.htm.

Powell, Walter, and Paul DiMaggio. *The New Institutionalism in Organizational Analysis.* Chicago: University of Chicago Press, 1991.

Power, Samantha. *A Problem from Hell: America in an Age of Genocide.* New York: Norton, 2002.

Preston, Julie. "U.N. Officials Scale Back Peacemaking Ambitions." *Washington Post,* October 28, 1993, A40.

Quelch, John, and Nathalie Laidler-Kylander. *The New Global Brands: Managing Non-Governmental Organizations in the 21st Century.* Mason, Ohio: South-Western College, 2006.

Rabinow, Paul. *French DNA.* Berkeley: University of California Press, 2002.

Ramsbotham, Oliver, and Tom Woodhouse. *Humanitarian Intervention in Contemporary Conflict.* Cambridge, UK: Polity, 1996

Randall, John, Jr. "The Churches and the Liberal Tradition." *Annals of the American Academy of Political and Social Science* 256 (1948): 148–64.

Reamer, Fred. *Social World Values and Ethics.* New York: Columbia University Press, 1999.

Redfield, Peter. "Doctors, Borders, and Life in Crisis." *Cultural Anthropology* 20, no. 3 (2005): 328–61.

——. "A Less Modest Witness: Collective Advocacy and Motivated Truth in a Medical Humanitarian Movement." *American Ethnologist* 33, no. 1 (February 2006): 3–24.

Reilly, Annemarie. "Beyond the 'Protection' of Human Rights." Paper prepared by Catholic Relief Services for a Humanitarianism and War Project Conference, 2000.

Reilly, Annemarie, and Jaco Cilliers. "Champions for Peace: The Role of CRS in Times of Violent Conflict." Catholic Relief Services—USCC, World Summit Conference, September 2000.

Reinisch, Jessica. "We Shall Rebuild Anew a Powerful Nation: UNRRA, Internationalism, and National Reconstruction in Poland." *Journal of Contemporary History* 43, 3 (2008): 451–76.

Reisman, Michael. "Kosovo's Antinomies." *American Journal of International Law* 93, no. 4 (1999): 860–62.

——. *The Laws of War: A Comprehensive Collection of Primary Documents on International Laws Governing Armed Conflict.* New York: Vintage, 1995.

Renwald, Sister Mary Casilda. "Humanitarianism and British Colonial Policy." Dissertation, St. Louis University, 1934.

Rice, Condoleezza. "The Promise of Democratic Peace: Why Promoting Freedom Is the Only Realistic Path to Security." *Washington Post,* December 11, 2005.

Rieff, David. *A Bed for the Night: Humanitarianism in Crisis.* New York: Simon and Shuster, 2002.

Rist, Gilbert. *The History of Development: From Western Origins to Global Faith.* New York: Zed Press, 1997.

Robert, Dana. "The First Globalization: The Internationalization of the Protestant Missionary Movements Between the World Wars." *International Bulletin of Missionary Research* 26, no. 2 (April, 2002): 50–66.

——. *Occupy until I Come: A. T. Pierson and the Evangelization of the World.* Grand Rapids, MI: William Eerdmans, 2003.

Roberts, Adam. "Humanitarian War: Military Intervention and Human Rights." *International Affairs* 69, no. 3 (1993): 429–49.

——. "NATO's 'Humanitarian War' over Kosovo." *Survival* 41, no. 3 (1999): 102–23.

Roberts, M. J. D. *Making English Morals: Voluntary Association and Moral Reform in England, 1787–1886.* New York: Cambridge University Press, 2004.

Rocha, Simone. "Afghanistan: When Military Forces and NGOs Provide a Disservice." *MSF Internal Newsletter* 85 (July–August 2004): 60–62.

Roggo, B. "After the Kosovo Conflict, a Genuine Humanitarian Space: A Utopian Concept or an Essential Requirement?" *International Review of the Red Cross* 837 (2000): 31–47.

Rohrer, Norman. *Open Arms: Wherever People Suffer, World Vision Is There.* Wheaton, IL: Tyndale Publishers, 1987.

Rorty, Richard. "Human Rights, Rationality, and Sentimentality." In *Truth and Progress: Philosophical Papers,* ed. Richard Rorty, 167–85. New York: Cambridge University Press, 1998.

——. "Who are We? Moral Universalism and Economic Triage." *Diogenes* 44, no. 1 (1996): 5–15.

Rosenberg, Emily. "Missions to the World: Philanthropy Abroad." In *Charity, Philanthropy, and Civility in American History,* ed. Lawrence Friedman and Mark McGarvie, 241–58. New York: Cambridge University Press.

——. *Spreading the American Dream: American Economic and Cultural Expansion, 1890–1945.* New York: Hill and Wang, 1982.

Rostow, W. W. *The Stages of Economic Growth: A Non-Communist Manifesto.* New York: Cambridge University Press, 1991.

Rotberg, Robert. "The New Nature of Nation-State Failure." *Washington Quarterly* 25, no. 3 (2002): 85–96.

Rozario, Kevin. *The Culture of Calamity: Disaster and the Making of Modern America.* Chicago: University of Chicago Press, 2008.

Rubenstein, Jennifer. "The Distributive Commitments of International NGOs." In *Humanitarianism in Question: Politics, Power and Ethics,* ed. Michael Barnett and Thomas Weiss, 215–34. Ithaca: Cornell University Press, 2008.

Ruggie, John. "International Regimes, Transactions, and Change: Embedded Liberalism in the Postwar Economic Order." *International Organization* 36, no. 2 (1982): 379–415.

Rutherford, Kenneth. *Humanitarianism under Fire: The U.S. and UN Intervention in Somalia.* Bloomfield, CT: Kumarian Press, 2008.

Sandos, James. *Converting California.* New Haven: Yale University Press, 2004.

Sandoz, Yves. "'Droit' or 'Devoir d'Ingerence' and the Right to Assistance: The Issues Involved." *International Review of the Red Cross* 288 (May–June 1992): 215–27.

Sartorius, Rolf, ed. *Paternalism*. Minneapolis: University of Minnesota Press, 1983.

Save the Children. *Provincial Reconstruction Teams and Humanitarian-Military Relations in Afghanistan*. London: Save the Children, 2004.

Scheizer, Beat. "Moral Dilemmas for Humanitarianism in the Era of 'Humanitarian' Military Interventions." *International Review of the Red Cross* 86 (September 2004): 547–64.

Schnyder, Gerald. "Les aspects juridiques actuels du problème des réfugiés." Hague Academy of International Law, *Recueil des cours* 114 (1965).

Scott, James. *Moral Economy of the Peasant: Rebellion and Resistance in South East Asia*. New Haven: Yale University Press, 1977.

——. *Seeing Like a State: How Certain Schemes to Improve the Human Condition Have Failed*. New Haven: Yale University Press, 1999.

Sen, Amartya. *Development as Freedom*. New York: Anchor Books, 1999.

Shah, Timothy. "For the Sake of Conscience: Some Evangelical Views of the State." In *Church, State, and Citizen*, ed. Sandra Joireman, 115–144. New York: Oxford University Press, 2009.

Shapcott, Richard. "Anti-Cosmopolitanism, Pluralism, and the Cosmopolitan Harm Principle." *Review of International Studies* 34, no. 2 (2008): 185–205.

Sharma, Sanjay. *Famine Philanthropy and the Colonial State: North India in the Early Nineteenth Century*. New York: Oxford University Press, 2001.

Shawcross, William. *The Quality of Mercy: Cambodia, Holocaust, and Modern Conscience*. New York: Touchstone Books, 1985.

Shephard, Ben. "'Becoming Planning Minded': The Theory and Practice of Relief 1940–1945." *Journal of Contemporary History* 43, no. 3 (2008): 405–19.

Shorter, Aylward. *Cross and Flag in Africa: The "White Fathers" during the Colonial Scramble, 1892–1914*. Maryknoll, New York: Orbis Books, 2006.

Simeant, Johanna. "What is Going Global? The International of French NGOs `Without Borders.'" *Review of International Political Economy* 12, no. 5 (December 2005): 851–83.

Simma, B. "NATO, The UN, and the Use of Force: Legal Aspects." *European Journal of International Law* 10, no. 1 (1999): 1–22.

Singer, Amy. *Charity in Islamic Societies*. New York: Cambridge University Press, 2008.

Singer, Peter. "Famine, Affluence, and Morality." *Philosophy and Public Affairs* 1 (Spring 1972): 229–43.

——. *The Life You Save: Acting Now to End World Poverty*. New York: Random House, 2009.

——. *One World: Ethics and Globalization*. New Haven: Yale University Press, 2002.

Sjoblom, Gustav. "The Missionary Image of Africa: Evidence from Sweden, 1885–1895." Paper presented at the Henry Martyn Seminar, Cambridge University, February 20, 2003.

Skran, Claudena. "The International Refugee Regime: The Historical and Contemporary Context of International Responses to Asylum Problems." In *Refugees: The Asylum Dilemma in the West*, ed. G. Loescher, 8–35. University Park: Pennsylvania State University Press, 1992.

Slim, Hugo. "By What Authority? The Legitimacy and Accountability of Non-Governmental Organizations." *Journal of Humanitarian Assistance* 10 (2002). Available at www.jha.ac/articles/a082.htm, accessed July 12, 2010.

——. *A Call to Alms: Humanitarian Action and the Art of War*. Geneva: Centre for Humanitarian Dialogue, 2004.

——. "Doing the Right Thing: Relief Agencies, Moral Dilemmas, and Moral Responsibility in Political Emergencies and War." *Disasters* 21, no. 3 (1997): 244–57.

——. "Military Humanitarianism and the New Peacekeeping: An Agenda for Peace?" *Journal of Humanitarian Assistance* 22 (September 1995).

——. "Military Intervention to Protect Human Rights: The Humanitarian Agency Perspective." *Journal of Humanitarian Assistance* 11 (March 2002). Available at www.jha.ac/articles/a084.htm, accessed July 12, 2010.

——. "Not Philanthropy but Rights: The Proper Politicisation of Humanitarian Philosophy." *International Journal of Human Rights* 6, no. 2 (Summer 2002).

——. "Protecting Civilians: Putting the Individual at the Humanitarian Centre." In *The Humanitarian Decade: Challenges for Humanitarian Assistance in the Last Decade and into the Future*, Vol. II., 154–69. Office of the Coordinator of Humanitarian Assistance. New York: United Nations Press, 2004.

——. "Relief Agencies and Moral Standing in War: Principles of Humanity, Neutrality, Impartiality, and Solidarity." *Development in Practice* 7, no. 4 (1997): 342–52.

Smillie, Ian. *The Alms Bazaar: Altruism Under Fire—Non-Profit Organizations and International Development.* Exeter, England: International Development Research, 1995.

Smillie, Ian, and Larry Minear. *The Charity of Nations: Humanitarian Action in a Calculating World.* Bloomfield, CT: Kumarian Press, 2004.

Smith, Gayle. "Ethiopia and the Politics of Famine Relief." *MERIP Middle East Report*, no. 145 (March–April 1987).

Smith, Timothy. "Historic Waves of Religious Interest in America." *Annals of the American Academy of Political and Social Science* 332 (November 1960): 9–19.

Sogge, David. 1999. "ICVA's Near-Death Experience: Temptation and Redemption in the 'Humanitarian International.'" *Development in Practice* 9, no. 4 (August 1999): 449–56.

Solana, Javier. "Press Statement." NATO Press release 040, March 24, 1999.

Spellman, Elizabeth V. *Fruits of Sorrow: Framing Our Attention to Suffering.* Boston: Beacon Press, 1997.

Sphere Project. *Humanitarian Charter and Minimum Standards in Disaster Response,* 2004. http://www.sphereproject.org/index.php?option=content&task=view&id=27&Itemid=84

Spurr, David. *Rhetoric of Empire: Colonial Discourse in Journalism, Travel Writing, and Imperial Administration.* Durham: Duke University Press, 1993.

Stanley, Brian. "Africa through European Christian Eyes: The World Missionary Conference, Edinburgh 1910." In *African Identities and Global Christianity in the Twentieth Century,* ed. Klaus Korschorke, 165–80. Wiesbaden, Germany: Harrassowitz Verlag, 2005.

——. *The Bible and the Flag: Protestant Missions and British Imperialism in the Nineteenth and Twentieth Centuries.* Leicester, U.K.: Apollos Press, 1990.

——. "Christianity and Civilization in English Evangelical Mission Thought, 1792–1857." In *Christian Missions and the Enlightenment,* ed. Brian Stanley, 1–21. Grand Rapids, MI: William Eerdmans, 2001.

——. "Church, State, and the Hierarchy of 'Civilization': The Making of the Commission VII Report, 'Missions and Governments' Edinburgh, 1910." In *The Imperial Horizons of British Protestant Missions, 1840–1914: The Interplay of Representation and Experience,* ed. Andrew N. Porter, 58–84. Grand Rapids, MI: William Eerdmans, 2004.

——. "Defining the Boundaries of Christendom: The Two Worlds of the World Missionary Conference, 1910." *International Bulletin of Missionary Research* 30, no. 4 (October 2006): 171–76.

——. "Edinburgh 1910 and the Oikoumene." In *Ecumenism and History,* ed. Anthony Cross, 89–105. Carlisle, U.K.: Paternoster Press, 2002.

——. "Twentieth-Century World Christianity: A Perspective from the History of Missions." In *Christianity Reborn: The Global Expansion of Evangelicalism in the Twentieth-Century,* ed. Donald M. Lewis, 52–83. Grand Rapids, MI: William Eerdmans, 2004.

——. "Welcoming Lecture: Christian Mission and the Unity of Humanity." Available at www.martymission.cam.ac.uk./CInaguralpage1.html, accessed July 12, 2010.

——. *The World Missionary Conference, Edinburgh 1910.* Grand Rapids, MI: William Eerdmans, 2009.

Stedman-Jones, Gareth. *An End to Poverty? A Historical Debate.* New York: Columbia University Press, 2004.

Stein, Janice. "Humanitarian Organizations: Accountable—Why, to Whom, for What, and How?" In *Humanitarianism in Question: Politics, Power, Ethics,* ed. Michael Barnett and Tom Weiss, 124–42. Ithaca: Cornell University Press, 2008.

Stirrat, Jock. "Competitive Humanitarianism: Relief and the Tsunami in Sri Lanka." *Anthropology Today* 22, no. 5 (October 2006): 11–16.

Stockton, Nicholas. "Accountable Humanitarianism and MSF." In *Médecins Sans Frontières, My Sweet la Mancha,* 95–105. Geneva: Médecins Sans Frontières International, 2005.

——. "In Defence of Humanitarianism." *Disasters* 22, no. 4 (1998): 352–60.

Sugino, Kyoichi. "The 'Non-Political and Humanitarian Clause' in UNHCR's Statute." *Refugee Survey Quarterly* 17, no. 1 (1998): 33–59.

Suhrke, Astri, M. Barutciski, P. Sandison, and P. Garlock. *The Kosovo Refugee Crisis: An Evaluation of UNHCR's Emergency Preparedness and Response.* January, 2000.

Sullivan, Robert. "The Politics of Altruism: An Introduction to the Food for Peace Partnership between the United States Government and Voluntary Relief Agencies." *Western Political Quarterly* 23, no. 4 (December 1970): 762–68.

Swinburne, Richard. *Responsibility and Atonement.* Oxford: Clarendon Press, 1989.

Sznaider, Natan. "The Sociology of Compassion: A Study in the Sociology of Morals." *Cultural Values* 2, 1 (1998): 117–30.

Sztucki, Jerzy. "The Conclusions on the International Protection of Refugees Adopted by the Executive Committee of the UNHCR Programme." *International Journal of Refugee Law* 1, no. 3 (1989): 285–318.

Taithe, Bertrand. "Algerian Orphans and Colonial Christianity in Algeria, 1866–1939." *French History* 20, no. 3 (2006): 240–59.

———. "The Red Cross Flag in the Franco-Prussian War: Civilians, Humanitarians, and War in the Modern Age." In *War, Medicine, and Modernity,* eds. Roger Cooter, Mark Harrison, and Steve Sturdy, 22–47. London: Diane, 1998.

———. "Reinventing (French) Universalism: Religion, Humanitarianism and the 'French Doctors.'" *Modern and Contemporary France* 12, no. 2 (2004): 147–58.

———. "Religious Responses, Humanitarianism, and Colonialism from the Algerian Drought and Famine to the French Doctors." In *Natural Hazards: Responses and Strategies in Global Perspective,* ed. Christof Mauch, Christian Pfister, 137–64. New Brunswick, NJ: Lexington Books, 2007.

Tanguy, Joelle. "Foreign and Humanitarian Aid: Paradox and Perspectives." Speech delivered at a panel discussion organized by the Institute for International Liberal Education, New York, March 8, 2000. Available at www.doctorswithoutborders.org/publications/article.cfm?id=1352&cat=speech, accessed July 12, 2010.

———. "When Intervening in the Name of Humanity, Be Cautious." Public Affairs Report, Institute of Governmental Studies, University of California-Berkeley, 2000, 41, no. 1.

Taylor, Charles. *A Secular Age.* Cambridge, MA: Harvard University Press, 2007.

Terry, Fiona. *Condemned to Repeat? The Paradox of Humanitarian Action.* Ithaca: Cornell University Press, 2002.

Thomas, George M. *Revivalism and Cultural Change: Christianity, Nation-Building, and the Market in the Nineteenth-Century United States.* Chicago: University of Chicago Press, 1989.

Thornberry, Cedric. "Saving the War Crimes Tribunal." *Foreign Policy* 104 (Fall 1996): 72–85.

Todorov, Tzvetan. *The Conquest of America: The Question of the Other.* Norman: University of Oklahoma Press, 1999.

Torrelli, Maurice. "From Humanitarian Assistance to 'Intervention on Humanitarian Grounds'?" *International Review of the Red Cross* 288 (May–June 1992): 228–48.

Tronto, Joan. *Moral Boundaries: A Political Argument for an Ethic of Care.* New York: Routledge, 1993.

Tsui, Ed, and Thant Myint-U. "The Institutional Response: Creating a Framework in Response to New Challenges in OCHA." In *The Humanitarian Decade: Challenges for Humanitarian Assistance in the Last Decade and Into the Future, Volume Two,* 1–14. New York: UN Office for the Coordination of Humanitarian Affairs, 2002.

Twain, Mark. *On the Damned Human Race,* New York: Hill Wang, 1962.

UNHCR. Executive Committee of the High Commissioner's Programme, "Forty-Eighth Session Annual Theme: Repatriation Challenges." UN doc. A/AC.96/887, September 9, 1997, *International Journal of Refugee Law* 9, no. 4 (1997): 679–87.

———. Executive Committee of the High Commissioner's Programme. "Note on International Protection." August 31, 1983.

———. *State of the World's Refugees: In Search of Solutions.* New York: Oxford University Press, 1995.

United Nations. *Agenda for Peace,* New York: United Nations, 1992.

———. "Report of the Secretary-General pursuant to General Assembly resolution 53/35: The fall of Srebrenica," A/54/549, November 15, 1999.

Urquhart, Brian. "Who Can Police the World?" *New York Review of Books* 41, no. 9, May 12, 1994.

Uvin, Peter. *Aiding Violence: The Development Enterprise in Rwanda.* Bloomfield, CT: Kumarian Press, 1998.

Vallaeys, Anne. *Médecins Sans Frontières: La biographie.* Paris: Fayard, 2004.

VanDeVeer, Donald. *Paternalistic Intervention: The Moral Bounds of Benevolence.* Princeton, NJ: Princeton University Press, 1986.

van der Veer, Peter. *Imperial Encounters: Religion and Modernity in India and Britain.* Princeton, NJ: Princeton University Press, 2001.

Van Zandt, Steven. "Don't Rebuild Haiti: Reimagine it." *Politico,* February 2, 2010. Available at www.politico.com/news/stories/0210/32333.html, accessed July 12, 2010.

Varg, Paul. "Motives in Protestant Missions, 1890–1917." *Church History* 23, no. 1 (1954): 68–82.

Vaux, Tony. *The Selfish Altruist.* London: Earthscan, 2001.

Waldie, Paul. "Good Intentions Gone Wrong." [Toronto] *Globe and Mail,* February 9, 2010. Available at http://ijdh.org/archives/9075/.

Walker, Peter. "Chaos and Caring: Humanitarian Aid Amidst Disintegrating States." *Journal of Humanitarian Assistance,* 1996. Available at www.jha.ac/articles/a010.htm, accessed July 12, 2010.

———. "Crisis and Normality, Two Sides of the Same Coin." Presentation given to the Brookings Institution/Ford Foundation Workshop, Towards a New Poverty and Development Agenda: Contributions of the INGO Community, May 30–31, 2007.

Warner, Daniel. "The Politics of the Political/Humanitarian Divide." *International Review of the Red Cross* 81 (1999): 109–18.

———. "Voluntary Repatriation and the Meaning of Return to Home: A Critique of Liberal Mathematics." *Journal of Refugee Studies* 7, nos. 2/3 (1994): 160–74.

Watenpaugh, Keith David. "League of Nations' Rescue of Armenian Genocide Survivors and the Making of Modern Humanitarianism, 1920–27." *American Historical Review* (December 2010): 1315–39.

Weber, Olivier. *French Doctors: Les 25 ans d'épopée des hommes et des femmes qui ont inventé la médecine humanitaire.* Paris: Robert Laffont, 1995.

Weiss, Thomas G. *Humanitarian Intervention: Ideas in Action.* Cambridge: Polity Press, 2007.

———. "Principles, Politics, and Humanitarian Action." *Ethics and International Affairs* 13, no. 1 (1999): 1–22.

Weiss, Thomas, and Amir Pasic. "Reinventing UNHCR: Enterprising Humanitarians in the Former Yugoslavia, 1991–1995." *Global Governance* 3 (Spring 1997): 41–57.

Weitz, Eric. "From the Vienna to the Paris System: International Politics and the Entangled Histories of Human Rights, Forced Deportations, and Civilizing Missions." *American Historical Review* 113, no. 5 (2008): 1313–43.

West, John G., Jr. *The Politics of Revelation and Reason: Religion and Civil Life in the New Nation.* Lawrence: University of Kansas Press, 1996.

Whaites, Alan. "Pursuing Partnership: World Vision and the Ideology of Development—A Case Study." *Development in Practice* 9, no. 4 (1999): 410–23.

White House. *National Security Strategy.* September 2002. Available at www.whitehouse. gov/nsc/nss/2002/index.html.

Wilberforce, William. *An Appeal to Religion, Justice, and Humanity of the Inhabitants of the British Empire, in Behalf of the Negro Slaves in the West Indies.* London: J. Hatchard and Son, 1823.

Wiles, Peter. "The Kosovo Emergency: The Disasters Emergency Committee Evaluation." Paper presented at the conference, "Kosovo and the Changing Face of Humanitarian Action," Uppsala, Sweden, May 2001.

Wiles, P., et al. "Independent Evaluation of Expenditure of DEC Kosovo Appeal Funds." Phases I and II, April 1999—January 2000. Disasters Emergency Committee, London, 2000.

Williams, Peter C. *The Ideal of the Self-Governing Church: A Study in Victorian Missionary Strategy.* Leiden, Netherlands: E. J. Brill, 1990.

Wilson, Francesca. *In the Margins of Chaos: Recollections of Relief Work in and between Three Wars.* London: John Murray, 1944.

Wilson, Richard, and Richard Brown, eds. *Humanitarianism and Suffering: The Mobilization of Empathy.* New York: Cambridge University Press, 2009.

Wiseberg, Laurie. "The International Politics of Relief: A Case Study of the Relief Operations Mounted during the Nigerian Civil War 1967–70." Ph.D. dissertation, UCLA, Department of Political Science, 1973.

Wood, James. "Between God and a Hard Place." *New York Times, Week in Review,* January 24, 2010, 11.

Woodbury, Robert. *Dividing Elites: Religious Liberty, Protestant Competition, and the Global Spread of Democracy,* Project on Religion and Economic Change World Paper no. 2, March 5, 2009.

World Vision International. "New Vision Journey Findings—Executive Summary," mimeo, 2002.

World Vision International Council. *World Vision's Ministry of Mission Challenge: Directions for the Future.* Discussion paper, September 16–19, 1986.

Wright, Neil. "UNHCR and International Humanitarian Cooperation in the Former Yugoslavia." *Refugee Survey Quarterly* 18, no. 3 (1999): 50–54.

Young, Kirsten. "UNHCR and ICRC in the Former Yugoslavia: Bosnia-Herzegovina." *International Review of the Red Cross,* no. 843 (2001).

Young, Michael. *Bearing against Sin: The Evangelical Birth of the American Social Movement.* Chicago: University of Chicago Press, 2006.

Young, Robert. "John Stuart Mill, Ronald Dworkin, and Paternalism." In Mill's *'On Liberty': A Critical Guide,* ed. C. L. Ten, 209–27. New York: Cambridge University Press, 2008.

——. *Postcolonialism: An Historical Introduction.* Malden, MA: Blackwell Publishing, 2001.

Zabriskie, Alexander. "The Rise and Main Characteristics of the Anglican Evangelical Movement in England and America." In *Anglican Evangelicalism,* ed. Alexander Zabriskie. Philadelphia, 1943.

Index